T0392252

Thoughtful Proclaimer

A bottom-up guide to preparing Bible messages
that transform you from the inside out

Elizabeth Wright Anderson

WESTBOW
PRESS®
A DIVISION OF THOMAS NELSON
& ZONDERVAN

Copyright © 2017 Elizabeth Wright Anderson.

All rights reserved. No part of this book may be used or reproduced by any means, graphic, electronic, or mechanical, including photocopying, recording, taping or by any information storage retrieval system without the written permission of the author except in the case of brief quotations embodied in critical articles and reviews.

This book is a work of non-fiction. Unless otherwise noted, the author and the publisher make no explicit guarantees as to the accuracy of the information contained in this book and in some cases, names of people and places have been altered to protect their privacy.

WestBow Press books may be ordered through booksellers or by contacting:

WestBow Press
A Division of Thomas Nelson & Zondervan
1663 Liberty Drive
Bloomington, IN 47403
www.westbowpress.com
1 (866) 928-1240

Because of the dynamic nature of the Internet, any web addresses or links contained in this book may have changed since publication and may no longer be valid. The views expressed in this work are solely those of the author and do not necessarily reflect the views of the publisher, and the publisher hereby disclaims any responsibility for them.

ISBN: 978-1-5127-9721-3 (sc)
ISBN: 978-1-5127-9720-6 (e)

Library of Congress Control Number: 2017912263

Print information available on the last page.

WestBow Press rev. date: 10/21/2017

Unless otherwise noted, all Scriptures are from The Holy Bible: English
Standard Version. Wheaton, IL: Standard Bible Society, 2016.

Scripture quotations marked ESV are from the ESV® Bible (The Holy Bible, English Standard Version®), copyright
© 2001 by Crossway, a publishing ministry of Good News Publishers. Used by permission. All rights reserved.

Scripture quotations marked NIV are taken from the Holy Bible, New International Version®, NIV®. Copyright
© 1973, 1978, 1984, 2011 by Biblica, Inc.™ Used by permission of Zondervan. All rights reserved worldwide.

Scripture quotations marked NRSV New Revised Standard Version Bible, copyright © 1989 National Council
of the Churches of Christ in the United States of America. Used by permission. All rights reserved.

Scripture quotations taken from the New American Standard Bible® NASB, Copyright © 1960, 1962, 1963, 1968,
1971, 1972, 1973, 1975, 1977, 1995 by The Lockman Foundation.Used by permission. www.Lockman.org

NET Bible® copyright ©1996-2006 by Biblical Studies Press, L.L.C. http://netbible.com All rights reserved

Scripture quotes marked NKJV are taken from the New King James Version®. Copyright
© 1982 by Thomas Nelson. Used by permission. All rights reserved.

Scripture quotes marked KJV are taken from the King James Version of the Bible.

Scripture quotations marked NIV are from The New International Version. Grand Rapids, MI: Zondervan, 2011.

Scripture quotations marked NRSV are from The Holy Bible: New Revised
Standard Version. Nashville: Thomas Nelson, 1989.

Him we proclaim, warning everyone and teaching everyone with all wisdom, that we may present everyone mature in Christ. -Colossians 1:28

With thanks to Jesus Christ who saved and called me and to the Holy Spirit who inspired and empowered the writing of this book.

With special thanks to the thoughtful proclaimers He placed in my life to encourage me:

To the Gospel Messengers who preached around the Midwest circa 1947 and whose ministry had a profound influence on my spiritual formation from many years before I was born (including the Welsh evangelist, my uncle, David Lawrence; my pastor "Uncle" Carl Pfaff; and the evangelist Mr. Morgan whose story of the lost sheep touched my heart lead to my salvation).

To my dad, Jon Wright, who valued preaching and the Word above all.

To Pastor Constance Jordan-Haas who taught me that my call was where my greatest joy and the world's greatest needs intersected.

To Dr. Martin Sanders who joyfully taught preaching at Alliance Theological Seminary and made proclamation seem easy and fun.

To Professor Jeffrey Arthurs and Randy Pelton who unwittingly launched the writing this book by instilling in me an enthusiasm for teaching preaching as part of the Doctor of Ministry program, Preaching the Literary Forms of the Bible, at Gordon-Conwell Theological Seminary.

To my Community Bible School class who lovingly put up with years of experimental messages and let me know what went well and what didn't, as I read and tried to put into practice every book on preaching I could.

To Pastor Bill Gestal who unknowingly encouraged me to make this book my best gift to God by hauling a boxload of a not so very good early version of this book all the way to ECWA Theological Seminary in Jos, Nigeria.

To Melanie Turner whose sweet encouragement made this book a little more light-hearted and accessible to a younger generation.

It is my prayer that the next generation of proclaimers will find this work a helpful guide.

TABLE OF CONTENTS

PREFACE

The most important thing that proclaimers of God's Word can do is find God, the Commander's, intent for Scripture and let it transform their lives. Then, they must make that intent clear and memorable to others showing them how to live transformed lives in light of God's message to them and offering them motivation to live out God's intent through the power of the Holy Spirit based on a grateful response to Christ's sacrifice.

The Thoughtful Proclaimer Bible message preparation method is a step-by-step guide to interpreting, applying, and proclaiming God's purposes for His Word. It is accessible to experienced as well as new proclaimers of Scripture. The method is a spiritually enriching as well as a thorough way of discovering the primary purpose of a passage for the objective of preaching and teaching. The method is called thoughtful because it explicitly focuses on Scripture transforming the proclaimer while the proclaimer prepares transformative messages for others.

The proclaimer may be a busy pastor, lay preacher, Bible teacher, missionary, youth leader, or other person looking for a practical yet thorough method of finding and sharing God's purpose for Bible passages. Thoughtful proclaimers come from various backgrounds. Some are leaders recently called to teach or preach though they have little previous experience doing that. Others may be trained pastors who have been preaching for years but are looking for a deeper, spiritually enriching method of preparing their sermons. Still other Christian communicators will find the methods refreshing and the step-by-step explanations helpful.

This book incorporates classic Bible study style techniques, time-honored spiritual disciplines, step-by-step exegesis made accessible to laypeople, and novel practices in teaching and sermon planning. *The Thoughtful Proclaimer* offers something for all sorts of Bible proclaimers regardless of training or experience. It uses an innovative, inductive, question-based exegesis method and incorporates devotional aspects to enhance study and message preparation making the process spiritually edifying.

Further, the method incorporates helpful communication methods and sermon planning devices such as the Commander's intent, the point for proclamation, a message catchphrase, and an anchor image to ensure that our messages hit the mark and are memorable.

Seminaries teach preachers and teachers to study the Bible, its languages, and its backgrounds. Seminarians learn to read and apply the ancient texts to modern times and prepare biblical messages for their congregations. Lay Bible studies often provide people with questions to help them study particular passages and related Bible references to help them form personal theological understanding of what a passage means for them. *The Thoughtful Proclaimer* does both by guiding the proclaimer to ask the types of questions one needs to ask and answer to understand and apply a Scripture passage. Asking questions stimulates spiritual contemplation and scholarly study. Sample questions at the end of the appropriate chapters will stimulate thoughtful preparation; the entire method is summarized in a Thoughtful Proclaimer Worksheet available in the appendix B. The best message preparation tools available to date are our hearts and minds.

The thoughtful proclaimer method starts with choosing a passage, determining its God-given purpose, understanding what God, our Commander's intent, is for that passage, and helping us apply that purpose to our own and our listeners' lives.

Finally, the method guides us through turning the purpose of the passage into a point for proclamation from which we can build a redemptive message that speaks to believers in Christ and those who are not yet convinced of God's love for them. The method assumes that all passages of the Old and New Testaments were given to us by God for a purpose and are useful for teaching, rebuking, correcting, and training in righteousness.[1]

> He said to them, "Therefore every teacher of the law who has become a disciple in the kingdom of heaven is like the owner of a house who brings out of his storeroom new treasures as well as old." (Matthew 13:52)

If we are called by the King of the universe to proclaim His holy Word, we will want to go deep into the mine of Scripture to bring out the gold and jewels buried there. We want God to use our hard work to transform the hearts and minds of our listeners and make a difference in our lives as we prayerfully toil to prepare a sermon or lesson.

Learning to ask the right questions leads us to understand God's purposes for His Word and allows us to speak genuinely into the lives of others. *The Thoughtful Proclaimer* Bible message preparation method allows us to grow in our knowledge of the Bible and in our relationship with Jesus as we wrestle with and study His Word in preparation for sharing it with others in a way that calls us all to fuller lives in Christ.

---

[1] 2 Timothy 3:16.

INTRODUCTION

In the presence of God and of Christ Jesus, who is to judge the living and the dead, and in view of his appearing and his kingdom, I solemnly urge you: proclaim the message; be persistent whether the time is favorable or unfavorable; convince, rebuke, and encourage, with the utmost patience in teaching. For the time is coming when people will not put up with sound doctrine, but having itching ears, they will accumulate for themselves teachers to suit their own desires, and will turn away from listening to the truth and wander away to myths. As for you, always be sober, endure suffering, do the work of an evangelist, carry out your ministry fully. (2 Timothy 4:1–5 NRSV)

Knowledge of ancient Hebrew and Greek is of value to those who have it. The ability to analyze the grammar and diagram books of Scripture is a great goal. Days and days with nothing to do but read scholarly writings about the Bible would be a blessing. But the most important task for those God calls and gifts as proclaimers of His Word is to proclaim the message. To do this, we must grow in the knowledge and grace of our Lord Jesus Christ and be prepared to answer His call.

We study "to show ourselves approved" to proclaim God's purposes for inspiring each passage of Scripture.[1] This book calls God's purpose for inspiring a passage of Scripture the Commander's intent. Once we know what God meant to say and begin to apply it to our lives, the rest of our preparation involves finding the best way to share the message with others. Finding God's intent for a passage gives direction to our preaching and teaching so it can be understood, remembered, and transformative.

The Thoughtful Proclaimer is a practical form of theological exegesis that utilizes inductive thinking and questions; we call it inductive theological exegesis.[2] Theology is the study of God and His purposes while exegesis is plainly articulating what the Word of God says and means. Theological exegesis looks at the totality of Scripture to understand the particular meaning of a passage under consideration.

Using questions, we will study the biblical language and context (both the biblical context and the historical and cultural background of a text). We'll look at all this not to gather information but to understand the intended message of the passage for ourselves and for the people who trust us enough to listen to us.

---

[1] 2 Timothy 2:15.

[2] Some technical words and phrases specific to this method are defined at the end of this introduction in the glossary or footnotes.

The Three Steps of a Thoughtful Proclaimer

> Truly I tell you, whoever does not receive the kingdom of God as a little child will never
> enter it. (Mark 10:15)

Listen—A Contemplative Exegesis

The first step to transformed messengers is contemplative exegesis—reading the passage. The most important part of contemplative exegesis is listening; we listen and let the Bible speak. We allow it to say what it says, not what we wish it said or thought it said. We listen after we pray for the guiding presence of the counselor Jesus promised to send who breathed out the Scripture we are studying.[3]

Setting aside all else like a child listening to a beloved story, we quietly attend to the Word. Setting aside the fact that we will be speaking on this passage in a few days, forgetting the interesting but unrelated detours our minds want to wander to, and ignoring our to-do lists, we listen with an open mind. If we can't put a thought, doubt, or argument with God aside, we write it down for later and try to read with the trust of a child on her loving father's knee or with the rapt attention of a lover receiving a letter from someone dear who is far away.

Next, we schedule an interview with the Holy Spirit. The thoughtful proclaimer asks questions of a passage, a sort of structured interview. We ask all sorts of questions of the text; some we plan, and others come up as we are reading. The questions are personal, cultural, contextual, historical, grammatical, and implicational. Some questions will require us to ask the experts (to look things up in books and commentary), but most of our answers will come directly from Scripture.

Live—A Transformative Hermeneutic

The Bible transforms us so we can bring transformation to others. Personal transformation requires prayer and time living with the Word and living it out. Preparing a message for others requires sensitivity and honesty. Creativity takes mental space. It is generally best not to try to squeeze message preparation into one day or we will find ourselves serving up only the answers to our questions (or worse, the answers to the questions a commentary writer thought to ask) rather than a well-developed, honest, relevant message. If we follow the recipe provided in this book, our parishioners and class members will be discussing and savoring the memory of God's message at lunch instead of serving roast preacher.

During the live phase, we will consider our listeners and decide on the purpose of our passage, the Commander's intent. We will then live out the message so we can speak on it honestly. We'll let the passage percolate through our minds and lives until, like perked coffee, it is good and strong. The Commander's intent is first applied, lived out, by the proclaimer who lives under His authority.

Love—A Redemptive, Purposeful Homiletic

The Christian life and thus Christian proclamation is all about Christ's love and the offer of redemption. Our souls are redeemed by Christ for all eternity, but God continues to redeem our

---

[3] "When the Spirit of truth comes, he will guide you into all the truth … He will glorify me, for he will take what is mine and declare it to you" (John 16:13–14). "And I will ask the Father, and he will give you another Helper, to be with you forever, even the Spirit of truth …" (John 14:16–17). "All Scripture is breathed out by God and profitable for teaching, for reproof, for correction, and for training in righteousness" (2 Timothy 3:16).

broken lives and mold us to be more like Him. We live in a broken world; we are broken people in need of a redeemer whether we are hearing about the grace of God for the first time or have been believers for decades. We preach the gospel for those the Holy Spirit is calling, and we preach it for those who need to hear about forgiveness and second chances a second, third, and fourth time.

We love our listeners by offering them redemption and messages that have clearly articulated life-changing purposes. We love our listeners so much that we make sure our lessons and sermons are for them. If we are called to proclaim the Word, one of the most loving things we can do is ensure that our messages have one well-articulated reason for being listened to. (Hopefully, that reason will be the same reason God placed our passage in Scripture.) Often, the teacher or preacher tells us what the Bible says but forgets to help us understand why God said it. What does He want us to do about it?

If we were parents in Canada, there would be some important things we'd want our children to learn. Loving our listeners means we tell them what they must know. We don't leave them wondering why they bothered to come this week at all. Canadian parents don't just inform their children that water freezes at zero degrees centigrade; rather, they warn them to be careful walking on ice. We love our listeners not only by telling them about the Bible but why it says what it says. We offer guidance to apply it. If we love others, we will make sure our message has a point.

Finally, we will give our message a handle, something for our people to hang onto. Using the best methods, we help our main point, our point for proclamation, stick in the minds of our people so they can't forget. A parent might shout, "Stay off the ice!" Most of us won't yell, but we will offer a sticky, memorable catchphrase, a piece of a verse, good story, or visual image they can remember. Something practical like a "Keep Off the Ice!" warning sign. We want our listeners to take God's Word home so they can meditate on it for a week or a lifetime.

Using the Thoughtful Proclaimer Method

As with anything as significant and holy as understanding and conveying the message of God to His people, there is no rushing our preparation. Being a thoughtful proclaimer takes some time, but it is time well spent as we grow in our faith and the knowledge of God. Because this method incorporates listening, living out, and loving our people, there is no way of knowing how long each step will take; that will depend on many things including our skill level and the difficulty of our passage.

The steps in this method are mostly written in order, but in real life, message preparation is more Spirit led and might not progress in a strict order. We may move back and forth between the steps of listening and living several times until we get the Commander's intent (see chapter 2) and our point for proclamation just right or as right as it will be this week.

Finally, the appendix has a reproducible Thoughtful Proclaimer Worksheet. Though lists of questions are supplied at the ends of the chapters and in the worksheet, I hope asking questions will become second nature to you. After some months of practice, you will know what questions are needed for which passages, and you will not need the questions at the end of the chapters. But when you come across a difficult passage, you can always take out the Thoughtful Proclaimer Worksheet and work prayerfully through it to find the Commander's intent.

GLOSSARY

This book is based on some key themes. There is benefit from being introduced to them.

ANCHOR IMAGE

An anchor image is a memory device used to help anchor the purpose of a passage, the main applicable transformational point of a message, in the mind of the listener. A picture is worth a thousand words, and an anchor image whether it is a picture, a prop, or an image we create with a verbal description, illustration, or story is of inestimable value for anchoring our message in our listeners' minds. See chapter 13, "Make It Memorable," to find out more about anchor images.

CANON

We use the word *canon* in this book to refer simply to the whole Christian Bible (minus the Apocryphal and Deuterocanonical books included in some Bible versions). "The original meaning of the term canon can be traced to the ancient Greeks, who used it in a literal sense: a *kanon* was a 'rod, ruler, staff, or measuring rod.'"[i] The word *canon* today can mean either the standard or rules by which books were chosen by the church as Scripture, or it can refer to Scripture itself—the actual books of the Bible that we now consider to be our rule and authority.[1] The methods in this book are meant to apply to every book of the Bible—to the entire canon of Scripture. In fact, it is the whole canon of Scripture that we will trust to be our guide in understanding the most difficult passages.

COMMANDER'S INTENT

The Commander's intent is a military term we will borrow (God being the assumed commander). The Commander's intent communicates the will of a military commander regarding the main task to be accomplished and the ultimate purpose of a mission. It is the most important piece of information in a military order and is kept front and center over long and complicated sets of plans for a mission. For a military mission to be successful, every member of the mission must understand the Commander's intent. All those under God's authority, all those who seek to proclaim His message, must be sure they are clear on God's intent for the passages they hope to teach. Chapter 2 goes into more detail on the Commander's intent.

---

[1] The history behind the formation of the canon is beyond the scope of this book. If you are interested in the formation of the canon, I recommend *How We Got the Bible* by Neil R. Lightfoot, *A General Introduction to the Bible* by Norman Geisler and William Nix, and *The NT: Its Background, Growth, and Content*, by Bruce M. Metzger.

Exegesis

Exegesis is the interpretation of a passage on its own terms (the Greek *exēgeomai* means "to lead, draw out"). To perform exegesis is to study a written text for the purpose of achieving an accurate understanding of the author's original meaning. Thoughtful proclaimer biblical exegesis is a word-by-word, phrase-by-phrase, and paragraph-by-paragraph analysis of the meaning of a passage in light of its many contexts. Attention is paid to word meaning, sentence form, paragraph structure, context (historical and biblical), and theology.[ii]

This book assumes that God wants us to understand a biblical text and apply it. Further, it assumes that by asking the right questions and prayerfully answering them well, we will find that task of exegesis easier and more edifying.

We will use the word *exegesis* to refer to a way of analyzing not only Scripture but also ourselves and the culture we are surrounded by and are speaking to. Using the word *exegete* in reference to people may be unusual, but it is actually very descriptive because we are interested in explaining our text and in interpreting that text to others. We need to know what the Bible says and a lot about our audience, their presuppositions, the things they believe, and the way they live. Chapter 3 and section 2 contain step-by-step procedures and questions to help us do exegesis of a passage.

Expository Preaching and Teaching

Expository preaching or teaching starts with the biblical text rather than with a subject. Rather than choosing something we want to teach about and finding a text to support it, expository preaching takes the text as primary and preaches or teaches on it. The text is given primacy rather than the preacher or a topic.

The purpose of an expository message is to clearly explain the original, God-intended meaning of a passage and apply it to the needs of today's congregation.[iii] Expository preaching is not the presentation of one's exegesis or study to a congregation unless those facts introduce or highlight the point for proclamation. Rather, expository preaching synthesizes the interpretation of a passage in light of related and adjacent passages to speak to the lives of listeners in their present condition.

Not all biblical preaching is necessarily expository in this sense. Expository preaching has a point, which is the same point as the scriptural passage, and its application to life is based on that point. We call it the point for proclamation, our preachable and teachable version of the Commander's intent. The reason for expository preaching should be the transformation of listeners' hearts, minds, and lives in accordance with what God intended a passage to do.[2] (See more about expository preaching and teaching in chapter 2.)

Hermeneutics

Hermeneutics is the methodology used to apply an ancient text to a modern setting. It covers the principles and theories of how texts can be applied based on understanding the roles of and relationships between the author, the text, and the original and subsequent readers.[iv]

---

[2] Expository proclamation generally focuses on one primary passage though other verses and passages may be used to elucidate the God-intended purposes of the passage more clearly or fully. Expository preaching can be topical if the topic is the God-intended, main purpose of the passage and if it is explained primarily in light of the rest of the passage being taught. Topical messages based on themes, words, parts of verses, or a multiplicity of related passages that contain the same word are generally not expository though they may be biblical.

A hermeneutical principle for the thoughtful proclaimer is that all Scripture is interrelated and has value for us today. We trust that God had a reason for giving us His Word and that our heavenly Author's intent for a passage is knowable if only imperfectly. We use Scripture as the primary interpretive tool for other Scriptures that are less clear.

A primary hermeneutical principle in *The Thoughtful Proclaimer* is the idea that identifying the heavenly Author's intent for a passage is paramount to understanding the purposes of Bible passages for today. The assumptions behind this hermeneutic is that the Holy Spirit inspired the author of the Bible and that He can also empower the prayerful exegete to understand His text. Further, understanding the intent of the earthly author for writing or speaking his passage is one key to unlocking a passages meaning.[3] (Section 3, chapters 9–10 are on hermeneutics.)

HOMILETICS

Homiletics is that "discipline that deals with the preparation, structure and delivery of sermons [homilies]."[v] This book focuses on finding the one primary purpose of a single passage and developing a sermon or teaching based on that point and on what the Scriptures say regarding that point. This book is not a textbook on how to preach so much as a handbook on how to find and apply the primary purpose of a passage to our lives to preach and teach it to others. We will address several ways to develop the Commander's intent and the purpose for proclamation into a message in the final chapters of this book. (Section 4, chapters 11–14 are on homiletics.)

INDUCTIVE REASONING

Inductive reasoning moves from the specific to the general and is a way of drawing a conclusion from a collection of information. Inductive reasoning uses observations to build a case for something that appears true based on what we see or hear. Inductive Bible study is a method of asking and answering questions to draw conclusions based on the answers we find in Scripture. Inductive reasoning is a way of understanding Scripture because the Bible means for us to understand it based on its own witness (especially if we base our conclusions on the entirety of the canon and not one only one passage).

The thoughtful proclaimer method uses induction in two of its senses. First, this method is inductive in that it interprets the larger and more general purposes of God by looking at individual passages and comparing what we observe there to what we observe in related Bible passages.

The second sense of the word induction is a method of study accomplished by asking and answering questions to gain the general meaning; this is typical of inductive Bible study methods. Rather than relying on other people's writings about texts, the thoughtful proclaimer emphasizes reading the text carefully and many times to truly hear what it says about itself. We then study it inductively by asking questions to understand the text, ourselves, our listeners and how that text applies today. (See chapter 3 for more on inductive exegesis; the questions at the ends of chapters 4–7 will help us get started asking suitable questions for inductive exegesis.)

---

[3] A hermeneutical principle of this book is that God wants to redeem His people and that He can redeem and offers eternal life to those who call on Him in repentance. This redemption is available to those who believe in Jesus Christ. God is able to redeem, make something good from broken lives, families, and communities for those who call on Him. And we know that for those who love God, all things work together for good for those who are called according to his purpose (Romans 8:28).

POINT FOR PROCLAMATION

The point for proclamation is a clear statement that captures the core of the Commander's intent for a passage as it pertains to preaching or teaching it to others. The Commander's intent point for proclamation is the primary preaching/teaching point of a Bible message to which all other points, illustrations, or Scriptures relate. It is the transformational message we want our listeners to understand and remember long after they have forgotten our sermon or teaching. (Chapter 13 helps us formulate points for proclamation.)

CATCHPHRASE

The point for proclamation catchphrase is a short, pithy phrase, parable, slogan, verse, or quote that is memorable and that briefly represents or characterizes the point for proclamation. It can be used as a message title or repeated throughout the teaching or preaching so the listeners have something to grab onto that they can repeat and remember. This phrase will bring up the Commander's intended point for proclamation in the minds of the listeners when they think of it. (The last half of chapter 13 gives guidance on how to turn a thorough point for proclamation into a memorable catchphrase.)

PROCLAIMER

Proclaimers are those who sense a call from God to publicly announce and explain the truth of God's Word. Proclaimers may be evangelists, preachers, or Bible teachers. Their settings may be among youth, abroad, in churches, Bible studies, or classrooms. Proclaimers are often people in leadership roles and are seen as authorities on Scripture by their constituents. They are entrusted by God with speaking for Him and must seek to live as examples of this message played out in life.[4]

It may seem that we should draw a distinction between the sort of preparation needed for teaching versus preaching. However, since both roles claim to speak for God about His Word, this distinction is not entirely necessary for training purposes.[5] The teacher may be expected to go into more depth regarding biblical languages and culture to make a point, and the preacher may be expected to be more pastoral or evangelistic in emphasis. Stylistically, there may be differences in the presentation, though this is not always so, and in any case, it has less to do with preparation than presentation.

The New Testament uses preaching and teaching almost interchangeably. Paul called his own preaching "teaching" quite frequently.[6] The writer of Acts likewise called Paul's preaching

---

[4] "'And in the last days it shall be,' God declares, 'that I will pour out my Spirit on all flesh, and your sons and your daughters shall prophesy, and your young men shall see visions, and your old men shall dream dreams; even on my male servants and female servants in those days I will pour out my Spirit, and they shall prophesy'" (Acts 2:17–18).

[5] "The verb *didasko* appears consistently in the sense of teach or instruct. Sometimes parallel to *euangolidzomai* [to proclaim or preach the good news] (Luke 20:1; Acts 5:42; 15:35) or *karusso* [to announce, make known, or mention publicly] (Matt 4:23; 9:35; 11:1; Acts 28:31)." Horst Robert Balz and Gerhard Schneider, *Exegetical Dictionary of the NT* (Grand Rapids, MI: Eerdmans, 1990), 317.

[6] "That is why I sent you Timothy, my beloved and faithful child in the LORD, to remind you of my ways in Christ, as I teach them everywhere in every church" (1 Corinthians 4:17).

"teaching."[7] Jesus' ministry was described by Luke as "doing preaching and teaching."[8] Matthew said Jesus did both preaching and teaching.[9] The Old Testament primarily calls doctrinal instruction of any sort "teaching" (unless it comes as prophecy, which appears to be a more direct word from God).[10] Though there is not much of a difference in the preparation, there may be a difference in the roles for which the Holy Spirit gifts people.[11] The word *proclaimer* covers all the bases for our purposes. We seek to be thoughtful proclaimers; no proclaimer should consider that his or her role is less important or requires less preparation.[12]

THEOLOGICAL EXEGESIS

There are many types of exegesis. Theological exegesis specifically seeks to understand a text in light of the rest of Scripture, the entire canon. Rick Byargeon, associate professor of the Old Testament at Southwestern Baptist Theological Seminary, wrote that the value of theological exegesis was its ability to provide a sense of unity regarding God's revelation.[vi] Theological exegesis is necessary for us to move "beyond the descriptive (what it meant) to the normative (what it means)."[vii] We ask how the meaning of this text is affected by other texts of Scripture. Using theological exegesis rather than interpreting texts outside the context of the whole canon helps keep us from theological and interpretative error.[13] Theological exegesis is always important, but it particularly shines in Old Testament interpretation. The thoughtful proclaimer method utilizes a specific form of theological exegesis we are dubbing inductive theological exegesis.

---

[7] "But during the night an angel of the LORD opened the prison doors and brought them out, and said, 'Go and stand in the temple and speak to the people all the words of this Life.' And when they heard this, they entered the temple at daybreak and began to teach. Now when the high priest came, and those who were with him, they called together the council, all the senate of the people of Israel, and sent to the prison to have them brought" (Acts 5:19–21).

[8] "In the first book, O Theophilus, I have dealt with all that Jesus began to do and teach, until the day when he was taken up" (Acts 1:1–2).

[9] "When Jesus had finished instructing his twelve disciples, he went on from there to teach and preach in their cities" (Matthew 11:1).

[10] See for example: "For Ezra had set his heart to study the Law of the LORD, and to do it and to teach his statutes and rules in Israel" (Ezra 7:10). "They shall teach my people the difference between the holy and the common, and show them how to distinguish between the unclean and the clean. In a dispute, they shall act as judges, and they shall judge it according to my judgments. They shall keep my laws and my statutes in all my appointed feasts, and they shall keep my Sabbaths holy" (Ezekiel 44:23–24).

[11] "And God has appointed in the church first apostles, second prophets, third teachers, then miracles, then gifts of healing, helping, administrating, and various kinds of tongues. Are all apostles? Are all prophets? Are all teachers? Do all work miracles?" (1 Corinthians 12:28–29). "And he gave the apostles, the prophets, the evangelists, the shepherds and teachers, to equip the saints for the work of ministry, for building up the body of Christ" (Ephesians 4:11–12).

[12] Romans 12:3–8; 1 Corinthians 12:4–11; Ephesians 4:11–13; 1 Thessalonians 5:19–22; Hebrews 2:4.

[13] For example, the Mormon practice of baptism for the dead is based on one obscure text in 1 Corinthians 15:29 according to Bruce Corley, Steve Lemke, and Grant Lovejoy, *Biblical Hermeneutics: a Comprehensive Introduction to Interpreting Scripture*, 2d ed. (Nashville: Broadman & Holman, 2002), 310–11.

Section 1

PRACTICAL PREPARATION

CHAPTER 1

THOUGHTFUL PROCLAIMERS ARE CHANGED BY THE WORD

When Joshua was by Jericho, he lifted up his eyes and looked, and behold, a man was standing before him with his drawn sword in his hand. And Joshua went to him and said to him, "Are you for us, or for our adversaries?" And he said, "No; but I am the commander of the army of the LORD. Now I have come." And Joshua fell on his face to the earth and worshiped and said to him, "What does my LORD say to his servant?" And the commander of the LORD's army said to Joshua, "Take off your sandals from your feet, for the place where you are standing is holy." And Joshua did so. (Joshua 5:13–15)

You Are Standing on Holy Ground

Kick off your shoes. Studying the Bible to preach and teach what God is saying to the world from His Word is sacred work. When you ask of a Bible passage, "What are you saying, Lord?" you are entering holy ground. Nothing is more significant than asking God, "What is the message you have for your servants from this passage?" We are asking for the Holy Spirit to clearly show us why He inspired the passage we plan to teach. We are standing in that holy moment in a new place and time asking what the Lord's message, written long ago, means for us individually and for the people in our care. It is a great privilege to have the opportunity of relaying God's message to His children. Getting it right is important, but it is just as important for us to allow the Word we preach and teach to transform us. That is why we call this method "thoughtful."

What Exactly Are Thoughtful Proclaimers?

Thoughtful proclaimers are people who believe the Bible can change lives, families, and the world and that that's not too much to ask of God. Thoughtful proclaimers are not looking for the easy road to a good Bible message; they're looking for the right road. They are not seeking to merely read the Bible; they are compelled to share its message. They don't want to teach just what the Bible says but to encourage people to understand what God means for them to be, do, feel, and think. Thoughtful proclaimers want to proclaim God's Word more effectively, to share with people the good news that Jesus Christ offers to lost souls and broken lives.

Thoughtful Proclaimers Have Differing Educational Backgrounds

There is no educational requirement to be a thoughtful proclaimer except to keep learning and growing in faith and knowledge of Jesus Christ and God's Word. For some of us, that means hours with our Bibles in prayerful study. For others, it means Bible classes or advanced degrees. For most of us, it means reading often and widely on a variety of subjects to improve our skills, broaden our perspectives, and make our messages more appealing. Thoughtful proclaimers are not ever content to stop growing.

A. W. Tozer is widely regarded as one of the twentieth century's greatest preachers, but his schooling ended with grammar school. With no high school education and certainly no formal theological training, he practiced ministry for forty-four years and wrote forty books. He ministered as a pastor, author, conference speaker, and denominational leader. His biographer, James Snyder, claimed he was a reliable spiritual mentor. He added that many regarded him, even during his lifetime, as a twentieth-century prophet.[i] Tozer educated himself by reading all the time. As a young minister, he traveled twice a week to a library for armloads of books and borrowed many theological books from other ministers.[ii] Despite his lack of a diploma and regardless of his voracious reading habits, his view was, "A man should think twice as much as he reads."[iii] His ministry flowed out of him not just because he studied so hard but because he was under the control of the Holy Spirit.[iv]

The messages of thoughtful proclaimers' messages are built on the bedrock of Bible study and prayer, but our minds are fed also by significant reading of all kinds. Thoughtful proclaimers are big on reading but even bigger on thinking, meditating, and praying.

Thoughtful proclaimers are changed by God's Word as they study it. The natural product of studying the Bible is for the Bible to do its work on our hearts and minds. As proclaimers of the Word, we get so focused on what God wants us to say or teach that we forget whom God wants to make us into.[1] The first step in message preparation is messenger preparation.

> And we also thank God constantly for this, that when you received the word of God, which you heard from us, you accepted it not as the word of men but as what it really is, the word of God, which is at work in you believers. (1 Thessalonians 2:13)

---

[1] "Finally, be strong in the LORD and in the strength of his might. Put on the whole armor of God, that you may be able to stand against the schemes of the devil. For we do not wrestle against flesh and blood, but against the rulers, against the authorities, against the cosmic powers over this present darkness, against the spiritual forces of evil in the heavenly places. Therefore take up the whole armor of God, that you may be able to withstand in the evil day, and having done all, to stand firm. Stand therefore, having fastened on the belt of truth, and having put on the breastplate of righteousness, and, as shoes for your feet, having put on the readiness given by the gospel of peace. In all circumstances take up the shield of faith, with which you can extinguish all the flaming darts of the evil one; and take the helmet of salvation, and the sword of the Spirit, which is the Word of God, praying at all times in the Spirit, with all prayer and supplication. To that end keep alert with all perseverance, making supplication for all the saints, and also for me, that words may be given to me in opening my mouth boldly to proclaim the mystery of the gospel, for which I am an ambassador in chains, that I may declare it boldly, as I ought to speak" (Ephesians 6:10–20).

Resonating with the Spirit

When the jazz musician John Coltrane blew into a saxophone, his breath, which was relatively light, caused a little reed to vibrate, which caused the horn to produce sound, which was further magnified by the horn's bell shape and became the jazz music with which he delighted audiences. In physics, we would call this *resonance*. When a driving force (the breath of a musician) is at a frequency close to the natural frequency of something (a reed), the resulting oscillation is greatly increased; this increase in oscillation is called resonance.[v] When the Holy Spirit breathed His message into the writers of the Bible,[2] the ink that flowed from their pens became something far more than scratches and marks; it became the Word of God.

Just as the breath of a musician turns into music, the words of God we study resonate with the Holy Spirit indwelling us[3] to form a melody to be played for our listeners. That melody, when it resonates in the ears and hearts of our listeners, is again transformed by the Holy Spirit into something even more significant. Our little tune can be used by God to transform lives. The ripples go out from that place like sound waves and are used by God to change the world.

God Speaks through the Bible

God has spoken to us primarily in two ways: first, through Scripture and through the words of His Son when He was on earth,[4] and second and less clearly, through His Spirit and His creation.[5] The Bible is our chief source for proclamation to others because it is the clearest message we have from God. The Bible is not just a well-respected, ancient document but the Spirit-breathed Word of God infused with God's power to transform us.

God spoke the world into being with His words.[6] The apostle John called Jesus Christ the

---

[2] "All Scripture is breathed out by God and profitable for teaching, for reproof, for correction, and for training in righteousness" (2 Timothy 3:16).

[3] "And when [Jesus Christ] had said this, he breathed on them and said to them, 'Receive the Holy Spirit'" (John 20:22).

[4] "All Scripture is breathed out by God and profitable for teaching, for reproof, for correction, and for training in righteousness" (2 Timothy 3:16). "Long ago, at many times and in many ways, God spoke to our fathers by the prophets, but in these last days he has spoken to us by his Son, whom he appointed the heir of all things, through whom also he created the world" (Hebrews 1:1–2).

[5] "And I will ask the Father, and he will give you another Helper, to be with you forever, even the Spirit of truth, whom the world cannot receive, because it neither sees him nor knows him. You know him, for he dwells with you and will be in you" (John 14:16–17). "Do you not know that you are God's temple and that God's Spirit dwells in you?" (1 Corinthians 3:16). "For it has seemed good to the Holy Spirit and to us to lay on you no greater burden than these requirements" (Acts 15:28). "If we live by the Spirit, let us also keep in step with the Spirit" (Galatians 5:25). "For what can be known about God is plain to them, because God has shown it to them. For his invisible attributes, namely, his eternal power and divine nature, have been clearly perceived, ever since the Creation of the world, in the things that have been made. So they are without excuse" (Romans 1:19–20). "For all who are led by the Spirit of God are sons of God. For you did not receive the spirit of slavery to fall back into fear, but you have received the Spirit of adoption as sons, by whom we cry, 'Abba! Father!' The Spirit himself bears witness with our spirit that we are children of God, and if children, then heirs—heirs of God and fellow heirs with Christ, provided we suffer with him in order that we may also be glorified with him" (Romans 8:14–17).

[6] "And God said …" (Genesis 1:3, 6, 9, 11, 14, 20, 24, 26).

Word.[7] Words of God are powerful, sharper even than a scalpel or sword.[8] The Bible calls the commandments "living oracles."[9] There is no greater source for our proclamation than the Word of God. By focusing on the Bible in our message preparation, we drink deeply from the well of His Word and grow closer to the Savior.

It is possible to have much Bible knowledge and yet not be growing closer to the source of the Bible, God. But it is not possible to truly be preaching or teaching in a Spirit-filled way while not trusting in the subject of the Bible, Jesus Christ, as Savior. There are experts on the Bible just as there are experts on Shakespeare. You might know all about the history, culture, and times Shakespeare lived in. You might have memorized large passages of Shakespeare's writing. You might understand the literature, the style, and the grammar of Shakespeare and be steeped in Elizabethan English. But you can never really have a relationship with Shakespeare. You cannot pray to Shakespeare for wisdom to understand his writing. Other than enjoying his plays, Shakespeare cannot transform you and certainly cannot offer you eternal life.

That is how proclaimers differ from biblical specialists. We aim to know the author of the Bible better by our study. We can't really understand the message of the Word without trusting that the author is the King of the universe. We can proclaim God's purposes if we are willing to step out in that faith and live according to those purposes. In this way, we can show them to be true in our own hearts and lives. In this way, we are honest, true proclaimers of God's message—not perfect by any means, but on the journey.

Ask the Lord to use you to apply His message to your life, and ask Him for the wisdom to proclaim that message to others.[10]

God Speaks through Us

> The saying is trustworthy and deserving of full acceptance, that Christ Jesus came into the world to save sinners, of whom I am the foremost. But I received mercy for this reason, that in me, as the foremost, Jesus Christ might display his perfect patience as an example to those who were to believe in him for eternal life. (1 Timothy 1:15–16)

God speaks through us. What a privilege and responsibility. God allows us to be His mouthpieces though we are not perfect or deserving of that honor. We are blessed to bless others. But to be that blessing, we have to be willing to be clay in the Potter's hands to be formed as He

---

[7] "In the beginning was the word, and the word was with God, and the word was God. He was in the beginning with God. All things were made through him, and without him was not anything made that was made. In him was life, and the life was the light of men. The light shines in the darkness, and the darkness has not overcome it" (John 1:1–5).

[8] "For the word of God is living and active, sharper than any two-edged sword, piercing to the division of soul and of spirit, of joints and of marrow, and discerning the thoughts and intentions of the heart" (Hebrews 4:12).

[9] "This is the one [Moses] who was in the congregation in the wilderness with the angel who spoke to him at Mount Sinai, and with our fathers. He received living oracles to give to us" (Acts 7:38).

[10] "And this is the confidence that we have toward him, that if we ask anything according to his will he hears us" (1 John 5:14). "You ask and do not receive, because you ask wrongly, to spend it on your passions" (James 4:3).

wills.[11] Hardened clay is impossible to form into something useful; nothing blocks God's ability to mold us into what he wants us to be more than a hard heart. Personal repentance is key to great proclamation. Acknowledging that we are sinners saved by God's grace makes us the perfect people to share that grace with others.

Two men came to the temple to pray, Jesus told us. One was very righteous and thanked God he was not like the other, an awful sinner. In contrast, the tax collector next to him would not even dare lift his eyes toward heaven; he just beat his breast and cried out for mercy before God. Jesus sad,

> I tell you, this man went down to his house justified, rather than the other. For everyone who exalts himself will be humbled, but the one who humbles himself will be exalted. (Luke 18:14)

We pray and confess before we read and study, and we are engaged in two-way communication, prayer, and meditation the entire time we prepare and as we speak. Preaching and teaching God's Word is not a performance and not a prepared speech; it is a Spirit-filled, living, breathing event. We place ourselves in the hands of God to be molded and used throughout the process of listening, living, and loving others by proclaiming God's message to a hurting world.

In general, the better prepared we are, the more we can be used. Though Jesus told His disciples not to be anxious about what they would say in their defense when they were attacked for their faith,[12] nowhere are we encouraged not to prepare to teach the Word. In fact, we are charged with being ready "in season and out of season" to preach the Word.[13] I'm personally partial to the King James Version of 2 Timothy 2:15: "Study to show thyself approved unto God, a workman that needeth not to be ashamed, rightly dividing the Word of truth." Think of *study* as God working the clay to make it easier for Him to mold us.

The Importance of Asking Questions

> The brothers immediately sent Paul and Silas away by night to Berea, and when they arrived they went into the Jewish synagogue. Now these Jews were more noble than those in Thessalonica; they received the Word with all eagerness, examining the Scriptures daily to see if these things were so. Many of them therefore believed, with not a few Greek women of high standing as well as men. (Acts 17:10–12)

Inductive Bible interpretation for proclamation allows preachers and teachers to make Spirit-led discoveries. When we listen, we begin to formulate questions—personal, spiritual, and exegetical. By asking questions, we prepare messages that are richer and fuller for our

---

[11] "But now, O LORD, you are our Father; we are the clay, and you are our potter; we are all the work of your hand. Be not so terribly angry, O LORD, and remember not iniquity forever. Behold, please look, we are all your people" (Isaiah 64:8–9; cf. Jeremiah 18:6; Isaiah 45:9; Romans 9:21).

[12] "[Jesus said to the disciples:] 'When they deliver you over, do not be anxious how you are to speak or what you are to say, for what you are to say will be given to you in that hour. For it is not you who speak, but the Spirit of your Father speaking through you'" (Matthew 10:19–20). "Then Peter, filled with the Holy Spirit, said to them, 'Rulers of the people and elders …'" (Acts 4:8).

[13] See 2 Timothy 4:1 in the preface and 2 Timothy 14 at the head of chapter 3.

congregation. Our primary source for proclamation is to be Scripture rather than the writings of other people or scholarly research. Thoughtful proclaimers focus first on reading the Word and listening to it with their minds and hearts. This is a simple way of examining Scripture, like the method used by the Bereans in Acts 17. Though the thoughtful proclaimer method is easy to understand, in practice, it is challenging. But the hard work will reap good results for preaching, teaching, and personal devotion.

Reading books and studying commentaries can broaden our understanding of a passage and give us help with application, ideas for illustrations, and information regarding language and backgrounds. But commentary reading is not usually the best way to spend our devotional time. Our time is limited, so we must choose wisely. Learning how to ask good questions helps us come to exegetical and theological conclusions based on our observations of a text in its context and in the context of Scripture as we have it. Asking questions helps expand our thinking and allows us to meditate on a passage devotionally even as we study it exegetically. After all that is done, if we need to ask an expert, we can consult our commentaries.[14] The thoughtful proclaimer method is more about the Bible changing the preacher than about the preacher becoming an expert on Near Eastern history or Hebrew verb conjugations.

It Is Christ We Proclaim

> Him we proclaim, warning everyone and teaching everyone with all wisdom, that we may present everyone mature in Christ. (Colossians 1:28)

Before we had the Bible on our phones, it used to be in book form (!), and many of us kept articles, church bulletins, pages ripped from devotionals, and the occasional funeral card tucked inside. Sometimes, these important pieces of paper dropped out of our Bibles and were lost. When we are preparing a message on a passage of the Bible that doesn't directly mention Jesus Christ, He can easily slide out unnoticed onto the floor like those old clippings.

Biblical messages that stick closely to a particular passage can miss the mark when it comes to proclaiming Christ. It is easy to become so focused on our individual passage, its purpose, and other related passages that we forget the preeminent purpose of the book that contains our text. We must keep Christ in focus as we study a passage especially if it does not speak directly to the gospel message.

Having Christ-centered questions to help us study keeps Him from falling out of our messages. The Thoughtful Proclaimer Questions at the end of many of the chapters to come will help us as we study our passages and remind us to keep Christ in all our messages, even those from the Old Testament.

The other side of the coin is that preachers who are gospel focused can use evangelism as an excuse for not proclaiming the whole Word of God—both the Old and the New Testaments. The passage we are proclaiming is the boss and we are its servants. Though we keep Christ in focus, we must not use our evangelistic fervor as an excuse for sloppy exegesis and incomplete preaching of God's complete Word of truth in the many forms He inspired it.

---

[14] See chapter 6 for advice on commentaries or see *How to Read the Bible for All It's Worth* and *How to Read the Bible Book by Book*, by Douglas Stuart and Gordon Fee.

Authority and the Need for Interpretation

This book is based on an understanding that the Bible in its entirety is authoritative for the life and practice of a Christian; understanding what the Bible is not only saying but also meaning is of utmost importance. The purpose of a passage, our Commander's intent, is authoritative if it is perfectly understood, but that may not always be possible. Theological exegesis interprets all texts in light of the complete canon of Scripture.

A book like this that claims to be able to help humans understand the intentions of God needs to explain carefully what it means by calling the Bible authoritative. By claiming that we are finding the Commander's intent for a passage, we may invite the accusation that we are being somehow prideful or worse—warmongering or militaristic. In fact, the opposite is true: by looking for the Commander's intent, we are taking a step of humility, love, and care. We are people carefully attempting to live under the authority of the loving God of Abraham, Isaac, Jacob, and Moses, the personal Savior of our souls. We call on the counsel of the Holy Spirit. Like good servants, we aim to understand the master and follow His command to love our neighbor as ourselves.[15]

John Stott wrote,

> Our claim, then, is that God has revealed himself by speaking; that this divine ("God-breathed") speech has been written down and preserved in Scripture; and that Scripture is, in fact, God's Word written down, which therefore is true and reliable and has divine authority over us.[vi]

N. T. Wright further delineated this idea well by explaining,

> The "authority of Scripture" is a shorthand expression for God's authority, exercised somehow through Scripture; [and] that Scripture must be allowed to be itself in exercising its authority, and not be turned into something else ... let the Bible be the Bible, and so to let God be God—and so ... enable the people of God to be the people of God, his special people, living under his authority, bringing his light to his world.[vii]

So, what do we mean when we commit to making the Bible our authority and look for the Commander's intent? On one hand, we are simply saying Scripture is our authority when it is interpreted in light of its historical, cultural, literary, canonical, and redemptive contexts. That is a long string of adjectives in front of the word *contexts*, but those adjectives in no way diminish the authority of Scripture. In fact, they describe the Bible we have, which is an English (or other language) translation of a library of God-breathed or inspired sacred texts recorded in many genres over thousands of years in the contexts of different cultures and in several ancient languages. We ignore those facts to our own and the world's peril. If this were not so, we would not need to interpret the Bible or preach it or teach from it at all, but God calls us to preach and to teach on His Word.[16]

---

[15] For the whole law is fulfilled in one word: "You shall love your neighbor as yourself" (Galatians 5:14). See also Leviticus 19:18; Matthew 19:19, 22:37–40; Romans 13:9; and James 2:8.

[16] See 2 Timothy 4:2 at the end of the preface where "preach the word" is translated "proclaim the message."

As preachers and teachers, it is our divine appointment to study the Bible humbly and responsibly and aim to get it right. We listen to God and converse with Him in prayer over each passage. We look at the other things God has spoken in the book we call the Word of God. We say all this with humility knowing we are not perfect in our ability to interpret and apply but desiring to aim by the anointing power of the Holy Spirit to understand and proclaim God's intention as best we can.

In fact, a great deal of the Bible does not directly claim authority at all but was written rather as narrative,[17] poetry, prophecy, and ancient, culturally bound law. The Bible is in fact mostly descriptive rather than prescriptive. It is best taken at face value, as it was originally meant to be understood, in its own historical context and in the literary form that contains it. Those few rules we read in the Bible are often culturally bound or situational in their context and intent. Preachers and teachers must carefully study to determine what God's universal intent is for those passages. That is the purpose of this book—to find God's intent for each passage.

Aim for the intention of God, Not Your Own

> For we are not peddlers of God's word like so many; but in Christ we speak as persons
> of sincerity, as persons sent from God and standing in his presence. (2 Corinthians 2:17)

The Bible doesn't get to mean what we want it to mean; it means what the author(s) wrote it to mean. The authors' meaning (inspired by the heavenly Author) is the point of control. As proclaimers, we have a lot of power bestowed on us by our listeners, and we must not abuse it. Interpretation is as much art as science, but that does not give us an excuse to artfully distort God's intentions into what we want. If you are a persuasive speaker, that can be a temptation.

Charles Hodge warned many years ago (1871–1873),[viii] in his *Systematic Theology*, "No man has a right to lay down his own opinions, however firmly held, and call them 'first truths of reason,' and make them the source or test of Christian doctrines."[ix] Serious Bible interpretation, inductive theological exegesis in fact means the opposite.

The Bible most often does not clearly spell out how we are to live in its narrative histories and poems. This means we must seek the intent, not just the letter, to interpret it well. The Bible is most often describing a broken world and sinful people but not providing us with examples to follow. The Bible rarely offers moral commentary or principles to live by at the end of its stories. Rather, it describes sinful people who look a lot like us. The Bible, rather than being a book of rules (though there are those too), is a book to show how a just and loving God deals with a broken world.

If I say the Bible is my authority and my message contains God's intentions, must my listeners trust my interpretation and blindly follow it? Good preaching and teaching grow mature believers who, like the Bereans in our introduction, have learned from us how to discern for themselves if what we are saying is true. Our responsibility is to teach others to discern truth from error even

---

[17] Narrative is something that is narrated such as a story or historical account of an event.

more than it is to be right all the time.[18] Teaching the Commander's intent does not make us commanders; it makes us stewards.

> Who then is the faithful and wise servant, whom his master has set over his household, to give them their food at the proper time? Blessed is that servant whom his master will find so doing when he comes. (Matthew 14:25–26)

Again, N. T. Wright remarked on the authority of Scripture,

> We must let Scripture be itself, and that is a hard task. Scripture contains many things that I don't know, and that you don't know; many things we are waiting to discover; passages which are lying dormant waiting for us to dig them out … we must determine— corporately as well as individually—to become in a true sense, people of the book.[x]

Proper Interpretation Encourages Empathetic Proclamation

> If I speak in the tongues of men and of angels, but have not love, I am a noisy gong or a clanging cymbal. And if I have prophetic powers, and understand all mysteries and all knowledge, and if I have all faith, so as to remove mountains, but have not love, I am nothing. If I give away all I have, and if I deliver up my body to be burned, but have not love, I gain nothing.
>
> Love never ends. As for prophecies, they will pass away; as for tongues, they will cease; as for knowledge, it will pass away. For we know in part and we prophesy in part, but when the perfect comes, the partial will pass away. (1 Corinthians 13:1–3, 9–10)

Thoughtful proclaimers do not base a message on one passage but carefully consider the context of the entire Bible. They highlight the important things. They don't emphasize things they don't understand despite prayer and study. The Bible is one book containing a library of books. Incorrect views occur when a passage is taken out of context or when we view a passage from one book without considering the message of the library, the fullness of Scripture.

We cannot know the Commander unless we consider His overall intent for His Word. Unfortunately, in trying to speak the truth, we may forget to speak it in love and thus negate the message altogether. In focusing fully on our passage, we may forget the gospel message—the ultimate context. God's purpose, His intent, is not to condemn the world but for all of us, even those we erroneously consider to be "bigger sinners" than ourselves, to be reconciled to Himself.[19]

> For God so loved the world, that he gave his only Son, that whoever believes in him should not perish but have eternal life. For God did not send his Son into the world to condemn the world, but in order that the world might be saved through him. Whoever

---

[18] "But solid food is for the mature, for those who have their powers of discernment trained by constant practice to distinguish good from evil" (Hebrews 5:14).

[19] "All this is from God, who through Christ reconciled us to himself and gave us the ministry of reconciliation; that is, in Christ God was reconciling the world to himself, not counting their trespasses against them, and entrusting to us the message of reconciliation. Therefore, we are ambassadors for Christ, God making his appeal through us. We implore you on behalf of Christ, be reconciled to God. For our sake he made him to be sin who knew no sin, so that in him we might become the righteousness of God" (2 Corinthians 5:18–21).

believes in him is not condemned, but whoever does not believe is condemned already, because he has not believed in the name of the only Son of God. (John 3:16–18)

In our zeal for the gospel and Scripture, we can lose sight of the big ideals Jesus insisted on.[20] We can take on the role of Old Testament prophet, but we know that is a role we must never assume. The authority we claim is not God's authority because that belongs solely to Him. It is not personal authority to command and accuse people. Rather, we claim the authority of one who would be the servant of all, a humble proclaimer.[21] We teach as best we can and admit we see God's purposes only dimly; we speak on behalf of our Savior and the one who loves the World using Scripture as our guide and to the best of our ability.[22]

The proper response to tragedy or loss is always sincere sympathy and sorrow. The deepest emotions and fears of people are universal. Even in the case of loss caused by sinful decisions, our biblical response is not to point fingers but to repent of our sins and be grateful for God's mercy on us. As proclaimers, we may warn others from time to time that sin carries judgment on earth as well as in eternity. But if ever misfortune occurs, it is never our prerogative to put ourselves in the place of God and claim to know the cause. In Luke 13:1–5, Jesus warned the disciples of this very sin of trying to figure out why bad things happen.

> There were some present at that very time who told him about the Galileans whose blood Pilate had mingled with their sacrifices. And he [Jesus] answered them, "Do you think that these Galileans were worse sinners than all the other Galileans, because they suffered in this way? No, I tell you; but unless you repent, you will all likewise perish. Or those eighteen on whom the tower in Siloam fell and killed them: do you think that they were worse offenders than all the others who lived in Jerusalem? No, I tell you; but unless you repent, you will all likewise perish." (Luke 13:1–5)

In the case of natural disasters or widespread calamities, the proclaimer calls the people of God to lament.[23] This is not a time for judgment or finger-pointing but rather for personal repentance of the righteous. Some who arrogantly claim prophet status go as far as to claim that the people who have suffered deserve the misfortunes that befell them. Even the prophet Jeremiah, who spent the majority of his life warning sinners of coming judgment, is called the weeping prophet because of his great sadness over the sins of the people and the consequences

---

[20] For example, the greatest of all the commandments: "Jesus answered, 'The most important is, "Hear, O Israel: The LORD our God, the LORD is one. And you shall love the LORD your God with all your heart and with all your soul and with all your mind and with all your strength."'" (Mark 12:29–30).

[21] "And he sat down and called the twelve. And he said to them, 'If anyone would be first, he must be last of all and servant of all'" (Mark 9:35).

[22] "For now we see in a mirror dimly, but then face to face. Now I know in part; then I shall know fully, even as I have been fully known. So now faith, hope, and love abide, these three; but the greatest of these is love" (1 Corinthians 13:12–13).

[23] Joel 1:13–20 tells us that in the day of disaster, the ministers of the altar were to put on sackcloth and lament (v. 13). They were to call the people together to fast and pray (v. 14) and to call on the LORD for help (v. 19). "'Yet even now,' declares the LORD, 'return to me with all your heart, with fasting, with weeping, and with mourning; and rend your hearts and not your garments.' Return to the LORD your God, for he is gracious and merciful, slow to anger, and abounding in steadfast love; and he relents over disaster. Who knows whether he will not turn and relent, and leave a blessing behind him, a grain offering and a drink offering for the LORD your God?" (Joel 2:12–14).

allowed by a long-suffering God when His children rejected Him.[24] When people are hurting, a true prophet, like a loving parent, weeps with those who suffer loss despite the fact that he may have warned of the ramifications of sin prior to seeing its result. If we warned a well-loved son to drive carefully as he left the house, would we stand at his bedside in the hospital after an accident shaking our finger at him and saying, "Repent, you sinner"? Yet there are plenty of preachers who don't even go to the bedside but rather stand behind a pulpit far away and pronounce judgment on the brokenhearted and hurting.

If all sinners got what they deserved, the world would be wiped clean of every human being. The example Jesus gave us was to judge the self-righteous accusers of the woman caught in adultery much more harshly than He judged the woman: "Let the one who is without sin cast the first stone."[25] To her he said, "Go and sin no more."[26]

Just as Paul turned his suffering in chains into an opportunity to spread the gospel, we can transform chains and suffering into an opportunity for good by encouraging our listeners to focus not on judging others but rather on good deeds, reconciliation, and personal salvation.[27]

We should always remain aware of our own sinful status and the forgiveness Christ paid for so dearly. We weep with those who weep and rejoice with those who rejoice. We are not prideful, and we do not assume to speak for God beyond what He has clearly written in His Word, and then with great humility.[28]

"To Thine Own Self Be True" Self-Examination[xi]

> Or how can you say to your neighbor, "Let me take the speck out of your eye," while the log is in your own eye? (Matthew 7:4)

When I weigh something on my kitchen scale, I take care to set it to zero first. We must always balance our scale if we hope for it to be accurate. Whenever interpreting the Bible, we should examine not only our text but also our presuppositions. Our first responsibility as thoughtful proclaimers is self-examination. We need to make ourselves aware of the chips on

---

[24] "[The LORD said:] 'And I will declare my judgments against them, for all their evil in forsaking me. They have made offerings to other Gods and worshiped the works of their own hands" (Jeremiah 1:16). "Jeremiah also uttered a lament for Josiah [when he died in battle]; and all the singing men and singing women have spoken of Josiah in their laments to this day. They made these a rule in Israel; behold, they are written in the Laments" (2 Chronicles 35:25). "My people have been lost sheep. Their shepherds have led them astray, turning them away on the mountains. From mountain to hill they have gone. They have forgotten their fold. All who found them have devoured them, and their enemies have said, 'We are not guilty, for they have sinned against the LORD, their habitation of righteousness, the LORD, the hope of their fathers'" (Jeremiah 50:6–7).

[25] "And as they continued to ask him, he stood up and said to them, 'Let him who is without sin among you be the first to throw a stone at her'" (John 8:7).

[26] "She said, 'No one, LORD.' And Jesus said, 'Neither do I condemn you; go, and from now on sin no more'" (John 8:11).

[27] "[Paul wrote:] I want you to know, brothers, that what has happened to me has really served to advance the gospel, so that it has become known throughout the whole imperial guard and to all the rest that my imprisonment is for Christ. And most of the brothers, having become confident in the LORD by my imprisonment, are much more bold to speak the word without fear" (Philippians 1:12–14).

[28] "Rejoice with those who rejoice, weep with those who weep. Live in harmony with one another. Do not be haughty, but associate with the lowly. Never be wise in your own sight. Repay no one evil for evil, but give thought to do what is honorable in the sight of all. If possible, so far as it depends on you, live peaceably with all" (Romans 12:15–18).

our own shoulders that color our perspective. Before we ever attempt to eradicate the sliver in someone else's eye, Jesus tells us to remove the giant log from our own.[29] In stopping to point out the error of someone else's path, we can easily trip and fall.[30]

We need to take careful note of our social, political, economic, and cultural views. We are all biased; we tend to see in others the sin we are most blind to in our own lives. We cannot take a scalpel and excise these thoughts from our brains, but we can make ourselves aware of them. We can bow in repentance.

> Who can discern his errors?
> Declare me innocent from hidden faults.
> Keep back your servant also from presumptuous sins;
> let them not have dominion over me!
> Then I shall be blameless,
> and innocent of great transgression.
> (Psalm 19:12–13)

Inductive reasoning is easily prone to being self-focused; we can end up asking only the questions we want to answer. A good method is to focus also on the questions others might ask. Read the passage as if you are from a different culture or life situation. For example, read Psalm 23 as if you are poor and starving. Read Revelation as though you have suffered severe persecution. Balance your presuppositions and cultural biases by using your imagination and putting yourself in someone else's shoes as the reader. If you are conservative, think like a liberal. If you are trusting, think like a skeptic.

> To thine own self be true,
> and it must follow, as the night the day,
> Thou canst not then be false to any man.

> —Shakespeare (*Hamlet*, act 1, scene 3)

---

[29] "Why do you see the speck that is in your brother's eye, but do not notice the log that is in your own eye? Or how can you say to your brother, 'Let me take the speck out of your eye,' when there is the log in your own eye? You hypocrite, first take the log out of your own eye, and then you will see clearly to take the speck out of your brother's eye" (Matthew 7:3–5). "Why do you see the speck that is in your brother's eye, but do not notice the log that is in your own eye? How can you say to your brother, 'Brother, let me take out the speck that is in your eye,' when you yourself do not see the log that is in your own eye? You hypocrite, first take the log out of your own eye, and then you will see clearly to take out the speck that is in your brother's eye" (Luke 6:41–42).

[30] "Brothers, if anyone is caught in any transgression, you who are spiritual should restore him in a spirit of gentleness. Keep watch on yourself, lest you too be tempted" (Galatians 6:1).

As expected, Pastor Tom's Shakespeare illustration went right over their heads. *xii*

Deductive Reasoning Can Help Us through Apparent Inconsistencies in Scripture

Being a thoughtful proclaimer means interpreting Scripture based on other Scripture. Though our method is primarily inductive in nature, we sometimes must use deductive reasoning to understand a difficult, confusing, or seemingly conflicting passage. Deductive reasoning moves toward a necessary conclusion from a known truth.[31] We use deductive reasoning when we have a passage that seems to run counter to a known attribute of God for example.[32] This is especially true when our personal theology is at odds with the apparent meaning of a passage

In *Reading the Word of God in the Presence of God*, Vern Poythress wrote,

> Our growth in communion with God includes growth in knowing God and knowing the Bible as his Word. In this growth, we profit from interaction between three interlocking foci: (1) theology, as a summary of the teaching of the Bible as a whole; (2) interpretation of individual passages of the Bible (sometimes called "exegesis"); and (3) hermeneutics, the study of principles for and practice of interpretation. Troubles can arise if we absolutize any one of the three foci and refuse to let it be informed by insights from the others.[xiii]

We use deductive reasoning to understand passages that run counter to what we know from the rest of Scripture to be true. So when Paul quoted God as saying, "Jacob I loved, but Esau I hated" in Romans 9:13, we know this statement runs contrary to what we have read in 1 John 4:10—that God loved us. Our first job is to check our assumptions. If our assumption is true, we

---

[31] We remember from our glossary that inductive reasoning moves from the specific to the general, from an observation to a hypothetical conclusion.

[32] But what do we do when we read something in Scripture that doesn't make sense? Hide our eyes? Say, "I don't believe that part"? Say, "I always hated Paul anyway"? Just ignore it? No. When I run into trouble and it looks like the coach has suddenly turned against his own team, I do a couple of things. First, I consult other Scriptures, all of Scripture as much as possible. Scripture out of context is dangerous. I then see what God is like in the rest of Scripture and who He is in light of how He has acted in history. He has not given me any reason to doubt Him before! If I'm still a bit confused, I consult biblical authorities, but not first—first, I look at everything I can know about God from His own Word and His own actions.

must keep looking. For example: God loves all people; Esau is a person; therefore, "Esau have I hated" is not a logical statement, so we must look further.

Of course, Paul knew we would be shocked by the words "Esau I hated." And that is just why he included them: "What shall we say then? Is there injustice on God's part? By no means"![33] Paul went on to explain the purpose for his dramatic quotation of Malachi 1:2–3. Paul was pointing out that God did in fact love us all though we must note He was in charge. His ways were inexplicable. In fact, we later learn that His love for the descendants of Jacob was for the very purpose of bringing the descendants of Esau (that refers to the rest of us) to Himself.[34] God's love is not based on our will but on His mercy.

We read that God even raised up the evil Pharaoh (which didn't seem like a very loving thing to do considering he had enslaved the Hebrew people) so all people would hear His name: "For this very purpose I have raised you up, that I might show my power in you, and that my name might be proclaimed in all the earth."[35] And He blessed Jacob in a different way than He blessed Esau (whom he did bless mightily despite saying, "Esau I hated").

Through Jacob's descendants, all people would be brought to God: "Even us whom he has called, not from the Jews only but also from the Gentiles? As indeed he says in Hosea, 'Those who were not my people I will call 'my people,' and her who was not beloved I will call "beloved.""[36] By His love for Jacob, He made Esau and the rest of us His beloved.

The Bible Is Not a Fortune Cookie

When we wake in the morning and read a few verses with our coffee, the verse or paragraph has been excised from its place in the canon and is often not being read in light of its historical underpinnings. We may prayerfully take it to heart as our word from God for the day. That is what I call devotional reading, and it should not necessarily be considered as exegetically sound until we check it out. As thoughtful proclaimers, we need to take more care in our interpretation if we are to speak to others on God's behalf.

Let us suppose that I've been fretting all night about my grown child who is not following the Lord. I open my Bible and read Proverbs 22:6: "Train up a child in the way he should go; even when he is old he will not depart from it." I feel comforted. It seems like an answer to prayer. God seems to have promised me that my child would return to Himself when he was older. But is that what I should preach on this week? Is that a promise? What about God's children who turned away from Him? My devotional reading may be good comfort, but I've missed the literary genre of proverbs and turned it into a promise.[37] I've not considered the rest of Scripture on the subject; I've turned the Bible into a fortune cookie. It is a comfort, but it is not suitable for a sermon or a teaching.

We must carefully guard against confusion arising from less-solid devotional readings of

---

[33] Romans 9:14.

[34] "I will make you [Jesus Christ and by extension the Jews] as a light for the nations, that my salvation may reach to the end of the earth" (Isaiah 49:6b).

[35] Romans 9.

[36] Romans 9:24–25.

[37] See chapter 6 for more on literary genre and context.

Scripture for the purposes of preaching and teaching. Because we advocate a spiritually edifying form of Bible interpretation, it must be firmly reiterated that our inductive theological exegesis takes into account historical, cultural, literary, grammatical, and especially canonical exegesis (a study of the fullness of Scripture on the subject). We are not advocating teaching and preaching what may be called merely devotional meanings; we should not preach to others the personal applications and situational meanings that we are apt to apply to Scripture when we read a few verses out of context in light of our current life situations. It is a temptation to read into a passage our own biases, hopes, and dreams with little or no regard to what the Bible means. We can be tempted to ignore Scripture's many genres, contexts, and cultural-historical underpinnings and the canonical context as a whole.

Thoughtful proclaimers, especially when preparing messages for others, should not read the Bible as if it were a fortune cookie left over from last night's take-out dinner.[38] Verses plucked out of context can be much like the fortune in a cookie. But a fortune cookie does not know you, cannot offer you eternal salvation, and did not create the universe![39] As thoughtful proclaimers, we owe Scripture our diligent study, not just a quick read-through. When we teach or preach on a passage, we must consider its context and original meaning and the original author's perspective.

If the Bible means the same thing today that it meant when it was penned thousands of years ago, we must find out what it meant when it was penned or preached in Bible times. The true meaning of the biblical text for us is directly related to what God originally intended it to mean when it was first breathed out by the Holy Spirit; that is what we try to determine.[xiv] The application may differ from then to now, but the meaning remains.[xv]

Our aim will be to turn a complete passage into one point, a finely honed arrow whose shaft is long and straight and cuts through a significant portion of Scripture and considers what the Bible says on the subject elsewhere focusing on the meaning back then and its relevance today.

Your hard work may make the message look like it was easy to prepare, but you will know you are speaking the universal message, not a fortune-cookie message.

A Theology of Proclamation

1. Effective message preparation must first be "messenger" preparation.

    If I had cherished iniquity in my heart, the LORD would not have listened. But truly God has listened; he has attended to the voice of my prayer. (Psalm 66:18–19)

    Do not be conformed to this world, but be transformed by the renewal of your mind, that by testing you may discern what is the will of God, what is good and acceptable and perfect. (Romans 12:2)

---

[38] For those whose culture and diet differ from mine, fortune cookies have Chinese proverbs or predictions placed inside before they are baked.

[39] My favorite fortune cookie said, "A fool and his money are soon parted." On the back, it read, "Your Lucky Numbers are 55, 76, 89."

2. Proclaimers are ambassadors for God and His Word and should preach and teach as such. Our ultimate message is that of the reconciliation and redemption available to all people because of Christ's death and Resurrection.

All this is from God, who through Christ reconciled us to himself and gave us the ministry of reconciliation; that is, in Christ God was reconciling the world to himself, not counting their trespasses against them, and entrusting to us the message of reconciliation. Therefore, we are ambassadors for Christ, God making his appeal through us. We implore you on behalf of Christ, be reconciled to God. For our sake he made him to be sin who knew no sin, so that in him we might become the righteousness of God. (2 Corinthians 5:18–21)

3. The Old and New Testaments were given to us to proclaim so we can build up believers. They must be understood in concert to be understood properly.

All Scripture is breathed out by God and profitable for teaching, for reproof, for correction, and for training in righteousness, that the man of God may be complete, equipped for every good work. (2 Timothy 3:16–17)

4. The second goal of proclamation is for the listeners to be transformed to be more like Christ and grow spiritually so they can discern the will of God for their lives.

And he gave the apostles, the prophets, the evangelists, the shepherds and teachers, to equip the saints for the work of ministry, for building up the body of Christ, until we all attain to the unity of the faith and of the knowledge of the Son of God, to mature manhood, to the measure of the stature of the fullness of Christ, so that we may no longer be children, tossed to and fro by the waves and carried about by every wind of doctrine, by human cunning, by craftiness in deceitful schemes. Rather, speaking the truth in love, we are to grow up in every way into him who is the head, into Christ, from whom the whole body, joined and held together by every joint with which it is equipped, when each part is working properly, makes the body grow so that it builds itself up in love. (Ephesians 4:11–16)

5. If we proclaim the purposes of God found in His Word, our proclamation will accomplish what God intended. Our effort is necessary, but it is ultimately God who touches and transforms hearts.

So shall my word be that goes out from my mouth; it shall not return to me empty, but it shall accomplish that which I purpose, and shall succeed in the thing for which I sent it. (Isaiah 55:11)

6. The Word of God is spiritually alive and actively changing those who will hear it if it is taught in truth. Seek to sound a clear signal, make a straight path, and proclaim winningly the message of each passage.

For the word of God is living and active, sharper than any two-edged sword, piercing to the division of soul and of spirit, of joints and of marrow, and discerning the thoughts and intentions of the heart. And no creature is hidden from his sight, but all are naked and exposed to the eyes of him to whom we must give account. (Hebrews 4:12–13)

This is the one who was in the congregation in the wilderness with the angel who spoke to him at Mount Sinai, and with our fathers. He received living oracles to give to us. (Acts 7:38)

7. If God is our Lord and King, every part of His Word contains a trace of His intent for us. No parts of Scripture should be ignored as all are necessary to Christian understanding.

For whatever was written in former days was written for our instruction, that through endurance and through the encouragement of the Scriptures we might have hope. (Romans 15:4)

Thoughtful Proclaimer Personal Examination Questions

- What do I need to confess to God today? What have I done wrong? What have I left undone that God has called me to do?
- Are there people I need to forgive before I plan to proclaim to others?[40]
- Do I have any logs in my eye that I need to remove so I can see clearly before pointing out the specks in others' eyes?[41]
- Are there areas where I am being a hearer only and not a doer of the Word?[42]

---

[40] "Pray then like this: 'Our Father in heaven, hallowed be your name. Your kingdom come, your will be done, on earth as it is in heaven. Give us this day our daily bread, and forgive us our debts, as we also have forgiven our debtors. And lead us not into temptation, but deliver us from evil. For if you forgive others their trespasses, your heavenly Father will also forgive you, but if you do not forgive others their trespasses, neither will your Father forgive your trespasses" (Matthew 6:9–15). "And whenever you stand praying, forgive, if you have anything against anyone, so that your Father also who is in heaven may forgive you your trespasses" (Mark 11:25).

[41] "Why do you see the speck that is in your brother's eye, but do not notice the log that is in your own eye? Or how can you say to your brother, 'Let me take the speck out of your eye,' when there is the log in your own eye? You hypocrite, first take the log out of your own eye, and then you will see clearly to take the speck out of your brother's eye" (Matthew 7:3–5).

[42] "But be doers of the word, and not hearers only, deceiving yourselves. For if anyone is a hearer of the word and not a doer, he is like a man who looks intently at his natural face in a mirror. For he looks at himself and goes away and at once forgets what he was like. But the one who looks into the perfect law, the law of liberty, and perseveres, being no hearer who forgets but a doer who acts, he will be blessed in his doing" (James 1:22–25).

CHAPTER 2

DISCOVER THE COMMANDER'S INTENT

For as the rain and the snow come down from heaven
and do not return there but water the earth,
making it bring forth and sprout,
giving seed to the sower and bread to the eater,
so shall my word be that goes out from my mouth;
it shall not return to me empty,
but it shall accomplish that which I purpose,
and shall succeed in the thing for which I sent it.
(Isaiah 55:10–11)

Our job as people sent by God to communicate His message is to proclaim what He purposed for His Word and claim for ourselves Isaiah's prophecy—that God's Word will succeed in doing what God sent it for. We seek to understand the purpose of a passage just as a soldier seeks to understand his commander's intent for a mission. We develop our Commander's intent for a Bible passage into a point for proclamation, the central theme for our sermon or lesson.

The invasion of France on June 6, 1944, had been planned for years. British, Canadian, and American airborne forces planned and "rehearsed for months a precise series of glider and parachute landings designed to secure bridges, road junctions, and other key terrain that would enable the ground invasion forces to advance rapidly inland."

But when the airborne invasion forces took off from England, all those "months of planning appeared to vanish instantly. Parachute forces dropped into unmarked landing zones, gliders landed in the wrong areas, and thousands of soldiers from different units were mixed in the night. It appeared that a military disaster had occurred."

"Yet only hours later, the original military objectives were being accomplished by ad-hoc units that faced fierce German resistance. The commander's intent had saved the day. Leaders and soldiers at all levels understood that no matter where they landed, they had to form units and seize the bridges and key terrain. The plan was a failure, but good commander's intent and superior training allowed improvisation and initiative to save the mission."[1]

What Is a Commander's Intent?

The term *commander's intent* has become popular and is being used in business and other nonmilitary settings. Chip and Dan Heath popularized it in their excellent book *Made to Stick*.[ii] When I read about it, I was convinced we were looking for the Commander's intent when we study a Bible passage for the sake of preaching or teaching it. We are trying to make sense of an ancient book as it pertains to us in the battles and hubbub of modern life. We need to figure out our marching orders though everything has changed from when they were given to how they play out today. Those who come to hear us speak want to know what God has for them to do, be, think, and say today; they come to be transformed by the Word of God.

I read what I could about the commander's intent in the *Military Review* and publications from the War College. Then just to be sure, I had dinner with Major Eric J. Schmitz, U.S. Army, and talked to him about what commander's intent means in a military context. It works like this: an army order travels from the top down through many levels of subordinate authority after it is issued. The order morphs and changes as it is delivered to different types of troops with different parts of a job to accomplish. The commander's intent has to cover simultaneously offensive and defensive actions, stability, support, and even civil authority. Those who receive the order for a mission have differing levels of training and education. Somehow, this order has to communicate to everyone what needs to be accomplished. That is the commander's intent. Though the times, places, circumstances, weather, and details may surprise them, the troops are charged with accomplishing the commander's intent.

Depending on how the order is delivered, the commander's intent may be spelled out clearly or it may need to be interpreted and adapted for those further down the ranks or in different situations. Those under authority need to hear the commander's intent in a way they can understand. Those next in line in the chain of command must ensure that their commander's intent is clearly understood by all subordinate personnel and carried out. The commander's intent is the purpose statement for the mission.[iii]

Chip and Dan Heath said it this way in *Made to Stick*.

> The Combat Maneuver Training Center, the unit in charge of military simulations, recommends that officers arrive at the Commander's Intent by asking themselves two questions: If we do nothing else during tomorrow's mission, we must _____. The single, most important thing that we must do tomorrow is _____.[iv]

The Commander's Intent Grows Out of the Purpose of the Passage

The idea of a commander's intent is a powerful metaphor for the thoughtful proclaimer who seeks to interpret the Bible for its God-given meaning and purpose; the bottom line, good for all circumstances, must be accomplished intent. There are no extraneous, outdated, or unnecessary passages in the Bible. Depending on how we carve up a book into teachable passages, we may identify different related purposes, but we aim to find the Commander's intent that a well-defined passage has.

The application of the Commander's intent will look different to different people in different times, places, and circumstances, but the Commander knew what He had in mind when He placed that passage in His Word. The deeper meaning of a passage doesn't change though the circumstances and the people communicating it will.[1]

To help us hone in on the Commander's intent or purpose for a passage, we will consider the sub-purposes behind the writing of a passage: what did the intent look like for people back then? The sub-purposes to think about are:

1. the purpose of the original author in Bible times
2. the purpose of the Holy Spirit for breathing out the passage
3. the purpose that the Holy Spirit had in mind for this passage when read in our time and culture
4. the purpose of the passage for my personal transformation
5. the purpose of the passage for my audience's transformation

We can also look at the purposes of the passage by studying them in their larger biblical context: What is the purpose of the passage in the surrounding chapters? What is the purpose of the biblical book containing the passage? What is the purpose of the book in salvation history and the big story of redemption?[2]

Our reason for proclaiming our sermon or teaching is directly related to the Commander's intent, which is built on a foundation of the sub-purposes. The theme or subject of the passage is not equivalent to the Commander's intent. We want to determine the theme or subject of the passage, but the Commander's intent is the reason the passage was inspired by God and thus exists.

The Commander's Intent is why a particular passage is in the Bible. We are not looking for what the inspired author wrote *about* (which is equivalent to the theme or the "big idea"[3]); rather, we are looking for *why* the inspired author wrote and what he meant for us to hear, do, feel, and be as a result of studying the passage. Another way of looking at the Commander's intent is to examine what the inspired author wrote *for*.[4]

The Thoughtful Proclaimer Method Has Roots

How do we determine the Commander's intent without a lot of subjectivity and confusion creeping in? We will discuss this in much more detail and offer several methods to help us crack

---

[1] For example, if we are preaching on sacrifices in Leviticus or laws in Deuteronomy, we will need to take the time to ask questions about why something was done in a particular way. We will need to learn a lot about the culture. We will need to study the rest of the Bible on the matter. Does something in the New Testament replace or supersede the sacrifice in the Old? Why would God have made that particular rule? Who did it protect? Why was it necessary? The Commander didn't change, nor did His ultimate will, but the circumstances have. What is the deeper intent of the Commander for that passage? How does it apply to us today?

[2] Reading 1 and 2 Kings for example, we may wonder why God showed us the failings of so many earthly kings and the downfall of Judah. What does that have to do with the coming of the heavenly King?

[3] See Haddon Robinson's excellent book *Biblical Preaching: The Development and Delivery of Expository Messages* and chapter 10 of this book for more on Haddon Robinson's "Big Idea."

[4] In the hermeneutical world, there is no end to acronyms. If you read other books on Bible interpretation for preaching, you will find many of them. Do not confuse the Commander's intent with the CIT, which other interpreters use as an acronym for the central interpretative theme. The Commander's intent is the purpose of the passage, not the central subject/theme.

difficult passages in chapter 10. For now, credit must be given to Haddon Robinson, who had a "big idea" about using what he called the subject and the complement of a passage to determine the central unifying idea of a passage.[5]

Despite the variation between our method and Haddon Robinson's methods, the thoughtful proclaimer method has its roots in this important concept, especially the notion that a passage's multiple ideas and purposes must be honed to one sharp point, which is used to determine the big idea of an expository message.

THE PURPOSES OF THE PASSAGE ->COMMANDER'S INTENT

The Commander's Intent Will Be Developed into a Point for Proclamation and Finally a Sermonic Catchphrase

The commander's intent is handed down to the troops in a way they can understand, remember as needed, and apply. Just so, the Commander's intent will be adapted into something that suits our audiences as a point for proclamation. Like boiling down vinegar, the universal Commander's intent must be reduced further until it is sweet and thick. We then throw in a pinch of application, and we have the Commander's point for proclamation.

The point for proclamation is our sermon proposition, the point of our arrow. We structure our message around the point for proclamation, which won't have every minor sub-point of our message in it. However, every sub-point of our message will address, support, or illustrate our point for proclamation.

From the point for proclamation, we will come up with a succinct, memorable, and universal catchphrase. The catch phrase can be used as a title, opening, conclusion, or the phrase that we say repeatedly mention throughout our message. It is the unforgettable phrase, the proverb, or snippet of a key verse; the thing that rings in people's ears and helps them remember everything else we said.[6]

---

[5] Haddon H. Robinson is the Harold John Ockenga Distinguished Professor of Preaching, senior director of the Doctor of Ministry program, and former interim President at Gordon-Conwell Theological Seminary. Wikipedia biography https://en.wikipedia.org/wiki/Haddon_Robinson (accessed 5/21/16).

[6] For example, Paul is usually pretty clear about his purposes, so we will look at his letter to the Philippians. In Philippians 1, we find Paul in prison and writing to the people of the church of Philippi. Their situations are very different from each other, yet Paul and the people of Philippi know suffering. The Commander's intent I observe is to advance the gospel, or more fully, the idea that our suffering can advance the gospel.
The Commander's point for proclamation could vary by proclaimer and audience. When I spoke on this a few years ago, my title was, "Break the chains of suffering by allowing your suffering to advance the Gospel." My subpoints based on Philippians 1 were: 1) Paul's imprisonment (chains) advanced the gospel and turned suffering into something positive, 2) Suffering is often just meaningless, 3) Self-advancement can end in failure and suffering, 4) Suffering can be used to advance the gospel (instead of being meaningless), and 5) Turn your suffering around, take the focus off of self, by using your circumstance to advance the gospel. It will then cease to be meaningless suffering. The Commander's point for proclamation catchphrase was, "Break the chains of suffering by advancing the gospel."

SEVERAL PURPOSES OF THE PASSAGE ->PRIMARY PURPOSE OF THE PASSAGE->COMMANDER'S INTENT->POINT FOR PROCLAMATION -> CATCHPHRASE

The Commander's Intent Is the Core of the Biblical Message

Cornelius Plantinga Jr.[7] wrote,

> What the Bible says, God says. That is why the Bible is an expert on how we must think and act. That is why the Bible has power to influence and help us. That is why the Bible has the right to give us orders that we must obey. God speaks through the Bible. And of course God is the supreme authority in the universe. After all, he thought it up in the first place.[v]

> For the commandments, "You shall not commit adultery, you shall not murder, you shall not steal, you shall not covet," and any other commandment, are summed up in this word: "You shall love your neighbor as yourself." Love does no wrong to a neighbor; therefore love is the fulfilling of the law. (Romans 13:9–10)

The Commander's intent for Romans 13:9–11 (though this is far too short a passage to preach on) is "Love fulfills the law." The point for proclamation might be "We live out God's will by loving others." The catchphrase might be "Love covers it all."

In *Made to Stick: Why Some Ideas Survive and Others Die*, Chip and Dan Heath talked about the importance of finding the core message.[vi]

> Finding the "core" means stripping an idea down to its most critical essence. To get to the core, we've got to weed out superfluous and tangential elements. But that's the easy part. The hard part is weeding out ideas that may be really important but just aren't the most important idea. The Army's Commander's intent forces its officers to highlight the most important goal of an operation. The value of the intent comes from its singularity.[vii]

Our Authority Comes from Accurately Portraying the Commander's Intent in Our Point for Proclamation

Donald Grey Barnhouse, pastor of Philadelphia's Tenth Presbyterian Church for thirty-three years, said, "When I take the Bible into my hands I think of it as originating with God, given by Him to man in the very order, terms, phrases and words in which He wanted us to have it."[viii]

---

[7] Cornelius Plantinga Jr. was president of Calvin Theological Seminary in Grand Rapids, MI. He is the brother of philosopher Alvin Plantinga. He taught systematic theology at Calvin Seminary and was dean of the chapel at Calvin College. Plantinga wrote several books including *Not the Way It's Supposed to Be*, the *Christianity Today*, Book of the Year in 1996, and *Engaging God's World*, a *Christianity Today*, Book of the Year in 2003.

J. Kent Edwards[8] wrote, "The doctrine of inspiration guarantees that as long as I restrict my preaching to what the Bible says, I will never be embarrassed."[ix]

At the top of every Thoughtful Proclaimer Worksheet (see the Appendix for Thoughtful Proclaimer Worksheets), I write: "Do not hesitate to proclaim the whole will of God.[9] Remember: If I use Scripture as my authority and the gospel as my motivating call for change, I can speak with full conviction and confidence." At the top of all my message notes, I write out the point for proclamation. Throughout the message and especially at the end, I give my listeners the Commander's point for proclamation catchphrase.

Haddon Robinson said,

> Ministers can proclaim anything in a stained-glass voice at 11:30 on Sunday morning following the singing of hymns. Yet when they fail to preach the Scriptures, they abandon their authority. No longer do they confront their hearers with a Word from God.[x]

When we have identified the Commander's intent, we can speak with authority. Dr. Albert Mohler, Jr.[10] said,

> The preacher's authority is a delegated authority, but a real authority. We are assigned the task of feeding the flock of God, of teaching the church, of preaching the Word. We do not speak as one who possesses authority, but as one who is called to serve the church by proclaiming, expounding, applying, and declaring the Word of God. We are those who have been called to a task and set apart for mission; as vessels who hold a saving message even as earthen vessels hold water …

> Our authority is not our own. We are called to the task of preaching the Bible, in season and out of season. We are rightly to divide the Word of truth, and to teach the infinite riches of the Word of God. There are no certainties without the authority of the Scripture.[xi]

Trusting the authority of the Word of God does not mean that we should act "authoritatively"; in fact the opposite is true. We only have authority when we are speaking the Word of God. Trusting the authority of the Word of God does not make us an "authority" on every non-biblical matter we might otherwise choose to speak on, be that psychology, self-esteem, parenting, how to have the perfect marriage or some other popular preaching topic du jour. In a culture that has been brought up on distrust of all authority, we must claim our authority sparingly and humbly but nonetheless firmly as far as it is a reflection of God's authority. The authority we can claim is the message a passage of Scripture gives us.

Having authority allows us to be relevant, convincing, and passionate—not pushy. Claiming

---

[8] J. Kent Edwards wrote Deep Preaching: Creating Sermons that Go Beyond the Superficial, Effective First-Person Biblical Preaching: The Steps from Text to Narrative Sermon, and It's All in How You Tell It: Preaching First-Person Expository Sermons. He is the professor of Christian ministry and leadership at Talbot School of Theology at Biola University, the founding pastor of Oasis Community Church in Yorba Linda, California, and the president of Cross Talk Global.

[9] Taken from Acts 20:27.

[10] Albert Mohler was the president of the Southern Baptist Theological Seminary in Louisville Kentucky.

God as the authority, we may at times admit to our questions and doubts because we know our listeners may have those same questions and doubts. We are not the authority; we point to God and His Word as the authority. Our job is to demonstrate and persuade our audience they can trust God and His Word.

The Commander's Intent Supports Expository Preaching

Haddon Robinson defines expository proclamation as:

> the presentation of biblical truth, derived from and transmitted through a historical, grammatical, Spirit-guided study of a passage in its context, which the Holy Spirit applies first to the life of the preacher [and teacher] and then through him to his congregation.[xii]

This definition perfectly describes what we aim to do in the thoughtful proclaimer method. Walter Russell Bowie[11] gave this memorable description of the difference between great expository preaching and not-so-great expository preaching:

> No sort of preaching can be more misunderstood and more poorly done than [expository preaching] … Properly it is the direct elucidation and interpretation of a particular part of Scripture, most characteristically of a lengthy part; and the trouble with many preachers is that when thus confronted with a wide area of the Scripture, they become bewildered and cannot see it as a whole. So what they do is make a few groping comments on each successive verse, like a blind man tapping his way with a stick. But in order to guide the thought of a congregation effectively, the Scripture must be seen in its full perspective and in the entirety of meaning within which the several elements find their sure relationship. It is not a mechanical matter of stating one detail after another; it is a creative grasp of what the whole passage says and a setting forth of this with such selection, abridgment, or rearrangement of the details as will make the great pattern unmistakable.[xiii]

Finding the Commander's intent and focusing it into a clear point for proclamation keeps us from tap, tapping our way blindly through a passage with no clue where we are meant to end up. Like the North Star, it guides our way as we prepare our message. "You can't have five North Stars, you can't have five 'most important goals,' and you can't have five Commander's intents."[xiv] Identifying God's purpose for a passage, His intent for placing it in that place in Scripture, is the most important thing we can do. If all else fails—the wind blows our notes away, the projector fails destroying our opening video, or we completely forget our conclusion or realize at the last minute that it doesn't support our point—we still have a message because we know our point is God's point for that passage. Talk about that.

The process of finding and articulating our Commander's point for proclamation demonstrates its ultimate value in expository teaching. I hate to denigrate myself unless I can get a good laugh out of it, but one day, I was speaking on Psalm 1 and did exactly what Walter Russell Bowie

---

[11] Walter Russell Bowie was an Episcopal priest and pastored three churches including Grace Church in New York City. He was professor of pastoral theology at Union Theological Seminary and a professor of homiletics at his alma mater, Virginia Theological Seminary. He was a member of the editorial team for the Interpreter's Bible series as well as for the Revised Standard Version of the Bible.

described above. I tapped my way verse by verse through the psalm. I had no one Commander's intent in mind; I had no point for proclamation. Instead, I created mental images and gave examples of each verse. "Blessed is the 'one' who …" I thought it was a pretty good message until a pastor in the audience came up and said, "That was a good expository message." I asked him what he meant because I instinctively realized my message had not been expository. He meant it as a compliment, but I felt like he had stabbed me in the heart with his ball point pen. He clarified his mistaken view that an expository message is one in which the speaker goes verse by verse and explains each one. I had to find another place and time to speak on Psalm 1 because I knew an expository message should have one central point, the point the author intended.[12] Expository preaching is not a verse by verse commentary unless you can show how each verse points to the point for proclamation. The preacher or teacher should make sure that point is made, illustrated, explained, and applied.

The goal is to make the author's purpose the one I proclaim. My message is to convince, proclaim, prove, or explain the Commander's intent for a passage in a way that causes my listeners to live differently in light of what they have heard. Remember—there can be only one North Star.

"Wait a minute! … I distinctly remember
ignoring this same sermon two years ago!"

xv

---

[12] For Psalm 1, the Commander's intent I identified was, "The secret of happiness is based on who you spend your time with." I clarified that by saying who you listen to or walk with, what you sit and watch, and whose path you follow will determine your life course. Those who bring blessing on themselves spend their time listening to sound teaching rather than wasting it or spending it on worthless things. My catchphrase was, "Who ya gonna listen to?"

CHAPTER 3

PRACTICE INQUISITIVE EXEGESIS

Now the Berean Jews were of more noble character than those in Thessalonica, for they received the message with great eagerness and examined the Scriptures every day to see if what Paul said was true. (Acts 17:11 NIV 2011)

When my oldest son was a toddler and just learning to speak, we took a trip to the Miami Zoo. His first glimpse of an elephant left him awestruck but not speechless. In a reverent tone, he breathed two words: "Big dog."

That is inductive thinking. Big and small were categories my son already knew, and this living, breathing thing in front of him was really, really big. He knew only a few types of four-legged animals. And it was definitely not a cat. Inductive thinking comes naturally to humans; that is how we learn as children and how we continue to learn as adults. When we hear something or read something, we retain a certain amount. But when we figure something out for ourselves, it sticks. Our mind is transformed. We develop a new category. We grow. My son did not remember the terminology of big dog, but the thing we adults know of as an "elephant," that he never forgot.

Inquisitive Bible Interpretation

Thoughtful proclaimers are inquisitive or train themselves to be. We learn by asking questions, thinking deeply, and coming to conclusions. The thoughtful proclaimer method coined the term *inductive theological exegesis,* which has as its goal finding the inspired purpose for a passage for preaching and teaching. There is an awkward gap between traditional Bible exegesis and actually determining the main purpose of a passage for proclamation.[1] If we study the moss on the bark of individual trees, we can get lost in the forest and lose focus on the path before us. On the other hand, without disciplined exegesis, we are left to depend upon subjective, emotional responses and can be misled by such things as bright and shiny memory verses that catch our eye (like fortune-cookie devotions).

In narratives, it is easy to get lost in the excitement of a story. We might know what a passage says, but it is another thing to be able to assess what God's purpose for that story is for our audience. Why is that story in the Bible? Is it simply there to teach a moral? How are we to highlight a character like David as a moral exemplar knowing in a few chapters he will commit adultery and murder?[2] What should we do with those dark passages about Jephthah killing his daughter to keep a vow to God?[3] What about didactic[4] passages that seem to swiftly move from subject to subject? Which is the main idea, and which are the subordinate ideas in biblical poetry? What about seemingly archaic Old Testament laws and sacrifices; should we ignore them because nothing jumps out and says "preach me, preach me!"

If we learn to do inductive theological exegesis and use the methods described in chapter 10 for finding the Commander's intent, we should be able to interpret almost all passages of the Word of God for our listeners' edification. Very few passages will be left out of our teaching.

Making God's Word Contagious

> One who heard us was a woman named Lydia, from the city of Thyatira, a seller of purple goods, who was a worshiper of God. The Lord opened her heart to pay attention to what was said by Paul. And after she was baptized, and her household as well, she urged us, saying, "If you have judged me to be faithful to the Lord, come to my house and stay." And she prevailed upon us. (Acts 16:14–15)

The thoughtful proclaimer method of inductive theological exegesis is personal and transformational, and the personal transformation that occurs in the proclaimer is contagious to

---

[1] Though we will study the structure, ideas, words, and context in depth, we will not spend a lot of time addressing the manuscripts that lay behind our current Bibles except in very obvious cases when mentioned in the footnotes of our Bibles or when our translations differ markedly. We may study the origins of quotations, hymns, or historical references the original authors placed in our passages. For the most part, we will look at the text in front of us and look forward to today rather than backward at the various manuscripts that lay behind it. For example, we may ask questions about Mark 16:9–19, which modern Bibles tell us was not in the earliest manuscripts. We will not worry about whether Isaiah was originally one book or several books or whether a text calls God Yahweh or El. We will probably notice that some Bible translations set Philippians 2:6–11 off and wonder about that and why that is. When the study is important to the passage's message, we will spend time on it, but if it does not substantially affect our message, we will not. This does not mean that textual variants and form criticism is not important; they are very important, but they are quite often not germane to our mission as proclaimers and thus a distraction.

[2] 2 Samuel 11–12.

[3] Judges 11:27–40. "And at the end of two months, she returned to her father, who did with her according to his vow that he had made. She had never known a man, and it became a custom in Israel that the daughters of Israel went year by year to lament the [killing of the] daughter of Jephthah the Gileadite four days in the year" (Judges 11:39–40).

[4] Didactic material in the Bible is that which is clearly intended to teach or give moral or spiritual instruction. In some sense, all of Scripture is didactic but here I mean material like the epistles or Jesus' "sermon on the mount" rather than poetic material, or story (narrative), or history, or apocalyptic passages.

those who hear them teach and preach. The process of listening well to God's Word and then asking and answering pertinent questions about a Bible passage and other passages related to it changes us by the power of the Holy Spirit (who breathed the Word into being) speaking to us in His Word, the Word of God.[5] When we study God's Word in the power of the Holy Spirit with a willingness to allow God to transform us, we get excited, and our excitement is contagious. When we spend time in the Word to really understand the message, our proclamation is winning and people catch our enthusiasm.

The truths of the Word of God are hidden in plain sight. Because the Holy Spirit inspired the Book, we know it is meant to be understood, applied, and shared. When our natural, God-given curiosity and prayerful thoughtfulness work with the leading of the Holy Spirit, inductive thinking brings cognitive learning and transformational spiritual growth. More important for our congregations, it leads us to find the primary transformational purpose for a passage—and that purpose is what we will preach.

Jesus often taught in parables to make people stop and think. He could have told them what he wanted them to know, but He told them a story instead. Jesus stimulated inductive thinking by asking questions such as, "What is the kingdom of God like?" And when their minds were open and pondering, He answered the question: it is like a tiny mustard seed that grows into a great big bush. It is like a pinch of yeast that spreads, grows, and ends up turning flour and water into loaves of bread ready for the oven.[6] The purpose of the passage is that the kingdom of God is a living, growing thing. Jesus could have told his listeners outright that the kingdom of God, when it is real, multiplies and grows, but instead, He encouraged them to figure it out for themselves, and in so doing, those whom the Spirit of God willed understood it. They were excited, they spread the good news, and the kingdom of God did grow.[7]

Like those who became followers of Jesus, whom the Spirit allowed to really hear His parables, the teacher catches something transformational from the Scripture as he or she studies and meditates on it. When we have caught it, we pass that germ on to the congregation, and everyone who hears us catches the message. When transformed proclaimers share the Word of God with others, the lives of their listeners are transformed as well. The truth grabs you and doesn't let you off the hook. This is the opposite of inoculation, which is when a watered-down message or a message that has been changed from the original in some slight way is preached weekly in insignificant amounts and vaccinates the congregation from ever actually catching the excitement or being caught by the gospel of Jesus Christ.

---

[5] "All Scripture is breathed out by God and profitable for teaching, for reproof, for correction, and for training in righteousness" (2 Timothy 3:16).

[6] "He [Jesus] said therefore, 'What is the kingdom of God like? And to what shall I compare it? It is like a grain of mustard seed that a man took and sowed in his garden, and it grew and became a tree, and the birds of the air made nests in its branches.' And again he said, 'To what shall I compare the kingdom of God? It is like leaven that a woman took and hid in three measures of flour, until it was all leavened'" (Luke 13:18–21).

[7] "And they devoted themselves to the apostles' teaching and the fellowship, to the breaking of bread and the prayers. And awe came upon every soul, and many wonders and signs were being done through the apostles. And all who believed were together and had all things in common. And they were selling their possessions and belongings and distributing the proceeds to all, as any had need. And day by day, attending the temple together and breaking bread in their homes, they received their food with glad and generous hearts, praising God and having favor with all the people. And the LORD added to their number day by day those who were being saved" (Acts 2:42–47).

Learn to Ask the Right Questions

The work of an inductive exegete includes learning what kinds of questions to ask to discover the author's meaning.[i] A secondary task is putting the answers together in a way that allows us to teach others the relevance of God's message for us. Related to this is knowing which questions, if left unanswered, will not harm the meaning of the text for the purposes of proclamation in our particular setting. After all, we could spend seventy hours a week prepping for a message and never get around to living it out.

According to Gordon Fee, biblical authors intended their readers to understand what they wrote.[ii] The Word of God was written through human authors in human languages to transform humans. Gordon Fee claimed there is divine and human intentionality, and the task of exegesis is to understand the divine-human intention locked in the text.[iii] God promises that the Holy Spirit will help us to understand His Word: "But the Helper, the Holy Spirit, whom the Father will send in my name, he will teach you all things and bring to your remembrance all that I have said to you" (John 14:26).

Learning to think like an inductive Bible exegete allows us to be mightily used of God to proclaim His message. We should discipline ourselves to listen well to the passage. What questions does it want us to ask of it? What personal questions do we have? What questions will our listeners have? What do we observe? What do we need to know to understand it? What does the rest of the Bible have to say about the topics it mentions?

Consider the relevant subjects that must be understood. When we read something, we unconsciously ask literary questions of it. We read the news differently than we do a novel, and we read a cereal box differently than we do a poem. We ask literary questions of the Bible since it is a library of different books in different genres. We consider the literary genre of our passage. We ask questions about the structure of the argument, the flow of the poem, or the elements of the plot. We ask grammatical questions about words and ideas and how they were linked by the author. We want to know about the history surrounding the passage, the author, and the situation the earthly author's early listeners faced.

We want to know about their cultures, the structure of their societies, and how they worshiped or understood God. We want to understand the passage contextually in light of other passages of Scripture. And of course we want to think theologically.[8] What does this passage have to do with God's message of salvation and the roles of God, the Holy Spirit, and Jesus Christ implicitly or explicitly? What theological doctrines does this passage teach or illustrate?

Finally, we want to ask questions for our listeners and consider how they will hear and will react to the passage. How will this passage inform or disagree with their cultural presuppositions and understanding?

Thoughtful Proclaimer Inductive Theological Bible Exegesis

Though we have made great advances in linguistics, ancient history, and the ancient texts (such as the discovery of the Dead Sea Scrolls), our understanding of who God is and what He

---

[8] Theology is the study of God. "Its purpose is the investigation of the contents of belief by means of reason enlightened by faith (*fides quaerens intellectum*) and the promotion of its deeper understanding." (Cross, F. L., and Elizabeth A. Livingstone, eds. *The Oxford Dictionary of the Christian Church*. Oxford; New York: Oxford University Press, 2005.)

meant to convey in Scripture has not changed. Approaches to Bible interpretation have changed over the centuries,[9] and we use different styles to preach and teach, but the purpose of the Bible has always been to transform lives and reconcile all people to God.[10]

Theological interpretation has a spiritual element in conjunction with the intellectual side of exegesis. It means we have to be listening well to the Holy Spirit as we read and study. Kevin Vanhoozer[11] explains in the *Dictionary for Theological interpretation of the Bible*,

> Theological interpretation of the Bible ... is oriented to the knowledge of God. For much of their history, biblical studies, theology, and spirituality were all aspects of a single enterprise, that of knowing God. Knowing God is more than a merely academic exercise. On the contrary, knowing God, like theological interpretation of the Bible itself, is at once an intellectual, imaginative, and spiritual exercise. To know God as the author and subject of Scripture requires more than intellectual acknowledgment. To know God is to love and obey him, for the knowledge of God is both restorative and transformative.
>
> The saving knowledge of God results in the transformation of the reader into the likeness of Jesus Christ. In the final analysis, theological interpretation of the Bible may be less a matter of knowing God than of engaging with the living God and being known by God (Galatians 4:9). Theological interpretation of the Bible achieves its end when readers enter into the world of the biblical texts with faith, hope, and love. When we make God's thoughts become our thoughts and God's Word become our word, we begin to participate in the world of the text, in the grand drama of divine redemption. This is perhaps the ultimate aim of theological interpretation of the Bible: to know the triune God by participating in the triune life, in the triune mission to Creation.[iv]

Thoughtful proclaimer inductive theological exegesis is a variation of theological Bible interpretation, which uses inductive thinking and questions as its primary tool for study. In this way, theological Bible interpretation becomes accessible to anyone serious about good exegesis, and it becomes more personal and less dependent on the scholarly writings of others. Though we are concerned with contextual and grammatical concerns, we will not to be overly concerned with the world behind the text, which requires a great amount of knowledge of ancient texts and ancient languages.

Our thoughtful proclaimer method is more concerned with what God is doing in and through the text than what the scribes, copyists, and translators were doing with the text. We ask why

---

[9] For a good overview of other historical methods of Bible interpretation, see *God Sense: Reading the Bible for Preaching* by Paul Scott Wilson.

[10] "Therefore, if anyone is in Christ, he is a new Creation. The old has passed away; behold, the new has come. All this is from God, who through Christ reconciled us to himself and gave us the ministry of reconciliation; that is, in Christ God was reconciling the world to himself, not counting their trespasses against them, and entrusting to us the message of reconciliation. Therefore, we are ambassadors for Christ, God making his appeal through us. We implore you on behalf of Christ, be reconciled to God. For our sake he made him to be sin who knew no sin, so that in him we might become the righteousness of God" (2 Corinthians 5:17–21).

[11] Kevin Vanhoozer is research professor of systematic theology at Trinity Evangelical Divinity School in Illinois. Much of his work has focused on systematic theology, hermeneutics, and postmodernism. Of interest to the thoughtful proclaimer is Vanhoozer's 1998 book *Is There a Meaning in this Text? The Bible, the Reader, and the Morality of Literary Knowledge* (Grand Rapids, MI: Zondervan).

God inspired the text? We look at what God wants to do with the text? What is God's intention, our heavenly Commander's Intent, for the text.

The thoughtful proclaimer method takes the focus off scholarly study and puts it on God. The Bible is not meant to be a history book, a science book, a psychology book, or an instruction manual on parenting. The Bible speaks to all those things and much more, but it is a book about how God wants to save us as evidenced by how He acted in history to save the world despite humans who consistently rejected Him. When we are at a loss about how to apply a particular Scripture, we will often find it is because we are focusing on the broken and sinful characters in the story rather than on God.

Four Reasons for Using Inductive Exegesis

1. Inductive Exegesis Produces Relevant Sermons—Know Your Audience

Inductive theological interpretation of Scripture includes understanding not only the Bible but also the values, hurts, and motivations of the people we teach. We talk to our audience, our neighbors, young people, and older people about their views. We share our message before we preach it to others at a dinner party or over coffee and get their thoughts.

Keep a list in your mind of the types of people in your audience and hold these people in your mind's eye as you study your passage and prepare your message. Some are sick or have sick family members. Some have suffered loss. Some go to church not to hear from God but to please a family member or friend. Others want to learn and long for scholarly information about the Bible. Still others just need a message of encouragement. Some are seeking someone to point out their sin and show them a way out of it. By asking the sorts of questions our people want asked of a passage, our message remains relevant.

Thoughtful proclaimers will also ask a passage their own questions and confront their doubts and difficulties with a text. We ask these questions for ourselves and in consideration of the doubts of others. In this way, we identify with the difficulties our listeners face when they hear us teach Scripture. Inductive exegesis does not lead to preaching or teaching that is full of pat answers or dogmatic pronouncements; rather, it acknowledges the problems our listeners might have with Scripture.

In his classic book *The Homiletical Plot: The Sermon as Narrative*, Eugene Lowry[12] gave a clue as to why inductive interpretation was so well suited to sermon development.

> Every explicit [sermon] theme presumes an implicit problem…One might say that my sermon involves both an "itch" and a "scratch" and sermons are born when at least implicitly in the preacher's mind the problematic itch intersects a solution scratch— between the particulars of the human predicament and the particularity of the gospel.[v]

Lowry believed that preparation for preaching required us to probe for the causes of our motives, fears, and needs. We need to find out where people itch before we scratch. God's Word has the diagnosis, but first, we need to know where our people hurt.

As we form our applications, we want to keep our audience lovingly in mind. To speak to our

---

[12] Rev. Eugene Lowry was professor of preaching for over thirty years at Saint Paul School of Theology in Kansas City, MO. He was a distinguished professor, speaker, and scholar. Besides his writings, he also has jazz recordings.

audience, we must honestly acknowledge that as fellow humans, we too sometimes doubt God, disagree with Him, and even lack faith in the Bible's veracity. This is where the humanity of proclaimers helps explain and apply Scripture honestly and humbly to their listeners.

We must set aside our doubts at times but we must never forget that others may have them too. It is the specialty of the thoughtful proclaimer to be willing to acknowledge to himself his own human condition, his doubts, and his failure at times to truly trust God.

2. Inductive Exegesis Fits Our Specific Community

> Every Christian reader comes to the Bible with the spectacles provided by the tradition that is alive in the community to which he or she belongs, and that tradition is being constantly modified as each new generation of believers endeavors to be faithful in understanding and living out Scripture. This is the hermeneutical circle operating within the community. —Lesslie Newbigin[vi]

The beauty of inductive theological exegesis is that our exegesis fits the community we live in. Our message preparation is done in the community of listeners. The Bible can be read by everyone despite the disparate nature of communities and cultures. Thoughtful proclaimers will often have "spectacles" similar to those of their communities, so their interpretation will be contextual. Their messages are incarnational, meaning that when they speak, they are a little like Jesus walking through their towns. They use the eyes of Christ to see the situations their members and friends are living in.

Because inductive interpretation of the text takes place in the same settings where the message will be taught, the interpreter shares an understanding with the listeners. This yields a more relevant message than if the interpretation had been done by reading and studying what scholars or others have said about the passage when it was applied to their communities, times, and places.

Reading a commentary on Psalm 23 that teaches about ancient Middle Eastern shepherding practices is interesting and can yield a good message. But reading Psalm 23 with a congregation that lives in a desert (either real or metaphorical) allows us to apply the psalm in a personal way. If we live and teach among those who suffer hunger and fear daily, our personal inductive study will yield a message that fits that community.[13] "Even though I walk through the valley of the shadow of death, I will fear no evil, for you are with me" means one thing in the metaphorical jungle of New York City and another to those living in a tropical jungle in the Congo.

When we are dependent on commentaries rather than inductive exegesis for our applications, we may base our understanding on a commentator's community rather than our own. Thus as we consult commentaries, we should be aware of the commentary writer's point of view, "spectacles."[14] If our perspective is taken from those commentaries rather than from the Scripture itself studied

---

[13] "The LORD is my shepherd, I shall not want. He makes me lie down in green pastures. He leads me beside still waters. He restores my soul. He leads me in paths of righteousness for his name's sake. Even though I walk through the valley of the shadow of death, I will fear no evil, for you are with me; your rod and your staff, they comfort me. You prepare a table before me in the presence of my enemies; you anoint my head with oil; my cup overflows. Surely goodness and mercy shall follow me all the days of my life, and I shall dwell in the house of the LORD forever" (Psalm 23).

[14] Many scholarly commentaries until lately have had a white, Western, mainline perspective. Some commentaries now take the perspective of particular denominations or have distinct political or cultural perspectives. Just as we would consult different news sources to get a balanced view, if we do consult commentaries we should consult a variety of them.

in our own contexts, we may be distracted from the message Scripture has for our particular community.

This is not to say different communities can make the Bible say different things; the Bible is big and broad enough to fit all the communities and cultures of the world for all time. If the community of faith reading the Word asks questions and understands their audiences, the message, particularly the application, will be appropriate for their communities.[15]

The British theologian and missionary to India, Lesslie Newbigin,[16] wisely commented,

> We can never claim that either our understanding or our action is absolutely right. We have no way of proving that we are right. That kind of proof belongs only to the end. As part of the community that shares in the struggle, we open ourselves continually to Scripture, always in company with our fellow disciples of this and former ages and in the context of the struggle for obedience; and we constantly find in it fresh insights into the character and purpose of the one who is "rendered" for us in its pages. We read these pages, naturally, as part of our real history, secular history, the history of which we are a part.[vii]

No other form of exegesis makes good use of this natural and unavoidable phenomenon of studying the Bible as part of a group as does inductive Bible interpretation. The thoughtful proclaimer method grew more or less out of the idea that Bible study was done best by asking and answering questions about Scripture in the midst of community at a time in history in a particular culture and in a local society. We study the times in which the Bible was written and edited and study our own times and consider how our spectacles affect our view. Thoughtful proclaimers anticipate and consider questions from their listeners or those in the surrounding community. These natural question and answers—scholarly and personal, historic and relating to the current culture—help us make the Bible more explicable to real people whether in Minot, North Dakota or Kolkata, India.

3. Inductive Exegesis Is Evangelistic—Know Your Collective Culture

> Now when they heard this they were cut to the heart, and said to Peter and the rest of the apostles, "Brothers, what shall we do?" And Peter said to them, "Repent and be baptized every one of you in the name of Jesus Christ for the forgiveness of your sins, and you will receive the gift of the Holy Spirit." (Acts 2:37–38)

To evangelize, we need nonbelievers to hear our messages and trust them. Messages that are

---

[15] I began seminary on the morning of September 11, 2001, about thirty miles north of the Twin Towers that were destroyed by a terrorist attack in New York City. Prior to that day, my reading of the book of Revelation was focused on a coming Day of the LORD, a nebulous end times. When I studied Revelation soon after the attack on American soil so near to my community, an attack that left friends and neighbors without spouses and their children without parents, my reading of Revelation was suddenly changed. Revelation, which had been a black-and-white sort of picture for me, was suddenly in Technicolor. I read Revelation an apocalyptic book, and I understood it in a completely different way. No longer were the bowls and scrolls pointing to some dim, metaphorical future; I read Revelation as if it had been written about right now, poetry that put into words the fears and hopes in my heart.

[16] Lesslie Newbigin was a British theologian, missionary to India, and author. He is my favorite philosopher and apologist. I recommend his books highly.

prepared inductively can be attractive to believers and nonbelievers alike because they are rooted in asking questions. We ask questions for the unbeliever, and more important, we question the assumptions of the culture and of unbelievers.

Timothy Keller examined his audience as well as his culture to help people understand where their belief system broke down.[17]

> There are many working definitions of "culture," but I think one of the best is that culture is a collective heart. It is a set of commanding commitments held and shared by a community of people. Now my hearers—both Christians and non-Christians—live in the highly secular, late modern (some would say postmodern) cosmopolitan culture of Manhattan. This ethos is pulling on the hearts of all its residents. It is the source of so many of their deep aspirations, unspoken fears, and inner conflicts.[viii]

> I think it may be possible to say that every sermon should have three aspects or purposes. First, you need to preach the text in its Scriptural context; second, you need to preach Christ and the Gospel every time; and finally, you need to preach to the heart. Put another way, you should preach the truth, not just your opinion; you should preach the good news, not just good advice; and you should preach to make the truth real to the heart, not just clear to the mind.[ix]

Some readers may note that John Stott taught that the preacher stands "Between Two Worlds."[18] Stott quoted Karl Barth's practice: "What do you do to prepare your Sunday sermon?" Barth answered, "I take the Bible in one hand and the daily newspaper in the other."[x] Stott said Spurgeon even wrote a book entitled *The Bible and The Newspaper.*[xi]

Keller took this idea much further. He is a student not just of current events but of literature and philosophy; he is especially a student of the philosophies underlying the culture of his audience.

> The so-called "cultural references," [I use] then, are simply my way of entering the world of my hearers, helping them understand at a deep level what is shaping their daily work, their romantic and family relationships, their attitudes toward sex, money, and power. I seek to make plain the foundations of our city's culture in order to help people understand themselves more fully and imagine what it means (or would mean) to live a Christian life here.[xii]

Inductively study your listeners. Ask the questions they would ask and the ones they don't know they should be asking. Talk to nonbelievers and questioners and ask their questions of the text and of the world.[19] When we understand the collective heart of a people, we can offer them the good news of salvation. To a people who don't see their need, the offer of salvation seems moot. But if we can show them where their assumptions fall short and cut them to the heart, we can show them where the message of salvation can complete their message and heal their souls.

---

[17] Timothy Keller is a pastor, theologian, and Christian apologist. He is best known as the founding pastor of Redeemer Presbyterian Church in New York City. He is a prolific author; he is involved with the Gospel Coalition.

[18] John Stott wrote a book by this name in 1982.

[19] For more on this point see chapter 9, "Understand Your Listeners."

4. Inductively Determined Application Is Transformational

Jesus Christ is the same yesterday and today and forever. (Hebrews 13:8)

Bible application through inductive interpretation is valid because it is not just descriptive of the past (Bible times) but asks how the past describes the potential of the future (now). It works because of the unchangeable nature of God.[20] Since God is the same yesterday, today, and forever, we can learn what He is like now by reading about how He operated in ages past. By observing the mighty acts of God both past and present, we can learn about who God really is and what He can and will do in the future. The thoughtful proclaimer assumes that because God is who He says He is—loving and unchangeable—what the authors of the Bible wrote is still true today. Most important, God's unchangeable nature means His message of salvation for all people is still as relevant today as it was at any time since Creation.

Inductively determined application is based on the fact that though language, culture, and technology change, human nature does not. Brevard Childs wrote,

> The divine imperatives are no longer moored in the past, but continue to confront the hearer in the present as truth. Therefore it is constitutive of Biblical Theology that it be normative and not merely descriptive, and that it be responsive to the imperatives of the present and not just of the past.[xiii]

Bible application is contextual. Many claim the Bible needs no interpretation, but some are so steeped in its truth that they do not see that its application is not at all clear to others. They often focus solely on the New Testament for their messages. In a sense, they are right because God is the same as He always was, but besides God's character and the state of the human heart, most everything else has changed since the Bible was written. When we inductively interpret the Bible (both the Old and New Testaments) in its contexts (see chapter 6), the truth and application can be determined in a relevant, evangelistic, and applicable way for a whole new community.

---

[20] "Remember your leaders, those who spoke to you the word of God. Consider the outcome of their way of life, and imitate their faith. Jesus Christ is the same yesterday and today and forever" (Hebrews 13:7–8). "So the Jews said to him, 'You are not yet fifty years old, and have you seen Abraham?' Jesus said to them, 'Truly, truly, I say to you, before Abraham was, I am'" (John 8:57–58). "'I am the Alpha and the Omega,' says the LORD God, 'who is and who was and who is to come, the Almighty'" (Revelation 1:8).

CHAPTER 4

PLAN YOUR PROCLAMATION

Let the words of my mouth
and the meditation of my heart
be acceptable in your sight,
O LORD, my rock and my redeemer.
(Psalm 19:14)

Beware Fingerprints

It never fails—when I rush to set the table for a dinner party, I see fingerprints. The glasses we so carefully washed and put away weeks earlier have somehow gotten covered in fingerprints. Any policeman could tell you that we leave fingerprints on whatever we touch. Fancy restaurants even have staff to wipe fingerprints off glassware with a linen towel just before they set them on the table. No one wants to drink from a glass covered in someone else's fingerprints.

And the words of the LORD are flawless,
like silver purified in a crucible,
like gold refined seven times.
(Psalm 12:6 NIV)

When we study God's Word to understand the Commander's intent for proclaiming, we want to keep our fingerprints off. Once we teach or preach the Word, our fingerprints are all over the message, but in the planning stages, our aim is to let the Word of God be itself, to keep it pure and free from our contaminating prints.

The first place where thoughtful proclaimers leave fingerprints is in text selection. It really can't be helped, but to do the least damage to God's message, we aim to stick to the way the original earthly author would direct us to cut up his text. The author wrote an entire book, but the Holy Spirit planned only a few hours for us to teach it.[1]

---

[1] "For we are his workmanship, created in Christ Jesus for good works, which God prepared beforehand, that we should walk in them" (Ephesians 2:10).

Preaching with a Plan Works Best

> Go therefore and make disciples of all nations, baptizing them in the name of the Father and of the Son and of the Holy Spirit, teaching them to observe all that I have commanded you. And behold, I am with you always, to the end of the age. (Matthew 28:19–20)

Preaching and teaching is ultimately about winning and growing disciples of the Lord Jesus Christ. Proclaiming in order to grow disciples takes planning. A survey conducted by the Haddon Robinson Center for Preaching at Gordon-Conwell Theological Seminary showed that more experienced preachers (those who had been in pastoral ministry longer than six years) indicated that they planned their preaching anywhere from four to six months before they preached while others followed a one-year plan.[i] The Holy Spirit can better guide our planning six months to a year in advance than He can when we are stressed at the last minute. In general, it is not a good policy to wait until the week you preach to plan what your passage will be.[2]

God Knows What Will Happen ahead of Time

If you are not accustomed to planning your preaching well in advance, you might worry that things will pop up that will throw your schedule off. This is rarely the case if God is in the planning for the preaching and teaching schedule. During the course of six weeks one spring when I was teaching a Bible study, a mass shooting of twenty children and their teachers in a nearby community occurred.[ii] And our class was canceled for the first time in many years due to a massive hurricane that flooded the area and caused great damage to our class members' homes and vehicles.[iii] These were not one-week disasters, and they were not events that could be ignored. I was teaching through 1st and 2nd Kings that year. That was the hardest year of speaking preparation I have ever had not because the year had been scheduled out almost a year in advance but because of the long and often gory passages I had to find God's intention for. (You can use the same points for proclamation only so many times. I used, "God is the only really good King" and "We need a good King—so God sent Jesus" early on.) Yet God faithfully shaped the Commander's intents of those multichapter Old Testament passages to fit the local disasters that shook the community. My year had been planned, but the Holy Spirit had planned my teaching so the passages fit the emotional climate and the events.

As the director of adult spiritual formation for a church, I taught a Sunday morning adult Bible class. I was amazed Sunday after Sunday at how even through changes in the pastoral staff, God orchestrated the adult class themes and passages I had planned the summer before to perfectly coincide with the sermon themes and passages that various pastors spoke on each week throughout the year. It would perhaps have been preferable for the pastoral staff and the adult spiritual formation team to work together, but since that was not an option, God directed our steps.

> The mind of man plans his way,
> But the LORD directs his steps.
> (Proverbs 16:9 NASB)

---

[2] "For which of you, desiring to build a tower, does not first sit down and count the cost, whether he has enough to complete it? Otherwise, when he has laid a foundation and is not able to finish, all who see it begin to mock him, saying, 'This man began to build and was not able to finish'" (Luke 14:28–30).

At times—holidays, weddings, funerals, church events, extraordinary circumstances, and so on—we might choose a passage outside the biblical series plan (see "Proclaiming Whole Books" later in this chapter). Our plan is good, but it is not carved in stone as were the Ten Commandments. "The fact that you plan your texts and themes in advance doesn't mean the Lord can't break in and give you a prophetic word for that hour based on a different text," advised Warren Wiersbe. "We can be aware of the Holy Spirit's leading as we plan and we want to be attentive to His direction as we preach weekly."[iv]

Decide on Your Purpose for Preaching or Teaching

To plan our preaching well, we must decide on our reasons for preaching, our theology of preaching. Whether we realize it or not, we all have an underlying reason for preaching or teaching that determines to an extent what we decide to preach and when.

"Let's split the preaching responsibilities...
I'll make them smile...You make them squirm." [v]

Scott Gibson, in *Preaching with a Plan: Sermon Strategies for Growing Mature Believers*, suggested, "If more preachers came to the responsibility of preaching—text selection, planning, sermon construction—with the understanding that they are nurturing disciples, their preaching might be different."[vi]

Take a week or two to study a book of the Bible; divide it up and plug it into your calendar. In this way, you will be able to spend time reading the whole book through as well as some commentaries on the book that will help you to see the author's development of thought. When it's time to prepare your messages, you will have already done the background work.

Proclaiming Whole Books of the Bible Offers Benefits

The law of the LORD is perfect,
reviving the soul;
the testimony of the LORD is sure,
making wise the simple.
(Psalm 19:7)

Preaching sequentially through whole books of the Bible puts the fewest fingerprints on the messages.[3] Granted, we have to divide the book, but we are not picking and choosing something from a different book each week. We may choose the book, but we allow the author and the Holy Spirit to choose the message.

This idea of preaching through whole books or major sections of the Bible for several weeks or months—especially long Old Testament books—is not a popular thesis. Many feel they should preach only what they consider to be the best and most relevant portions of Scripture; we have only an hour a week after all. The idea is that we find a need in our congregations and search for a passage that addresses that need. In the following section, you will encounter my belief that there would be fewer needs if we preached and taught a fuller and more accurate Word of God. The earliest church, the one that spread over the known world in just a few years, had only the Old Testament to preach from!

It is not so much what our church members need as what books of the Bible they haven't heard enough of that should take priority as we plan. If we preach sequentially through the books of the Bible or at the very least biblically sequential series, the Bible itself will take care of providing what people need. This works with the thoughtful proclaimer method because you and I will have taken the needs of the people into account as we consider our points to proclaim. Our job is to give our people a balanced diet of the whole Word. If we call it preaching or Bible teaching, it needs to be proclamation of the Word primarily as we have it in complete books, not shredded into bits and pieces. We can trust God that His Word will take care of the people's needs even in a series on Leviticus.

Deep Roots Are More Resilient

In the Burgundy region of France, it is illegal to irrigate grapevines. In the documentary *A Year in Burgundy*, retired winemaker Dayday Porchulav wrote of burgundy grapevines,

> You can't coddle it, or it will become lazy like a couch potato. If the roots don't dig deep there's trouble … They have to go down four or five meters. Then if it's dry for a couple of months, no problem. The vine will survive. A vine can live 100 years if you treat it right.[vii]

Deep roots will keep our ministries and our congregations alive and resilient so they will last the long haul even during dry times. If we want to teach for many years, we should grow deep roots by using our time wisely, meditating personally on the Word of God, and growing mature Bible-believing congregations. If we are regularly being transformed by the Word, we can grow and produce fruit even in the driest of times.

Another way to grow deep roots is to tackle the difficult passages, the hard, dry, rocky passages, the passages most preachers skip over. Study and speak on the Law, the prophets, the long, gory Old Testament narratives, Psalms, Proverbs, and Revelation. If we are willing to do the heavy lifting, if we are willing to proclaim a holy God, if we are willing to be creative and work at being a little bit entertaining, we can preach the entire Bible and quiet the skeptics who want to hear only from the gospels and the epistles. In this way, our congregations will grow deep roots as well.

---

[3] *Lectio continua* is the method of preaching whole books of the Bible. Some even preach through the whole Bible.

But whoever drinks of the water that I will give him will never be thirsty again. The water that I will give him will become in him a spring of water welling up to eternal life. (John 4:14)

Preaching Sequentially Lends More Accuracy of Meaning

When we pick and choose passages from various books each week or preach on several passages because they have the same word or topic in them, we leave fingerprints all over the meanings and intentions of the books and can easily do harm to the biblical author's full message. To some extent, it is inescapable as we cannot usually teach a whole book at one time, but we can do our best to speak sequentially through the book. If we were standing next to one of the inspired earthly authors of Scripture (and one day we will be), we would find it hard to tell him we picked and chose bits and pieces from his book to preach on while leaving out the rest of what he wrote as one treatise under the Spirit's inspiration.

Preaching sequentially gives our listeners a broad sense of the Bible. When we pick and choose good bits from here and there in Scripture, we inadvertently give the impression to our listeners that parts of the Bible are good but that most of the Bible can be ignored or is too difficult to understand.

Some books, including Psalms, Proverbs, Job, and the major prophets, are collected sermons, songs, or wisdom sayings. Though they have a structure, they can more safely be taught through without hitting every single chapter in order. You might teach through several psalms, sections of Proverbs, or chunks of Job as long as you emphasize the author's intent for the entire book as you go (see Appendix E for a sample series on Jeremiah). Large sections from several chapters of the major prophets such as Isaiah can be preached as a sermon series especially if the history of Judah and Israel is taught as an adjunct to the oracles so they hang together.[4] But for most other books, sequential preaching will give the truest sense of the Commander's intent and the author's meanings.

Preaching Sequentially Simplifies Preparation and Benefits the Proclaimer

Doing thorough message preparation week after week can be a challenge. When we are preaching sequentially, most of our background study can be done weeks or months ahead. If we have studied a book well and then some crisis causes us to have limited preparation time one week, we are still able to give a biblical, in-depth, accurate message though we don't have time to prepare a delightfully illustrated one. Because of our previous background study, our cupboard will be stocked with supplies. Even when we don't have time to shop for fun facts, good stories, and visuals, we are able to serve a solid, accurate, and spiritually nutritious meal to our audiences.

We may initially shy away from the Old Testament thinking it would be too challenging to make relevant. However, once we do the cross-cultural and historical background study for an Old Testament book, it will not generally need to be redone every week. Taking time to study the whole book in some depth in advance will make preparation easier than trying to do good cultural, historical background work on a new book of the Bible every week.

---

[4] The appendix contains a sample plan for preaching through Jeremiah in one year. Because Jeremiah was not compiled in sequential order, as long as the context is given, it should be safe to preach it out of order.

Teaching through whole books of the Bible with a focus on the Commander's intent for the entire book allows the proclaimer to become biblically well founded in a shorter number of years. One of the thoughtful proclaimer method goals is for message preparation to be messenger preparation, and the sequential method of teaching and preaching does that well. Teaching through the books of history makes the prophets come alive. Teaching through Genesis gives roots to rest of the Bible. Understanding Deuteronomy makes the theology of Scripture clearer. Teaching Acts makes Paul's epistles more personal. The more books we teach, the deeper we can go toward understanding the whole canon as one big story; jumping around from passage to passage each week doesn't give us that kind of grounding.[5]

Preaching sequentially allows the proclaimer to be fruitful. James Montgomery Boice, one of my favorite homiletical commentary writers, died at the relatively young age of sixty-one. I was surprised to learn this because he had written so much. His sermon series were turned into preaching commentaries.[6] Maybe you do not aspire to writing fifty books during your ministry, but I hope you aspire to being fruitful in ministry for many years. I believe Boice's combination of in-depth study of Scripture and his heart to share the Word of God, book by whole book, allowed him to have a significant impact—one that reaches beyond the grave.

"I don't want to miss any of this great sermon series...
Could you preach on a different topic for the next 7...no...8 Sundays?"   *viii*

---

[5] You will get a lot of biblical jumping around as you cross-reference studies in their context, so you will have a continual widening and broadening of biblical material to study. You will begin to see the web of connected themes and ideas more clearly for having a home base in a single book of the Bible for some weeks or months.

[6] "The Rev. Dr. James Montgomery Boice served as Senior Minister of Tenth Presbyterian Church from 1968 to 2000. His ministry at Tenth [Presbyterian in Philadelphia] was marked by a unique combination of scholarly engagement and pastoral application." Tenth Presbyterian Church, "Boice Center," http://www.tenth.org/ministries/learning/boice-center (accessed 4/22/2016).

Preaching Sequentially Benefits Our Listeners

Understanding the big picture of whole books of Scripture benefits our listeners as well us. The Commander's intent for particular portions Scripture are always subordinate to His intent for the whole book of the Bible. If we tie the individual portion into the larger intent of the whole book each week, we give our audiences the Commanders intent of the whole book; they get to hear it repeated and hear its different nuances. In this way, our audiences become more fully biblically literate than if they hear only sermons extracted from different parts of the Bible each week. Despite the fact that those sermons may be topically tied, they will not be in the setting the biblical author intended. Though our students or congregations may become theologically versed in topics they will have difficulty becoming truly biblically literate. They may know a lot about theology from our sermons, but they won't have the scriptural grounding to know the difference between sound theology and "pop" theology.

Avoid leaving out the hard or disagreeable passages; that leaves listeners vulnerable to attacks from those who pick and choose difficult passages and use them against Christianity. The attacks on Christianity and Scripture so prevalent today are effective because most Christians do not know the whole of Scripture or how the New Testament informs and complements the Old.[7] We are told by those who pick and choose verses that God is vengeful, the Bible is misogynistic, it promotes slavery, and encourages cruel practices such as stoning adulterers. If we have modeled reading the Bible in bits and pieces taken out of context, those criticisms can be difficult to refute. But if we model thorough preaching and teaching of whole books of the Old Testament in conjunction with New Testament passages that inform and complement them, our parishioners will be less susceptible to the atheistic attacks they regularly face at work, school, and in the media. Modeling the understanding of Bible passages in their historical and cultural contexts and particular genres will help our listeners see the supposedly damning passages in a vastly different light.

Sequential (chapter by chapter or significant portion) preaching coupled with canonical exegesis—interpreting individual portions in light of the whole of the Bible—gives us a clearer picture of who God is. When we preach sequentially, we show our listeners how to balance God's love and justice, grace and truth, mercy and uncompromising holiness, love and vengeance. Focusing on only some of God's main attributes while blatantly ignoring others gives our listeners a very lopsided view of God and makes Him into a kindly old grandfather instead of God almighty.

So little preaching is done on the Old Testament perhaps because we find it easier to preach on the love, grace, and mercy of God without regard to His justice, righteousness, and

---

[7] In some denominations or churches, a lectionary is used to guide the choices for preaching. In a lectionary, Bible readings are carefully chosen based on the church calendar and Christian holidays. The lectionary richly sews together theologically related OT and NT passages. This can lend itself to good canonical preaching, but the nonlectionary user can do the same thing. Additionally, the passages are repeated every three years so the major themes of the Bible are regularly visited. The downside is that good historical and cultural exegesis has to be done on new books of the Bible each week though it is provided by commentaries, and though after a few years, you begin to learn the backgrounds of those passages, you are left using someone else's decisions as to what is important. The fingerprints on the lectionary are unfortunately gigantic as the Sunday selections of the Common Lectionary covers only 13 percent of the Bible and only 6 percent of the OT. Again, parishioners are left to assume the other 87 percent as irrelevant.

Sequential preaching using a style of tying the Old and New Testaments is superior to only covering 13 percent of the Bible in your ministry. The site lectionary.library.vanderbilt.edu has many resources for the preacher who uses the lectionary. From http://lectionary.library.vanderbilt.edu/faq2 (accessed 5/22/16).

uncompromising holiness. When we teach the Old Testament, we should always teach the New Testament along with it so we give a balanced view of God. The Bible is meant to be understood by all who read it, and showing others by example how to read it in its fullest context makes that possible for them.

"When people ask where our congregation was trained to endure disasters, we always point to your 40-week sermon series on the first chapter of Leviticus." *ix*

Preaching Sequentially Helps Prevent Exegetical Traps

When my son was little, he saw a gag where your finger is pushed through the bottom of a small jewelry box and laid on a piece of cotton. If you hold it correctly, it looks as if you're carrying a finger around in a little jewelry box. He was terrified. No matter how often you showed him the finger was indeed connected to the hand, that unattached-finger memory would not leave his little brain.

That is how I feel about topical messages. Verses out of context are like fingers in a box. I know they are attached to hands, but you can't see the hands, and it can be scary. You've heard it said that you can make the Bible mean anything you want it to. Well, this is true without chapter and book context and without canonical theological exegesis—the context of the whole Bible. This is why topical messages are of great concern.

Though all preaching is subjective to some extent, topical preaching, that is, choosing a theme or topic first and then finding the passages you want to use to teach it, is wholly subjective. In topical preaching, there is no one book of the Bible that is guiding the emphasis, that is the boss. Rather, the speakers are the bosses as they choose which passages, often from lists in a concordance, they want to use to support their messages. This method puts lots of fingerprints on the Scripture.

In topical preaching, it's easy to accidentally take a passage out of context or use it to support your meaning when perhaps that was not what its author meant to say at all. Because you can't do good contextual study on ten or twelve thematically related Scriptures, you are doing "fortune cookie" preaching or teaching on disconnected quotes.

In *Toward an Exegetical Theology: Biblical Exegesis for Preaching and Teaching*, Walter Kaiser[8] wrote,

> What is so lacking in this case is exactly what needs to be kept in mind with respect to every sermon which aspires to be at once both biblical and practical: it must be derived from an honest exegesis of the text and it must constantly be kept close to the text ...[x] So strong is this writer's aversion to the methodological abuse he has repeatedly witnessed—especially in topical messages—that he has been advising his students for some years now to preach a topical sermon only once every five years—and then immediately to repent and ask God's forgiveness![xi]

At times, a topical message is called for, and in a sense, a good expository message based on a point for proclamation derived from the Commander's intent is somewhat topical, though God and his writer chose the topic. But the reason that nonsequential preaching, especially topical preaching and teaching, is dangerous can be called exegetical traps; traps we can accidentally fall into when we choose what topic we want to speak on before we choose what passage we will speak on.[9] Exegetical traps include,

- Cherry Picking: looking for all the verses that seem to support our ideas and leaving the rest.
- Low-Hanging Fruit: speaking on only the easy or politically correct passages and leaving the rest.
- Stacking the Cards: building a case for our views by giving the passages that support our views greater weight than other passages.
- Proof Texting: making a point by using short passages to support a view. There is an old axiom in many a course on biblical interpretation: "A text without a context is a pretext for a proof text."[10]

In each of these cases, we make the erroneous choice of deciding what the truth is and then use the Bible to support our view. This is worse than fingerprints; it's cutting off fingers!

As thoughtful proclaimers, we must be careful to read the Bible with as little bias as possible.

---

[8] Walter Kaiser is an Old Testament scholar, writer, public speaker, and educator. Kaiser was the Colman M. Mockler distinguished professor of Old Testament and former president of Gordon-Conwell Theological Seminary in South Hamilton, MA; he retired in 2006.

[9] For more on this, read D. A. Carson's *Exegetical Fallacies*, 2d ed. (Grand Rapids, MI: Baker Academic, 1996).

[10] In his book *Practical Wisdom for Pastors*, Curtis C. Thomas gave a well known example of the exegetical trap of proof texting using James 2:24: "You see that a person is justified by works and not by faith alone." A teacher searching for a verse for a sermon text on faith could mislead the congregation. Thomas explained, "The problem with quoting only those biblical words is that there is more said in the immediate context. James is arguing that a man who has a dead faith, a faith that produces no works, has simply a head knowledge and not saving faith. Our faith has to be demonstrated by our works. James uses Abraham as an example of a man with faith who was willing to demonstrate his faith by offering up his son Isaac on the altar. And then James concludes with these phrases: "Abraham believed God, and it was credited to him as righteousness," and he was called God's friend. You see that a person is justified by what he does and not by faith alone ... As the body without the spirit is dead, so faith without deeds is dead' (James 2:23–26)."

Our goal is God's view, not our own or our denomination's view. We should read the Bible simply for what it says realizing we need to examine our hearts and our cultural, political, personal, and theological prejudices prayerfully and humbly. We must read the Bible for the Bible's message, not for a message we have predetermined to be there. Whatever passage we choose, we need to seek out the whole view of Scripture on that passage by checking every cross-reference at least briefly to assure ourselves we are indeed reflecting our Commander's intent on that subject.

> Is not my word like fire,
> declares the LORD,
> and like a hammer
> that breaks the rock in pieces?
> (Jeremiah 23:29)

It is difficult not to bias our understanding of Scripture. But God can't say anything new to us, if we have predetermined what we expect to hear. He can't light a fire under us or break a secret habit in us if we don't accept His Word with an open mind.

A friend of mine was preparing answers for an inductive Bible study group he was attending. He finished in one hour what took me and others about four. I asked him how he had done that, and he said he already knew the answers so it was easy. How often do we read a passage that should be quite difficult but read it according to the answers we already think we know?[11] Speaking of putting God in a box!

Divide a Book for Proclamation

> Do your best to present yourself to God as one approved, a worker who has no need to
> be ashamed, rightly handling the Word of truth. (2 Timothy 2:15)

As we pick a passage to proclaim, we are required to do a bit of surgery. Whenever I think of dividing a book into preachable passages, I think of this verse because the King James Version says, "rightly dividing the word of truth." Paul used the Greek word *orthotomeo*, "to give accurate instruction," "to teach correctly, to expound rightly."[xii] It is the opposite of "to pervert, twist, or deceive." When we divide a book of Scripture for teaching or preaching, we get our fingerprints all over it, so care must be taken to cut out a proper section so as not to change the intent of the passage.

Carve Up a Book without Butchering It

At my house, we can take a beautiful turkey and turn it to shreds. We can take a perfect beef roast, and by the time we are done with it, it is good only for soup. In some cultures, when you cut up a chicken, you hack it to bits with a cleaver. Bones everywhere. If you are a French chef, you may remove all the bones from the poultry leaving a bird *sans* bones. The end product has a

---

[11] "And we also thank God constantly for this, that when you received the word of God, which you heard from us, you accepted it not as the word of men but as what it really is, the word of God, which is at work in you believers" (1 Thessalonians 2:13).

lot to do with how sharp your knife is, your skill at carving, and most important, what you aim to do with the meat.

As thoughtful proclaimers, we need some tools and practice to help us carve up our text without butchering it. Teaching the Bible requires us to carve up biblical books carefully. We want our parts to be recognizable like a Thanksgiving turkey on a platter. We can't eat a whole turkey at one time, so we have to cut it up. Choosing where to start and stop can be very challenging. Large portions are obviously somewhat more difficult to handle, so many people choose too small of portions.

These small portions can be prone to exegetical traps. Each portion of Scripture chosen for preaching or teaching should contain a major biblical idea. Each portion of Scripture should be able to stand alone as far as meaning goes (though we won't let it—we will teach it in context). Likewise, the nearby passages should also be able to stand alone. If they cannot, they should be included as part of the passage immediately preceding or following it.

Proclaim Significant Portions

When I was little, my dad regularly fell asleep during sermons. I thought it was so funny. I'd poke him and whisper to him to wake up. He always said he was just praying! Poor Eutychus couldn't claim to be praying when he fell out the window that night as Paul preached on and on (Acts 20:7–12). Paul is the only preacher I know who actually killed someone with his long-windedness. Perhaps he bit off a longer portion of Scripture than what we might appreciate today. At least without a coffee break.

There is often no perfect way to divide a text into preachable portions, but we want to honor the writer of the text and his meanings and intentions when we make those decisions. In *God Sense: Reading the Bible for Preaching*, Paul Scott Wilson[12] wrote:,

> Determine the boundaries of the text, as a detective determines the perimeters of a crime scene. For example, does the portion of the text being examined have unity and coherence on its own, or do you need to consider a larger section? Ideally, the passage should represent a complete unit of thought, and special care needs to be taken concerning where to begin and end it.[xiii]

We should generally divide books into chunks that can be handled without putting people to sleep or confusing them. Each passage should be large enough so we can tie our idea to the central idea of the book yet small enough to be covered in one message or lesson. We want to preach on significant pieces of Scripture.

We can generally ignore or take chapter and verse demarcations with a grain of salt as they are not part of the original autographs except in a few cases.[13],[xiv] Think about whole paragraphs and groups of paragraphs. Ask yourself, *If I were the author of this book, where would I have put the*

---

[12] Paul Scott Wilson is the professor of homiletics at Emmanuel College at the University of Toronto.

[13] Chapter demarcations are often good places to stop and start, but other times, they can lead you astray, so don't depend on them. The writers of the Bible did not write in verses (except for poetry), and they did not include numbers for chapters. These divisions and their numbering systems were added much later to make it easier for us to find our way. The prose sections of the Bible were written in paragraphs and longer sections that are now best observed in translations that preserve them.

chapter -stops? Then check. *Did I leave any small orphan ideas behind? Are there passages after or before this text that have a similar theme or that can't stand on their own apart from this passage?*

A great example of leaving an orphan idea behind was in a sermon I heard on the post-resurrection appearance of Jesus making brunch on the beach (John 21:1–14). The pastor did an expository message and covered his passage very well. His theme and repeated refrain was that Jesus feeds us as he fed those disciples. While there is no right or wrong way to divide up a text, given the pastor's theme, "Jesus feeds us," I noticed that he didn't conclude and apply the passage in the way the apostle John did; he left out the last few verses that would have completed the message. How perfect it would have been had he included John 21:15–19 in his passage: "When they had finished breakfast, Jesus said to Simon Peter, 'Simon, son of John, do you love me more than these?' He said to him, 'Yes, Lord; you know that I love you.' He said to him, 'Feed my lambs'" (John 21:15). Jesus feeds us and calls us to feed His sheep.

Strive to honor the book and the surrounding context's thought or meaning. When excised, our text should not say something different from what it would have had it been left in the place the author meant it to be. Context must be considered in the choice of where to start and stop. All translations divide the chapters without regard to the author's actual thought. Use the words, thoughts, and ideas of the author to decide where passages should start or stop, not the chapter demarcations. The most important thing to consider is whether we have a significant portion to determine the author's intent for the whole book. No preaching portion should mean something that does not fit into the author's larger meaning for the whole book. If it seems to, expand your preaching portion.

You certainly have a gift for sermon titles.   xv

Different Genres of Literature Are Carved Up according to Their Types

Just as we carve up a piece of meat according to its type and what we are using it for, we divide books of the Bible differently depending on what genre of literature it is. Read your book several times in as short a time as possible to get the author's meaning. Then make a plan to carve up your passage without butchering the author's message—"Ask what 'therefore' is there for!" The same holds true for all conjunctions, logical moves, and inferences. Any time the next section is part of the thought of the last section, we need to take it into account (though not necessarily include it).

NARRATIVE

Robert Alter, professor of Hebrew and comparative literature at the University of California Berkley explained that to get the most out of narrative, we should analyze Scripture as we would any piece of well-written literature. To know where the boundaries of stories are and thus how we should divide them for proclamation, we need to observe the minute details. He wrote in *The Art of Biblical Narrative*,

> By literary analysis I mean the manifold varieties of minutely discriminating attention to the artful use of language, to the shifting play of ideas, conventions, tone, sound, imagery, arrangement, argument, narrative viewpoint, compositional units, and much else; the kind of disciplined attention, in other words, that through a whole spectrum of critical approaches has illuminated, for example, the poetry of Dante, the plays of Shakespeare, the novels of Tolstoy.[xvi]

The Bible, and the Old Testament in particular, adds no extraneous details. If you see something, say something. Be assured the author meant for it to be seen.

As you divide narrative passages into major sections, check to make sure they focus on the same theme, word, or idea. Make sure to include an entire story or at least an episode of a story or a scene. To decide where the story is best divided, pay attention to the story line, plot, climax, and conclusion as well as to key words, similar ideas, scenes, tone, narrative viewpoint (who is talking), and whatever other little details your detective eyes spot.

Narrative is like a journey on a train. Each peek out the window is interesting, but each peek can't be an entire train stop (sermon) or you'll never get to your destination. Yet you have to stop somewhere to sleep or your audience will just fall sleep right there in their seats.

Where you stop depends on several things. How long do you have for your trip (message series)? What is the reason for your trip (what is the need you are trying to address)? What is the main purpose, the Commander's intent, for your trip (the book you are teaching or preaching)?

Once you know the Commander's purpose or the book's controlling idea, you can better determine where to stop for the night (how to divide up your book). You may want to stop when the scenery (setting) changes or when the main idea changes.[14] If you see a group of similar, related, or identical key words or ideas that run throughout several scenes, you probably should put them together. If you're traveling along and suddenly a new person jumps into the seat beside you (a new character appears), you will know you have come to a stop. If your seatmate dies (a character drops out or literally dies), stop. A character change signals a good stopping place for your sermon.

The primary way to divide up narratives is according to plot lines. Every story has a plot line; it starts at the beginning, rises to a climax, and resolves. Sometimes, there is an interlude in the journey, a seemingly unrelated episode stuck in the middle of an otherwise coherent story. Of course, these interludes are not a mistake and are there for a reason. It's our job to figure out the reason.[15]

An Example of a Long Narrative

The Joseph story is quite long—Genesis 37–49. There are discrete episodes in the bigger story including Joseph's dreams, Joseph being sold, Joseph in Potiphar's house, Joseph in prison, Pharaoh's dreams, Joseph ruling Egypt, Joseph's brothers and the silver cup, Joseph revealing himself to his brothers, Jacob going to Egypt, Joseph and the famine, and Jacob blessing his sons. Changing how many episodes you include in your sermon will likely change your point for proclamation in some way. But whatever you choose as the point for proclamation, it must fit with the main point, the Commander's intent, of the entire Joseph story as well as the entire book of Genesis.

---

[14] The words *kingdom of heaven* and *kingdom of God* appear to be a key motif in Matthew (they appear thirty-seven times). Matthew's controlling idea appears to be describing the kingdom of heaven through a narrative story about Jesus' life. When you go to divide Matthew 19 and 20 for preaching, you might think you should stop at the end of chapter 19 but a better place to divide the passage for preaching and to see the Commander's intent in this case is when Jesus moves from one place to another. This is not so much because Jesus moved but because it seems the narrator noted Jesus' move to a new location as an indicator that we are on a new subject.

In 19:1, Jesus went to Judea, and in 20:7, he went to Jerusalem. Also, the tone and topic changes between the last verse of 18 and the first verse of 19. They change again between 20:7 and 20:8. The repeated refrain for this section is in 19:30 and 20:6, which is that in the kingdom of heaven (unlike on earth), the last shall be first and the first shall be last. This must be related to what Jesus has been teaching in this particular pericope, that in the kingdom of heaven, the roles of power are flipped.

In this larger preaching portion you will see illustrations of how the kingdom of heaven is. You will see something about marriage, divorce and creation-based theological ethics (Matthew 19:4–6). But Jesus considered this little interruption caused by the Pharisees as not just a distraction but another chance to teach on the kingdom of heaven that God is not in favor of easy divorce and that some people are willing to live celibate lives to advance the kingdom of heaven. In the kingdom of heaven, some people are willing to put themselves last. The Commander's intent is to show us the kingdom of heaven and how it differs from earthly kingdoms.

[15] An example of an interlude in a bigger story can be seen in chapters of genealogy or other short stories such as the story of Tamar and Judah in Genesis 38, which are inserted in the middle of the Joseph story. Though the story of Tamar and Judah seems at first to be unrelated to the Joseph narrative, it is there for a purpose, and it is our job to discover that purpose and decide how to handle it. The Tamar and Judah story serves to heighten the tension in the Joseph story and to give us a glimpse into the passing of time while Joseph is sold as a servant to Potiphar. But why is it placed in this spot in the narrative? What other the purposes can we identify? Judah's character poses a stark contrast to what we will hear of Joseph's character. If we look more closely, we may agree that Joseph, this story of Judah and Tamar, and all Genesis point out that it is in fact God's choice as to who is the elect. It is His choice alone; it does not belong to the parents. The stories of Joseph and Tamar reiterate for us that it is not the firstborn but the one God chooses whom He uses to bless others. God is in charge. God loves us despite our sin. Our poor performance in life does not alter God's plan.

Motifs as Clues to Dividing Narratives

Sometimes, you might find stories in separate parts of a longer narrative that have similar motifs. For instance, 1 Kings 17 and 2 Kings 4 contain the stories of different prophets—Elijah and Elisha—but they revolve around the motifs of lack and God's providential help. Both involve empty containers and women in rough circumstances whose sons die. If you keep your eyes open, repeated motifs are plentiful in the Old Testament. You might notice that Genesis has repeated stories about meeting at wells and being buried near trees. This is a good place to mention that romantic interludes (wells), death (trees), childbirth, and other major life events can help us find places to stop on our narrative journey too.

The Gospels and Acts

Since the four Gospels and the book of Acts are narrative, they are divided in the same way as the Old Testament narratives are. One difference is that parables will often be preceded by a narrative section that ties the two passages together. Frequently, Jesus told a string of parables or performed a group of healings that tied together. You can divide these or keep them together for preaching as long as you are aware that the meaning comes from the group of parables or the closely aligned events.

In the case of the New Testament narrative, look for ideas and purposes rather than scene changes alone. For example, we will talk a lot in coming chapters about the story of the Two Sons in Luke 15 in which Jesus was talking to tax collectors and sinners as well as Pharisees and scribes. This is integral to understanding whom Jesus' audiences were—sinners and religious people alike.[16] Stories in close proximity to one another are often related and you will see that all the stories in Luke 15, for example, are related. (More on this in chapter 12.)

EPISTLES AND HEBREWS

An epistle contains many ideas strung together like beads on a necklace. Sometimes, the beads are arranged randomly; other times, the beads are arranged in groups with similar topics. Other times, there is one central bead, one important idea central to the message of the book, and everything else points to it.

The problem can be finding good places to cut an epistle into preachable portions. But the hardest problem is often determining the Commander's intent for the passage since there can be several very important ideas close to each other. All those glittery, beautiful ideas can catch our eyes and distract us from the main theme of the passage. Which jewels are key to the purpose of the passage, and which support the main idea, the Commander's intent for this portion?[17] All the beads are important, but some are the key to the meaning of the whole book or the author's intent for writing.

Don't be confused by the sparkling verses; focus instead on the paragraphs. Paragraphs are very important in the epistles as each one is one bead or a group of beads with a single

---

[16] "Now the tax collectors and sinners were all drawing near to hear him. And the Pharisees and the scribes grumbled, saying, 'This man receives sinners and eats with them.' So he told them this parable: 'What man of you, having a hundred sheep, if he has lost one of them, does not leave the ninety-nine in the open country, and go after the one that is lost, until he finds it?'" (Luke 15:1–4).

[17] If my metaphor makes no sense at all, see Randal E. Pelton's book *Preaching with Accuracy*. Pelton uses a metaphor of lightbulbs—some are smaller and dimmer, while others shine more brightly and are more important.

idea. Usually, there will be more than one paragraph in a well-divided preaching portion. The paragraphs, if we put them together, should center on one idea.

Consider the author's intended meaning of the book and decide where he changes from one subordinate idea to the other. As misleading as they sometimes are, chapters can be pretty good clues to the dividing points in the epistles. Don't leave behind orphan paragraphs—they usually belong with another passage directly before or after. Look for transitions in the argument or message. When the subject changes, you can cut the passage, but you must look carefully at the passages before and after to see if there really is a subject change.

Don't be confused by the headings that have been added in our modern Bibles; they are not part of the Word of God, and though they may help us find a specific passage, they don't mark the beginnings or endings of large ideas that should be joined in preaching passages.[18] Headings also do not tell us the Commander's intent.

POETRY, PROPHETS, AND APOCALYPTIC LITERATURE

If narratives are divided by paragraphs, poetry is divided by stanzas and strophes. Strophes are often two lines that have similar meaning or whose meaning builds. Stanzas are groups of strophes or verses around a subject. They are indicated by spaces—like paragraphs—in translations including the ESV, NIV, and NRSV, but not the KJV.

For Psalms, consider including the relevant historical narrative portions if they can be determined.[19] Psalms can also be divided by use. For example, psalms of lament, psalms of penitence, psalms of thanksgiving, psalms of praise to the creator, festival songs, liturgy, and psalms of trust or meditation. Psalms can safely be taught as stand-alone messages. (No, you don't need to do a 150-week series because the topics are quite often separate.)

The book of Proverbs groups proverbs by subject. Teach on one proverb for young children, but show adults how the other proverbs and the rest of Scripture supports your chosen proverb or group of proverbs. Proverbs are also good for occasional use or devotionals rather than sequential teaching (a series covering every proverb would be a long series). Particularly in the case of Psalms and Proverbs, keep in mind genre as it pertains to meaning (see chapter 6).

Prophetic works should be thought of in terms of oracles, visions, and scenes.[20] In the prophets, if a visionary passage is too long, look for a thought segment focused on a theme such as judgment, idolatry, social injustice, religious formalism, repentance, or hope. If you are teaching an oracle or vision, include the narrative passage that goes with it. If you find repeated words or phrases or a string of similes, they might be considered together even though they run throughout several

---

[18] For example, if we were speaking on Hebrews, where would we stop our first message? The writer seems to have the same idea from Hebrews 1:1 to Hebrews 3:6; however, some would stop at the end of chapter 2. If you need help, use teaching aids that outline the book.

[19] For example, when you are reading Psalm 52 you might notice that it is preceded by, "To the choirmaster. A Maskil of David, when Doeg, the Edomite, came and told Saul, "David has come to the house of Ahimelech." Then it would be of great interest to read 1 Samuel 21 and 22.

[20] Oracles are authoritative pronouncements; they often start with a formula such as, "Thus says the LORD." An example is in Amos 1:3–5.

chapters.[21] A new thought sometimes starts with "In that day …" or "Thus says the LORD …," a rhetorical question, or a formula such as "for three … and for four."[22]

Be sure to include the related Old Testament historical settings when you teach the prophets because they are part of the same story. Don't try to blend the Commander's intent from the narrative passage from say Kings or Chronicles and a prophetic book or you will get really confused. Merely use the narrative/historic books as background information for what the prophet is preaching about. Always find the Commander's intent of the main passage you are speaking on rather than other cross-referenced passages. (See the Appendix G for several samples on preaching from the prophets.)

A SPIRAL CUT

Sometimes, a spiral cut works best. If you have ever had a spiral-cut ham, you know that the slices are all attached to the bone. The pieces are all connected. Despite all our tools, there are passages that must remain connected to preceding and following passages if we are truly going to represent the Commander's intent., So it is permissible and even advisable to have overlap. In some books of the Bible, the passages should all be hanging together in their meaning if we carve them correctly.

Since we have to divide books for preaching or teaching, we must include the context before and after our chosen passage in the development of our message if we want to slice it correctly. How much or how little of last week and next week's message you cover is up to the passage. Your decision may depend on whether you have found a major idea in your passage, one that supports the entire book's major theme and is developed throughout the book in ways that are impossible to surgically divide without losing a limb.

One example of where the spiral cut should be used is the book of Job. You have to keep the Commander's intent for the book in mind as you read and especially as you preach. The book of Job is like a spiral-cut ham that needs the bone to hold it together until the last minute—the bone being the central intent of the book. Job can of course be preached sequentially over many weeks, but since Job and his friends' speeches contain only partial truths, it might be better to serve some of the inner chapters in larger chunks while keeping the Commander's intent of the entire book from being lost.

A Case Study

The book of Romans is an excellent place to use the spiral-cut method; it contains one long, inductive argument; it is a difficult book to cut without destroying Paul's big-picture message. Paul's style of reasoning makes his point strong and irrefutable, but if we chop it up incorrectly, we butcher his meaning.

When you first teach on Romans, read it straight through a couple of times and try to forget what you thought you knew it said. In doing so, it becomes clear that Paul did not put the chapter divisions in his epistle. In fact, the chapter divisions diminish his argument and in some cases change Paul's message altogether. Romans 1 and 2 are cases in point.

---

[21] For example, in Amos, you see the "For three transgressions … and for four …" motif repeated. You could put them all together with the main judgment for each nation charged being a point in your message on justice.

[22] "Thus says the LORD: 'For three transgressions of Israel, and for four, I will not revoke the punishment, because they sell the righteous for silver, and the needy for a pair of sandals'" (Amos 2:6).

In chapter 1, Paul started with some specific sins his readers would be ready to heartily condemn. When his listeners began to judge those other evil sinners, Paul continued to narrow the entrance to the trap like a funnel. Soon, he lists sins his listeners (including you and me) would recognize in themselves.

> And since they [those horrible sinners from earlier verses] did not see fit to acknowledge God, God gave them up to a debased mind to do what ought not to be done. They were filled with all manner of unrighteousness, evil, covetousness, malice. They are full of envy, murder, strife, deceit, maliciousness. They are gossips slanderers, haters of God, insolent, haughty, boastful, inventors of evil, disobedient to parents, foolish, faithless, heartless, ruthless. Though they know God's righteous decree that those who practice such things deserve to die, they not only do them but give approval to those who practice them. (Romans 1:28–32)

Paul recounted a list of sins that his readers recognized in themselves. Then bam! Paul slammed the gate locking us all in.

> Therefore you have no excuse, O man, every one of you who judges. For in passing judgment on another you condemn yourself, because you, the judge, practice the very same things. We know that the judgment of God rightly falls on those who practice such things. Do you suppose, O man—you who judge those who practice such things and yet do them yourself—that you will escape the judgment of God? (Romans 2:1–3)

Paul could have simply said, "We have all sinned and deserve death." But the type of reasoning he used was a superior way of drawing his listeners into the trap. If we stop his message at the end of chapter 1, we completely miss the punch line, the point, which is, when we are pointing one finger at those who commit shameful sins, we are pointing four fingers back at ourselves. That kind of great logical reasoning continues throughout the rest of Romans. If we had followed the chapter demarcations, we would have destroyed Paul's first main point.

This morning, we begin a 12-week series I'm calling, "Irrelevant Points From Previous Sermons."

xvii

53

Classification of Books in the Bible with Primary Genre

THE LAW/PENTATEUCH: CONTAINS NARRATIVE AND LAW PASSAGES

1. Genesis
2. Exodus
3. Leviticus
4. Numbers
5. Deuteronomy

POETRY/WISDOM: POETRY AND PARABLE

18. Job
19. Psalms
20. Proverbs
21. Ecclesiastes
22. Song of Solomon

OT HISTORY: NARRATIVE

6. Joshua
7. Judges
8. Ruth
9. 1 Samuel
10. 2 Samuel
11. 1 Kings
12. 2 Kings
13. 1 Chronicles
14. 2 Chronicles
15. Ezra
16. Nehemiah
17. Esther

OT PROPHETS: PROPHECY, PREACHING, POETRY, AND NARRATIVE

A. Major Prophets

23. Isaiah
24. Jeremiah
25. Lamentations
26. Ezekiel
27. Daniel

B. Minor Prophets

28. Hosea
29. Joel
30. Amos
31. Obadiah
32. Jonah
33. Micah
34. Nahum
35. Habakkuk
36. Zephaniah
37. Haggai
38. Zechariah
39. Malachi

GOSPELS: NARRATIVE

40. Matthew
41. Mark
42. Luke
43. John

NT HISTORY: NARRATIVE

44. Acts

EPISTLES
PAULINE
45. Romans
46. 1 Corinthians
47. 2 Corinthians
48. Galatians
49. Ephesians
50. Philippians
51. Colossians
52. 1 Thessalonians
53. 2 Thessalonians
54. 1 Timothy
55. 2 Timothy
56. Titus
57. Philemon

GENERAL
58. Hebrews
59. James
60. 1 Peter
61. 2 Peter
62. 1 John
63. 2 John
64. 3 John
65. Jude

NT PROPHECY
66. Revelation

Questions for Picking Passages

Big-Picture Questions for Planning

- What does God wants to accomplish in and through my ministry?
- What does my congregation need in terms of teaching or preaching?
- What is the general spiritual maturity level of my congregation? How might that affect what I choose?
- What time frame do I have for covering the material?
- Have I been shifting the focus back and forth between the Old and New Testaments to offer a balanced diet to my congregation?
- What types of biblical literature have I left out of my ministry and so need to cover? (Pauline epistles, prophecy, Gospels, Old Testament history, pastoral epistles, Genesis, Apocalyptic Literature, the Law, Psalms, wisdom literature, parables)

Preaching Calendar Planning Questions

- What are the teaching days in this year? (Make a planning/preaching calendar.)
- How many weeks will I give to this particular book?
- What are the holidays or special days? How will these interfere or be incorporated in the planning calendar? (For example : Can I make it to the passion narratives by Easter?)
- How can I best carve up my chosen book, to fit the calendar? (Will I choose to focus primarily on chapters, groups of chapters, stories, or paragraphs?)

- What about retreats and other special events?
- What other things in the calendar do I need to take into account?

Book-Level Questions

Read the whole book. Read it again. Read the first and last chapters. Read a commentary that gives you the historical context of the book. Research the original purpose of the book. This generally needs to be done only before the start of a sequential series.

- What is the main message of the book I have chosen to preach or teach?
- Who wrote this book, and what can I say about the human author?[xviii]
- Whom was this book written to?
- When was this book written?
- Was this book written about a special occasion, event, or occurrence?
- Why was this book written, and what purpose did the human author have?
- What was happening in Israel, the church, or world history at the time this book was written?
- What was happening or is about to happen?
- What is this book's place in the canon of Scripture?
- What would be missing from the Bible if this book were not there?
- How does this book fit into the story of salvation?
- How was this book originally meant to be used (preached, sung, used for festivals, read aloud, read personally, read in church)?
- How did the author or editors organize or divide this book? Why?

This Week's Passage Pinned Down

- What are the boundaries of the text to be preached, and why did I choose them? (Generally speaking, ignore chapter and verse and focus on the message of story.)
- Does my passage carry a complete thought? Does it carry the important idea for this section, or is the idea here subordinate to other ideas in the text? If so, do I have a big enough idea?[xix]
- Can the surrounding passages stand alone, or should they be included with the passage I have chosen?
- Will I be speaking on the same subject next week? Should I combine the two passages?
- What specific portion within the larger portion I plan to speak on, is meant to carry the main emphasis of the larger passage?
- What is the main message of this passage?
- What verse or phrase contains the Commander's intent for this passage? (It may be way too early for this question, but think about it.)
- Should I include verses from the next passage or previous passages to complete the thought of the passage?
- Do I need to use the spiral-cut method, or does the passage contain a full enough idea on its own to convey a significant purpose of the author?

- What are the broad confines of the message? Which verses are included? How much Scripture can I include to support the main message and not get off topic?
- Should I focus this week primarily on the whole chapter in my passage, a section, a group of chapters, a theme in the book, one or several of the included paragraphs, a story, a group of stories, several episodes based on themes or key words, related subjects, or arguments?
- Am I thinking whole paragraphs, whole thoughts, whole ideas?
- Are there any key words or repeated phrases or ideas that continue past my chosen section?
- Am I fairly conveying the author's message in the way I've divided this passage?

Section 2

LISTEN: CONTEMPLATIVE, INDUCTIVE THEOLOGICAL EXEGESIS

CHAPTER 5

LISTEN! LISTEN!

> Listen, listen to me,
> and eat what is good,
> and you will delight in the richest of fare.
> Give ear and come to me;
> listen, that you may live.
> (Isaiah 55:2b–3a NIV)

We must guard against the rush to write that can happen when we are preparing to preach or teach. We want to jump to find our sermon title and writing a teaching outline before we've even finished reading the passage. We're busy. We think we get it.

Stop. Turn off your engines. Cool your jets. It's not time to write a message yet. This is contemplative exegesis. We aren't ready to decide on the Commander's intent for His passage until we have soaked the passage into every pore. Paul Scott Wilson put it this way.

> We do not listen to the text at this stage to hear what we should preach. We hear what the text says in its own time and place. Contemplative Exegesis is a process of questioning a biblical text in a manner that helps the interpreter encounter it afresh and think it through.[i]

Listen! Listen! You might have heard the Hebrew for the Word *listen*. It is *shema*[1]—which means "hear" or "listen," but it can also mean "obey." This is the prerequisite for every message. Hear, listen, and be prepared to obey. Then you are ready to proclaim.

---

[1] *Shema* is often translated "listen diligently," but I like the more emphatic translation, "Listen! Listen!" (NIV). The verb *shema* is used 1,050 times in the OT (TWOT). Notably it is the first word in the Jewish prayer called the Shema. "Hear, O Israel: The LORD our God, the LORD is one. You shall love the LORD your God with all your heart and with all your soul and with all your might. And these words that I command you today shall be on your heart. You shall teach them diligently to your children, and shall talk of them when you sit in your house, and when you walk by the way, and when you lie down, and when you rise. You shall bind them as a sign on your hand, and they shall be as frontlets between your eyes. You shall write them on the doorposts of your house and on your gates" (Deuteronomy 6:4–9).

Good Listening Takes Time

But whoever listens to me
will dwell secure and will be at ease,
without dread of disaster.
(Proverbs 1:33)

When a woman is pregnant, people say she is eating for two. We are listening for a lot more than two. We are listening for a lot of different people. We are listening for ourselves. We are listening for the people to whom this passage was written or spoken. We are listening for our congregation. We are listening for the culture, the people of the world we live in. Listen! Listen! This is a big job.

If we get no other message preparation done, we should at least sit quietly and listen to what the Word of God really says. It is unfortunately possible to teach about the Word of God without actually having heard its message in our hearts. Thomas Long, professor of preaching at Candler School of Theology at Emory University in Atlanta, wrote,

> Fundamentalists, charismatics, social activists, feminists, evangelicals, traditionalists, liberationists—all of us, in fact—go to the texts of the Bible and return with trophies that are replicas of our own theological image. It is no easy task genuinely to listen to the voice of Scripture rather than merely to hear the sound of our own echoes.[ii]

We are listening for the heart message of our Commander, not the echo of our own viewpoint.

Let the Bible Speak

For our first several readings through the passage and its context, we set aside our questions, doubts, misgivings, and disagreements with God and His Word. Instead of interrupting the Holy Spirit's message, write your questions down to grapple with prayerfully after you have done your initial listening. Set aside mental interruptions to listen to God speak through His Word. Taking a leap of faith does not mean not having questions or doubts; it means trusting that the Bible is worth listening to without interrupting it.

When we practice this discipline of reading without thinking about our message (or our upcoming dental appointment), we will find it to be very rewarding. Set aside the sermons you've heard, the stuff you've read, the notions you have about this text. Read it with fresh eyes. Haddon Robinson wrote this in his text on biblical preaching.

> Expositors approach their Bible with a childlike desire to hear the story. They do not come to argue, to prove a point, or even to find a sermon. They read to understand and to experience what they understand.[iii]

I'm betting that both Mary and Martha heard every word Jesus said when he was teaching in their home. Their home was probably small, and Martha thought she was listening as she bustled about. But Martha was so busy serving Jesus that she didn't have time to truly listen to Him. She wasn't abiding in the vine; she was too busy serving the wine. And that is why poor Martha was anxious, bitter, and jealous of Mary, who just sat there at Jesus' feet soaking in the blessing. (You will see below in the writings of Guigo the monk that after we listen carefully, we can meditate on the Word while going about our everyday, mindless tasks.)

I can hear Martha clanging the pans and slamming the cupboards and muttering at her lazy sister, and I know exactly how she felt. All too well do I know it.[2]

> The Lord answered her, "Martha, Martha, you are anxious and troubled about many things, but one thing is necessary. Mary has chosen the good portion, which will not be taken away from her." (Luke 10:41–42)

Choose the good portion, sit at Jesus' feet, and listen to the Word. Abide in Christ. Finish your prayer's request, lay aside your worries, and sit like a child on your father's knee. Listen. Stop arguing with God about what He isn't doing (listen like a child, not like a teenager). Stop telling the Bible what it says or what you think it should say. Just stop. Let the Bible speak for itself. If the Bible really is the words of God, of course we should spend time reading and meditating on it. I wonder how Jesus must feel when we proclaim the Word without first listening, listening.

Practice *Lectio Divina*

In *Praying Scripture for a Change: An Introduction to Lectio Divina*, Dr. Tim Gray shared the writings of Guigo, a Carthusian monk.[3]

> One day when I was busy working with my hands I began to think about our spiritual work, and all at once four stages in spiritual exercise came into my mind: reading, meditation, prayer, and contemplation. These make a ladder for monks by which they are lifted up from earth to heaven. It has few rungs, yet its length is immense and wonderful, for its lower end rests upon the earth, but its top pierces the clouds and touches heavenly secrets.[iv]

> Reading is the careful study of the Scriptures, concentrating all one's powers on it. Meditation is the busy application of the mind to seek with the help of one's own reason for knowledge of hidden truth. Prayer is the heart's devoted turning to God to drive away evil and obtain what is good. Contemplation is when the mind is in some sort lifted up to God and held above itself, so that it tastes the joys of everlasting sweetness.[v]

This method of reading Scripture is called *lectio divina*, sacred reading. It is an ancient technique for listening to God speak to us in Scripture, a way of reading Scripture in the context of contemplative prayer. Dr. Tim Gray explained the secret of the saints; he quoted St. Cyprian: "Diligently practice prayer and lectio divina. *When you pray, you speak with God; when you read, God speaks to you.*"[vi] In his delightful book, Gray described for us how we too like the saints of old can meditate prayerfully on Scripture. The monks meditated on Scripture and prayed all day as they worked in the vineyard. Here are the steps they used.[vii]

---

[2] Luke 10:38–42.

[3] Dr. Tim Gray is a Catholic theologian, president of the Augustine Institute, and professor of Scripture at St. John Vianney Seminary in Denver.

Lectio: Here, the words of Scripture are examined closely and their connections and patterns are noted similar to how the grapes of a vineyard are examined and collected with care.

Meditatio: In this phase of reading, Scripture is squeezed to extract its meaning. This is similar to how grapes are squeezed for their juice.

Oratio: In oratio, our conversation with God about the Word allows us to ponder it in our hearts with a growing desire for the One who has spoken to us. Oratio is similar to how grape juice ferments over time in an oak barrel to produce the sweet wine.

Contemplatio: In contemplatio, we "taste the goodness of the Lord" similar to how the wine is opened and its sweetness consumed.

Operatio: This is when we make operative, we practice, some resolution. We bring the wine of God's Word to fruitfulness in our life and the world.

Gray wrote,

> The monks who relished the idea of Scripture being a spiritual vineyard surely grasped just how analogous winemaking is to lectio divina. Perhaps this is why so many monasteries specialized in making wine. The monks found that lectio divina, like winemaking, was always worth the effort.[viii]

Thoughtful Proclaimers Abide in the Vine

> Abide in me, and I in you. As the branch cannot bear fruit by itself, unless it abides in the vine, neither can you, unless you abide in me. I am the vine; you are the branches. Whoever abides in me and I in him, he it is that bears much fruit, for apart from me you can do nothing. (John 15:4–5)

Jesus could turn water into wine. But for the rest of us, taking dirt and gnarly roots and turning them into something special and unforgettable to serve to others (such as a sermon) is a long process. First, we need to bear fruit, and then, we must skillfully turn it into wine. Jesus and His beloved disciple John used the word *abide* to describe the relationship of the branch to the vine, the relationship of believers to Jesus Christ. "Jesus said … 'If you abide in my Word, you are truly my disciples'" (John 8:31). All believers are like grapevines that must be attached to the vine to bear fruit. Without abiding in Christ and the Word, we cannot bear fruit. If we don't bear fruit, we are worth nothing for Him.[4]

Thoughtful proclaimers are servants who work in a vineyard to grow the fruit and then use their skill and time to turn it into wine. The difference between spoiled grapes and fine wine is not luck or chance or even giftedness; the difference is hard work, learned skills, artistic talent, and God's miraculous blessings of rain, sun, and fermentation. Winemakers aren't born; they learn their craft. They must learn about the history of a region and its vines, the soil, geology, geography, and weather. They must know how to grow and select grapes and then press, store, and age the juice. They must know to add sugar and yeast to ferment the juice and then blend, bottle, label, and age the wine.

---

[4] And he told this parable: "A man had a fig tree planted in his vineyard, and he came seeking fruit on it and found none. And he said to the vinedresser, 'Look, for three years now I have come seeking fruit on this fig tree, and I find none. Cut it down. Why should it use up the ground?' And he answered him, 'Sir, let it alone this year also, until I dig around it and put on manure. Then if it should bear fruit next year, well and good; but if not, you can cut it down'" (Luke 13:6–9).

Just as a winemaker can't know everything there is to know about making wine without learning from others, we need to learn about the process of taking the fruit and with God's help transforming it into something special, a message to proclaim.[5]

We need a recipe.

RECIPE FOR THOUGHTFUL PROCLAMATION

Listen, and let the Bible speak. Pay attention to context. Dig deep into the ideas. Dig deep into the actual words. Paraphrase the passage. Work to understand your listeners. Decide on our Commander's intent for the passage. Let it simmer for a bit. Consider how best to proclaim it redemptively to those listening. Make it memorable with a single point for proclamation, a catchphrase, and an anchor image. Pull it all together into a transformational message to teach.

We can have the finest educations, the most creative spirits and active intellects, and be inspirational and entertaining speakers but if we are not abiding in the vine, in Christ, the fruit needed for the first step will be missing, and anything we preach or teach will be worth only the paper it is written on. It may be an artificially flavored grape drink, but it will not be wine.

In his book *Messiology: The Mystery of How God Works Even When it Doesn't Make Sense to Us*, George Verwer[6] reminded us that God occasionally does for a time use pastors, missionaries, and preachers who are not abiding in Him, who are secretly living in sin, whose personal lives don't jibe with their ministry calling.[ix] It is God's prerogative to use whom He wants, and He does so for His own purposes.

But that is not the plan. The plan is for the laborers in the field to be listening to the Master's instruction. Thoughtful proclaimers do not plan routinely to depend on miracles of God's mercy and grace for a good and meaningful sermon when they haven't done their work or are living far from God. Thoughtful proclaimers stay close to Christ and the Word, learn the needed skills, and do the work needed to produce the product God can best use.

Then we can depend on God's mercy and grace for a good and meaningful message. Though God calls and uses those He wills, the humble and grateful laborer who hangs on His master's every Word is the most useful to Him.[7]

All believers in Jesus Christ must abide in the vine to bear fruit and grow. But some of us are blessed to be called to preach and teach, to make that fruit something spiritually mysterious that God can use to cause others to bear fruit. The growth of the fruit requires no effort on the part of the vine when it is firmly rooted. But turning that fruit into wine, a message, is a joint effort between the heavenly vine and the earthly winemaker.

---

[5] "But the fruit of the Spirit is love, joy, peace, patience, kindness, goodness, faithfulness, gentleness, self-control; against such things there is no law. And those who belong to Christ Jesus have crucified the flesh with its passions and desires" (Galatians 5:22–24).

[6] George Verwer is the founder and former international director of Operation Mobilisation, www.om.org. OM is an international mission conglomerate that has brought the gospel, Christian books, and practical help worldwide for over fifty years.

[7] "The end of all things is at hand; therefore be self-controlled and sober-minded for the sake of your prayers. Above all, keep loving one another earnestly, since love covers a multitude of sins. Show hospitality to one another without grumbling. As each has received a gift, use it to serve one another, as good stewards of God's varied grace: whoever speaks, as one who speaks oracles of God; whoever serves, as one who serves by the strength that God supplies—in order that in everything God may be glorified through Jesus Christ. To him belong glory and dominion forever and ever. Amen" (1 Peter 4:7–11).

The process of turning fruit from a vine into wine is partly natural, partly miraculous, time consuming, and a lot of work just as preparing a biblical message is. Writing a message that transforms hearts requires great skill and hard work along with God's supernatural gifts of faith, insight, and creativity. Just as the fermentation occurs on its own, in secret, in the dark, so the fermenting of Scripture into a message requires us to spend time in secret, Sabbath, and contemplation; sometimes a lot of it.

Though I don't know much about viticulture, I do know about trying to produce spiritual wine, a message, without abiding in the vine. I know about trying to conjure up a message when I haven't been abiding in Christ. It doesn't work. I don't recommend it. The message can be organized, interesting, humorous, and inspiring, but it will not have that sparkle that comes only from the fermentation, from the anointing of the Holy Spirit.

> You did not choose me, but I chose you and appointed you that you should go and bear fruit and that your fruit should abide, so that whatever you ask the Father in my name, he may give it to you. (John 15:16)

"We don't know what you're doing in here, but we've been waiting five minutes to talk to you about the broken hand dryer in the ladies' room."

Accept the Guidance of the Holy Spirit

We impart a secret and hidden wisdom of God, which God decreed before the ages for our glory. As it is written,

> What no eye has seen, nor ear heard, nor the heart of man imagined, what God has prepared for those who love him" these things God has revealed to us through the Spirit. For the Spirit searches everything, even the depths of God. (1 Corinthians 2:7, 9–10)

Only by the Spirit of God can we discern who God is, believe what He has done, and understand the intent of His Word. God's Spirit, the Holy Spirit, is given to those who will take the leap of faith, those who will believe even with perhaps an imperfect belief because our belief can be only imperfect this side of eternity.

By our natural self, without faith, without asking in prayer for guidance from the Holy Spirit, we will not be able to discern all things concerning faith and the Spirit in the Word. We cannot fully understand Scripture unless we decide to trust in the God of Scripture and his Son, Jesus Christ. We have a secret weapon in our arsenal—the Holy Spirit. Since the Spirit of God inspired the original writers, we can understand the mind of our writers by listening closely and prayerfully to the Holy Spirit as we read. The Holy Spirithe will guide our hearts and minds as we listen and read.

When we prepare to speak, God can fill our thoughts and pens with the truth of the Scripture we are studying. When we preach and teach, the Holy Spirit can anoint us with His power. We should not try to do it alone.

> I still have many things to say to you, but you cannot bear them now. When the Spirit of truth comes, he will guide you into all the truth, for he will not speak on his own authority, but whatever he hears he will speak, and he will declare to you the things that are to come. He will glorify me, for he will take what is mine and declare it to you. All that the Father has is mine; therefore I said that he will take what is mine and declare it to you. (John 16:12–15)

Read Many Translations

If you unearthed an old love letter from your father to your mother, how would you read it? What would you be wondering? If your best friend called after a long absence with big news, how would you listen? What questions would you ask? In the same way, the author of a biblical book (and surely the Holy Spirit) deserves our undivided attention. He deserves that we read His words through, hanging onto each idea, looking for words of love, envisioning the far-flung place in which he wrote, and picturing each character and circumstance in our mind's eye.

When we prepare to teach on a passage, we should first read it repeatedly, but since our love letter was written in an ancient and foreign language, we face a great challenge. We want to read it in its original language if possible. Barring that, we will read it in as many good translations as we can, trying hard to understand not only the gist of it but also to understand it fully.

Read the passage fully and in depth; seek guidance from the Holy Spirit. Try to focus on the passage and ignore any study notes (written by people, not God) at this point. You will be doing other studies later, but for the time being, just listen to the passage. Listen! Listen! Make note of your questions, things that are pertinent, difficult, or need clarification of some sort. But for the most part, just listen to God speak through His Word.

If you are proficient in the original language, read it in the original. If not (and even if you are), read translations that were done by committee and which have different translational perspectives.[8] J. I. Packer put it this way: "No definitive version of the Bible is possible, any more than a definitive performance of Beethoven's Ninth Symphony or C sharp minor quartet is possible, there is more in it waiting to be expressed than any one rendering can encompass."[xi] For this reason, we listen to many translations to get the fullest message.

For English translations at the time of this writing, start with the ESV, NIV (1984), NIV (2011), NASB (1995), NRSV, NKJV, The NET Bible, KJV, and for the OT, read also the New JPS Tanakh (85).[9]

TYPES OF TRANSLATIONS:[XII]

Formal Equivalence (literal)			Functional Equivalence (dynamic)					Free
1. KJV	NASB	RSV	NIV	NAB	GNB	JB	NEB	LB
2. NKJV	NASU	NRSV ESV	TNIV	NJB	REB	NLT		The Message

A COMPARISON OF TRANSLATIONS USING 1 CORINTHIANS 10:13

Greek: We but not to the without measure to boast but according to the measure the rule that rules we the God measure to reach as far as even you.

---

[8] The perspectives translators use vary. Some are more functional or aim for dynamic equivalence (like the NIV). They attempt to translate thought by thought and strive for translations that read more like normal English. Other translations lean toward word-for-word translation (NASB, ESV). You might think that the word-for-word translation is better, but there is great value in dynamic equivalence, which better handles idioms and full thoughts. Both methods yield good results and are important for our understanding. The NRSV attempts to translate the KJV but uses better original texts, thus eliminating most unoriginal matter in the KJV. (From Gordon D Fee and Douglas Stuart, *How to Read the Bible for All It's Worth*, Grand Rapids, MI: Zondervan, 2003, chapter 2).

[9] If you have access to the Internet, phone apps, or computer programs that offer many choices, use them but beware of your choices as there are many translations available and more coming all the time. If in doubt, ask a professor of Greek or Hebrew whom you trust for advice. For more advice on choosing good translations, read *How to Read the Bible for All It's Worth*, by Gordon Fee and Douglas Stuart, published by Zondervan (you'll want the newest edition).
Generally, translations that include the word *New* or those done more recently are better for two reasons. First, there have been many advances in the study and understanding of ancient languages, and despite our confidence, some words and phrases are difficult to translate. Second, our modern languages change rapidly, and what might make sense to a person of seventy may mean something different to a person of fifteen. However, not everything new is better, and the best approach, barring reading in the original language, is to read many translations. Note that there are three major NIV translations—the NIV 1984, the TNIV, and the NIV 2011—and there are differences among them, so consider reading both the NIV 84 and what they are now calling the NIV.
The JPS New Tanakh reflects the traditional Jewish interpretation of the Hebrew Bible ignoring Christological interpretations present in many non-Jewish translations.

KJV 1611: But we will not glory beyond our measure, but according to the measure of the province which God apportioned to us as a measure, to reach even unto you.

KJV 1900: But we will not boast of things without our measure, but according to the measure of the rule which God hath distributed to us, a measure to reach even unto you.

NKJV 1982: We, however, will not boast beyond measure, but within the limits of the sphere which God appointed us—a sphere which especially includes you.

NRSV 1989: We, however, will not boast beyond limits, but will keep within the field that God has assigned to us, to reach out even as far as you.

NASB 1995: But we will not boast beyond our measure, but within the measure of the sphere which God apportioned to us as a measure, to reach even as far as you.

ESV 2001: But we will not boast beyond limits, but will boast only with regard to the area of influence God assigned to us, to reach even to you.

NIV 1984: We, however, will not boast beyond proper limits, but will confine our boasting to the field God has assigned to us, a field that reaches even to you.

NIV 2011: We, however, will not boast beyond proper limits, but will confine our boasting to the sphere of service God himself has assigned to us, a sphere that also includes you.

NET 2005: But we will not boast beyond certain limits [The words "will confine our boasting" are not in the Greek text, but the reference to boasting must be repeated from the previous clause to clarify for the modern reader what is being limited.], but will confine our boasting [*Greek* "according to the measure of the rule which God has apportioned to us as a measure"; for the translation used in the text see Luow & Nida 37.100] according to the limits of the work to which God has appointed us [see parenthetical above] that reaches even as far as you.

Do not read paraphrases such as *The Message*, *The Amplified Bible*, *The Living Bible*, or *The Good News Bible* at this time (though you may read them later as you prepare your message and after you have done thorough exegesis through Chapter 10).[10] Depending on the length of the passage, you may read it enough times that parts of the passage become committed to memory.

Read the Surrounding Context

In preparation, read the whole book. Read the chapters that surround your passage even if you just preached on them last week. In this way, you are certain to understand the author and the Commander's intent in light of the context.

Take the Bible at Face Value

Why do we need to interpret the Bible anyway? In reality, we don't if by that we mean change what it says in some way. By interpret, we mean we want to know what the Bible means. We want to know what it meant to its original culture and audience because that will help us know how

---

[10] As a serious Bible teacher, I have been very cautious about watching or reading dramatizations on the Bible. Even audio dramatic readings have perspectives. If you do partake of Bible dramatizations or paraphrases, be careful to note in your mind that they are just that. Even my own dramatic telling of a Bible narrative takes some liberty for the sake of humor, understanding, or to make a point.

to apply it ourselves. The best methods for good interpretation are listening well and taking the Bible at face value.[11]

We interpret the Bible to truly take it at face value. We are digging in to each word, verse, idea, and paragraph. We are working to understand the contexts. We ask questions: What is it saying? Why is it saying that? To that end, we sometimes need to ask, how is it saying it (its genre)? Who did the Spirit inspire to say it (its author)? Who was he saying it to first (the history)? What was happening in their world (the culture)? What else did that author say (the surrounding context)? How does what this passage says fit into the rest of the Old or New Testaments? How is this passage part of the big story of redemption?

Even with our most careful reading, we will at times have trouble understanding what a passage means. We also have to look a bit deeper when things get cloudy—when passages seem to contradict each other, when stories don't have clear morals, or when a passage seems to say something we are pretty sure God wouldn't have said.[12] Some passages, especially apocalyptic material and prophetic oracles, contain difficult to interpret metaphors. In those cases, we may need some help to get at the face value of the passage. In such cases, I'm always glad I have my commentaries, though even then, I read several commentaries to get different perspectives.

Learn to Ask Good Questions

If you were to examine a rare jewel, you would do so from every angle and in different light. The same is true of a Bible text. You want to look at it from all angles, some obvious, some less expected. You want to shine a light onto all the edges and even look through to the inside. Oletta Wald, Bible teacher and author of *The New Joy of Discover in Bible Study*, wrote, "Observation demands concentration! The purpose of observation is to saturate yourself thoroughly with the content of a passage. Like a sponge you should absorb everything that is before you."[xiii]

As you begin to ask and answer questions, look for themes to develop from your answers and watch for answers that are repeated as this may indicate a trend. Be aware of things that stand out more than others do—things that are odd, things that are troubling. Note that every question in

---

[11] I say "face value" instead of "literally" because taking the Bible literally has negative connotations for some of us since it has often been taken to mean read "without regard to context." When we take the Bible in context, as we will see in chapter 6, we cannot forget the historical and cultural aspects of its origins and especially what the Bible says on an issue in the rest of the canon. Simply referring to the literal reading of the Bible tends to make one think that we do not care to know what the Bible really means but only what it says, and that is wrong. We care greatly about what Scripture means to say in the Spirit-inspired, supra-cultural entirety. We want to know why God would want us to preach or teach on this passage to our audience. So for example, we look at the genre of a passage. When I read hyperbole, metaphor, poetry, or description, I take it at face value but not literally. When I read the Old Testament laws, I understand them in their historical context, in light of the New Testament teaching, and according to how the author would apply them today if he were around and under the inspiration of the Holy Spirit. Because the Bible is so important, we want to know what it means to say rather than reading words on a page. We look for the Commander's intent that lies behind the words in the passage.

[12] For example, I had a major anxiety attack, heart palpitations, and nearly fainted the first time someone alluded to the possibility that the opening of Genesis might not be a datable scientific account according to commonly held modern standards. I eventually had to teach on it, so I read it … a lot … for a whole summer, just the first four chapters until it was in my blood. I listened to God speak through His Word, and I prayerfully attempted to forget all the things I had been told and had read and assumed and thought I'd die and go to hell if I didn't believe. And I can say it was very refreshing and enlightening to take God's Word at face value without trying to make it say things it never meant to say when it was written many thousands of years ago.

this book will not make sense for every passage. Some questions may seem redundant, but they are just different ways of looking at the same jewel.

What seems particularly important? What stands out to you? What verses seem to be key? What words, phrases, or ideas are repeated or seem important or difficult? Does the passage have a theme? What is the passage about? Who are the characters? Is it focused on the future, the present, or the past? What other questions can you think of?

Be a Good Steward of Your Time

> And the Lord said, "Who then is the faithful and wise manager, whom his master will set over his household, to give them their portion of food at the proper time? Blessed is that servant whom his master will find so doing when he comes. Truly, I say to you, he will set him over all his possessions … Everyone to whom much was given, of him much will be required, and from him to whom they entrusted much, they will demand the more." (Luke 12:42–44, 48)

Your job is not to find out every geographic detail or ancient religious or cultural background point but to discern the Commander's intent for your passage and how it can be applicable today. To do this, you will likely benefit from knowing something about the people, the times, and the temptations of the original audience for the message, but not everything.

Ask every question that seems pertinent and then a few more. Write down your observations and answers when they are relevant to the meaning. If you don't know the answer, consider if finding the answer is important to the theme and message of the passage. If not, wait to answer it until you have free time. Not every question you have will need to be answered. Most importantly, use your questions and your study to know God better, to understand the Bible more fully, and to empathize with your audience well.

There is a balance between the importance of biblical background and the fact that God inspired each passage knowing we would be preaching on it 3,500 years later. That is not an excuse not to do our historical and background homework, but it is true. Cultural and historical background can sometimes add color, interest, depth, and nuance, but only occasionally does it completely change meaning. This is especially true if you are preaching sequentially through a book and you've done your commentary study on the culture and background of the text at the beginning. Discern when the cultural, geographical, or historical facts are important to the meaning of the text and when they are more incidental to it (see chapter 6).[13]

Use Commentaries Sparingly

My son is a cook (I say chef). He works in a restaurant that makes almost everything from scratch. It takes time and it's expensive, but it's good. A few sauces in the restaurant have become popular, so they have bottled them for sale, but they don't taste nearly as good coming from a

---

[13] "The aim of the grammatico-historical method [of exegesis] is to determine the sense required by the laws of grammar and the facts of history." In this text, we are more focused on what Walter Kaiser calls syntactical-theological exegesis; we use grammar and history as tools, but our goal is to find the meaning and what a passage teaches us about God and what He wants from us. See Walter Kaiser, *Toward an Exegetical Theology: Biblical Exegesis for Preaching and Teaching* (Grand Rapids, MI: Baker Academic, 1981), 69.

bottle. When I eat at my son's restaurant, I ask for the sauce to be made fresh by the chef. (When your son is the chef, you can do that!) The same is true for shortcuts in preaching and teaching. That's why we do it from scratch—it's just better.

Spending time coming to our own conclusions about the Commander's intent is better than spending a lot of time reading other people's conclusions or listening to other people's sermons on the passage. Fresh messages are always better than leftovers. Commentary reading is most appropriate in the planning stages before you begin a book, not when we are preparing the message. If we find we need to look up an answer in a commentary or textbook, we should do so but remember that our time is limited; we could probably spend weeks on one passage, but we have a matter of hours. On the other hand, when it is important to God's message to know something that is not evident, asking experts and gleaning from others who've done the hard work can help us listen well.

As much warning as I give about spending too much time in commentaries, I advise you to read the book introduction in a good study Bible or one- or two-volume commentary such as *The Bible Knowledge Commentary* after you have read the book through and yet before you write your first message on the book.[xiv] At the time of this writing, I recommend the *ESV Study Bible* for this purpose.[xv] We don't want too much information or commentary at this time as it may influence our thinking regarding the Commander's intent. We need just enough information so we can correctly discover whom the passage was written to, when it was written, what the circumstances were, and general information regarding context (see chapter 6). Right now, in the Listen! Listen! phase, we are striving to let the Bible speak for itself. If after studying the passage in depth we still have questions or have misunderstood something, we can always go back to the commentaries to ask an expert.

Putting a laser focus on the text, context, and Scripture and leaving commentaries and footnotes or application notes until later will help us be more spiritually connected to the passage and personally creative in our preaching and teaching. It will give us a sense of satisfaction as we learn and discover the Bible's meaning on our own, and we will take ownership of our interpretations. When we learn this way, our preaching and teaching has gravitas, and our audience can tell we know what we are talking about. If we have looked something up in a commentary or book, we can share that information if needed to make our point to our listeners. We never want to be caught proclaiming a commentary or someone else's message; we are called to proclaim Scripture.

I once heard a very accomplished Bible study teacher claim she read three hundred pages a week to prepare for her teaching. I believe had she spent three quarters of that time in the Word of God, she would have been better off. Though commentaries and other aids can be very helpful tools for the Bible teacher or preacher, consider that God, who inspired the passage, usually gave us everything we really needed to know about that passage for the purposes of proclamation right in His Word.

It might be nice to know what the weather was like when Jesus broke the loaves and fishes and fed five thousand, but is it necessary to the meaning of the passage? (I use that illustration because I actually did look up that detail, and it did help me set the scene for the story; however, it was possibly not the best use of my time.) We are only stewards of our time as our time is really God's.

"I don't mind God knowing the true intentions of my heart
as long as He doesn't spill the beans."   *xvi*

Good Questions for Great Listeners—Let the Bible Speak

Read many translations without interrupting the Word of God speaking to your heart. Read until you feel you understand what is being said. Read until you can repeat what is being said. Use these questions as a springboard for your own observations.

Personal Questions Regarding the Passage

- What stands out to me about this passage?
- Why did God put this passage in the Bible?
- What is this passage about?
- What questions do I have for God after reading this passage?
- What don't I understand here?
- What parts of this passage or its message don't I like?
- What about this passage goes in the opposite direction from the way most people suppose it should go?
- What is God saying here that is counter-cultural?
- What is God saying to me personally in this passage?
- Where do I need transformation to live out what God is saying to me in this passage?
- What work does the Holy Spirit need to do in my life because of what I've read here?
- What does Jesus Christ want to change in me before I am honestly able to recommend it to others?
- Why did the Holy Spirit inspire this passage?
- What is the Holy Spirit's message in this passage?
- What are the bright, shiny memory verses that stand out to me in this passage?

Make General Observations

- Can I picture the writing or preaching of this passage?
- Do we know who wrote this book? What do we know about him?

- What can we tell about the human author if he is not identified?
- Is the audience this was written to different from the characters in the story?
- Who is the audience?
- Is this book focused on the past, the present, or the future?
- Did this book cause anything to change or happen when it was written?
- Who are the characters in this story or passage? What are they like? How are they like us? How are they different from us?
- What are the characters doing?
- Where is God in this passage?
- Was this passage written for an occasion or circumstance or to address a particular problem? What was it?
- How is this circumstance, occasion, or problem similar or different from today?
- What do I need to know more about to understand this passage?
- Which questions can I answer from the text and its context?
- Which questions can't I find the answers to in the book I'm studying? (Make a note of them.)
- What would I want to ask the author of this passage if he were here with me?
- What appear to be the key verses that convey the main meaning in this passage? (Note: the key verses are not necessarily the bright, shiny memory verses.)

CHAPTER 6

CONTEXT, CONTEXT, CONTEXT

When my youngest son, Charles,[1] was about seven, he walked onto Miami Beach to buy a cold drink at a stand about fifty feet away from where we were all standing. He didn't come back. We became more and more terrified. We spoke to the police, who helped us look for one little boy out of hundreds and hundreds of children.

My parents walked up and down the street in front of the hotels and cafes that lined that strip of beach. My older children walked up and down the boardwalk between the street and the beach. I went up to every person I could find hoping to appeal to their hearts to help us keep an eye out for a lost little boy and to keep him from being abducted on a very busy beach lined with bars and hotels.

We looked for hours. The police drove up and down the beach in their jeeps questioning people. The authorities were not ready to give up hope, but clearly, our son had disappeared. The fear that was looming was that he was no longer on the beach but had been taken by a stranger into one of the cheap, sleazy hotels that lined the beach.

Hours later, we were feeling quite sick when we saw little boy walking down the sidewalk with a coconut under each arm. He was not on the beach but on the road next to the beach. It was Charles with sunburned cheeks looking for the car. How did he get so lost? He hadn't paid attention to his surroundings as he walked to the stand. He didn't take note of where he was. He went for a cold drink and then saw a volleyball game. And then a coconut. And then he wandered so far, he didn't know where he was along that strip of miles of beach and thousands of bathers. Just lots of half-naked people lying on towels. The next thing he knew, his parents were nowhere to be found.

If we don't pay attention to where we are, we can get lost. This is true of all sorts of reading, but certainly when we are reading the Bible for the purpose of teaching its meanings to others, we must not get lost. We have to study the biblical surroundings. Take note of where we are. Study not only our chosen passage but also those around it. Study the entire book. Find out why the book is where it is in the canon of Scripture. Ask ourselves about the larger message of the book. Ask ourselves how that book fits in with the gospel story, the big story of redemption. Only in this way can we prevent losing the context of the message of Scripture and missing its real purpose.

Context is the basis for all interpretation. In all modes of communication whether written,

---

[1] Charles is the chef who makes great sauces.

spoken, or symbolic, context is the key to understanding it properly. Meaning always flows from the larger literary unit down to the smaller. The meaning of a word depends on its sentence, and the meaning of the sentence depends on the paragraph. The paragraph depends on the chapter that contains it, and the chapter depends on the book. The book is part of the whole of Scripture and cannot be understood without keeping creation, the gospel, God's love and holiness, and eternity in mind. To understand a verse or a passage, we have to examine its context in ever-widening circles.[i]

You've chosen the passage you are going to proclaim, and you are ready to get started. For the many weeks you will speak on this book of the Bible, you will want to keep your eyes on the signposts. Never allow yourself to get lost—that is where bad theology and all sorts of error begin to creep in. The difference between good and bad preaching or teaching is often a matter of paying attention to the signposts. The good news is, the more work you do on context up front, the less work you will be doing weekly. You're excited. It's going to be great. Now where do we start?

Contextual Signpost 1: Read the Book of the Bible

Imagine traveling to Spain. You fly there, you check into your hotel, and you head to one of the greatest art museums in the world, the Prado. You line up for tickets. The great moment arrives; you are going in to view paintings by the old masters. You walk into the gallery and someone says you have to wear special glasses that block your view of everything except a few inches to the left and right. Someone takes you by the arm and leads you to a piece of art, and you look at it. All you can see is a hand, some dark stuff, maybe an eye. Bits and pieces. You decide you don't like art very much after all. Your enthusiasm vanishes.

That is what we do to our listeners when we speak on bits and pieces of Scripture without showing them what the book the passage comes from is saying. We show them a foot and describe it in detail but never show them the whole painting. Show them the painting and then describe the delicacy of a foot or hand or eye or whatever bits and pieces are in your passage. Keep stepping back and appreciating the whole book and its place in the Bible and especially the big story of redemption as you describe the bits and pieces.

A few weeks or even months before we plan to speak on this book, we should start our exegesis on the whole book. Before we read more than the book introductions in commentaries, we should read the book at least once. If it is short enough, read it several times. Read the first chapter and the last chapter repeatedly to understand the author's road map—know where he starts and where he finishes, and look for the purpose of his writing.

Randal E. Pelton[2] recommended paying particular attention to the first and last chapters of a book to find the author's intentions for the whole book.[ii] Note that books that the Old Testament books that have a first and second book (like 1st and 2nd Samuel) are actually one book, though they were divided to fit onto two scrolls. If we keep our eye on the first and last chapters

---

[2] Randal E. Pelton teaches preaching at Lancaster Bible College and teaches in the doctoral program at Gordon-Conwell Theological Seminary where he was one of my teachers. He is senior pastor of Calvary Bible Church in Mount Joy, Pennsylvania. I recommend his blog PeltonOnPreaching.com and his book *Preaching with Accuracy*.

throughout our teaching of Job, for example, we will not forget God's intention for a book where not everything that glitters is true gold.[3]

Outline the book, or if it is a book that is very difficult to outline, review the book outlines others have made (these are often found in the initial chapters of commentaries). Consider where the best stopping and starting places will be. Consider if you will need to do a spiral cut, and keep looping back to help the message hold together.

Consider offering an introductory teaching or sermon to show your audience the whole painting, the whole book. This will help your audience understand its context. But whether you do this or not, every week, remind yourself and your listeners of the big picture, the purpose of the book. In this way, we demonstrate to our listener how to read their Bibles.

Contextual Signpost 2: Study the Surrounding Passages

> Not many of you should become teachers, my brothers, for you know that we who teach will be judged with greater strictness. (James 3:1)

The first thing our realtor taught us was location, location, location. She meant that the cost and the value of every property are influenced most by its location. The most important thing in biblical interpretation is quite similar—context, context, context. Always look at the context (location) of a passage and its surrounding passages. Just another advertisement for sequential preaching—it's easier if you preached the passage that precedes this one last week.

Because of my love for Scripture (and the fact that my childhood church used to give us prizes for memorizing it), the verses that often pop into my head may or may not be out of context. For example, we all need to be aware that some of the verses we may claim for ourselves were originally promises meant for Israel in a particular historical context. Being a teacher of the Word means we are held to a high standard of truth and accuracy. When we proclaim a passage as though we are the resident biblical authority and yet do not consider what its author meant for it to be saying in light of the passages around it, we commit an error. Usually, conscientious expositors may make this mistake by forgetting the surrounding signposts or making assumptions based on their preconceived notions of what that text is about.

When someone leaves a sandwich on the counter in the kitchen, our basset hound will eat it in one bite. If you leave any food anywhere in the house where Beauregard can possibly get it (and he's pretty determined), he will. We call that a rookie mistake.[4]

Similarly, reading a verse or a passage without considering its broader context—the passages around it—is a mistake only a beginner should make, but in fact, it's easy to do especially if you are preaching from the lectionary, using *lectio selecta* (where each week you are choosing a completely new passage), or doing a topical preaching series rather than a sequential teaching

---

[3] Very briefly stated, the intention you find in the first and last several chapters of Job is that God is God and must be trusted.

[4] A mistake only a beginner would make.

through a book.[5] This is why the thoughtful proclaimer method generally recommends against these forms of topical preaching.

The context will never lead us astray when we are trying to understand the meaning of a word, the message of a paragraph, or the intent of the author for his book. If when looking at the surrounding context we see repeated themes, ideas, or words, we can be sure the author didn't do that accidentally but to help point us to his message and ours. As we have already mentioned, conjunctions such as "therefore" are there for a reason. No passage is an island; every passage is connected to a continent that contains it and informs its message.

Contextual Signpost 3: Consider the Canonical Context

> And [Jesus] said to them, "O foolish ones, and slow of heart to believe all that the prophets have spoken! Was it not necessary that the Christ should suffer these things and enter into his glory?" And beginning with Moses and all the Prophets, he interpreted to them in all the Scriptures the things concerning himself. (Luke 24:25–27)

We have several canonical contexts to consider. First, we must consider the context of our text in the book that contains it. We must look at our text in relation to the Testament, Old or New, in which it exists. We should look at how our text, our Commander's intent, is viewed in both the Old and the New Testaments.

As we consider the canon as a whole, we must constantly remember the different contexts and viewpoints of the people who wrote the books and of our two different testaments. The Old Testament was the witness of Israel and was written in a variety of literary styles. It is based in the historicity of the world and particularity of a people who became biblical Israel.

The New Testament is the witness of the Christian church. The Old Testament reflects the redemptive events of the people of Israel. The New Testament is a witness to God's redemption of all people through Jesus Christ. We must juggle the synagogue vs. church, Hebrew-Aramaic vs. Greek, ancient Near Eastern cultures vs. first-century Greco-Roman cultures, the theology of promise vs. the theology of fulfillment. We have to remember to consider the theology of creation, how everything was effected by the fall, and how all of that is being transformed into the kingdom of God.

When we study a passage, we need to consider where it is in the canon. Is it in the New Testament or Old? Where is it in the specific books of the Christian canon? Why was it put in this place? What does that have to do with its meaning?

On the writers of the two testaments, Brevard Childs[6] observed,

> The writers of the New Testament began from their experience with Jesus Christ from whom they received a radically new understanding of the Jewish [Old Testament] Scriptures. Then on the basis of this transformed Old Testament, the New Testament

---

[5] Here we have another reason to prepare your message from sequential Bible passages and not from a list of verses on you name it from the concordance. If your sermon is an exposition of twenty verses on forgiveness, you need to read twenty passages and surrounding context to make sure the author's message is your message.

[6] Brevard Childs was an Old Testament scholar and Professor of Old Testament at Yale University. He is noted for his pioneering work in interpreting the Bible based on the text of the biblical canon as a whole and finished product.

writers interpreted the theological significance of Jesus Christ to the Christian church by means of the Old. Moreover, the historical uniqueness of Jesus of Nazareth was not only related theologically to Israel's traditions of the past, but extended into the future by means of eschatological and liturgical actualization.[iii]

The dialogical [characterized by a dialogue between different voices] move of biblical theological reflection that is being suggested is from the partial grasp of fragmentary reality found in both testaments to the full reality that the Christian church confesses to have found in Jesus Christ, in the combined witness of the two testaments. It is not the case that the New Testament writers possess a full knowledge of Christ which knowledge then corrects the Old Testament. Nor is it adequate to understand interpretation as moving only in the one direction of Old Testament to New. Rather both testaments bear testimony to the one Lord, in different ways, at different times, to different peoples, and yet both are understood and rightly heard in the light of the living Lord himself, the perfect reflection of the glory of God. (Hebrews 1:3)[iv]

Childs's approach calls on us to wrestle with the Old and New Testaments using our two vehicles of revelation—the Word of God and the Holy Spirit—which cannot be separated or played against one another.[v] Every passage we seek to interpret should be seen in light of the full canonical truth of which it is a part. The New Testament is not a correction of the Old Testament but an extension of it that is based on the deep and ancient roots of the Old Testament.

Cross-References

The Protestant reformers taught that Scripture interprets Scripture (*Scriptura scripturam interpretatur*) and that Scripture is interpreted by Scripture alone (*sola scriptura*). The Bible is the best commentary on itself. We can learn much about a subject by looking at that subject mentioned or referred to in other parts of Scripture. Some things that seem clear in one passage are not as clear once we look at the fullness of Scripture on the matter. Vice versa, some things very unclear in one place are clearer in other parts of Scripture.[7]

The New Testament is based on the Old Testament, and Christianity is generally very Jewish in background but also very Greek. Additionally, the meanings and theology of Old Testament books are linked; for example, the prophets have their context in the books of history and Deuteronomy. Walter Kaiser represented the view of John Bright, a preeminent Old Testament scholar, as follows.

Every Biblical text has within it some facet of theology expressed in such a way as to be part and parcel of the fabric of its contents. While that theology cannot be torn from that text, it, nevertheless, often has [other Biblical] roots which were laid down antecedent [as a precursor] to that text.[vi]

For example, when Isaiah said, "Your country lies desolate" in Isaiah 1:7, he was referring to

---

[7] We can find cross-references in a good study Bible or online resource. Consider investing in software (even software that works on a phone). The ESV study Bible is quite good and has many cross-references (those little alphabetical footnotes in the text). The Thompson Chain Reference Study Bible or Nave's Topical Bible can be helpful for cross-references, but they can also inadvertently entangle us in tangentially related topics not central to a passage.

other passages such as Deuteronomy 28:15: "All these curses shall come upon you and pursue you and overtake you till you are destroyed, because you did not obey the voice of the LORD your God, to keep his commandments and his statutes that he commanded you." One verse is a cross-reference to the other; they explain or are on the same subject as one another, desolation or a curse.

We study themes and doctrines in our text by looking at other Scriptures that mention those themes and doctrines explicitly or where there is an implicit linkage. By looking at cross-references, we can more fully understand the broader biblical intent of our theme. Additionally, we can understand the development or fulfillment of the theology surrounding the passage's focus throughout Scripture. This canonical study helps guard against misunderstanding the Bible or reading our predispositions into it.[8]

Considerations for the Use of Cross-References

There are several very important considerations to be aware of when using cross-references:

DON'T FORGET THE CONTEXT OF THE CROSS-REFERENCE

As we look at the footnotes and cross-referenced passages, we have to read them in their own contexts as well. It is possible to be misled by cross-references if we don't understand the context (surrounding passages and book purposes, canonical place, literary genre, historical, cultural, and situational contexts) in which something is written.

KEEP THE PRIMARY PASSAGE IN CHARGE OF THE COMMANDER'S INTENT AND POINT FOR PROCLAMATION

In history, conscious intention is everything. —Baruch Halpern[9, vii]

Though it is good for the interpreter of one passage to compare the related passages in other books (the cross-references), it must be done with the authorial intention, historical situation, and theological point of view of the primary passage we are teaching in mind. Be sure to focus primarily on the message of the passage you are reading without confusing it with the message of

---

[8] Sometimes, cross-references will help us be more firm on some issues and less dogmatic about others, for example, when we look canonically at the subject of women and the church. We see Paul's strong message to the Corinthian church and to Timothy: "the women should keep silent in the churches. For they are not permitted to speak" (1 Corinthians 14:34), and "I do not permit a woman to teach or to exercise authority over a man; rather, she is to remain quiet" (1 Timothy 2:12). But as we look further, we see Paul exhorting women to cover their heads when they pray or prophesy (1 Corinthians 11:5). We see Paul's friends and students, Priscilla and her husband Aquila teaching the evangelist Apollos (Acts 18:26). We read that Paul visited female prophets in the early church (Acts 21:9). When Paul wrote to the church at Philippi, he chastised the Christian sisters Euodia and Syntyche to get along, and he told the other church members to help them return to their gospel ministry (Philippians 4:3). Clearly, cross-references where Paul mentions the spiritual gifts of apostle, prophet, evangelist, and pastor teachers are meant for all believers (Romans 12:3–8; 1 Corinthians 12; Ephesians 4:11–14). The cross-references begin to weaken the dogmatic case we may have built had we been preaching on 1 Corinthians 14:34 alone. (Though clearly, one verse is not a large enough passage to speak on, nor does that one verse represent Paul's purpose for the passage, which has to do with orderly worship.) As we look at references outside Paul's teachings, we see Peter preaching (Acts 2:17–18) and quoting the prophecy of Joel: "And in the last days it shall be, God declares, that I will pour out my Spirit on all flesh, and your sons and your daughters shall prophesy, and your young men shall see visions, and your old men shall dream dreams; even on my male servants and female servants in those days I will pour out my Spirit, and they shall prophesy" (Acts 2:17–18; Joel 2:28).

[9] Baruch Halpern is the Covenant Foundation Professor of Jewish Studies at the University of Georgia. He uses archaeological information to help interpret the meaning of biblical texts.

other passages that cover the same or similar events in other parts of Scripture. Though we must grapple with the entire canonical teaching on our subject, keeping our focus on one passage will prevent us from slipping into topical preaching. (See chapter 4 for warnings about this.)

Though it is always good to read the other versions of an event (in the synoptic Gospels, prophets, OT narrative, and Acts/epistles), we need to keep in mind that they were written by different authors for different purposes; therefore, the Commander's intent is often different. For example, preach on Matthew, not the synoptic Gospels or John. Teach on Kings, not Kings/ Chronicles/Prophets. Any harmonizing of events or passages from different books ought to be done with one passage firmly in command of the intent.[10]

Scrambled eggs are very different from hard-boiled eggs though they are both eggs. If you blend your message from the events or parables or sermons from separate books, you will have a scrambled authorial intent, and a scrambled Commander's intent is not what biblical interpreters want to serve. Look at the cross-references for additional information, support, and background, but keep the author of your primary passage in charge.

Link passages only by theological subject, not simply similar wording

We need to be careful not to link assorted biblical texts simply because they have similar wording or common subject matter (usually called the proof-text method) while ignoring the full meaning of the linked texts in their respective contexts.[viii] Walter Kaiser warned, "This [haphazard linking of texts based on common wording] must be resisted since it fails to establish that all the texts being grouped together do indeed share the same theological or factual content."[ix] If we want to proclaim the Commander's intent, we must study how God's intention is expressed in the entirety of the book our text is plucked from and how that intent is addressed in the fullness of Scripture. Cross-references, then, must be carefully checked to ensure they really are on the same theological subject.

Don't Get Distracted

Warning: it is very easy to fall in love with your cross-reference and let that muddy your message. With so many great Bible passages, we must guard against getting lost in the trees. We look up cross-references to increase our understanding of the primary text and its themes, not to divert our attention from it. The focus of our message needs to remain on our passage.

In the same vein, our expository message should focus on one passage primarily. Though you and I will thoroughly study the cross-referenced passages, we will share them with our listeners only when we can build a better case for the Commander's intent by showing how other Scriptures support it. We can add cross-references to our message in order to support or explain the

---

[10] The danger of harmonizing the gospels or OT books can be seen for example in trying to harmonize 1 and 2 Kings and 1 and 2 Chronicles. The general facts in them are the same, but their purposes are different. The historical sources both writers used were the same as there is almost word-for-word congruity in some places. But the author of 1 and 2 Kings sought to highlight the severity of the crimes of the kings of Judah and Israel (and by extension the sins of the Hebrew people) and the justice of God.

For the Jews in exile in Babylon, 1 and 2 Kings explained why God had left His people to their own devices and how they had gotten what they deserved. And 1 and 2 Chronicles was written about one hundred years after Kings to a different audience and with different intentions. Chronicles portrays a God of mercy for the people in exile looking for a redemptive message and hope. For the Christian, the message of Kings is that of the downward spiral of sin; the message of Chronicles is that the grace of God is ours through repentance and belief.

Commander's point for proclamation. Sometimes another passage articulates the Commander's intent or our point for proclamation better than a verse or phrase within our preaching passage does. Sometime an outside cross-reference adds clarification; other times they overwhelm our confuse our listeners.[11]

We must guard our audiences' minds against confusion that so easily arises when we throw too much at them. You wouldn't make dinner for company by throwing all the food you have in the refrigerator and cupboards into the frying pan and cooking it up. Neither would you serve a twenty-course meal of all different sorts of random foods in no particular order. Give your people something they can identify, digest, and remember.

Contextual Signpost 4: Literary Genre

Returning home late one night, we heard a woman shrieking from an upstairs window, "Help! Let me out! Let me out! Help!" We immediately called 911 and watched with hearts pounding to see what would happen when the police arrived. To our dismay, the police broke into the house and came out a few minutes later alone. No rescued victim, no handcuffed perpetrator. We asked them why they were leaving without doing anything. The screaming for help had come, they informed us, from a parrot that wanted out of its cage. We had been hoping for a mystery with a dramatic rescue with us as the heroes. The actual genre of the episode was comedy, and the joke was on us.

Genre is the most basic contextual signpost. If we don't take genre into account, we can easily misconstrue the Commander's intent and the application of a passage. The term *literary genre* refers to larger literary units of Scripture such as narrative (history), law, gospel, epistle, apocalypse, poetry, wisdom, and prophecy. Every passage has a literary genre.[x] The term *literary form* refers to smaller literary units in the larger genres (for example, parables found in narrative gospels,[12] poetry as part of narrative or prophetic literature,[13] hymns or liturgies found in epistles,[14]

---

[11] New preachers and Bible teachers who are serious about being very biblical commonly include too many outside references, all their favorite verses, or a plethora of salvation verses. Serial preachers are those who preach three to four sermons on three or four topics one after the other at the same time. People leave unsure of what they are supposed to be thinking about or doing, and they can even be annoyed. Just when they think the message is over and they can go have lunch, the preacher jumps into a new topic, as though he's thinking, *This might be the last time I ever get to preach, so I better get it all in there.*

[12] "And he told them many things in parables, saying: 'A sower went out to sow'" (Matthew 13:3).

[13] "A voice cries: 'In the wilderness prepare the way of the LORD; make straight in the desert a highway for our God. Every valley shall be lifted up, and every mountain and hill be made low; the uneven ground shall become level, and the rough places a plain. And the glory of the LORD shall be revealed, and all flesh shall see it together, for the mouth of the LORD has spoken.'" (Isaiah 40:3–5).

[14] "Great indeed, we confess, is the mystery of godliness: He was manifested in the flesh, vindicated by the Spirit, seen by angels, proclaimed among the nations, believed on in the world, taken up in glory" (1 Timothy 3:16).

genealogies found in narrative,[15] legal codes,[16] songs,[17] prayers,[18] laments, annals, prophecies, prophetic utterances, sayings, church orders,[19] sermons, dialogues, or romance[20]). For the purpose of interpretation, both the general genre and the specific literary form used should be kept in mind.

1 Corinthians 15 is written in the literary genre of epistle. It is didactic in nature—it was intended to convey information for instruction or edification. But inside of it are some different literary forms. For example, in 1 Corinthians 15:33, Paul quotes a Greek play, Menander's comedy *Thais*, which the Corinthians were familiar with; in fact, it may have become a common saying by this time: "Do not be deceived: 'Bad company ruins good morals.'"[xi] Later in this same chapter Paul adds poetry that reflects Old Testament passages from Isaiah and Hosea.[21] This poetry uses figurative language as does most Hebrew poetry.

> Death is swallowed up in victory.
> O death, where is your victory?
> O death, where is your sting?
> (1 Corinthians 15:54–55)

The Holy Spirit Inspired His Message in a Specific Genre for His Purposes

The God-breathed form or genre is part of Scripture's power and meaning. Genre is an integral part of the inspired message and of the actual transformative power of Scripture. Though all Scripture is inspired, some literary forms may be more inspiring for some people at various times and situations. There are times when only a psalm will do, when a proverb is needed, or when a parable drives a message straight to the heart like a sharp dagger. The same words can have different meaning when written in different genres.

---

[15] "The book of the genealogy of Jesus Christ, the son of David, the son of Abraham. Abraham was the father of Isaac, and Isaac the father of Jacob, and Jacob the father of Judah and his brothers, and Judah the father of Perez and Zerah by Tamar … and Salmon the father of Boaz by Rahab, and Boaz the father of Obed by Ruth, and Obed the father of Jesse, and Jesse the father of David the king. And David was the father of Solomon by the wife of Uriah." (Matthew 1:1–6).

[16] "And Moses summoned all Israel and said to them, 'Hear, O Israel, the statutes and the rules that I speak in your hearing today, and you shall learn them and be careful to do them. The LORD our God made a covenant with us in Horeb … He said: 'I am the LORD your God, who brought you out of the land of Egypt, out of the house of slavery. You shall have no other gods before me''" (Deuteronomy 5:1–7).

[17] "And they sing the song of Moses, the servant of God, and the song of the Lamb, saying, 'Great and amazing are your deeds, O LORD God the Almighty! Just and true are your ways, O King of the nations! Who will not fear, O LORD, and glorify your name? For you alone are holy. All nations will come and worship you, for your righteous acts have been revealed'" (Revelation 15:3–4).

[18] "Jabez called upon the God of Israel, saying, 'Oh that you would bless me and enlarge my border, and that your hand might be with me, and that you would keep me from harm so that it might not bring me pain!' And God granted what he asked" (1 Chronicles 4:10).

[19] "So then, my brothers, when you come together to eat [LORD's Supper or "love feasts"], wait for one another—if anyone is hungry, let him eat at home—so that when you come together it will not be for judgment. About the other things I will give directions when I come" (1 Corinthians 11:33–34).

[20] Ruth.

[21] Isaiah 25:8 and Hosea 13:14. Most commonly, the OT quotes in the NT are from the Greek Septuagint translation of the OT because that was the commonly used Scripture of the NT church of the first century.

Genre Adds Clues to Meaning

If a snippet of Scripture is dissected from its literary form, it becomes something less than it would be as part of the whole. Individual verses removed from their context of genre are like body parts excised from a person, soaked in formaldehyde, and placed in jars on a biology teacher's shelf. They once played a key role in a life, but now, though we're examining them thoroughly, we cannot perceive how they actually were meant to function. For example, when the genre of epistle is ignored and bits of Paul's fairly complicated treatises are excised into individual sound-bites, the truth is twisted into something God did not intent to say—as when Romans 8:28[22] becomes "everything always turns out for the best" or when 1 Corinthians 10:13[23] becomes "God never gives us more than we can handle."

Genre can help clarify the true meaning of a difficult passage. For example, Exodus 13:12 states, "All the firstborn of your animals that are males shall be the LORD's"; that seems in opposition to Hosea 6:6: "For I desire steadfast love and not sacrifice, the knowledge of God rather than burnt offerings." Both are OT passages, but their genres are different; one is law and the other is prophecy. In the context of time, we note that in Exodus, God was setting up a nation and a sacrificial system, whereas in the Hosea passage, He was making a prophetic corrective to misunderstood purposes of a law.

Another common error that highlights the importance of literary genre occurs in the handling of proverbs. A proverb is neither a promise nor a law.[xii] If it is treated that way, it may prove immensely discouraging when things do not seem to work out as the so-called "promise" suggests. For example, Proverbs 3:9–10 sounds like a promise, but we know it to be a generally true principle: "Honor the LORD with your wealth and with the firstfruits of all your produce; then your barns will be filled with plenty, and your vats will be bursting with wine." Do you know of people who honor the Lord and are generous yet who often have trouble making ends meet? The two verses in Proverbs 26:4–5 seem to give contradictory advice: "Answer not a fool according to his folly, lest you be like him yourself. Answer a fool according to his folly, lest he be wise in his own eyes."[xiii] The genre of proverb is meant to make us think about our actions, not to prescribe a particular universal action for all occasions.

Biblical poetry is best taken as poetry given by God for comfort, praise, worship, or encouragement. We should be careful about turning even biblical poetry into propositional truths. In the temptation of Jesus, Satan ignored genre when he quoted a poem from Psalm 91:11–12 as a propositional truth to tempt Jesus into jumping from the top of the temple:[24] "For he will command his angels concerning you to guard you in all your ways. On their hands they will bear you up, lest you strike your foot against a stone" (Matthew 4:6). Jesus correctly used Scripture when He used a law from Deuteronomy in response: "You shall not put the Lord your God to the test" (Matthew 4:7).[25]

---

[22] "And we know that for those who love God all things work together for good, for those who are called according to his purpose" (Romans 8:28).

[23] "No temptation has overtaken you that is not common to man. God is faithful, and he will not let you be tempted beyond your ability, but with the temptation he will also provide the way of escape, that you may be able to endure it" (1 Corinthians 10:13).

[24] Matthew 4, Mark 1, Luke 4.

[25] Deuteronomy 6:16.

Even narrative portions of Scripture are misunderstood when genre is not considered. Casual (and sometimes even serious) students of Scripture are often thrown off guard when Jephthah executed his daughter after a rash vow to God.[26] We must always remember that narratives are in general descriptive, and not prescriptive. Narrative Scripture can incorrectly be forced to mean something it was never intended to mean. Gordon Fee and Douglas Stuart suggested, "People force incorrect interpretations and applications on narrative portions of the Bible as much as or more than they do on any other parts."[xiv]

Noting the Subgenre in the Genre Adds Color and Interest

As we observed in 1 Corinthians 15 above, there is often a subgenre or literary form in a passage that is important to appreciating the passage. Historical narrative may contain other material such as poems and hymns, proverbial sayings and maxims, stories and fables, and other literary genre used to enhance the effectiveness of the story.

The eyes of my early morning high school Bible study students began to glaze over as we read Acts 13 together. Though we generally had lively discussions, that morning, they began to doze, and I was relieved to know that even Paul's sermons could sometimes cause people to nod off. They had not realized that the passage we were reading had turned from a narrative event to a report of Paul's sermon in the synagogue at Antioch. Once they realized they were listening to a sermon recounted as part of an event, they were able to appreciate and discuss the passage.

Genre Should Influence the Form and Mood of the Proclamation

Because a passage's genre is itself part of its message, it should be considered when we decide the style we will use to preach a sermon on it. In *The Sermon as Symphony*, Mike Graves[27] recommended the following steps to best utilize knowledge of literary genre to enhance God's message as it is expounded. First, ask what the text is saying (this is typically what we do in the exegesis step—the thoughtful proclaimer would also ask, why is the passage saying what it is saying). Second, ask what the text is doing. By that, he meant, we should discover how the text was saying what it wanted to say. What are the forms and genres used? What is the mood of the passage? What is the movement of the message of the passage? For example, is the point the author is making being made through story or inductive argument or poetry? Third, ask yourself, *how can my message say and do the same thing in a way the author would approve?*

Graves gave three ways the sermon could say and do the same thing the passage is saying and doing: mood, message form or structure, and delivery style.[xv] Graves felt that mood was the most important of the three. Though Graves was speaking of a sermon, the same thing can apply to a classroom situation—how can you evoke the mood or tone of the passage?

Literary genre, then, is key to proper interpretation of Scripture and is part of the inspiration given by the Spirit. Literary genre helps us choose what and how God wants us to teach or preach on a passage. An effective sermon on a psalm describes the psalmist's message and may

---

[26] Judges 11:29–40.

[27] Mike Graves is professor of preaching and worship at Saint Paul School of Theology.

recreate the visual and emotional impact as well as the rhetorical effect[28] of the psalm on the listeners.[xvi] Literary genre not only influences our understanding of Scripture and helps clear up misunderstanding, confusion, and misapplication it can enhance how we proclaim it.

Contextual Signpost 5: History and Culture

Vern S. Poythress[29] wrote,

> Some of the books of the Bible indicate that they were originally written to particular recipients, such as the church at Corinth, Philippi, or Colossae. But God, who knows the end from the beginning (Isa. 46:10), also had us in mind: For whatever was written in former days was written for our instruction, that through endurance and through the encouragement of the Scriptures we might have hope (Rom. 15:4). We enrich our understanding when we keep in mind both sets of recipients.[xvii]

A very basic outline of biblical interpretation for proclamation comes from the answers to these questions: What does it say? What does it mean? Why did God say it? So what? Observation, interpretation, application. It sounds so easy, right? Sometimes it is, and when it isn't, that is not because God is trying to be tricky but because our sacred text was written over the course of thousands of years in at least three languages and many dialects by many authors and editors and to a myriad of different audiences. Most of it is written as stories from ancient history. A lot of it is written as poetry. Some of it is written as prophecy that points to the prophets' political-geographical-historical situations and to Christ's day, to today, or even into the future and the last days or eternity.

Much of the New Testament was written as letters to people we don't know about who were living in situations we must try to figure out from the one-sided conversation we hear. The clues regarding how things were different in biblical times compared to now are often there if we look, and if we can't find them, we can try to ask the experts. But what we should not do is ignore the differences.

We know what history is, but what is culture? H. D. McDonald[30] writing on culture said, "It is the climate of opinion, and network of ideas and values which form the social environment within which each individual lives his life."[xviii] Our culture is invisible to us. The culture of the people the Bible was originally written about and to includes the way they did things. The social rules and norms they had. The way they ate, slept, married, buried, raised their children, and lived their lives. The thought patterns they had. What they thought was good and just or bad and unfair.

Besides the fact that we are historically and culturally distant from the people and times of the Bible, we have our own cultural complications. We often think our cultural norms are in fact

---

[28] Rhetorical effect is the effective use of our speech to convey both the content and the mood or feel of something. Rhetorical effect is a style that persuades.

[29] Vern S. Polythress has taught at Westminster Theological Seminary for thirty years. He is the professor of New Testament Interpretation and has six academic degrees and has been called one of the brightest minds on theological reflection of our day.

[30] Dr. H. D. McDonald is a former vice principal and senior lecturer at the London Bible College. He has spent time as a visiting professor at a number of institutions in the United States and Canada and has written many books on theology.

right and doing things another way is wrong. We might even think those who don't think like us are inferior. Christianity today is found in all sorts of cultures, and so when we apply Scripture, we have to examine not only its culture but the culture of those we speak to as well.

So, interpretation means examining the culture of biblical times and the current culture of our particular groups and then reasking those questions: What does it say? Why does it say it? What does it mean? Not only do we have to translate the languages from Greek or Hebrew to English; we also have to translate the cultures from then to now.

A word of warning is needed. When instead of understanding and considering the culture of biblical times we remove the historical and cultural context of a passage, we are in effect flattening Scripture—taking the air out of it. Turning a three-dimensional, real-life, historical, and culturally bound story into a one-dimensional book of inscrutable principles that are often not what God intended. For example, Deborah, a prophet and judge of Israel, sat under a palm tree to make her proclamation and issue her orders.[31] This is a very interesting thing to think about, but it is cultural, not prescriptive. There is no indication we should hold high court in Florida. How does Jesus washing the feet of His disciples and widows washing the feet of the saints translate to today? For that matter, how does enrolling widows for care by the church translate?[32]

We make it our job to understand the differences between then and now so we can accurately make the exegetical and theological moves needed to understand the Commander's intent. Moving from what it said to those people at that time to what it is saying to us now is the first step in interpretation; it requires us to know something about the people the message was written to. What were they like? What was the situation? Why were they being written to or about? When did they live? What was happening in the world at that time? What does it matter? What were the invisible presuppositions that made up their culture that are very different from the invisible suppositions that make up ours? What difference do they make to God's intent and purpose for the passage? Why did God choose those particular people to make his point for all of us? Most of this we learn just by reading the Bible.

Genesis 30 is a case in point as we see Leah and Rachel fighting over who could give birth to more children. When discussing this in a Bible study, a class member dryly observed that Jacob wasn't thinking of the high cost of college education or he'd have been more careful! Family planning was probably not the Commander's intent for the passage. There is a wide chasm of time and difference between the Bible and us. This historical and cultural distance can at times cause misunderstanding. Though human nature and God's nature are the same since Adam and Eve, pretty much everything else has changed.

We can learn a lot without studying outside works; our time can be best spent by focusing most of it on the Bible. The Bible was given to us to be read with the Holy Spirit at our elbow. We read prayerfully in God's presence looking for His message. But we are blessed to be able

---

[31] "Then the people of Israel cried out to the LORD for help, for he had 900 chariots of iron and he oppressed the people of Israel cruelly for twenty years. Now Deborah, a prophetess, the wife of Lappidoth, was judging Israel at that time. She used to sit under the palm of Deborah between Ramah and Bethel in the hill country of Ephraim, and the people of Israel came up to her for judgment" (Judges 4:3–5).

[32] "Then he poured water into a basin and began to wash the disciples' feet and to wipe them with the towel that was wrapped around him" (John 13:5). "Let a widow be enrolled if she is not less than sixty years of age, having been the wife of one husband, and having a reputation for good works: if she has brought up children, has shown hospitality, has washed the feet of the saints, has cared for the afflicted, and has devoted herself to every good work" (1 Timothy 5:9–10).

to ask the experts when we have hard-to-resolve questions about historical or cultural contexts. When we read 1 Corinthians 8 about not eating food sacrificed to idols, we understand Paul's meaning—think of other people and how what we do affects them and their spiritual growth. But reading commentary can also help us understand the historical-cultural context of idol worship as practiced in Paul's day in Corinth and that helps us find correlations in our own world.[33]

Practices that are no longer culturally acceptable are treated casually by biblical authors. But when you and I see Abraham, the father of our faith, sleeping with Sarai's maid, we are a bit shocked.[34] When we notice that Jacob married two sisters, we squint our eyes and purse our lips. Though polygamy wasn't acceptable in Jesus' day, nor in most of ours, in America at least, in many other cultures around the world today, it is very much the "proper" social norm.[35] When we read tales of war and royal succession that are not culturally in tune with our modern western minds, we realize that we should judge Bible characters and times by the cultural norms of Bible times.[36] The practice of understanding the past in light of its own history and culture is imperative in Bible interpretation and application. It protects us from accidentally assuming that ancient cultural norms should be mandated for modern-day Christians.[37] Also, it prevents us from dismissing the Bible, particularly the Old Testament, as archaic, evil, misogynistic, and completely irrelevant.

In *The IVP Bible Background Commentary: New Testament*, Craig Keener wrote, "God is so involved in the multicultural matrix of history that he did not disdain to step into it himself."[xix] The Word of God actually became a flesh-and-blood human being at a particular point in history where a particular culture was practiced and particular languages spoken. That is the way God works, and that is the way God speaks to us today through His Word printed on paper and bearing the visible signs of being thousands of years old.

Sometimes, archaeology will shed a light on something in Scripture that helps us see it a new way.[38] Sometimes, the study of linguistics makes a translation more clear.[39] Sometimes, world and

---

[33] According to Craig S. Keener, *The IVP Bible Background Commentary: NT*. Downers Grove, IL: InterVarsity Press, 1993. (1 Corinthians 8:7). Meat was unavailable to most Corinthians who were not well to do except at the pagan festivals, when it was doled out to the masses. Many of the socially powerless (the "weak") thus inevitably associated meat with idolatry (8:8). Here, Paul probably stated the view of the "strong," the Corinthian elite, with which he concurred except for his response: "But take care that this right of yours does not somehow become a stumbling block to the weak" (1 Corinthians 8:9).

[34] See Genesis 17.

[35] See Genesis 28–31.

[36] Read Kings and Chronicles.

[37] Things like slavery for example may have been the norm but are not prescribed. Consider the following passages: "A woman shall not wear a man's garment, nor shall a man put on a woman's cloak, for whoever does these things is an abomination to the LORD your God"; "When you build a new house, you shall make a parapet for your roof, that you may not bring the guilt of blood upon your house, if anyone should fall from it" (Deuteronomy 22:5, 8). Some have taught that the point of the first is to place limits on fashion where the point of the second is irrelevant when actually the second one, consider the safety of others when building your home, is far easier to interpret and apply than the first, especially since to our eyes, the robes of Abraham and Sarah both are assumed to look fairly similar.

[38] Consider *The Archaeological Study Bible: An Illustrated Walk Through Biblical History*, Walter Kaiser, Jr. and Duane Garrett, eds. (Grand Rapids, MI: Zondervan, 2005).

[39] The reason we use newer translations is that our understanding of ancient and modern linguistics changes. Read the notes in the beginning of your Bible to see which manuscripts the translators relied on and what their policies on translation were.

Near East history will shed light on passages. We are blessed to have experts who spend lifetimes learning about those times.

The most important tool we have in our historical-cultural toolbox is our imagination. Imagine yourself as part of the congregation when Jesus read Isaiah in the synagogue.[40] Imagine you are Jeremiah sinking in the mud in the well where you've been thrown for proclaiming God's message.[41] Pretend you are David, who has slept with Bathsheba, killed her husband, and now you hear Nathan's parable about the lamb; let the gravity and personal affront of what David did dawn on you just as it dawned on him.[42] Pretend you are in the church at Ephesus when the letter from Paul is read.[43] With Abraham, saddle your donkey, gather your workers and ride out after the kings who stole Lot and his family.[44]

[40] "And he came to Nazareth, where he had been brought up. And as was his custom, he went to the synagogue on the Sabbath day, and he stood up to read. And the scroll of the prophet Isaiah was given to him. He unrolled the scroll and found the place where it was written, 'The Spirit of the LORD is upon me, because he has anointed me to proclaim good news to the poor. He has sent me to proclaim liberty to the captives and recovering of sight to the blind, to set at liberty those who are oppressed, to proclaim the year of the LORD's favor.' And he rolled up the scroll and gave it back to the attendant and sat down. And the eyes of all in the synagogue were fixed on him. And he began to say to them, 'Today this Scripture has been fulfilled in your hearing'" (Luke 4:16–21).

[41] "So they took Jeremiah and cast him into the cistern of Malchiah, the king's son, which was in the court of the guard, letting Jeremiah down by ropes. And there was no water in the cistern, but only mud, and Jeremiah sank in the mud" (Jeremiah 38:6).

[42] "And the LORD sent Nathan to David. 'There were two men in a certain city, the one rich and the other poor. The rich man had very many flocks and herds, but the poor man had nothing but one little ewe lamb, which he had bought. And he brought it up, and it grew up with him and with his children. It used to eat of his morsel and drink from his cup and lie in his arms, and it was like a daughter to him. Now there came a traveler to the rich man, and he was unwilling to take one of his own flock or herd to prepare for the guest who had come to him, but he took the poor man's lamb and prepared it for the man who had come to him.' Then David's anger was greatly kindled against the man, and he said to Nathan, 'As the LORD lives, the man who has done this deserves to die, and he shall restore the lamb fourfold, because he did this thing, and because he had no pity.' Nathan said to David, 'You are the man!'" (2 Samuel 12:1–7).

[43] "Blessed be the God and Father of our LORD Jesus Christ who has blessed us in Christ with every spiritual blessing in the heavenly places, even as he chose us in him before the foundation of the world, that we should be holy and blameless before him. In love he predestined us for adoption as sons through Jesus Christ, according to the purpose of his will, to the praise of his glorious grace, with which he has blessed us in the Beloved" (Ephesians 1:3–6).

[44] "So the enemy took all the possessions of Sodom and Gomorrah, and all their provisions, and went their way. They also took Lot, the son of Abram's brother, who was dwelling in Sodom, and his possessions, and went their way. Then one who had escaped came and told Abram the Hebrew, who was living by the oaks of Mamre the Amorite, brother of Eshcol and of Aner. These were allies of Abram. When Abram heard that his kinsman had been taken captive, he led forth his trained men, born in his house, 318 of them, and went in pursuit as far as Dan. And he divided his forces against them by night, he and his servants, and defeated them and pursued them to Hobah, north of Damascus. Then he brought back all the possessions, and also brought back his kinsman Lot with his possessions, and the women and the people" (Genesis 14:11–16).

"THAT HAPPENS IN ALMOST EVERY SERMON." xx

How can we cross this historical-cultural divide? Study the history of the times of the Bible. The study of history and culture will make our messages more accurate and our interpretation less liable to error, and it will make our messages come alive.

A word of caution is needed: this is where you can lose time, however, so use discretion. Often, a simple study Bible has all the background necessary for understanding a text. If you have more questions, you can search for more answers, but don't waste time running down rabbit trails unrelated to the clear road to the Commander's intent for the passage.[45] Preach and teach context when it is necessary to understanding the passage.

I once spent a morning looking at Google Earth plotting Paul's journey toward Malta where he was shipwrecked. It was fun, but after I spoke, no one left the church wanting to live for God because I knew all about the route of Paul's trip to Rome. When we spend a lot of time on backgrounds and culture, some of our listeners will like it, some will think we are smart, but only rarely will background information bring anyone to his or her knees in repentance or inspire them to live for Jesus Christ.

---

[45] Some recommendations for tools to use to understand Bible backgrounds, history, and culture follow: Use a Bible timeline that explains what was happening on the world scene at that time. Read the pertinent parts of commentaries such as *The Bible Background Commentary* two-volume series (Old Testament by John H. Walton, Victor H. Matthews, and Mark W. Chavalas; New Testament by Craig S. Keener, both published by Intervarsity Press). Consider the geographical elements. Look at maps. Use study Bibles such as *The Archeological Study Bible: An Illustrated Walk Through Biblical History and Culture* from Zondervan by Walter Kaiser Jr.; *The ESV Study Bible*, or *The Harper Collins Study Bible: Student Edition* (A New Annotated Edition by the Society of Biblical Literature). Other valuable resources include *Chronological and Background Charts of the Old Testament* by John C. Walton. Where dates and details are concerned, you must compare several because they will differ. Consult also Bible dictionaries and books on manners and customs during biblical times.

Contextual Signpost 6: Redemption and the Gospel

> And the eunuch said to Philip, "About whom, I ask you, does the prophet say this, about himself or about someone else?" Then Philip opened his mouth, and beginning with this Scripture he told him the good news about Jesus. And as they were going along the road they came to some water, and the eunuch said, "See, here is water! What prevents me from being baptized?" (Acts 8:34–36)

> We do not preach so that people may encounter the Bible, but so that people may encounter Christ. —Paul Scott Wilson[xxi]

The great story of redemption is the ultimate and most consequential contextual guidepost. All others are subsumed in this. All Scripture is ultimately for the purpose of reconciling the creation to the Creator, to "make you wise for salvation through faith in Christ Jesus" (2 Timothy 3:15).[46] Though we aim to teach, disciple, encourage, reprove, guide, comfort, and promote good works; we seek an even greater, ultimate goal than all these tasks—to reconcile our listeners to God.

> Long ago, at many times and in many ways, God spoke to our fathers by the prophets, but in these last days he has spoken to us by his Son, whom he appointed the heir of all things, through whom also he created the world. (Hebrews 1:1–2)

Have you ever watched a good movie the second time and seen important clues in it you had missed before? Have you ever read a book that you already knew the ending of and as you read it thought, *Ahh, I know why that's happening!* Similarly, since we know how the Bible turns out, we examine every detail to discover how it points to Christ, salvation, and the coming culmination of the kingdom of God in heaven.

If the Bible is about redemption, we will be looking for sinners as we read narrative, not moral exemplars and moral exhortation. The Old Testament, in particular is not a book full of examples of good character. The good character in the Bible belongs to God. We must look instead at how every passage points to, exemplifies, or demonstrates our need for a perfect Savior to take our sins on himself and reconcile us to God. Timothy Keller recommended that we build into our minds the impulse to look for Christ in every passage of Scripture.[xxii] Everything we read in the Word points to Christ in some way.

> For the law of the Spirit of life has set you free in Christ Jesus from the law of sin and death. (Romans 8:2)

This context of Christ and salvation must be searched for and taught. It will fit perfectly into every Commander's intent and point for proclamation we preach because all Scripture points to our imperfection, sin, and need for salvation, for power to change, comfort, hope, and joy. No more pop-psychology sermons or teaching that encourages us to pull ourselves up out of the slough. Salvation and the power of the Holy Spirit to redeem and transform is the underpinning

---

[46] 2 Timothy 3:15–4:2.

for all the sermons we preach. Whether implicitly or explicitly, whether in the middle or at the end, preach Christ.

Brevard Childs guarded the Old Testament wanting it to be read for its own message first, but he wrote,

> Yet it also seems to me true that after the task of biblical theological reflection has begun in which the original integrity of both testaments has been respected, there is an important function of hearing the whole of Christian Scripture in the light of the full reality of God in Jesus Christ. In other words, there is a legitimate place for a move from a fully developed Christian theological reflection back to the biblical texts of both testaments … It … has to do with the ability of biblical language to resonate in a new and creative fashion when read from the vantage point of a fuller understanding of Christian truth. Such a reading is not intended to threaten the sensus literalis of the [Old Testament] text, but to extend through figuration a reality which has been only partially heard.[xxiii]

Graeme Goldsworthy[47] wrote that the narrative in the Hebrew canon was "brutal in realism."[xxiv] (My son, when he was small, informed me that the Bible should be rated R.) Goldsworthy continued,

> A characteristic of the salvation-historical narrative is that the human involvement in the outworking of God's plans is never without blemishes. This serves only to emphasize the reality of God's grace as he continues to achieve his purposes. The progress of salvation history is not without occasional serious interruption due to the waywardness and rebelliousness of the people of God. These setbacks serve only to demonstrate why history needs to be salvation history.[xxv]

The Holy Spirit empowers us to live out what the Bible prescribes, but our grateful response to Christ's sacrifice on our behalf is the motivation for every good deed and every transformation. In *Christ Centered Preaching,* Bryan Chapell[48] wrote, "We offer service to God not to gain his affection but in loving thankfulness for his affection."[xxvi] Our desire as believers who are maturing in the faith is to please and to glorify Him. Elyse Fitzpatrick[49] wrote, "Are there commands and obligations in Scripture? Yes, of course—they're all over. But they come to us in the context of what God has already done for us in Christ."[xxvii] "Instead of saying, 'Jesus died for your sins. How could you act this way?' the message ought to be, 'Jesus died for our sins, and that's our motivation to live a Godly life.'"[xxviii] "How would our lives be different if we believed that, when God looked at us, he was completely pleased and saw nothing but perfection? Those of us who have been justified by Christ live in the light of that."[xxix]

---

[47] Graeme Goldsworthy is an Australian Anglican theologian specializing in the Old Testament and biblical theology.

[48] Bryan Chapell, pastor of Grace Presbyterian Church, has a radio and online Bible-teaching ministry and is president emeritus of Covenant Theological Seminary in St. Louis.

[49] Elyse M. Fitzpatrick is a retreat and conference speaker and the director of Women Helping Women Ministries.

Other Considerations: Geography and the Collective Memory

But the Helper, the Holy Spirit, whom the Father will send in my name, he will teach
you all things and bring to your remembrance all that I have said to you. (John 14:26)

My husband and I went to Yellowstone for our thirty-fifth wedding anniversary. That was
our honeymoon destination and where we had taken a family vacation with two toddlers. My own
family had gone there every summer until I was in college. Yellowstone is more than a place for
us; it is an inherited memory. My children, now adults, want to go to Yellowstone because they
want to be part of new family memories that are continuing to be formed.

Just as it is not a coincidence that we went to Yellowstone for our anniversary, there are no
coincidences in the Bible. Places mentioned in the Bible have significance. The significance of
geography should not be overplayed, but it should be noted because it is part of our collective
Judeo-Christian heritage, our family memory. When we hear about one place, all our memories
flood in.

We pay attention to geography because the biblical author did. The author does not always
specify the name of the place where something happens, but when he does, it is significant and
not for the sake of future people making Bible maps. It is an indication that the story we are
hearing is real and in a place and time, and often, other related things happened or will happen
in that place throughout the Bible. The biblical authors expect us to make those connections and
see what happened there before in our mind's eye.

Occasionally, it is helpful to study maps because they give us a sense of distance and travel as
in the case of Mary and Joseph traveling to Bethlehem or Paul sailing around Malta. It is not so
much that we need to study maps, however, but that we need to study the meanings and memories
of Bible places.

Just one example of many is the Mount of Olives. When Jesus spent His last several nights
there and especially when he was betrayed by Judas there, we recall David's dramatic betrayal by
his son, Absalom, in 2 Samuel 15.[50] When Absalom staged a coup, David escaped the City of
David by going along with many of his people barefoot and with his head covered to the Mount
of Olives.[51] The Mount of Olives, the mountain east of Jerusalem, is where Ezekiel saw the glory
of the Lord rise and leave the temple.[52] It is where Zechariah said the Lord's feet would stand
when the mountain was split open on the Day of the Lord.[53] It is significant, then, that when
Jesus described for the disciples the signs of the coming of the end of the age, He did so on the
Mount of Olives.[54] When Jesus rode the colt of the donkey back into Jerusalem on what we call

---

[50] Matthew 26:30; Mark 14:26; Luke 22:39.

[51] "But David continued up the Mount of Olives, weeping as he went; his head was covered and he was barefoot. All the
people with him covered their heads too and were weeping as they went up" (2 Samuel 15:29).

[52] "And the glory of the LORD went up from the midst of the city and stood on the mountain that is on the east side of
the city" (Ezekiel 11:23).

[53] "On that day his feet shall stand on the Mount of Olives that lies before Jerusalem on the east, and the Mount of Olives
shall be split in two from east to west by a very wide valley, so that one half of the Mount shall move northward, and the
other half southward" (Zechariah 14:4).

[54] "As he sat on the Mount of Olives, the disciples came to him privately, saying, 'Tell us, when will these things be, and
what will be the sign of your coming and of the end of the age?'" (Matthew 24:3; Mark 13:3).

Palm Sunday, he rode from the Mount of Olives.[55] The garden of Gethsemane is on the Mount of Olives, and so this is also where Jesus underwent his agonizing prayer and where He was seized by the soldiers and taken to trial.

Many other things likely happened there in Scripture, but because the Mount of Olives, or the mountain east of Jerusalem, is not named, we can assume that the place name and geography was not important to the meaning of the passage in those cases.

Named biblical places are significant to our corporate memory. Mountains, wells, trees, and threshing floors for example are often named and mentioned repeatedly. Even directions such as up, down, and over can have significance if we pay attention. For example, the book of Jonah goes down, down, down and then comes up, up, up—these are small geographical changes with great spiritual significance.[56] The importance of Jerusalem is signified by the fact that Jerusalem is always *up* no matter where you start. If you notice something that seems significant, don't ignore it; look it up in a good Bible dictionary, encyclopedia, and concordance and see why the author highlighted that place.[57]

Typology and Messianic References

According to Christian exegesis, biblical typology deals with the parallels between historical (usually OT) figures or events and a later analogous fulfillment. Often, New Testament events and figures are typologically understood and interpreted according to an Old Testament pattern. Some examples of repeated typological themes in Scripture are creation and new creation, Adam and Christ, the Exodus and Salvation.[xxx]

In observing types, we are not out searching for them but rather stumbling on them as we read and study. Much like the geographic names that have a collective history, "types" are things we see that foreshadow a greater fulfillment in the New Testament, the church, and in the Second Coming of Christ. Salvation history repeats itself as it begins to come to fruition and become more explicit in Scripture.

The most obvious of these is of course the Old Testament type of Messiah fulfilled in Jesus Christ. The Bible tells us that David, for example, is a type for Christ. There are other types related to this one such as kingdom and royalty types that point us forward to the kingdom of God, the kingdom of heaven, or the church.

---

[55] Matthew 21:1–11; Mark 11:1–10; Luke 19:28–39.

[56] The ups and downs of Jonah. God called Jonah to get up and go to Nineveh because it had come up before him as a very wicked place. He was to preach against Nineveh. Jonah got up, but then he ran away down to Joppa, away from the presence of the LORD. He went down into the ship. Then he went down to take a nap and lay down. Then the sailors wanted the sea to calm down, and Jonah told the sailors to pick him up and throw him in because that would calm down the sea. So they threw him in and he went down.
The turning point was when Jonah was brought up from the pit, and the LORD vomited Jonah out on dry land. He got up and went up to Nineveh. He said, "In my distress I called to the LORD, and he answered me. From deep in the realm of the dead I called for help, and you listened to my cry. You hurled me into the depths, into the very heart of the seas, and the currents swirled about me; all your waves and breakers swept over me. I said, 'I have been banished from your sight; yet I will look again toward your holy temple.' The engulfing waters threatened me, the deep surrounded me; seaweed was wrapped around my head. To the roots of the mountains I sank down; the earth beneath barred me in forever. But you, LORD my God, brought my life up from the pit. When my life was ebbing away, I remembered you, LORD, and my prayer rose to you, to your holy temple" (Jonah 2:2–7 NIV).

[57] A concordance is an index to a book showing the location of each word with the words arranged in alphabetical order.

We need to take care not to overdo our typological study and begin to see analogies where they may not exist. Keep your eyes open, but don't go looking for typology specifically; they are usually obvious enough if you look at the fullness of Scripture and your cross-references. For example, Jesus himself pointed to Jonah being three days in the fish's belly just as He would be three days and nights in the grave.[58]

For the apostle John, water was a type or metaphor for the new life and the Holy Spirit. The water that poured out of Jesus' side on the cross foreshadowed living water flowing from the hearts of believers, the living water available to all who will drink it (as Jesus told the woman at the well) and be born again of water or water and blood. John made this explicit in his epistle when he wrote that Jesus Christ came by water and blood and the Spirit. It may be that Jesus' act of turning water into wine was a foreshadowing of all the above.[59]

Bill Bright, the great Old Testament scholar, warns, "Let us say it clearly: The text has but one meaning, the meaning intended by its author; and there is but one method for discovering that meaning, the grammatical-historical method."[xxxi] Though we affirm that the original meaning of the text as written by the earthly author is the objective point of control for our interpretation, at times, the Holy Spirit, and not the original author himself, may have had broader vistas in mind. Though we need to take care, we certainly cannot ignore obvious references. The book of Isaiah, for example, points to Christ, the suffering servant. The Psalms, which though written about earthly kings and kingdoms, remind us of our heavenly King and the kingdom of God.[60]

There are four types of messianic prophecies for example: Christ's First Coming or Advent, His Second Coming, both the First and Second Comings, and Christ's redemptive career.[xxxii] The people of the Old Testament did not know of a dying Savior but hoped for a King and Redeemer.[xxxiii] Isaiah first revealed this though we must assume he did so under divine authorship and not because he knew of Jesus and his death and Resurrection.

Messianic Passages[xxxiv]

THE LAW
> Genesis 3:15: The Seed of the Woman
> Genesis 2:18: The Seed of Abraham
> Genesis 49:10: The Seed of Judah
> Numbers 23 and 24: The Predictions of Balaam
> Deuteronomy 18:15–19: A Prophet Like Moses

THE PROPHETS
> Isaiah 7:1–17: Born of a Virgin

---

[58] "Then some of the Pharisees and teachers of the law said to him, 'Teacher, we want to see a sign from you.' He answered, 'A wicked and adulterous generation asks for a sign! But none will be given it except the sign of the prophet Jonah. For as Jonah was three days and three nights in the belly of a huge fish, so the Son of Man will be three days and three nights in the heart of the earth. The men of Nineveh will stand up at the judgment with this generation and condemn it; for they repented at the preaching of Jonah, and now something greater than Jonah is here'" (Matthew 12:38–41).

[59] John 19:34, 2:6–9, 3:5, 4:7–28, 46, 7:38, 13:5; John 19:34; 1 John 5:6–12.

[60] Cf. "For this I will praise you, O LORD, among the nations, and sing to your name. Great salvation he brings to his king, and shows steadfast love to his anointed, to David and his offspring forever" (Psalm 18:49–50).

Isaiah 8:9–10: The Promise of Immanuel
Isaiah 9:6–7: Unto Us a Son Is Given
Isaiah 11:1–2: The Stump of Jesse
Isaiah 40:3–5: The Herald of the King
Isaiah 42:1–6: The Servant of Jehovah
Isaiah 49:1–13: The Discouragement of the Servant
Isaiah 50:4–9: The Training of the Servant
Isaiah 52:13–53:12: The Suffering of the Servant
Isaiah 61:1–3: The Mission of the Servant
Jeremiah 23:5–6: Messiah the King
Micah 5:2: Bethlehem Ephrathah
Zechariah 9:9–10: Riding on a Donkey
Zechariah 11:1–17: The Two Shepherds
Zechariah 12:10: The Final Recognition of Messiah
Zechariah 13:7: The Good Shepherd
Malachi 3:1: The Messenger of the King

THE WRITINGS
1 Chronicles 17:10b–14: The Davidic Covenant
Psalm 2:7–12: The Son of God
Psalm 16:1–11: The Death of Messiah
Psalm 22:1–31: The Suffering & Exaltation of Messiah
Psalm 80:17: The Man of Thy Right Hand
Psalm 110:1–7: A Priest after the Order of Melchizedek
Proverbs 30:4: The Name of God's Son
Daniel 9:1–27: The Messianic Timetable

Covenant

> Now as they were eating, Jesus took bread, and after blessing it broke it and gave it to the disciples, and said, "Take, eat; this is my body." And he took a cup, and when he had given thanks he gave it to them, saying, "Drink of it, all of you, for this is my blood of the covenant, which is poured out for many for the forgiveness of sins." (Matthew 26:26–28)

Christianity is based on God's covenant love for His people. Understanding what a covenant is and what the new covenant does gives us a fuller understanding of the message of Scripture. You really can't overestimate the importance of covenant in the Bible. The word is used 325 times in the ESV Bible. The Hebrews and the first Christians understood covenant as the basis for all God's promises and blessings and for salvation.

A covenant is a special promise based on some rules. Through God's covenants to Noah, Abraham, Moses, and David in the Old Testament, we begin to see their place and ours in the eternal plan. The Old Testament is filled with covenants that have a bearing on our salvation.

There are always two sides to a covenant, and in biblical covenants, God is always on one side. God's promises, His covenants, cannot be broken. This covenantal plan was clarified for us by the psalmists, prophets, Paul, and the writer to the Hebrews.

The Ten Commandments were actually the stipulations of a covenant between God and His covenant people.[61] If these laws were broken, the result was death. That is why the people of God sacrificed an animal to atone for their sins; the covenant had been broken, and a debt was due.

The new covenant, according to Hebrews 8:13, made the old covenant, the law, obsolete.[62] Jesus Christ is the mediator of the new covenant, which offers eternal life rather than death. Christ's shed blood redeems or buys back those who deserved death for breaking the stipulations, the laws, of the old covenant.[63]

The importance of Christ's sacrifice and suffering on the cross is understood only if we understand the covenant that God made with us and which we have broken. Only then can we comprehend that we are deserve death. Without acknowledging our broken covenant obligations, we cannot appreciate our need for forgiveness; we are left with cheap grace.

> And I will establish my covenant between me and you and your offspring after you throughout their generations for an everlasting covenant, to be God to you and to your offspring after you. (Genesis 17:7)

Four hundred and thirty years before the giving of the law to Moses, God made a covenant with Abraham and his descendants. We, as believers, are heirs to that covenant promise by faith.[64] If we belong to Christ, we are Abraham's offspring, heirs according to the promise of God.[65] The entire gospel is based on this idea of covenant.

> As sin reigned in death, grace also might reign through righteousness leading to eternal life through Jesus Christ our Lord. (Romans 5:21)

> That is why it depends on faith, in order that the promise may rest on grace and be guaranteed to all his offspring—not only to the adherent of the law but also to the one who shares the faith of Abraham, who is the father of us all. (Romans 4:16)

---

[61] Exodus 34:28; Deuteronomy 4:13–14: "And he declared to you his covenant, which he commanded you to perform, that is, the Ten Commandments, and he wrote them on two tablets of stone. And the LORD commanded me at that time to teach you statutes and rules, that you might do them in the land that you are going over to possess."

[62] Hebrews 8:13.

[63] "For if the blood of goats and bulls, and the sprinkling of defiled persons with the ashes of a heifer, sanctify for the purification of the flesh, how much more will the blood of Christ, who through the eternal Spirit offered himself without blemish to God, purify our conscience from dead works to serve the living God. Therefore he is the mediator of a new covenant, so that those who are called may receive the promised eternal inheritance, since a death has occurred that redeems them from the transgressions committed under the first covenant" (Hebrews 9:13–15).

[64] "Just as Abraham 'believed God, and it was counted to him as righteousness'? Know then that it is those of faith who are the sons of Abraham. And the Scripture, foreseeing that God would justify the Gentiles by faith, preached the gospel beforehand to Abraham, saying, 'In you shall all the nations be blessed.' So then, those who are of faith are blessed along with Abraham, the man of faith" (Galatians 3:6–9).

[65] Galatians 3:29.

For all the promises of God find their Yes in him. That is why it is through him that we utter our Amen to God for his glory. And it is God who establishes us with you in Christ, and has anointed us, and who has also put his seal on us and given us his Spirit in our hearts as a guarantee. (2 Corinthians 1:20–22)

As proclaimers, we claim this anointing given us by the Spirit, which we have as a pledge that the covenant has been kept not by our own good works but by Christ's work on the cross.

Teaching and Preaching on Prophecy

I set watchmen over you, saying,
"Pay attention to the sound of the trumpet!"
But they said, "We will not pay attention."
(Jeremiah 6:17)

Prophets sound the trumpet. They are watchmen; they sound the warning, they point to the future, and for us, they also highlight the sins of the past and the ramifications. The writings of the prophets are like binoculars. If we look through the small end (the normal way) and out into the distance, we will see things very far away but only in small vignettes, snippets of things that are not yet in our reach. Sometimes, these snippets are hard to put together in a coherent picture. But if we look through the small end at things fairly close, things we can walk to and touch, we will see that the binoculars bring them sharply into focus. Looking through the large end (the wrong way) things look as if they could jump right into our laps. That is what the books of the prophets do; they show us the long view of the future in bits and pieces, but they also show us shockingly clear pictures of ourselves. They magnify the sin in our communities and the current world.

Just as the normal purpose of binoculars is to see things far away, the purpose of the prophets is to talk about situations both in their day and sometimes in their future. To interpret the books of the prophets, we need first to understand their particular historical, social, and canonical contexts. The prophets were speaking the words God had given them in a very direct way to the people of their time. They each had a message from God, a warning to people in a specific place and time dealing with a specific future problem or crisis. To apply these messages to our day, we need to understand what they meant in their day.

Sometimes, the prophets are calling for repentance. Sometimes, they are warning people of what will happen.[66] Portions of the prophets' books are a record of what they preached. Like many Scriptures, they were meant to be read aloud as proclamation to a specific person or group; they were occasional.[67] In the writings of the prophets as in other occasional literature, historical backgrounds and canonical context matter to the original meaning.

---

[66] Some prophetic books were written to a pre-exilic audience, an exilic audience, or a postexilic audience. The watershed events of Scripture are the Creation/Fall; the flood; the giving of the Abrahamic covenant/birth of the Hebrew nation; the Exodus/giving of the law/Mosaic covenant; crossing the Jordan/settling in Canaan; the kingdom of David/divided kingdom; the fall of Israel and the exile of Judah; the Crucifixion/Resurrection; the Ascension/sending of the Holy Spirit/beginning of the church/NT writing; and (still in the future) the Second Coming. The books of the prophets are situated roughly around the times of the exiles. Along with the book of Daniel, they are the final books written in the OT.

[67] The epistles and the prophets and some of the psalms are occasional literature in that they were written to a specific community and situation in the original author's time. To best understand occasional literature, we have to understand the occasion and the audience.

Always study the historical context of the prophets in the books of history such as 1 and 2 Kings and 2 Chronicles to help you understand the Commander's intent for a prophetic passage. Look also for New Testament passages that may quote the prophet as these may indicate a secondary Christological or church meaning.

To understand the message of the prophets, we need to be aware of the fall of Israel (Samaria) in the north to the Assyrians, the fall of Judah in the south to the Babylonians, and the exile of the people of Judah. We must understand covenant and how the people the prophets originally wrote to had broken it. To understand covenant, we must refer to Deuteronomy and its law code and the theology of blessing and cursing based on covenant keeping.[68]

In studying the prophets we will need to recognize the original audience—those whom the message was addressing. Was it a person, a community, or a nation? Often, the covenant people of God can be defined roughly as the kingdom of God today for purposes of application. In his book on preaching Christ from the Old Testament, Sidney Greidanus[69] wrote that the church was the heir of the prophetic message since we were God's covenant people.[xxxv] The United States, I'm sorry to say, is not specifically the covenant people of God. Believers are the covenant people of God. So, if a prophecy is aimed at a particular nation, it is not appropriate to claim that prophecy for the United States or your nation of choice. The same goes for Old Testament promises that were aimed at Judah and Israel; they are not transferrable to America or wherever you are from.

Admittedly, long series on the prophets at first seem problematic for us to preach today in the sense that they seem fixated on judgment. But the prophets were actually fixated on mercy, love, and a bright hope beyond the immediate, looming danger. If we keep that fact in focus as we read, we can better understand their general message. Though the prophetic message at times is that it is too late, we know it is never too late for God because we are standing historically on the other side of their disaster. We know prayer in faith moves mountains. The biblical prophets' message is the same message as what the New Testament writers have for us, and New Testament theology is a great help in understanding the prophets' message as we teach it today.

In *Preaching from the Old Testament*, Elizabeth Achtemeier[70] recommended that we consider pairing our text from the prophets with a New Testament text when we preach it.[xxxvi] Some ways to preach prophecy or to pair texts include these.

- Historical Redemptive—the Old Testament as types and shadows pointing forward in history to the time when Israel's Messiah would be revealed in the person and work of Jesus Christ (promise-fulfillment)

---

[68] "Know therefore that the LORD your God is God, the faithful God who keeps covenant and steadfast love with those who love him and keep his commandments, to a thousand generations, and repays to their face those who hate him, by destroying them. He will not be slack with one who hates him. He will repay him to his face. You shall therefore be careful to do the commandment and the statutes and the rules that I command you today" (Deuteronomy 7:9–11).

[69] Sidney Greidanus is a pastor and biblical scholar best known for his emphasis on preaching Christ from the Old Testament.

[70] Elizabeth Achtemeier was a leading evangelical voice in the Presbyterian Church (USA). She was a nationally known preacher, lecturer, scholar, and member of the faculty at Union Theological Seminary in Richmond, VA. She was a visiting professor at Gettysburg Lutheran Seminar, Pittsburgh Theological Seminary, and Duke Divinity School. She taught Old Testament at Lancaster Theological Seminary in Pennsylvania. She authored twenty books and was a frequent contributor to many other publications.

- Covenantal—the relationship between God and His people then and now
- Theology—what do we learn about God?
- Doctrinal—the core doctrines of the Christian faith that can be traced to systematic theology (i.e., soteriology, eschatology, etc.)
- Compare/Contrast with the New Testament—for example, God's love versus His wrath.

The prophets should be understood in light of their context in the canon; they are a link between the old and new covenants. Even messianic prophecies had a message to people of their day, and that message is our priority if our text is from an Old Testament prophet. That message should be covered in good depth before shifting to the New Testament. When preaching about wrath and judgment, keep the focus on God's holiness.

THE PROPHETS SPEAK TO A GENERATION FOCUSED ON JUSTICE

But let justice roll down like waters,
and righteousness like an ever-flowing stream.
(Amos 5:24)

Preaching the prophets' message is like letting loose a big, lumbering, grizzly bear. It's that dangerous but so exciting. We usually put a big red collar around the sleeping bear's neck and parade him on a chain to stand and roar once a year at Christmas.[71] In effect, we are telling our parishioners, "You just don't know how powerful the Word of God really is. I'll give you a peek. Ta-da!" We read a messianic prophecy from Micah, and the people are duly impressed that the Bible back then had something to say about Jesus Christ's birth.[72] And then we lock the bear back up in our garage and feed him blueberries and leftover smoked salmon until next Christmas.

Let the bear out. Let him roam through your church and community wherever he wants all year long. When he roars at the injustice he finds, his hot breath will make your hair blow back. We've kept him in our locked garage claiming he couldn't survive on his own. He is so powerful that we're afraid that if he gets out, he'll never come back or our congregation will never come back when they comprehend the full impact of the prophet's message. Secretly, perhaps, we are afraid if we let him out, he might devour something we prize or cause a lot of trouble. We may be fired for letting the bear out. Here's to a nice long series on Amos, Jeremiah, or Isaiah. Let's let the prophets out and see what they do.[73]

Preaching on Habakkuk, Gordon MacDonald[74] said,

I'd like to suggest to you … that prophets are people who burn. When they get into a subject and speak into it, they speak with enormous energy and emotion. Whatever

[71] Isaiah 9:6, 52:7, 57:18–19; Zechariah 9:9–10.

[72] "But you, O Bethlehem Ephrathah, who are too little to be among the clans of Judah, from you shall come forth for me one who is to be ruler in Israel, whose coming forth is from of old, from ancient days" (Micah 5:2).

[73] For the brave at heart, there is a section on how to divide up Jeremiah into a church-wide series is the appendix.

[74] Gordon MacDonald is chancellor of Denver Seminary, pastor emeritus of Grace Chapel in Lexington, MA, and editor at large of *Leadership Journal*. He has written more than twelve books and coauthored others with his wife, Gail, and his son, Mark.

feeling they've got, you can expect it to explode like a Roman candle. They will go to any expense to express to you their horror at what they see and they feel. And often it's not just academic to them, so while they're giving you facts, figures and statistics, they feel it in their gut very personally. Prophets burn because they feel, first of all, the effect and the awesomeness of sin and evil and what it does to people. There's no coolness in the life of a prophet. And often, as they burned and they spoke, the crowd would listen to them and then walk away and ignore them.[xxxvii, 75]

Just like thoughtful proclaimers, prophets interpret Scripture, covenant, law, and their own communities for a new generation. The prophets are the bridge between the old covenant—the law—and the new covenant—faith in Jesus Christ. The prophets nurtured an alternative perception of reality in which God really was King, called for dramatic change to the dominant culture, and refused to accept the status quo. Social justice and idolatry were their two big preaching points, and those points are very close to the heart of people today.

---

[75] Gordon's text was Habakkuk 1–3. His topic was how the prophets relate to God and society, and his "big idea" was that we don't always want to listen when the prophet speaks.

xxxviii

The Big Story of Redemption

In a sense, the Bible is one big majestic story, what we call a metanarrative—a grand story that gives meaning to all the smaller stories or narratives it encompasses. As believers in Christ, we see the metanarrative of Scripture as the story of salvation from Creation through eternity in heaven. In a sense, this metanarrative encompasses all our stories too.

When we look at small narrative stories in Scripture, we situate them in their places in the grand narrative of salvation. Each story we choose to tell is cut out of its setting like a heart-shaped valentine cut out of pink paper. Each valentine we cut out needs to be an independent story that in some way is significant to the larger metanarrative.

We saw for example the story of Joseph being divided into smaller stories in chapter 5 on picking a passage. Each episode in the Joseph narrative could be delivered as a different sermon, but in making these divisions, we must take care that each sermon or episode fits into the larger meaning of the story of Joseph, the story of Genesis, the story of the Hebrew people, the Old Testament, and ultimately the story of salvation. Not that we have to tell each of those stories every time, but we must keep them in mind as we prepare.

Generally, we have three stories to manage: the story we are telling, the larger story of the book the author was telling, and the metanarrative of Scripture, the big story of redemption. We must always keep in mind that the story we have is God's story; He is the one telling it. What was He trying to say? Many times, if we are faithful to our chosen passage, we'll end up with a Commander's intent something like, "Don't miss the blessing like the folks in this story!" or "God's promises are true whether we like it or not." The Commander's intent is grounded in the metanarrative of redemption.

Bible narratives are history with a purpose; they are stories to teach about theology. For the most part, Bible stories are not children's tales, morality plays, or character-building stories. There is usually no narrator telling us what to think of the sometimes crazy things that happen. Jeffrey Arthurs[76] said, "Biblical narrative can be defined as a historically accurate, artistically sophisticated account of persons and actions in a setting designed to reveal God and edify the reader."[xxxix]

When we preach and teach the books of Old Testament history, we are less interested in what the people were doing and more interested in what God was doing behind the scenes. Most Old Testament narratives show very sinful human beings making bad choices. We know God is in the background, but it is the reader's job to find Him.[77] We know God's purpose in writing is not to teach us history but to influence us in some way. It is our job as proclaimers to consider what God is trying to do in each story. How is he trying to influence us? That is the Commander's intent. Jeffrey Arthurs believed that narrative could be preached and taught with an historical-redemptive purpose, but he also observed that where stories contain moral exhortation, it was legitimate to interpret them that way.[il]

Regarding narrative, Arthurs also remarked,

> It is hardly incidental that lifting up Christ and the glory of his Father is the best way to change behavior. Moralistic preaching without theological grounding feels like nagging with its never ending "do more, do better." [Moralistic application] uses guilt to motivate behavior, a questionable pastoral practice that produces only temporary change.[ili]

The better course is to point our listeners to God's mercy, covenant keeping, love, and the ultimate gift of the cross as motivation for living. Preaching Old Testament narrative passages is uniquely suited to redemptive purpose and redemptive application. Keep God's holiness and His loving, redemptive purpose always in mind. Always, always ground application in the power of the Holy Spirit and the motivating factor of a grateful heart.

---

[76] Jeffrey Arthurs is the chair of the Division of Ministry of the Church, professor of preaching and communication and, dean of the chapel at Gordon Conwell Seminary.

[77] In teaching on 2 Kings 14–16, I observed that despite the evil of its rulers and the massive amount of sadness and despair their leadership brought on the people, God was still there graciously blessing His children. Not because of their behavior—which was idolatrous—but because of His grace and compassion and because of their parents (they were descendants of David). God is slow to act, but He does act. And before He does, He blesses and blesses and blesses. We see here God's hand of love traced across a people who did not deserve it, a people who had largely been worshipping other gods, not their God, YHWH.

Contextual Questions

Here are some questions to get you started. Answer those that are relevant, and ignore the rest. Add your own questions of the text.

Book of the Bible

- Who was this book written to? Who is its audience?
- After reading this book, what appears to be its purpose?
- What do I learn about the purpose of this book from the first and last chapters?
- Why was this book written?
- What is its purpose according to commentaries?
- What do I see as the theme of the book that contains my passage?
- Were the people this book is about or the people it was written to religious? Worshippers of YHWH, of Jesus, or of idols?
- How were these people different from us?
- How does the purpose of this book relate to us? What might the purpose of this book be for us today?
- If the book is prophetic, what were the circumstances facing the people?

Surrounding Passages

- What do the surrounding passages have to do with the one I am studying?
- If this passage is a story, parable, psalm, or proverb, what other stories, poems, or sayings in the same book relate to it?
- How does the main idea of this passage fit into the larger context of the book that contains it?
- What does this passage mean to say in light of the larger context of the book that contains it?
- Are there repeated words or ideas that help me find the beginning and end of the story?
- Do other connected stories have the same theme or teaching?
- What is the climax of the story?
- What is the conclusion?
- What seems to be the purpose of the story?

Canonical Context

- How does this passage fit into the grand story of salvation?
- How does this passage relate to the surrounding books of the Bible?
- Why was this book included in the canon?
- What is different about the message of this book when compared to the messages of all the other books in the Bible?
- What are other parallel passages in both testaments? What do I glean from them?

- If this book is one of the prophets, what other books expand on the situation, and what do they say?
- If this book is one of the synoptic gospels, what can we glean from the others on this story?

Literary Genre

- What is the genre of this passage?
- What difference does the genre of this passage make to its meaning?
- What literary forms are embedded in the larger genre of this passage?
- Why did God inspire this message to be written in this genre?
- How might the literary form change the way I choose to proclaim this message?

Historical Background

- When was this book written?
- Why were these people being written to or about?
- What was the prevailing historical situation at the time (war, famine, plenty, etc.)?
- What was happening in the history of Israel, the church, or the world at the time this book was written?[ilii]
- What was the geopolitical situation at this time?
- What were the people feeling and experiencing?
- How is the meaning of the passage tied to its historical context?
- What is clearly different about then and now?
- What sorts of interpretation may be needed to apply this text to our context?

Cultural Background

- What seem to be the invisible presuppositions that made up their culture that are very different from the invisible suppositions that make up ours?
- What difference do they make to God's intent and purpose for the passage?
- How were the people this book was written to like us?
- How were they different from us?
- If this passage/book takes place in or describes a geographic location, where is it? What does it look like? What does it feel like? How might geography have affected culture?
- Did the people this book was written to or about live in a rural or relatively urban setting? How does that affect the meaning of the passage/book?
- Were they settled or nomadic people?
- Were they living in the pre-temple times, or was there temple worship?
- Were they pre-exilic, in exile, or postexilic?
- Were they enslaved or free?
- Were they Jewish or Christian or both?
- Were they persecuted or not?
- What were their marriage practices?
- In what types of houses did they live?
- How did they raise their families?

- What is the basic social structure in this book—extended family, limited family, nation?
- What were their invisible cultural beliefs?
- Did they worship YHWH (the LORD) or someone/something else? Why?
- What biblical background information on the culture is relevant to this passage?
- How do these observations affect our understanding of this passage?
- How do these observations affect the application of this passage?

Redemptive Theological Questions for Thought[78]

- What passages from the Old and New Testaments further inform me about this passage, and what do they say?
- What does this passage say about God, Christ, and the Holy Spirit?
- What does the passage say about God's love and holiness?
- What group or person represents God in this passage?[iliii]
- What does this passage reveal about human brokenness and the need for redemption or forgiveness?
- How does this passage point to sin or how we have fallen short of God's purposes for our lives?
- What does this passage say about God's work?
- What does it say about God's message to the world?
- What does it say about God's will for humankind?[iliv]
- What is God (in one of the three persons of the Trinity) doing in this passage?[ilv]
- What divine judgment rests on those in this passage and why?
- Why did God choose to act in this passage?[ilvi]
- What hope does this passage imply or offer?[ilvii]
- What does this passage say about how God will restore humanity to His purposes?[ilviii]
- What does God do behind the scenes in the larger story of the Bible to accomplish His will regarding the problem in this passage?
- What is said or implied about the future and God's promises?
- How does the idea of covenant play into this passage?
- Are there messianic overtones or types in this passage?
- Does the passage point to blood, forgiveness, or sacrifice?
- Where is grace displayed in this passage?
- What characters might point in some way to Christ?
- What characters point to the need for Christ?
- Where is Christ or forgiveness portrayed?
- Where might Christ be needed?
- Is there a story of redemption here either secular or spiritual?
- How does any story of redemption in this passage relate to Christ?
- How does this passage relate to Jesus Christ's earthly ministry?
- What message from God is this passage relaying?

[78] In his book *God Sense: Reading the Bible for Preaching*, Paul Scott Wilson helped to expand my thinking on these questions.

- Where is the Holy Spirit found in this passage? Is He behind the scenes, or empowering characters, or simply inspiring the author?
- How can the Holy Spirit empower us to do the thing called for in this passage?
- In what way does this passage speak to the person who may be running from God?
- In what way does it speak to the person seeking God?
- In what way does it speak to those who are sick, suffering, or unable to help themselves?
- In what way does it speak to the religious/legalistic person?
- In what way does it speak to the self-righteous person (vs. righteousness from God)?
- What does God do in this passage to provide or accomplish what is needed?[xlix]
- What is God doing in the larger context, canon, or salvation story to accomplish what is needed?[l]
- What theological truth does this passage convey?
- What does this passage say or imply about Christ?[li]
- How does this passage connect to the Crucifixion, Resurrection, or eternity?[lii]
- How does our gratefulness to Christ for His offer of salvation cause us to want to live out this passage?
- What passage from the other testament might you pair with your passage to deepen your message?

CHAPTER 7

DIG DEEP—IDEA LEVEL

In the way of your testimonies I delight
as much as in all riches.
I will meditate on your precepts
and fix my eyes on your ways.
I will delight in your statutes;
I will not forget your word.
(Psalm 119:14–16)

My nephew is a great carpenter and a very good mechanic. He started as a boy going out to the fire pit (they lived in the country) to rescue things and take them apart. Old rotary phones, radios, car parts, tools, whatever he could find that he could carefully destroy. As a child, he could rarely put them back together, but as he got older, his projects got much bigger—cars usually—and he worked on several at a time in various stages of destruction and construction. Through taking apart of everything he could find, he learned how things worked.

We use this same principle to understand how a passage works. Study the passage at each level—ideas, paragraphs, sentences, and phrases. We want to understand what the passage meant when it was written. How was it put together? Why? How does this help us identify the Commander's intent?

Meaning begins with the larger part (the books and chapters) and flows down to the smaller parts (paragraphs, sentences, and words). We'll first tear the passage apart to understand it well and make it our own.

Tear the Passage Down to the Studs: Grammatical Exegesis

Grammar, really? Syntax who? What is this all about? The word *grammar* conjures an image of desks, pencils, and children sitting in rows. *Webster's Dictionary* tells us, "Grammar is the study of the classes of words, their inflections, and their functions and relations in the sentence."[i] Syntax is how the words are arranged to form meaning—the phrasing, the connecting words, the thought patterns of the author. In *Kairos: A Beginning Greek Grammar*, Fredrick J. Long[1] wrote,

---

[1] Dr. Fredrick J. Long studies and writes on biblical and Greco-Roman literature, Greek grammatical and discourse analysis and translation, and biblical exposition. He is professor of New Testament at Asbury Seminary.

"We speak every day unaware of the grammatical and syntactical rules that govern our language."[ii] But in reality, grammar "helps us discern the point of a sentence and eventually groups of related sentences."[iii] According to Ramesh Richard,[2] "Logical relationships help us understand the case, the point, or the argument the author is making."[iv] And "Translators have divided biblical texts into paragraphs, each of which has one dominant, identifiable thought. In fact, the very definition of a paragraph is that it proposes one cardinal thought."[v]

Instead of focusing on the concepts grammar and syntax, it can be easier to just focus on words, sentences, and paragraphs. We ask how the words, sentences, and paragraphs are organized and why they are put together that way. It is often helpful to start with groups of paragraphs that carry one primary overarching idea.

Consider the Passage Structure

Almost every passage is structured differently. Certainly, every genre is handled differently. But with most passages, we will start by dividing a significant passage into the major sections or chunks. Each chunk will have a major theme or idea.

Write out headings for the main idea of each major chunk of your passage. Determine how the writer organized the ideas, the chunks. Add the important subordinate ideas that modify or explain that idea under the headings. Outline your passage. Do a detailed sentence diagram of the key verse or verses. Underline key words. Pay attention to nouns and verbs. Notice the connecting words or conjunctions that are surprisingly important to meaning.[3]

If there are short, complicated sections as there often are in the epistles, you can outline them including every word in detail. When I am dealing with a story, I like to retell the story for myself in broad strokes. Other times, I take each paragraph as a main point and then list everything under that main heading. Create whatever type of outline or diagram will help you understand the individual ideas best.

Didactic Material

Didactic writing is intended to teach something; it conveys instruction and information. The Old Testament is primarily narrative and poetry while the New Testament is narrative and didactic with apocalyptic material in Revelation. The epistles are didactic for the most part; they were written to specific situations in different times and to different cultures, so their messages grow out of those elements.

The epistles were written to teach the church; those we have were passed from church to church to be read. Often, the main interpretive tool we use for didactic literature is simply asking what the passage would mean in a different time and culture. Other times, we have to consider the situation or occasion that an epistle was written to address, though the writer may not tell us that directly, and then consider the situations familiar to us that would correlate to those in Ephesus or Colossae for example.

---

[2] Ramesh P. Richard is professor of global theological engagement and pastoral ministries at Dallas Theological Seminary.

[3] A sentence diagram shows what the subject of the sentence is, what the main verb is, and then it indicates what is said about that verb. The other words that modify the nouns and verbs go underneath. If this is new to you or you need a refresher, ask or search online for how to do a sentence diagram. See Appendix F for an example of one way I diagram a small group of verses.

Simply divide your didactic passage into chunks based on the paragraphs. Make the subject of each paragraph a major point in your outline, and then put all the subordinate sentences or subordinate ideas underneath. Place every clause under what it modifies. This is never seen by anyone but you; it is strictly to help you understand the passage's flow of thought. Feel free to use the words of Scripture in your outline, or you can use your own words.

NARRATIVE

"It was the best of times, it was the worst of times."[4, vi] That's how I feel about teaching on biblical narrative. Surprisingly, a large portion of the Bible, especially the Old Testament, is story. We all love a good story, but it's not always easy to find the main point. Bible stories are notorious for being ambiguous as to meaning. If God wanted us to know exactly what to do and how to live, why did He not just give us precepts and rules? Why tell stories? And such stories they are! We can conclude only that God wanted us to think about who He was and whose people we were. He wanted us to see just what kinds of messes people get into and where those messes and our sinful lives can lead us if we leave Him out. And quite frankly, stories stick in our minds and we never forget them, and they are very interesting to read! God is present in every story of our lives all the time, but sometimes, He is very hard to see. In the same way, he can be hard to see in Bible narratives as well, especially some Old Testament ones.

If the narrator comments on the story it is easier to identify the author's intentions, but this is often not the case. Robert Alter described the theological quest of the biblical writers as a desire "to reveal the enactment of God's purpose in history."[vii] If that is the biblical writers' desire, ours is to understand God's purpose in history as detailed in the events of the Bible.

Once we have determined the Commander's intent for a particular story, retelling that story and highlighting the Commander's intent is about the most fun preaching or teaching we can do. History rolls along and never stops, but the Bible tells history in a literary form through story after story. These stories, particularly those in the Old Testament, can be analyzed for form and language in detail just as fine dramas and plays can be.

Though each story is there for a purpose, the stories and sometimes their purposes are interlinked making it difficult at times to divide them into manageable parts to speak on. Noticing repeated themes and words as well as changes of setting or character will often tell us where to stop and start. (We can also use the spiral-cut method of dividing the stories if need be; see chapter 4).

Plot

To tear down our story, we can diagram the plot instead of creating an outline. Stories have plots. Biblical stories have plots too, though, as we said, some of the plots are interwoven and can be difficult to pin down. Look for the beginning, middle and end of the story. Identify the rising action, the conflict, the turning point, and the resolution of the primary narrative in a passage.

Jeffrey Arthurs said that plot affects us in three ways. First, it highlights ideas. Second, it induces suspense. And third, it fulfills or does not fulfill our expectations.[viii] Each of these effects can be a key to finding the Commander's intent for a narrative passage.

---

[4] This is how Charles Dickens starts his story *A Tale of Two Cities*.

Situate the Setting, Time, and Place

For biblical stories, the setting, time, and place are often important to the meaning if they are specified. The context of the story is helpful to know, whether that involves such settings as the early church, exile (being different from the prevailing culture), time of the divided kingdom, the nation of Israel (settled and city based), pre-Israel (nomadic), or Egypt (slavery). These settings give us clues to the meaning of the story.[5] Only in children's storybooks can we pull Samson out of Judges and make him a folk hero.[6] In Daniel 6 (exile), Daniel broke the new law (written specifically to trap him) by praying three times a day in his upper chamber with his windows wide open so everyone would be sure to see. This story, which culminates in Daniel being thrown to the lions, becomes a children's story of God's faithfulness to us when we pull it out of its more complicated context, situation, and setting. The grown-up version, the biblical version, has Daniel living as God's emissary in a pagan land, the land of Babylon, at that time controlled by Persia. He was there against his will, yet he was well respected and had a lot of power. Without the setting and situation, we lose the very purpose of the story, which seems to be God's power being displayed before the foreign rulers. Daniel was an ambassador for God in a strange culture, and that is why God performed such a strong miracle. Daniel surviving the lion's den changed the course of history for the Hebrews in order to display God's power not necessarily Daniel's bravery (though surely we see that as well.).

Consider the Characters and Narrator

God is the main character in every biblical story. even the stories of Moses and Paul. God is sometimes seen, sometimes unseen, and very occasionally glimpsed as the omniscient narrator. We often make Job the primary character of the book of Job, but in the final chapters, when God seemed to have had enough of the nonsense, He spoke clearly.

For most Old Testament narrative passages, however, there is no moral guide. The stories are told, as they happened, leaving us at times in shock that a holy book would contain such sordid tails. There is often no moral; no, "Go thou and do likewise". The characters in the Bible, especially in the Old Testament, are not moral exemplars even if at times they seem to be for a few chapters. If we just keep reading, we will find they are more like sinful humans than we care to admit.[7] We study the characters, then, hoping to see ourselves or dreading seeing ourselves. We look to see where God is in relation to the characters who so resemble us or our times. In the stories of faith and lack of faith we see how God operated behind the scenes and we learn how God's people stepped out in faith or hid in the shadows and the effect that had on the outcomes.

The names of the characters are important. Old Testament stories can be character heavy, and

---

[5] There are several places in the Bible where we find doublets—stories that though they have different settings strongly resemble each other. We see this, for example, in Genesis 16 and 21 when Hagar and Ishmael are cast out. Genesis 12 and 20 have Abraham calling Sarah his sister to keep himself from being killed by someone who wanted Sarah. Then in Genesis 26, Isaac tried the same trick to save his skin with his beautiful wife Rebecca. In the NT are two feedings of thousands, one of 5,000 and one of 4,000; these are obviously not mistakes. It seems they serve a purpose in jogging our memories. For example, when God stopped up the Jordan River so Joshua could take the people into the Promised Land, we are meant to remember when Moses took the people of Israel across the Red Sea at the start of this journey.

[6] Judges 13–16.

[7] Joseph perhaps comes closest to a moral exemplar of all Bible characters at least after he stopped being prideful and arrogant!

many of their names frequently sound and look alike, which makes them very confusing. This purposeful technique serves to slow us down and make us study the passage. To help you and your audience keep track of who is who, consider giving the characters nicknames which represent their actions. This will help both you and your audience keep up with the story.[8]

This method is somewhat justified as the Bible names often have meanings that are important to the story. It is often informative to look up the meanings of the names of major characters in the Old Testament. Abram means, "exalted father,"[ix] whereas Abraham means "father of a multitude"[x] (*Ab* meaning father or grandfather).

Though the Bible is a long book, its style of writing in the case of narrative is very spare on details and descriptions. If details are mentioned, they usually have significance. When we read of David's son's Absalom's long hair, we think of his egotism, and we eventually see that his beautiful locks and arrogant pride were his undoing.[9] When we read in 2 Samuel 25 that no one was as handsome as he was, we know that trouble is brewing.

POETRY AND THE PSALMS

How can you describe a rose?
Or does a flower, once dissected, still delight?

Alas, finding the author's intent for a poem requires more heart than science, and the mind's eye trumps the grammarian's analysis. Poetry speaks a different language and to a different part of the mind. Dissecting a rose requires that we keep in mind the beauty of the flower while we tear apart the petals for closer inquiry.

You can analyze your psalm or poem by dividing it into its strophes or stanzas and analyzing the general subject of each. When we preach the Psalms, however, we are better off using our hearts and our imaginations to see what the psalmist said rather than a lexicon to analyze the wording. Find the movement of thought, the design of the poem or psalm. Decide on the purpose that covers all the strophes in the poem.

Consider the setting and the original use of the psalm if it is known. To preach on poetry, we can use art, photography, other poetry, other Scripture, description, or song to evoke the message or the vision of the psalm. Poets use few words, but we might need longer descriptions to duplicate the effect for our listeners.

So, tear it down, but be careful not to reduce it to mere words until you've absorbed the feelings. Tear it down to images. Note that Hebrew poetry is written in parallel lines. The first line says one thing, and the second line repeats it, strengthens it, or says a little bit more about it. To contemporize a psalm, you will want to know what it meant to its original hearers.

---

[8] Elijah and Elisha are two prophets of Israel who are very different men, but they have very similar names that our audiences can easily confuse.

[9] "Now in all Israel there was no one so much to be praised for his handsome appearance as Absalom. From the sole of his foot to the crown of his head there was no blemish in him. And when he cut the hair of his head (for at the end of every year he used to cut it; when it was heavy on him, he cut it), he weighed the hair of his head, two hundred shekels by the king's weight. (2 Samuel 14:25–26); And Absalom happened to meet the servants of David. Absalom was riding on his mule, and the mule went under the thick branches of a great oak, and his head caught fast in the oak, and he was suspended between heaven and earth, while the mule that was under him went on. And a certain man saw it and told Joab, 'Behold, I saw Absalom hanging in an oak.' Joab said to the man who told him, 'What, you saw him! Why then did you not strike him there to the ground? I would have been glad to give you ten pieces of silver and a belt'" (2 Samuel 18:9–11).

Only when you have absorbed and appreciated the heart of the psalm should you look at its words. You will want to consider what feelings they evoke. You will want to consider which words or images you will use to evoke that same feeling for your audience. Review chapter 6, "Contextual Signpost 4: Literary Genre," the section, "Genre Should Influence the Form and Mood of the Proclamation." Hebrew poetry contains some extra things we might miss in translation, so after you've studied all you can in your own language, consult a commentary to prevent you from missing alliterations, word plays, etc.

General Principles of Bible Interpretation

The following are four sets of principles written by Walt Henrichsen and published in NavPress's 1979 book *A Layman's Guide to Interpreting the Bible*. This book is out of print, but Henrichsen's principles have been reprinted in NavPress's *The Navigator Bible Studies Handbook*.[xi] Here are the principles:

General Principles of Interpretation

1. Work from the assumption that the Bible is authoritative.
2. The Bible interprets itself; Scripture best explains Scripture.
3. Saving faith and the Holy Spirit are necessary for us to understand and properly interpret the Scriptures.
4. Interpret personal experience in the light of Scripture and not Scripture in the light of personal experience.
5. Biblical examples are authoritative only when supported by a command. (For example, the book of Acts records that an apostle to replace Judas was chosen by casting lots—i.e., drawing straws. This does not mean the Bible teaches that drawing straws is the only or even the best way of choosing church leaders.) *A corollary:* The believer is free to do anything that the Bible does not prohibit.
6. The primary purpose of the Bible is not to increase our knowledge but to change our lives. *Two corollaries:*
   a. Some passages are not to be applied in the same way they were applied at the time they were written. (For example, Deuteronomy 22:8 says one should always build a parapet around the roof of his house so that no one will fall off the roof. This was a wise instruction when people used their flat roofs as additional living space.)
   b. When you apply a passage, it must be in keeping with a correct interpretation.
7. Each Christian has the right and responsibility to investigate and interpret the Word of God for himself. (Of course, humility is in order—everyone from the rankest beginner to the most experienced scholar can be wrong.)
8. Church history is important but not decisive in the interpretation of Scripture. *A corollary*: The Church does not determine what the Bible teaches; the Bible determines what the church teaches.

9. The promises of God in the Bible are available to the Holy Spirit for believers of every generation. One should avoid a demanding, presumptuous attitude when claiming promises given to individuals. For instance, just because God promised Sarah a baby does not mean that every woman who "claims" Genesis 18:10 will have a baby.

Grammatical Principles of Interpretation

1. Scripture has only one meaning and should be taken literally. [Note: When this was written, the word *literal* had a positive connotation. In more recent times, the word *literal* has been misconstrued to twist and denigrate Scripture. So in this book, we use the words *at face value* or in a straightforward way, meaning we seek to understand the Bible as the original author and God intend for us to. We apply it today considering its previous contexts, the rest of Scripture (of which is only a part), and our context. The authors of this book agree with the meaning Walt Henrichsen had for this statement. See also number 8 below.]
2. Interpret words in harmony with their meaning in the times of the author.
3. Interpret a word in relation to its sentence and context.
4. Interpret a passage in harmony with its context.
5. When an inanimate object is used to describe a living being, the statement may be considered figurative. *A corollary:* When life and action are attributed to inanimate objects, the statement may be considered figurative.
6. When an expression is out of character with the thing described, the statement may be considered to be a figurative one.
7. The principal parts and figures of a parable represent certain realities. Consider only these principal parts and figures when drawing conclusions.
8. Interpret the words of the prophets in their usual, literal, and historical sense unless the context or manner in which they are fulfilled clearly indicates they have a symbolic meaning. Their fulfillment may be in installments, each fulfillment of prophecy being a pledge of what is to follow.

Historical Principles of Interpretation

1. Since Scripture originated in a historical context, it can be understood only in the light of biblical history.
2. Though God's revelation in the Scriptures is progressive, both Old and New Testaments are essential parts of this revelation and form a unit.
3. Historical facts or events become symbols of spiritual truths only if the Scriptures so designate them.

Theological Principles of Interpretation

1. You must understand the Bible grammatically before you can understand it theologically.
2. A doctrine cannot be considered biblical unless it sums up and includes all that the Scriptures say about it.

3. When two doctrines taught in the Bible appear to be contradictory, accept both as scriptural in the confident belief that they resolve themselves into a higher unity.

4. A teaching merely implied in Scripture may be considered biblical when a comparison of related passages supports the teaching.

Questions to Help Us Dig Deep—Idea Level

Dig Deep—Idea Level

- Divide the passage into its major sections or chunks.
- What are the major themes or ideas?
- How is the passage organized?
- Outline the passage chunks.
- Underline key words or ideas (nouns, verbs, and connecting words or conjunctions).
- Make a sentence diagram of one or two key verses.

Dig Deep—General Observations

- What appear to be the key verses or phrases?
- Diagram the key verse or verses if it will help make them clearer.
- What is the mood of the passage? Why was it written in that mood?
- What is the organizing principle of the passage? Is it inductive, deductive, informally arranged, or arranged with the main thought in the middle?
- Why did the writer organize his thoughts in this way?
- What ideas are repeated and why?

Dig Deeper by Genre

If the Passage Is Didactic:

- Outline the passage with subject headlines.
- Outline the passage in detail.
- Show how the discussion or argument develops.
- What is the mood of the passage?
- Is there any advice?
- Are there admonitions?
- Are there warnings?
- Are there promises?
- What are the emphatic phrases?
- Is there figurative language? Why was it used?
- If the passage is from an epistle, what situation was being addressed? Why?
- How is this situation similar to or different from situations we face today?
- Is the application the same or different for readers today?

- Why did the author organize his ideas as he did?
- What was the most important idea to the author? Where did he place it?

IF THE PASSAGE IS NARRATIVE:

- Where does the story begin and end? Identifying different places, characters, or moods may help.
- What is the setting of the story?
- When does the story occur?
- Where does it occur? What is significant about this time frame in the context of Scripture, Israel, or the church?
- What is the mood of the story?
- Who is the main character or protagonist?
- Who is the antagonist, the one who contends with or opposes the main character?
- Is God a protagonist or antagonist in this story?
- What is the significance of the main character's name?
- What is the conflict or problem between the protagonist and the antagonist?
- Does the Bible tell us anything about how the characters look? Why?
- What is the rising action, or what major events lead to the turning point or climax of the story?
- What is the turning point or the point of greatest tension between the protagonist and antagonist?
- What happens after the climax (the falling action)? What events lead to the story's resolution?
- How does the story resolve or conclude?
- Who has the power in this story? Who is powerless? Who is excluded from power? How does this power structure affect the story's meaning?
- What is the outcome?
- What ideas are highlighted?
- What elements create suspense?
- What words are repeated more frequently than usual?
- Where is God found in this story? What is He doing? Is He in front of or behind the camera?
- What is the theme of the story?
- What lesson did the protagonist learn?
- What could we learn from this story?
- Whom do we want to identify with? Whom do we not want to identify with?
- What message is the author trying to communicate?
- What other passages of Scripture link to this story or explain it?

IF THE PASSAGE IS A PSALM OR POETRY:

- What types of images or figurative language are used? What do they represent?
- Take note of parallel structure. How does it function (repetition, enhancements)?

- Where in the psalter (if this is a psalm) is the passage? What are the other psalms around it about?
- Note the literary form—how it is arranged. Try to determine why it is arranged that way. Does it start with a call to worship or praise phrase? Is it arranged alphabetically in Hebrew (i.e., Psalm 119)?
- Why is this message presented in this genre?
- Divide the passage into strophes or chunks.
- Outline the strophes by topic or image.
- Where is the main topic or intent of the passage mentioned? Is it in the beginning, the end, or right in the middle?
- How are the strophes arranged? Look at the macro- and the micro-arrangement of the strophes.
- Is this psalm a community psalm or an individual psalm? What difference does that make to its meaning?
- What is the mood? Is it one more of praise or lament?
- If praise, is it a song of thanksgiving or a hymn of praise?
- If a hymn of praise, is it praising the Creator or Redeemer of Israel or the world or the ruler of history?
- Is it a storytelling psalm? A psalm of penitence? A psalm of trust and meditation? A royal psalm? A renewal liturgy? A psalm of ascent, a song of Zion, or an enthronement psalm?
- Note the feelings expressed. Consider the writer's emotions. How was he feeling in each part? Do his emotions and feelings change throughout the psalm?
- Are some of the feelings or phrases troubling to you? Prayerfully note these, and then read carefully to see if they are giving emotions to God or are registering trust in His sovereignty.
- Note stories or experiences shared by the psalmist.
- Note key words. How many different words are used for the same basic idea? (Psalm 119, for example, uses many words for God's Word.)
- Does the psalmist use any theologically loaded power words such as *love* or *justice*?
- What is God's name here (God/Elohim, a general word for God, or LORD/YHWH, a personal name for God)?
- How is God portrayed?
- Note strong allusions or illustrations.
- Can the historical context be discovered? Look up historical or grammatical notes to understand the poetry more clearly.
- Are there any elements that could be derived from other Near Eastern cultures (including mythical references to other gods, etc.)?
- Do some elements reflect a simple view of the universe such as the image of chariots pulling the sun across the sky?
- Look up the cross-references or notes to other Scriptures. Note that often other passages will refer to Psalms.
- Read the Psalms with a Christian perspective. Look for Christ, prophecy, or covenant.

IF THE PASSAGE IS PROPHECY:

- How was this prophecy originally offered (preached, spoken, illustrated, written)?
- Is there figurative language?
- Can you identify what the figurative motifs are meant to point to?
- Who are the characters?
- What genres are included? Why?
- Why did God give this message to the prophet?
- What forms is this prophecy presented in?
- Is it addressed to a priest, a king, or a group? What significance does that have?
- If addressed to a group, is it a nation, an international group, or the kingdom of God?
- How was the prophecy fulfilled in its day?
- Does this prophecy also point to a future fulfillment (e.g., a return to the land or a messiah)?
- Does this prophecy point even further toward the future (e.g., the Day of the Lord)?

CHAPTER 8

DIG DEEP—WORD LEVEL

Study Individual Words

Dr. George Guthrie, professor of Bible at Union University in Jackson, Tennessee, told this story.[i]

> One of my favorite little stories is about a lady stockbroker. This lady stockbroker was making a lot of money for a sheikh, and the sheikh decided that he wanted to do something nice for this lady stockbroker, and so he said, "Well, let me buy you something. I want to buy you a very fancy car. I'd buy you a house. You've made me millions and millions of dollars. Let me just buy you a nice house."
>
> And she kept saying, "No, I was just doing my job. You don't need to do that." But he kept pestering her. So finally she said, "Well, I'll tell you what. I'll let you buy me a set of golf clubs. I've taken up golf and I enjoy playing golf, so if you want to buy me a nice set of golf clubs, that will be fine."
>
> Well, she didn't hear from him for several weeks and she thought, well, he's probably forgotten it and it has gone off his radar screen. But then she got a letter in the mail and it was from the sheikh, and the sheikh wrote to her and said, "Dear Madam, I want you to know that I'm working on the golf clubs. I've bought three so far and two of them have swimming pools."

A word study would have been helpful to determine if the stockbroker had been talking about golf clubs or *golf clubs*. Translating between different languages and different cultures can leave us with inadequate understanding if not misinterpretation. Thoughtful proclaimers want to understand fully and correctly what they proclaim. Therefore, we must keep in mind that languages and the actual meanings of words change with time and from place to place.

What Are Word Studies? Why Do We Do Them?

Unlike any other great book we could pull off the shelf, the Bible is composed of Spirit-inspired words penned by humans over the course of thousands of years through many cultures and all across the Near East. The Bible was purposefully inspired in ancient languages and dialects that are no longer the vernacular. For this reason, the serious proclaimer of those words will want to look closely at the ancient words, study them, and find out how they were used and what they once meant. We conduct what we call "word studies" on the most significant words in our passages to make sure we fully understand them.

No matter how good it is, no one translation can ever fully portray the meaning of a foreign language. Language is not a code in which one set of Hebrew letters can be translated into one English word. For that reason, we consult a number of the best translations made by the best teams of scholars, and when in doubt or for more information, we consult lexicons (special Greek, Hebrew, and Aramaic dictionaries) and theological or exegetical dictionaries and word-study books. We compare the usage of our particular word in various parts of Scripture (particularly those parts written by the same earthly author or written during a similar historic time).

Easy Word Studies for Thoughtful Proclaimers

The following are six simple steps for completing a word study.

1. Identify the word you want to study.
2. Study the word in its context in English in your passage and the surrounding passages.
3. See how other translations of the Bible translate that word in your passage.
4. Look the word up in the appropriate ancient language lexicon. (More about that in a bit.)
5. Look the word up in an exhaustive concordance and see how it is used in different places in the Bible.
6. If you want to know even more, you can also look the word up in a theological dictionary.

We can do our word studies online, with computer software, on a smartphone with special apps, on the Internet, or with print books. The thought process is the same. It's just a matter of which tool you can most easily access and which are the best you can find. You will need the following tools:

- An interlinear (or reverse interlinear) or analytical key to the Bible that has the original language and an English (or language of your choice) gloss for each word. (English recommendations below.)
- An exhaustive concordance in the same translation as your primary preferred translation or better, a complete, original-language concordance for Greek and Hebrew.
- Lexicons for the Old Testament (Hebrew/Aramaic) and the New Testament (Greek). A lexicon is like a dictionary but the word you look up is in a different language than the definition is written in.
- An expository or theological dictionary or word book for the Old and New Testaments. Expository dictionaries go into much more detail than do lexicons.

If you don't read Greek or Hebrew, you may be asking, "How will I look up Greek and Hebrew words?" Every word in the Bible has been assigned a special number.[1] You'll use the code numbers or software that will make looking up the words easier.

So, let's try it out.

A Sample Word Study

IDENTIFY A WORD TO STUDY FROM YOUR PASSAGE AND LOOK AT IT IN CONTEXT

Let's say we are speaking on Exodus 34. Verses 1–10 are provided in the footnote below. I have highlighted verses 6–7 because they stand out as significant to the meaning of the passage. Particularly in verses 6–7, we observe the word *love*.[2] The ESV translation calls it "steadfast love."

A bit of background context: In Exodus 34:1–10, Moses was given two new tablets with the Commandments written by God because the others were broken during the golden calf incident.[3] So this passage is given as part of a covenant renewal between God and His people. Twice in this passage, "steadfast love" is used to refer to God's relationship to His people. In light of the people's unreliable love for God, God's steadfast love for them seems quite significant. We will begin a word study.

COMPARE TRANSLATIONS

When we compare several translations of Exodus 34:6–7, we notice that they translate this word as "steadfast love" (ESV and NRSV), just plain "love" (NIV), "lovingkindness" (NASB), "loyal love" (NET), "goodness" (v. 6) and "mercy" (v. 7) (KJV), and "unfailing love" (NLT). In Hebrew, there are many different words for *love*, some of which mean joint loyalty or obligation as we see in our passage.

In fact, the word *love* is used 745 times in the English Standard Version of the Bible. In Greek, there are also many words for love including the love of a spouse, charitable love, brotherly love,

---

[1] There are two sets of number codes for the Bible. The older one, based on the KJV, is called Strong's, and the newer one, based on the Greek and Hebrew manuscripts, is called GK after its authors, Edward W. Goodrick and John R. Kohlenberger. The GK numbers are also called G/K depending on your materials. We will call them GK for simplicity's sake.

[2] "The LORD said to Moses, 'Cut for yourself two tablets of stone like the first, and I will write on the tablets the words that were on the first tablets, which you broke. Be ready by the morning, and come up in the morning to Mount Sinai, and present yourself there to me on the top of the mountain. No one shall come up with you, and let no one be seen throughout all the mountain. Let no flocks or herds graze opposite that mountain.' So Moses cut two tablets of stone like the first. And he rose early in the morning and went up on Mount Sinai, as the LORD had commanded him, and took in his hand two tablets of stone. The LORD descended in the cloud and stood with him there, and proclaimed the name of the LORD. **The LORD passed before him and proclaimed, 'The LORD, the LORD, a God merciful and gracious, slow to anger, and abounding in <u>steadfast love</u> and faithfulness, keeping <u>steadfast love</u> for thousands, forgiving iniquity and transgression and sin, but who will by no means clear the guilty, visiting the iniquity of the fathers on the children and the children's children, to the third and the fourth generation.'** And Moses quickly bowed his head toward the earth and worshiped. And he said, 'If now I have found favor in your sight, O LORD, please let the LORD go in the midst of us, for it is a stiff-necked people, and pardon our iniquity and our sin, and take us for your inheritance.' And he said, 'Behold, I am <u>making a covenant</u>. Before all your people I will do marvels, such as have not been created in all the earth or in any nation. And all the people among whom you shall see the work of the LORD, for it is an awesome thing that I will do with you'" (Exodus 34:1–10).

[3] While Moses was on the mountain receiving the commandments from the LORD, the people made a golden calf and began to worship it. When Moses saw what they had done, he threw the stone tablets God had written down and broke them. See Exodus 32 and Deuteronomy 9.

devotion, and greedy craving. When we are speaking on a passage about love, we want to know what kind of love our passage has in mind.

FIND THE GREEK OR HEBREW WORD BEHIND OUR WORD

It is clear from the different translations of the wore *love* in our passage that this important word has a nuanced meaning. We always want to get to the root of a key word and find out what the Greek or Hebrew word behind the English word is. We want the original word, not the English translation in order to teach or preach on this passage properly.

Using either an interlinear Bible[4] (with numeric codes for each Greek or Hebrew word) or preferably a reverse interlinear Bible (which has the English on top), or an analytical Bible with the original language and then an English gloss, we will find that the original word behind "steadfast love" is actually the Hebrew word *hesed*. If you do not know Greek or Hebrew, your interlinear Bible must have Strong's numbers or GK numbers so you can look up more information on the word you want. If you are using an analytical Bible, it should be keyed to a lexicon. The Strong's number for *hesed* is 2617 in the interlinear translation below.[5]

If you would like to use a book rather than the Internet or software, for the Old Testament, use John Joseph Owens's *Analytical Key to the Old Testament* (AKOT), which has a brief English gloss for each Hebrew word and the page number to find the words in the *Brown–Driver–Briggs Hebrew English Lexicon* (BDB) (which has an index to the Strong's numbers in the backs).[ii] For the NT, the best resource at the time of writing is William D. Mounce's *Interlinear for the Rest of Us: The Reverse Interlinear for NT Word Studies*, which contains its own Greek-English dictionary keyed to GK numbers.

The	LORD,	the	LORD,	a	God	merciful	and	*e* gracious,
•	יְהֹוָה 9	•	יְהֹוָה 10	→	לֵ֣א 11	רַחוּם 12	וְ 13	חַנּוּן 14
	yhwh		yhwh		ʾēl′	rǎ·ḥûm′	w	ḥǎn·nûn′
	3068		3068		410	7349		2587

slow to anger,		and	abounding	in	steadfast	*f*love	and	faithfulness,[7g]
אֶ֤רֶךְ 15 אַפַּ֙יִם 16		וְ 17	רַב 18	→	→	חֶ֥סֶד 19	וְ 20	אֱמֶת 21
ʾě′·rěk̲ ʾǎp·pǎ′·yim		w	rǎb̲			ḥě′·sěd̲	wě	ʾ*e*mět̲′
750 639			7227			2617		571

[4] Interlinear Bibles have the original manuscripts in Greek or Hebrew on the top line and the English underneath. Reverse interlinear Bibles have the English on top. Reverse interlinear Bibles are the easiest for non-Greek or Hebrew readers to use. Logos Bible software turns many translations into a reverse interlinear with the click of a button as seen above.

[5] We have chosen to display Logos software's reverse Inline Interlinear, which shows the ESV translation, the Hebrew manuscript beneath it (the little numbers beside the Hebrew letters tell you which order the Hebrew words actually go in), the transliteration to help you pronounce the Hebrew word, and the Strong's numbers so we can look the word up in lexicons and dictionaries that use Strong's numbers. Logos has many translations available in this reverse interlinear format.

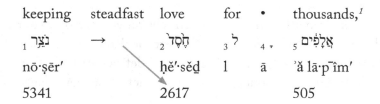

keeping	steadfast	love	for	•	thousands,[1]
נֹצֵר 1	→	2 חֶסֶד	3 לְ	4 ▾	5 אֲלָפִים
nō·ṣēr′		ḥĕ′·sĕd	l	ā	'ă lā·p îm′
5341		2617			505

LOOK UP THE WORD FOR STUDY IN A LEXICON

Lexicons provide modern definitions for ancient biblical words. Non-Greek and Hebrew (and Aramaic) readers will always need some way to link the foreign biblical word to the original language lexicon such as Strong's numbers or GK numbers or a key if they are using paper books. There are several lexicons keyed to the Strong's numbers on the market. Always use the most recent and best lexicon available. [6]

Note that some of the best lexicons are alphabetical according to the Greek or Hebrew but can be used by non-Greek and Hebrew readers with software or the Internet. If you are using any translation other than the KJV, you will benefit from buying newer tools that match your translation.[7]

If you have access to electronic or Internet lexicons or if you have a working knowledge of the Greek alphabet, consider the very complete *A Greek-English Lexicon of the New Testament and Other Early Christian Literature* by Arndt, William, Frederick W. Danker, and Walter Bauer published by the University of Chicago Press (nicknamed BDAG). And for the Old Testament, *The Hebrew and Aramaic Lexicon of the* OT (Leiden: E. J. Brill, 1994–2000) by Ludwig Koehler, Walter Baumgartner, M.E.J. Richardson, and Johann Jakob Stamm (nicknamed HAL). With software, you can use these fine lexicons without knowledge of the Greek of Hebrew.

---

[6] Strong's numbers are based on the KJV of the Bible, not the Greek and Hebrew ancient manuscripts, which are the basis of most of the better, newer translations. For this reason, Strong's numbers are incomplete, but nonetheless, they are generally quite helpful and widely available. Strong's numbers do not take into account homographs in the Bible, that is, words with the same spelling but different meanings. In English, we have homographs like bow and bow, but Hebrew has many more homographs. Dr. Strong, who worked out the system many years ago, also mixed Hebrew and Aramaic vocabularies (the two languages that make up the OT) into one numbering scheme, whereas modern lexicons treat them as different languages. Note that there are three words that sound the same as our word *hesed*, and two of them have the same S (Strong's) number due the fact that Dr. Strong's didn't separate homographs. One of these homographs that could cause trouble is our word. The word hesed1 GK H2875 means "disgrace" or "condemn." We are studying hesed2 GK2876. (The third homograph is GK2877 hesed3, a proper name). Finally, Strong's system suffers from some typographical and factual errors. For this reason, unless you work primarily in the KJV, you will want to use the newest and best lexical tools available to you.

[7] Dr. James Strong (1822–1894) and his many colleagues constructed an index of every original language word that underlays the King James Bible (the KJV is based on the Masoretic Text and the *Textus Recepticus*). Strong's index has been the gold standard for many years. However, Strong did not have available the texts now available to us that underlie translations such as the NIV and the ESV. For example, the New International Version (NIV) translations draw on manuscripts such as Biblia Hebraica Masoretic Hebrew Text, Dead Sea Scrolls, Samaritan Pentateuch, Latin Vulgate, Aramaic Targums, United Bible Societies' koine Greek editions, Nestle-Aland N.T.G. (based on Westcott-Hort, Weiss and Tischendorf, 1862). The English Standard Version (2001, ESV) draws on the Biblia Hebraica Stuttgartensia (B.H.S.) with Septuagint and the Nestle-Aland N.T.G. 27th edition. For this reason, Strong's numbers are not completely sufficient for those using newer translations though they are very helpful. For more on other translations see www.BibleStudy.org and Bible Translation Comparison Chart.

What Does "Hesed" Mean According to the Lexicon?

Using the Logos software reverse interlinear Bible in the diagram above, you see that your word for "steadfast love" is *hesed* in Hebrew—Strong's number 2617.[8] Your lexicon (in this case, we will use HAL, *The Hebrew and Aramaic Lexicon of the Old Testament*) defines *hesed* as joint obligation; lasting loyalty, faithfulness, favor; goodness, graciousness, Godly action, achievements; proofs of mercy.[iii]

However, in any one verse in which *hesed* is used, it cannot encompass all these definitions, so you must choose the most appropriate one. A word can mean only one thing at a time for the most part. (See "Semantic Range" below.) You will look for the definitions of *hesed* that fit your particular context and verse. If you happen to choose *Brown-Driver-Briggs Hebrew English Lexicon* (BDB), *The Hebrew and Aramaic Lexicon of the Old Testament* (HAL), or *A Greek-English Lexicon of the New Testament and Other Early Christian Literature* (BDAG), you will be able to see which one of these definitions actually fits the context of Exodus 34:6–7. You can visually scan down through the book or do a software search until you see Ex 34$_6$ or Ex 34$_7$ You will find that HAL has "abounding in faithfulness" and BDG has "kindness (lovingkindness) and fidelity."[iv]

Next Look at the Other Uses of Your Word in Scripture

A Bible concordance is an alphabetical listing of words in the Bible showing where they occur.[9] An exhaustive concordance is best for your use as it shows every word in the Bible with a brief context from every verse where it is found.[10] Your goal is to read through (if possible) all the uses of your word in the Bible. You are studying to find out how it is used in other parts of the Bible. (See "Semantic Range" below.)

Note that your exhaustive Bible concordance has to list the words in some way, either alphabetically in Greek or Hebrew, by the Strong's numbering system, the GK system, or electronically. If your exhaustive concordance is not in the original language, it must match our particular English translation of choice. So, if you used the NIV primarily, you would choose an NIV exhaustive concordance. (It doesn't matter which Bible translation you prefer to read, you will have to stick with one of them for your matching English concordance work. You have seen that many translators chose different English words to translate *hesed*, for example and you need to know which one to look up.) It is easiest to use the Greek or Hebrew word itself in an electronic concordance.

According to my exhaustive concordance, *hesed* is used 245 times in the Old Testament. When I skim through the verses listed in the concordance, I noticed that it is often used in describing the

---

[8] See footnote 6, which explains that there are three words that sound the same, and two of them have the same S number. *hesed*[1] GK H2875, means "disgrace" or "condemn." We are studying *hesed*[2] (GK number H2876).

[9] There are three main kinds of concordances. An exhaustive or unabridged concordance lists every occurrence of every word in every verse, including articles such as *the* and other insignificant articles, conjunctions, prepositions, etc. A good exhaustive concordance will also index the English words to the original biblical languages with those helpful S or GK numbers. A complete concordance lists every occurrence of every significant word in every verse ignoring insignificant words like articles and prepositions. A compact concordance lists only the most important occurrences of significant words in the most commonly read verses. Analytical concordances index the English words to their Hebrew/Aramaic and Greek roots.

[10] Some examples of exhaustive concordances are *The Strongest Strongs* by James Strong, John R. Kohlenberger III, and James A. Swanson; *The Strongest NIV Exhaustive Concordance* by Edward W. Goodrick and John R. Kohlenberger III; and *The NIV Exhaustive Bible Concordance*, Third ed. by John R. Kohlenberger III.

relationship of God to His people. Checking other translations, I found that the KJV translates it most often as mercy, though it is also translated as kindness, lovingkindness, goodness, favor, merciful, and mercies. The ESV translates it as love, kindness, steadfast love, loyalty, goodness, mercy, and favor. Now our curiosity is piqued. This is about us, about our God and how He feels about us.[11]

You will pay particular attention to how your word is used by the author of your Bible book if you know who that is. If you are reading a passage by Paul and look up one of Paul's words, youwill first want to know how Paul used that word and then how others used it. If you are studying a word in Lamentations, you woill want to know how Jeremiah used that word.

Find Words with Similar Meanings in the Other Testament

You are looking at both testaments for your context and understanding, even though they were written in different languages. So, you must consider which word the Greek New Testament used to refer to a topic and vice versa for the Old Testament. Your study of cross-references will help you. Software can help us. The best help for theologically important words will be an expository or theological dictionary.

Mounce's *Complete Expository Dictionary of Old and New Testament* says *hesed* is one of the richest, most theologically insightful terms in the Old Testament. It denotes "kindness, love, loyalty, mercy." Mounce compared it to the New Testament word *chrestotes* (GK 5983; S 5544), which means "kindness, goodness" and is used especially of God in Paul's letters.[v]

If you were looking at an Old Testament word, you might also want to know how the people of the first-century church understood it. The early church used a Greek Old Testament translation called the Septuagint.[12] For the most part, first century Jews did not speak biblical Hebrew but Aramaic or *koine* Greek.

In Exodus 34:6, instead of *hesed*, the Septuagint (Greek Old Testament) says God is *polyeleos*, "full of mercy." In verse 7, it says he "maintains righteousness and mercy" (*eleos*).[vi] This is how the early believers would have understood this passage.

Consult a Theological Wordbook or Theological Dictionary on a Word if It Is Theologically Important

When we come across a theologically loaded word (a term that refers to God or His relationship to His people) such as *hesed*, we will almost always want to look it up in one of two books. For

---

[11] A few paragraphs back, we were looking at the different translations of *hesed* in Exodus 34:6–7, but now we are looking at the different definitions of *hesed* in the other places it is used in the Old Testament.

[12] "This version [The Septuagint] with all its defects, must be of the greatest interest, (a) as preserving evidence for the text far more ancient than the oldest Hebrew manuscripts; (b) as the means by which the Greek Language was wedded to Hebrew thought; (c) as the source of the great majority of quotations from the OT by writers of the NT." "It derives its name from the popular notion that seventy-two (Septuagint means 70) translators were employed on it by the direction of Ptolemy Philadelphus, king of Egypt, and that it was accomplished in seventy-two days, for the use of the Jews residing in that country. There is no historical warrant for this notion. It is, however, an established fact that this version was made at Alexandria; that it was begun about 280 B.C., and finished about 200 or 150 B.C.; that it was the work of a number of translators who differed greatly both in their knowledge of Hebrew and of Greek; and that from the earliest times it has borne the name of 'The Septuagint,' i.e., The Seventy." M. G. Easton, Easton's Bible Dictionary (New York: Harper & Brothers, 1893).

the Old Testament, consult the *Theological Wordbook of the Old Testament* (or TWOT).[vii] For the New Testament, consult the *Theological Dictionary of the New Testament* known fondly as "Little Kittel" because the unabridged version of the *Theological Dictionary of the New Testament* is four volumes and goes into the development and backgrounds of words more deeply than is usually needed for teaching, a Bible study or writing a sermon.[viii]

Using the TWOT, we see the very interesting idea that the covenant mentioned in verse 10 is also mentioned in relation to God's steadfast love several other times in Scripture most notably in Exodus 20:6 and Deuteronomy 5:10 (both passages where the Ten Commandments are given). Exodus 34 is one of three passages where we are confronted with the idea of commandments and covenant being related to God's steadfast love. It seems God's *hesed* is somehow linked to humanity's obedience as well as God's mercy and long-suffering love. "The text of Ex 34:6–7 is fuller and more solemn, coming as it does after the great apostasy [the golden calf]. It was a tender revelation of God's self to Moses."[ix]

Sometimes, we might want to consult a Bible dictionary as well. In looking up the English word *mercy* (from the Septuagint), I found this quote, which seems to get at the root of *hesed*:

> In the Old Testament, the basis of God's mercy toward Israel is his covenant with Israel. Having established his covenant, he maintains it by his covenant love (Heb. *hesed*; …) and mercy[13] as well as by his judgments[14]. Since the covenant is established and maintained in history, God's mercy is known in specific historical acts.[15] Because God is known as merciful by his past acts of deliverance, his people can have confidence to call on him for deliverance in the present.[16] God's forgiving of his people's sins is a fundamental manifestation of his mercy.[17] The reversal from being forsaken by God to being received by his mercy is fundamental to the beginnings of biblical eschatology.[18] God's mercy toward his covenant people is sometimes portrayed as the love of a parent[19] or a husband.[20], [x]

Now we really understand the words *steadfast love*. We know the Hebrew word that was translated as "steadfast love," and we are aware that there is grace, mercy, and covenant associated with it.

Software and Internet Word Studies

The sample word study we just walked through noted the books one would use to conduct a thorough word study. Frequently, we are using computers, so we can use software such as Logos

---

[13] Exodus 33:19; Isaiah 63:7–9.

[14] Hosea 2:19 in Masoretic Text [MT] 21.

[15] e.g., Nehemiah 9:27–28; Isaiah 30:18–26; Jeremiah 33:24–26; Ezekiel 39:25–29.

[16] E.g., Psalm 57:1 [MT 2]; 123:1–4; Daniel 9:18.

[17] Psalm 25:6; 51:1–19 [MT 3–21].

[18] Cf. Hosea 1:6–7; 2:1 [MT 3].

[19] Psalm 103:13; Isaiah 49:15; Jeremiah 31:20.

[20] Hosea 3:1–3.

Bible Systems, Olive Tree Bible Software, Accordance, and others. Some of these systems come with the original language tools, and with others you purchase the tools you need separately.[21] The benefits of software are that it is portable; most work without an Internet connection, and many have apps that will work on a smartphone or pad. You can also try websites such as BibleHub.com or BibleStudyTools.com. A word of warning: "Free" can be good, but it isn't always best.[22]

Which Words Do I Choose for Word Studies?

There are many types of word studies. Sometimes, we simply define the word using a lexicon to understand the translated word more fully. Other times, we want to go much deeper into the background of a word to understand it well as we did above. We should choose to study in depth theologically loaded words or those used repeatedly in a passage or frequently in Scripture or words or concepts not easily understood by us. Consider studying imperative verbs.[23] Look for words that the passage meaning hangs on. Consider words that you have noticed are translated differently from one Bible to the next or words that seem to be problematic. Look for words that seem culturally loaded; for example, Zion, virgin, shepherd, scepter, remnant etc. Study difficult, puzzling, or unclear words. You will want to know what the Greek or Hebrew words meant when they were originally written.

Expository preaching in the first century.   *xi*

---

[21] I recommend Logos Software systems. Accordance is harder to learn. Olive Tree Bible has less current and less complete availability of books. With Logos, you can buy only what you need after purchasing a base system.

[22] Often, free commentaries and resources online are available for nothing because they are in the public domain, which means they were published before 1923 or are no longer covered by copyright laws.

[23] Imperative verbs express the will to influence the behavior of another. They may be in the mood of a command, entreaty, or exhortation. For example, in the phrase "Study that word!" the verb "study" is in the imperative verb. For further examples, see the appendix "Sample Grammatical Observations from Philippians 4:4–9."

The Importance of Semantic Range

Remember the golf clubs story? We learned from that the need to conduct word studies to help us determine if we are talking about golf clubs or *golf clubs*. Many words we use every day have what is called semantic range, and this is true of Greek and Hebrew words as well. We can hope to *run* away from that fact. Or we can *run* for president. How many ways can you think of to use the word *run*? All its meanings make up the word's semantic range. But we are interested in knowing only what *run* means in our particular context. If we want to know how to *run* a tractor, we don't need to know about your *runny* nose or the *run* in your stockings. For word meaning, context is king.

When you conduct a word study of an ancient word, you will find the whole semantic range of that word—all the different ways it could be used. You will need to study the context of your particular passage to decide on the correct meaning to choose.[24]

Walter Kaiser spoke to the need to narrow the semantic range down to one definition per use of a word as follows: "Any successful exegete must face the question of intentionality. We are most confident that the meaning of any given word (and therefore its text and context) will be discretely contained in a single intention of the author."[xii] God does not mean two very different things by one word in one verse, so we must decide using context which meaning is appropriate. Our lexicons can help, but in practice, it is up to us.

BiblicalTraining.org gives a great example of semantic range of the Greek word *charis*. In Ephesians 2:8–9, charis means "grace," "For it is by <u>grace</u> you have been saved, through faith—and this is not from yourselves, it is the gift of God—not by works, so that no one can boast." In Luke 1:30, however, the angel told Mary, "Do not be afraid, Mary; you have found <u>favor</u> with God." Here, charis means "favor." In Luke 6:32, *charis* takes on less of an "undeserved" meaning and more of a "good will earned" meaning, "If you love those who love you, what <u>credit</u> is that to you?"

Charis has a wide semantic range that must be considered. What if we translated Ephesians 2:8 with the wrong semantic meaning: "It is because of your good works that you earned your faith"? A lot is hanging on this, right? Let's do a quick word study of the word *charis* as it is used in Ephesians 2:8. Using an interlinear, we can see that it is Strong's number 5485. We could look up Strong's 5485 in a lexicon with Strong's numbers or look up *charis* electronically in *A Greek-English Lexicon of the New Testament and Other Early Christian Literature* (BDAG)[xiii] to see what they think. The same word is used in Ephesians 2:5, 7, and 8. We would expect that they are used in the same way. The primary meaning here is "a beneficent disposition toward someone, favor, grace, gracious care/help, goodwill." More specifically, the active form here in Ephesians 2 means, according to BDAG, "that which one grants to another, the action of one who volunteers to do something, not otherwise obligatory." And finally, we see that other passages and historical

---

[24] The tools we will use to help us most with semantic range are lexicons that indicate the exact verses where the words are used. (When in doubt, you can look the word up in a lexicon that lists every use of the word in Scripture like the HAL or the BDB or BDAG.)

references of *charis* in the active form denotes beneficent dispensations of the emperor or of Christ, who gives undeserved gifts to people.[25], [xiv]

Decrease the Number of Words You Need to Look Up

Unless you are using good software or become very good at word studies, you will want to study as few of the words in your text in depth as needed. If you are working sequentially through a book, you will find that the word studies become less frequent as you go because you begin to learn the vocabulary of the author and his subject matter—another great reason to work sequentially through entire books. For example, the apostle John used many loaded terms, but he used them repeatedly.

Do Word Studies on the Greek or Hebrew Word Only

I have been in several Bible studies in which the authors asked the students to look up an English word from a passage in a dictionary and look at its English meaning. Worse, they often ask you to write down all the definitions, the full semantic range. If you look up the word *darkness* in a dictionary, you will see the totality of its semantic range in English is very broad. [26] From now on, when you read *darkness* in 1 John 1:5 ("This is the message we have heard from him and proclaim to you, that God is light, and in him is no *darkness* at all"), you will look up (not darkness but) the real biblical word *skotia*.

We will see that the author John, in his gospel and epistles, often used *skotia* or "darkness" in a figurative way. Spiros Zodhiates, in his *The Complete Word Study Dictionary: NT* wrote,

> As light is not only the emblem of happiness but is also itself beneficial, darkness in like manner works unhappiness and death (John 12:35; 1 John 1:5, 2:8, 9, 11 [cf. Job 37:19]). Thus, *skotía* is not only a figurative term for sin itself, but also for the consequences of sin.[xv]

Such information is far more important for the expositor than a list of things the word *darkness* means in English.

Sometimes, it's easier to learn by example that the Bible was not written in English or whatever language you are likely reading it in. There are often several Greek or Hebrew words that are translated with one English word. This is because at times, Greek and Hebrew often have more words for one thing than English does. You want to know the Greek or Hebrew words, not the English one that was used for a translation. Let's say my passage for consideration is Luke 4:18–19 and I usually read the ESV. It says,

---

[25] Using other historical uses of the word in ancient literature such as the BADG does gives us a higher amount of confidence that the definition we are choosing is indeed the one the author intended when he penned the passage. Be very careful to use the same time frame however; you don't care what the word meant in classical Greek for example if you are reading koine Greek. See "Common Mistakes" later in this chapter.

[26] This is an unfortunately popular Bible study technique in some inductive methods, and I do not encourage it.

The Spirit of the Lord is upon me, because he has anointed me to proclaim good news to the poor. He has sent me to proclaim liberty to the captives and recovering of sight to the blind, to set at liberty those who are oppressed, to proclaim the year of the Lord's favor.

As proclaimers, let's find out more about the English word *proclaim*.

The Wrong Way to Do a Word Study

I see *proclaim* repeatedly, and I want to study it. It is used three times, and it seems to be a key word in my passage. I could look it up in an English dictionary, but that would tell me what *proclaim* means in English. I'd find that the third definition of *proclaim*—"to praise or glorify openly or publicly" (see footnote)—seems most helpful.[27]

If I consult my other translations and listen, listen, listen I will see that this word *proclaim* is translated differently. Studying only the English word *proclaim* I would therefore miss the multiple Greek words translated as "proclaim." We are again reminded that Greek and Hebrew are not codes with a one-to-one correspondence to English. Always find the ancient word behind the English word.

The Right Way to Do a Word Study

I'll do here what I should have done first (to review what we've done so far).

1. Compare several Bible translations.
2. Look at an interlinear or reverse interlinear Bible to determine the ancient words behind the English.
3. Look up the Greek or Hebrew word in a lexicon.
4. Look up the original language word in an exhaustive concordance to find its usage elsewhere in the Bible.
5. Check a good commentary and see if it mentions what's happening with these words.

If we look at Luke 4:18–19 in several translations, we see differences in the way the first, second, and third "proclaims" were translated.

I then use my interlinear or reverse interlinear Bible. When I do this, I notice that the Greek words for two of the uses of proclaim are different. I can see from my interlinear that the first proclaim in verse 18 isn't even there. The word is actually *euangelisasthai*, which comes from *euanglizo* and has the sense of "to bring good news." The second proclaim is *karuzai* from *karusso*, which has the sense of "to announce." Now I'm examining two different words, and I wouldn't have known that without checking an interlinear or Greek New Testament.

We next look up our word up in a variety of lexicons, theological dictionaries, or word study

---

[27] **pro•claim** \prō-ˈklām, prə-\ verb transitive
1a: to declare publicly, typically insistently, proudly, or defiantly and in either speech or writing: ANNOUNCE **b:** to give outward indication of: SHOW ⟨his manner proclaimed his genteel upbringing⟩
2: to declare or declare to be solemnly, officially, or formally ⟨proclaim an amnesty⟩ ⟨proclaim the country a republic⟩
3: to praise or glorify openly or publicly: EXTOL ⟨proclaimed the rescue workers' efforts⟩ **synonym** see DECLARE—
pro•claim•er noun (Merriam-Webster's Collegiate Dictionary. Springfield, MA: Merriam-Webster, 2003).

dictionaries that list words by their Strong's or GK numbers.[28] We learn that the first proclaim, *euangelizo,* in context actually means "to proclaim the Gospel or good news to the poor." The second proclaim, *karusso,* means "to announce publicly or preach." As proclaimers ourselves, we are gaining a sense of our mission. We then study the semantic range of the word *euanglizo* and consider which of those definitions fits the verse we are reading. We repeat this step for *karusso.*

We next use our exhaustive concordance to see where *euanglizo* and *karusso* are used elsewhere in the Bible. Finally, we will look up euanglizo and karusso in an expository or theological dictionary for deeper insight.

Some of the major words translated as "proclaim" are in Greek,

euanglizo—proclaim the gospel or good news to the poor
karusso—proclaim, preach
katangello—proclaim
apangello—report, announce, tell

Other Hebrew words translated as "proclaim" are

basar—publish, bear tidings, preach, show forth
qara—report, news, fame, rumor
shema—report, news, fame, rumor

Common Mistakes in Word Studies

The following are common mistakes when conducting word studies.

1. To conduct a word study or look up the English word when what we really want to study is the biblical word in another language. (We have already discussed this.)
2. To assume that a word means all its definitions at once. All words have semantic domains but can mean only one thing at a time.
3. To think that a word means its cognate. A cognate is a related word or a word that sounds similar. Perhaps you have heard that the word *power* in Greek is *dunamis,* which is the word we get our English word *dynamite* from. The story I heard mispreached over the years declares that *dunamis,* this power, is like the explosive power of dynamite. Interesting but misleading. Luke 4:14 describes how Jesus read the Isaiah scroll in the temple, which we were discussing a few paragraphs back in the "Proclaim" section. Jesus returned in the *dunamis* or power of the Spirit to Galilee.[29] The word has nothing to do with dynamite, explosions, or physical strength. The word *dynamite* has this root, but it was not invented in Bible times. My theory is that this is a common problem because when we are learning a language, we often memorize vocabulary by clinging to the cognates as memory aids. In his book on exegetical fallacies, D. A. Carson wrote, "Of course, what preachers are

[28] Remember not to look up "proclaim" but instead *euangelizo* and *karusso.*

[29] "And Jesus returned in the power of the Spirit to Galilee, and a report about him went out through all the surrounding country" (Luke 4:14).

trying to do when they talk about dynamite is give some indication of the greatness of the power involved. Even so, [Christ's power] is not dynamite, but the empty tomb."[xvi]

4. To decide what a word means by taking it apart, defining the prefix, root, and suffix, and then combining those definitions. The meaning of a word doesn't necessarily come from its etymology (e.g., the fact that the word *butterfly* contains "butter" and "fly" does not mean that butterflies are flies covered in butter). Try to stick with the lexical definition of the word.

5. To place too much meaning on any one word, even a key word in a passage, and think the word carries the meaning of the entire passage.[xvii] Just because you spent thirty minutes studying a word doesn't mean the Commander's intent for the passage is based on that word; the message is focused on the Commander's intent for the entire passage .

6. Just like English words, Greek and Hebrew words change meaning over time. The reason we suggest using the *Abridged Theological Dictionary of the New Testament* rather than the unabridged is that the unabridged version includes the meanings of Greek words over the history of the ancient Greek language. Knowing what the meaning of a Greek word was for Homer is not helpful in discovering what it meant in New Testament times.[xviii]

The point here is that a little Greek or Hebrew can be a dangerous thing. Use lexicons and dictionaries, but don't go beyond what the experts in them tell you. Trust the best translations. Use the newest and best scholarship and books available. And don't go out on a limb and teach something brand new that you just figured out and that no one else in the last two thousand years has ever guessed regarding the meaning of the ancient Greek or Hebrew words because you'll probably be wrong.

Write Your Own Paraphrase of the Passage

If we were skilled in Greek or Hebrew, we would just translate the passage. But if we don't know ancient Greek, Hebrew, and Aramaic, we can still make a reasonable paraphrase (at least for our own use) based on our grammatical study (see chapter 7), the word studies we have done in the last chapter, "Dig Deep—Ideas," and this chapter on defining key terms. At that point, we make the passage our own. If the passage is very long, for example, several chapters of the Old Testament historical narrative, paraphrase only the key verses or a key paragraph.[30]

We start our paraphrase by checking all the footnotes in a good study Bible to see if there are issues with the underlying manuscripts. Do different ancient manuscripts have variations in wording or the length of a passage?

We should write a paraphrase based on our study of the organization, the major ideas, subordinate ideas, and how the ideas are organized. We can include our own translations of words as well.

Compare the best translations. Then use your interlinear Bible, original language lexicon,

---

[30] At this point, you may be tempted to use someone else's paraphrase such as *The Message* by Eugene Peterson, *The Living Bible* edited by Kenneth N. Taylor, or others. *The Contemporary English Version*, while a translation, simplifies terminology and was meant for grade schoolers, second-language readers, and those who prefer its contemporary language. All three are good paraphrases of the Bible to read at later stages of your message development, but you will get more out of the process if you write your own paraphrase based on your own study first.

and the NET Bible notes.[31] If you are working through a whole book, I recommend purchasing the USB Handbook[32] for that book as it will be very helpful for your paraphrase.[xix]

Using your idea outline from chapter 7 and your thorough knowledge of the text, write what you understand to be the best translation, your paraphrase. The *Analytical Key to the Old Testament* that we used in our word study may be helpful for Hebrew passages. The New *Linguistic and Exegetical Key to the Greek New Testament* by Cleon L. Rogers Jr. and Cleon L. Rogers III can be helpful for the New Testament.[xx]

Compare the translation or paraphrase you made to the translations you have read. What differences can you find? Why are those differences there? Are the differences theologically significant? Since you are aiming for the author's natural meaning of the text, try not to put your own spin on it. It is better to use your paraphrase than someone else's as it builds your understanding of the text.

Listen with Your Heart

> Fellow believers, when we digest, absorb, and soak up the Word of the Lord, it becomes part and parcel of our daily lives. It is our delight. —A. W. Tozer

Okay, so that was a lot of digging. I'm exhausted. Just how well do we have to know this passage anyway? So well that it becomes part of us. A passage of Scripture is written in words, but there is much more to it than that. As important as all this studying of words and structures is, it is only a tool to help us dig out God's purpose, the Commander's intent for the larger passage.

Scripture or any other writing for that matter has meanings that are deeper than can be understood at first glance. Studying individual words, pulling out key words, and studying them in Greek or Hebrew, diagraming sentences, and studying the relationships between words are only the initial steps in understanding the practical meaning of the text.[xxi] Don't throw down this book yet—hear me out. Knowing exactly what the grammar and words say is the first step but not the most important step to understanding God's words to us.

In *Privilege the Text!: A Theological Hermeneutic for Preaching* Abraham Kuruvilla[33] wrote:

> Semantics is necessary for comprehension, but it is not sufficient, for there is a non-semantic part (i.e., the pragmatic element) to the interpretation of utterances and texts. This is to emphasize that there is more to understanding what authors are doing than just dissecting out the linguistic, grammatical, and syntactical [the way words are arranged] elements of what authors are saying. It is the non-literal nature of the doing that is the business of pragmatics.[xxii]

---

[31] The NET Bible or The New English Translation is a free, "completely new" online English translation of the Bible "with 60,932 translators' notes" sponsored by the Biblical Studies Foundation and published by Biblical Studies Press. Its notes are very helpful as you make your paraphrase. It is available at NET.Bible.org; *The NET Bible First Edition Notes*, Biblical Studies Press, 2006.

[32] *USB Handbook Series* (New York: United Bible Societies). These are useful for translators as well as amateur paraphrasers. They contain exegetical, historical, cultural, and linguistic information.

[33] Abraham Kuruvilla was Senior Research Professor of Preaching and Pastoral Ministries at Dallas Theological Seminary. His website is homiletix.org.

We study a passage of Scripture to learn the mind of Christ regarding that passage. We have the Holy Spirit as our guide.

> The natural person does not accept the things of the Spirit of God, for they are folly to him, and he is not able to understand them because they are spiritually discerned. The spiritual person judges all things, but is himself to be judged by no one. "For who has understood the mind of the Lord so as to instruct him?" But we have the mind of Christ. (1 Corinthians 2:14–16)

Haddon Robinson wrote,

> We are primarily concerned not [just] with what individual words mean, but with what the Biblical writers mean through their use of words. Putting this another way, we do not understand the concepts of a passage merely by analyzing its separate words. A word-by-word grammatical analysis can be as pointless and boring as reading a dictionary. If we desire to understand the Bible in order to communicate its message, we must grapple with it on the level of ideas.[xxiii]

When grappling with the ideas, we must include spiritual grappling. Some would say we are on dangerous ground. The specter of making the Bible mean whatever we want could be raised. However, the goal is not to make the Bible mean what we desire but to know what it really means. We want to know the deeper, fuller meaning that the authors had in mind—their intent—as best we can. We do this by observing all we can about a passage. But we don't leave it at the level of grammatical understanding. We will turn in the next section to the deeper meaning. We are going to live the message out.

Only through willing obedience can Scripture be really understood.[34] We're going to think of it in light of our own lives, the lives of our listeners, and the culture we live in, and then we'll meditate on it a bit. We'll analyze the entire passage using a few different methods to find the best fit. We want to know the Commander's intent and be ready to live it before we preach it.

> And you show that you are a letter from Christ delivered by us, written not with ink but with the Spirit of the living God, not on tablets of stone but on tablets of human hearts. Such is the confidence that we have through Christ toward God. Not that we are sufficient in ourselves to claim anything as coming from us, but our sufficiency is from God, who has made us sufficient to be ministers of a new covenant, not of the letter but of the Spirit. For the letter kills, but the Spirit gives life. (2 Corinthians 3:3–6)

---

[34] "They disagreed among themselves and began to leave after Paul had made this final statement: 'The Holy Spirit spoke the truth to your ancestors when he said through Isaiah the prophet: "Go to this people and say, 'You will be ever hearing but never understanding; you will be ever seeing but never perceiving.' For this people's heart has become calloused; they hardly hear with their ears, and they have closed their eyes. Otherwise they might see with their eyes, hear with their ears, understand with their hearts and turn, and I would heal them.'"'" (Acts 28:25b–27).

Questions for Digging Deep—Word Level

Identify and Define the Important Words

Find words that may require deeper study.

- key words
- difficult words
- repeated words
- unusual words
- words with similar meanings repeated
- words that all start with the same letter (in Hebrew) or that sound the same (in Hebrew, commentaries may be helpful here)
- words that are pronounced similarly but have different spellings
- words that have theological import
- words influencing the meaning of the text
- Here are some questions to ask.
  - What are these words in their original languages?
  - How do different translations translate these words?
  - What do they mean in their original language?
  - Where are they found in the rest of the testament that contains them (Old or New)?
  - What words in the other testament are similar? What do they mean?
- What significance did your word studies have in discovering the meaning of the text?

Write a Paraphrase or Translation of the Passage

- What textual difficulties do your Bible's footnotes reveal?
- Compare all the major Bible translations you use. What problems or differences do you notice when comparing the translations? How can you resolve them? (Commentaries may be helpful here.)
- Write out your personal paraphrase/translation of the passage or its key section.

Section 3

LIVE: A TRANSFORMATIVE HERMENEUTIC

CHAPTER 9

CONSIDER THE AUDIENCE: CULTURAL CONTEXT

On the Fourth of July in 1976, an estimated 400,000 people crammed onto Boston's Esplanade to hear the Boston Pops directed by Arthur Fiedler.[1] For over fifty years, Fiedler used his great skills as a musician, conductor, and showmaster to bring great music to the masses. His passion was to make world-class classical music available to a wider audience by making it less pretentious and more accessible to everyone. "This damned snobbism is the thing I've been trying to fight all my life, every chance I get," he once said.

The Boston Pops Orchestra recordings sold more than 50 million copies—more than any other orchestra in history. The Boston Pops made great music something people from all walks of life could call their own.

We have one more contextual signpost, one more context to examine, that is culture. We have to understand the people we are talking to. How can our passion for the masses be used to make faith in Christ accessible to people from all walks of life? Why would people from varying religious backgrounds or no religion at all want to hear our message and through us hear from God? How can we create a safe space with our message, our words, for the people who come to hear us, those who really need the message? What do we offer the skeptical, those who don't trust religion or feel comfortable with the idea of objective truth? What if we could make the Word of God attractive to people who previously knew very little about its message? Just as Arthur Fiedler brought the classics to the masses by making music more accessible and enjoyable, it is our job to make faith in Jesus Christ accessible to new generations.

Surprising and saddening to most of us is the fact that many people in our society see Christianity as a combination of judgmental convictions, sanctimonious moralism, and dangerous extremism. Others see all faiths as entirely subjective and even irrational. The view of many is, if it's good for you, fine, but it is presumptuous and arrogant of you to assume it is good for others. Faith, they think, is an entirely personal matter. Others see Christianity as one brand of religion among many valid belief systems. They don't see Christianity as objective truth, victorious life, goodness, or light. It's almost as though we were from two different planets—planet Us and planet

---

[1] The United States celebrated it's Bicentennial on July 4, 1976.

139

Them. We have to ask how we can join others in their world as Jesus did when He came to earth. What does it look like to be incarnational in our culture?

> Let each of you look not only to his own interests, but also to the interests of others. Have this mind among yourselves, which is yours in Christ Jesus, who, though he was in the form of God, did not count equality with God a thing to be grasped, but emptied himself, by taking the form of a servant, being born in the likeness of men. And being found in human form, he humbled himself by becoming obedient to the point of death, even death on a cross. (Philippians 2:4–8)

How can we reach into this other world? By talking to people, getting to know nonbelievers, making friends with those from other generations and cultures, keeping an eye on cultural trends, and asking the right questions including why our views are so different. When Jesus came into our world, He walked and talked with disciples, sinners, tax collectors, and even Pharisees.

We spend a lot of time studying and preparing to teach. Part of our work, our exegesis, should be spending time with all different kinds of people. If our preaching and teaching is directed only at other believers, those already in the church, those who speak our language and think as we do on many things, we aren't being incarnational as Jesus was.[2] We are preparing to give concerts to those who already like our music and inadvertently excluding the people who have never heard the greatest music of all.

Find out to whom people outside your own generation, church, or group listen to for information and to form their views. Find out how they think. Consider what they believe are the world's highest values and virtues are. Get to know what they are looking for in a church. Then invite them to a "concert" (your church or study) they can appreciate. When you speak, show them that you understand their viewpoint, include something new that they and those already established in your classes and congregations might not have heard before. I see some interesting lunch dates in your future.

Empathize with a Skeptic

Some people became Christians as children, know or associate only with Christians, and have never experienced any sort of doubt for as long as they can remember. If you are going to be a good missionary from planet Us to people from different generations or cultural spheres, you have to learn to ask their questions and understand their doubts and misgivings about Christianity. Those who can empathize with skeptics make great proclaimers. As you read Scripture, ask the hard questions, those a skeptic would ask. Allow yourself to disagree with the Bible momentarily for the sake of understanding what others find disagreeable in it. Don't be afraid to be honest with God about all your feelings. Pretend you are the neighbor who has never set foot in a church, or an angst-filled teenager, or your great-uncle the agnostic.

One of the greatest gifts I have received in preparation for teaching was a habit of my teenaged

---

[2] By incarnational, I mean representing God as Jesus did. Jesus was God with skin on, and that is what we need to be. "In your relationships with one another, have the same mindset as Christ Jesus: Who, being in very nature God, did not consider equality with God something to be used to his own advantage; rather, he made himself nothing by taking the very nature of a servant, being made in human likeness" (Philippians 2:5–7).

son, who would come into my office just as I finished a message and argue with me about what I was going to say. It drove me crazy, but after his arguments, I knew the weak spots in my message, the things some people wouldn't understand or wouldn't like. Listening for others and asking their questions is a great practice to develop even if you are using just your imagination.

The second gift that worked in my favor was a group of people who went through each passage with me before I spoke. These people were fairly homogeneous, but they were from different denominational backgrounds. Whatever you can do to interact with others, people from other cultures or spheres of life, will make your message speak to those who walk into your congregation looking for a message from God, a way to turn their doubt into belief.

Truly Understanding the Bible Requires a Step of Faith

Though we want to learn to empathize with nonchurched people, skeptics, and doubters, in reality, you must exercise faith to truly understand the Bible. To get beyond the basics of the Bible with a skeptic, we must on occasion ask them to set aside their doubt for a minute and listen to what the Bible says. Read the Bible with skeptics and doubters in mind; use your imagination to come up with what their disagreements will be. When we speak, we can ask our listeners to set those doubts or problems aside for the moment so they have a chance of hearing what God has to say.

Keep in mind that understanding and belief always require a leap of faith. Lesslie Newbigin wrote,

> If we are talking as the Bible talks about God, who is Creator and Governor of all things, who acts in specific ways, and whose purpose is the criterion for everything human, whether in the public or the private sectors, then there is an inevitable conflict.[i]

The conflict exists because to truly understand the God of Christian Scripture, we must be prepared to take a leap of faith, to step out into the unknown and reach for a God who can't be fully known.

> Faith alone is certainty. Everything but faith is subject to doubt. —Dietrich Bonhoeffer [ii, 3]

> [Jesus] made the disciples get into the boat and go before him to the other side … [hours later] the boat … was a long way from the land, beaten by the waves, for the wind was against them. And … he came to them, walking on the sea. But when the disciples saw him walking on the sea, they were terrified, and said, "It is a ghost!" and they cried out in fear. But immediately Jesus spoke to them, saying, "Take heart; it is I. Do not be afraid." And Peter answered him, "Lord, if it is you, command me to come to you on the water." He said, "Come." So Peter got out of the boat and walked on the water and came to Jesus. But when he [Peter] saw the wind, he was afraid, and beginning to sink he cried out, "Lord, save me." Jesus immediately reached out his hand and took hold of him, saying to him, "O you of little faith, why did you doubt?" And when they got into

---

[3] Dietrich Bonhoeffer was a German Lutheran pastor, theologian, anti-Nazi dissident, and key founding member of the Confessing Church. According to Wikipedia, he was born on February 4, 1906, in Wrocław, Poland. He died April 9, 1945, in a concentration camp in Flossenbürg, Germany.

the boat, the wind ceased. And those in the boat worshiped him, saying, "Truly you are the Son of God." (Matthew 14:22–33)

I love this story because Peter had faith but not enough on his own. He asked the "ghost" if it was really Jesus. Then he got out of his safe zone, the boat. He still didn't have enough faith, so he cried out to Jesus to save him. He would have sunk like a rock on his own. Even with his faith, he needed Christ's sure hand. This idea is key for speaking to a skeptic. Faith is not rock solid or it wouldn't be faith. We are asking for people to step out of the boat knowing they could sink. But if Peter had chosen to stay in that boat, he never would have experienced walking on water or felt Jesus' saving hand.

We have to call our listeners to take that first step outside of the boat though they don't know if Jesus is there or even if He is real. Acknowledge right away that you will say something that might sound countercultural. Ask people to set aside their judgments until they hear you out. They need to know that even the disciple Peter had only enough faith to take that first step. Then he began to sink until he cried out to Jesus for more.

What we all need is just a little bit of faith coupled with the humility to cry out for help. So, it is important for us to be practiced at listening with the ears of the doubters, those who've been hurt, those who have left the church, those who are angry at God, and those who can't bring themselves to believe in the supernatural. Ask questions, raise doubts, admit to misgivings and disagreements with God and with the Word of God. Write them down to grapple with prayerfully after you have listened well. These questions and doubts will help enormously as you prepare to speak to your listeners about their doubts or the doubts and arguments of society.

"There are some questions with no answers... and some problems with no solutions... As pastor, these will be your primary responsibilities." iii

Communicate That a Little Step of Faith Is Necessary to Understand the Bible

Communicate with skeptics that there is no perfect degree of faith this side of heaven. The Bible was written with the presupposition that everything it says is entirely true. Because the Bible is inspired by the Spirit of God it takes itself entirely at face value and holds itself up as the authoritative Word of God. Even so, the characters in the Bible were full of doubt at times.

David, Job, Habakkuk, Sarah, Mary were all real people who join us in admitting to doubts and fears about the goodness of God. We read the Word of God with the mindset that God is indeed God—the loving Creator, Governor, and Sustainer of all things. But as we preach and teach the Bible, we should balance these two truths; the Bible is written with no self-doubt but the characters in it, even the disciples, had some mistrust at times as to who God was or who He was not.

We balance these two truths in ourselves as we read. We believe the Bible is true and right in all it says yet we know there are people, and sometimes we ourselves, who have doubts about whether the Bible really is true, whether God really is good. We should cultivate a few friends to help us see the tough questions if we don't see them ourselves.

We assuredly do not understand fully what the Bible is saying in all places. We struggle with what it is instructing modern people to do. But we do find in its pages a close kinship with the characters who for all their distance from us in space and time are still very much like us in terms of their humanity, their doubts, and their fears. That will resonate with skeptics.

To understand who the God of the Bible is, we must, at least conditionally, accept what the Bible says about God to be His definition, His reality, His self-testimony. We have to believe Jesus is God and get out of the boat. Despite our doubt or that of our listeners, we can see Him and His mighty works in this messy and violent world as represented in the Book designed to show us God. We cannot truly understand the Bible if we are not willing to take the leap of faith to accept it as God's Word and believe it despite the fact that our earthly faith is never perfect.

The fallacy of skeptics is that they can't believe in God because He doesn't live up to their expectations of Him. That is circular reasoning. That is like saying you can't believe someone because they always tell the truth. In fact, if God really is God, would He fit into our man-made mold? Dietrich Bonhoeffer is often quoted as saying that, "A God who let us prove his existence would be an idol." Instead of explaining to Job why he had afflicted him, God recounted to Job who He really was. God showed Job the marvelous way He created the world and the wise, judicious way He governed it. God expanded Job's understanding of His governance of the world and caused him to perceive the limits of human understanding of the world order. God, by showing him creation, persuaded Job it was possible to believe He really was just and merciful and cared for every creature despite appearances.

When severe trials come, we cry out with Jesus His words on the cross, those words David also cried, in short, "Why?"[4] If we have ever asked why or questioned God's love for us, we can understand how our listeners sometimes feel. This ability to understand human frailty, the doubts about God and His love, and the temptations that beset us, make us powerful mouthpieces for God. Had we never doubted and never asked why, we would be useless for proclaiming. All the major characters in the Bible exhibited at one point or another a degree of fear, doubt, or sin.

In agreement with these basics, the thoughtful proclaimer is not afraid to ask questions. "If God is all love, then how could He …?" We come to Scripture not with ignorance or blindness but with respect for the Word of God and for others. We come with our testimonies of God's care for us. We have stepped out of the boat despite our fear so we can patiently lend others a hand as they too can put one cautious leg over the side. Sometimes we won't call for perfect faith but just for the first step.

---

[4] Psalm 22:1; Matthew 27:46; Mark 13:34.

BIBLE CONTEXT -> TEXT -> AUDIENCE'S CONTEXT-> COMMANDER'S INTENT

Learn to Ask Your Listeners' Most Challenging Questions

You are responsible for asking the questions your audience will have. If you speak to eighth graders, think like an eighth grader. If you speak to skeptics, be skeptical. If you speak to those who have left the faith and are now putting one toe cautiously inside the church door, adopt the mind-set of someone who has gone away from the fold and is searching for truth that works and accepts the prodigal home. If you speak to those who have remained in church all their lives and are still there more out of habit than choice, consider where they need to meet Jesus in their lives. Be aware that all kinds of people in all sorts of spiritual conditions are usually sitting together in the same row.

Aim every message at both the prodigal son who is thinking of leaving or has just returned home, the older brother who's been faithful all along and feels entitled to the blessing, the father who is trying to love them both well, and the self-righteous Pharisee who came to judge the others and especially came to criticize your sermon.[5]

Listening for your audience includes noticing where the story of redemption is in your passage, where forgiveness can be applied, and where salvation is spoken of or foreshadowed. Where is God's grace? What is God doing in this passage? Can God still work miracles? These are theological questions, but they are the questions that unbelievers in your congregation have come to hear answers to. Don't disappoint them.

For example, most of us instinctively reject the idea of a vengeful God. We may hear comments such as, "I couldn't believe in a God who would send people to hell" or "If there really was a God, He would never have allowed the holocaust." One late night on a long drive, I was listening to a podcast of a sermon from Redeemer Presbyterian. I realized that Timothy Keller too had faced people with questions like those. Permit me to share a part of this sermon as an example of preaching that takes the listener's misgivings into account.

In his sermon "Accepting the Judge," Timothy Keller explained why if there was no judge of the world there would be no hope for the world to improve and nothing could have value either good or bad.[iv] If there were no judge, the evil on this earth perpetrated by those in power would have no ramifications. (Keller had examined his audience and found their arguments against a God who judges the world as misguided.) In Keller's sermon, he paraphrased the Croatian theologian Miroslav Volf as follows:[6]

---

[5] We will be returning to Luke 15 in this chapter and in chapter 12.

[6] Miroslav Volf serves as the Henry B. Wright Professor of Theology at Yale Divinity School and director of the Yale Center for Faith and Culture at Yale University. Volf previously taught at the Evangelical Theological Seminary in his native Osijek, Croatia, and at Fuller Theological Seminary in Pasadena, California. His 1996 book *Exclusion and Embrace*, which has been paraphrased here, was named by *Christianity Today* as one of the 100 Most Influential Books of the Twentieth Century.

My thesis that the practice of nonviolence requires a belief in divine vengeance will be unpopular with many in the west, but imagine speaking to people, as I have, whose cities and villages have been first plundered, then burned, and leveled to the ground, whose daughters and sisters have been raped, whose fathers and brothers have had their throats slit.

Your point to them: we should not retaliate? Why not? [Keller interjects, What will ever keep them from retaliating?] I say this: the only means of prohibiting violence by us is to insist that violence is only legitimate when it comes from God. Violence thrives today, secretly nourished by the belief that God refuses to take the sword.

It takes the quiet of a suburb for the birth of the thesis that human nonviolence is a result of a God who refuses to judge. In a scorched land soaked in the blood of the innocent, that idea will invariably die, like other pleasant captivities of the liberal mind. If God were not angry at injustice and deception and did not make a final end of violence, that God would not be worthy of our worship.[v, 7]

Identify Your Listeners' Needs

To listen to Scripture well for the purpose of preaching and teaching, we must be aware of our listeners' needs. Scott Gibson quoted the nineteenth-century preacher John Kerr, who said,

> Therefore study people; know the souls before you. Know what they read; know their doubts, their besetting sins, their spiritual aspirations, their state of mind as influenced by the circumstances and current events. Then preach the truth in such measures, in such proportions, in such forms, at such times, as may seem best suited to bring men [and women] to Christ and to build them up in the Christian life.[vi]

Study your listeners. What are their needs? What are their fears? What are their doubts? What is happening in their world? Whom you are teaching will determine the kinds of questions you will ask in your cultural exegesis. Are you teaching an adult Bible class or leading a youth group? Is your congregation primarily biblically illiterate people, or have they been sitting under

---

[7] Let me further briefly paraphrase eleven pages of Keller's sermon. Keller preached that though we crave justice for those who commit atrocities and seemingly get away with it, none of us could withstand a judgment day that was truly fair—not those who rape and kill nor people like you and me who harbor sin in our hearts. If there were a judgment day, we would have no hope because the judgment of God focuses mainly on the heart, and it is conducted based on our knowledge, not an accounting of how many good deeds we've done. Keller claimed that something was wrong with our hearts that keeps us from doing all the good things we know we should do (1 Sam. 16). He asked if we have really done everything we know we should have done every single time. As we answer in our minds, Keller says, "Now that is terrifying." Our imperfection regarding the living out of what we know we should do means there is no hope for us. But, Keller continued, because of the Crucifixion, we have already had our judgment day. Jesus took on our judgment so we could have hope. Keller reminded us, however, that though Jesus was already judged for us, we are still being judged by people all the time for our looks, our bank accounts, etc. But in Christ, we can live between the judgments. Christians do not judge others because they know they are not superior to anyone; if justice were to be served, they would be in trouble. We can live humbly and with hope because neither the judgments of society nor the eternal judgment of God has power over us any longer. God has removed the curse. Keller concluded, accept Jesus as the weeping judge of your life. (Keller spoke to both the skeptic and the believer in this one message about being judged both for our sin and by society.) Timothy J. Keller, "Accepting the Judge" *The Timothy Keller Sermon Archive* (New York: Redeemer Presbyterian Church, 2013). Preached January 23, 2000. Logos.

your excellent teaching for a long time? Are you preparing for an evangelistically focused college Bible study or the new mothers' group? Are you ministering to people who have left the faith and are hoping God miraculously pulls them back to Himself?

The difficulty lies in the fact that some people listening to us—believers in Christ and those who are not yet believers—do not sense a need for change. They don't think they need Christ or at least live as though they don't. They do not see the Bible as an authority, or they act that way for practical purposes. Some will not acknowledge us as mouthpieces for an authority called God. Some in fact will consider our Commander to be a figment of our imaginations. They think they are plenty good enough, better than most, and that if there is a heaven, they will be going there. In their minds, all religions are equally valid or invalid. Often, Christianity is viewed as judgmental and backward, something much worse in a moral sense than no religion. Real Bible-believing Christianity is seen as a fundamentalist religion, a strong belief, which is dangerous and wisely avoided by intelligent and fair-minded people.

After we read our passage with an attitude of trying to hear it as the original audience did in Bible times, we should read it with our hearts, then one more time with the eyes of these people who we find filling our world. Those who are doubtful or agnostic, who seek justice and fairness for all yet who are hard pressed to define how that would work, for those who are suspicious of hypocrisy, cautious of authority, and perhaps those who feel a bit entitled to live in a perfect world where everything always works out for their immediate best.

Consider those hurt by the status quo, those who are unable to make it in the world as it now stands, those who have given up on the ideals they think we stand for as useless.

Whoever they are, get to know them, talk to them, read what they read, and listen to what they listen to. To identify their needs, ask yourself, *Why should they listen to me? What do I have that they need? How can I explain the intent of the passage in a winning and convincing way?* If you want good results, your preparation has to focus on the product, the people who need Jesus.

Include your listeners' questions but also ask some questions they may not have considered: Why do they need this message? What is God speaking about in this passage that points to their misunderstanding of the world as God designed it? What does God want to say to them from this passage? How should they respond to this message? What won't they understand?

What will most likely be their response to your message.

Watch Your Language! No Christianese

In an article in *Christianity Today*, Karen Swallow Prior wrote, "'I just wish Christians would learn to speak the world's language." She later wrote in her journal, "Learning the native tongue is one of the first tasks of any missionary to a foreign land. Why would it be any different within our own fractured culture?" She was referring to a serious misunderstanding that occurred when some Christians had announced that their city was a "battleground."[vii] They were referring to a spiritual battle, but nonbelievers, the press, and in fact, and the people of the town didn't understand the secret Christian code and felt attacked. They thought that a revolution of some sort was being called for, not a time of humble prayer and fasting. In an age of religiously motivated terrorism, comments like that are frightening.

A friend of mine who did not grow up in an evangelical milieu frequently asks me to translate when I say things that seem natural to me such as "I felt called to do that." For some of us, that sort of language is so habitual that we don't even notice that people don't understand what we're saying. When we preach and teach, we should be careful not to speak in Christianese or interpret what we are saying if we must.

Study Culture: Find the Sore Spots

What isn't working in our culture? Timothy Keller wrote,

> What in our passage crosses the cultural barrier so that everyone can agree? … What does the Bible say in this passage that goes against the commonly held beliefs of people today? … How can I graciously make the misguided cultural narrative of our listeners visible so that it can be discussed in light of Scripture?[viii]

Keller tells us that studying culture means finding the sore spots, the places "where people who don't believe in Christianity or God feel pinched, like feet in a pair of shoes that are too small, by their view of the world."[ix] "Preachers must know those sore spots and press on them with questions, offers, illustrations, and examples that make the tensions they feel more acute and the incongruities more troubling."[x]

To what end do we study our culture and make its inconsistencies apparent? We study our culture to show how the gospel of Jesus Christ and the Commander's intent for our passage provides a different and more complete perspective of the real world; we do so to show how the application of our passage can solve the problems created by following the invisible cultural path to its inevitable bitter end.

"How in the world did the early church rejoice with those who rejoice and mourn with those who mourn before Facebook?"[xi]

Questions for Studying Culture and Our Listeners

- What kinds of people make up my congregation?
- How does my congregation differ from me in their thinking and understanding of Scripture?
- What has been happening in the world lately that this passage reminds me of?
- What things will my audience have difficulty understanding?
- What things in this passage will my audience disagree with?
- Where does this passage differ from popular theological ideas my congregation or society holds?
- Who will stop listening to me and tune out?
- Why should they listen to me?
- Why should they hear this?
- How will I gain their attention or interest?
- What do they need? And do they know they need it?
- How can I make their need for this message clear to them?
- Why is this idea better than others in other religions or in secular society?
- Could my message come across as judgmental, hypocritical, politically incorrect, or mean spirited? How can I address that?
- Would a parable-like story or some other image of the application make the message more palatable for my listeners?
- Do I need to translate some ideas or common Christian or biblical words and phrases into a language that laypeople would understand?
- What invisible cultural belief or norm is touched on in this passage?
- What assumptions underlie the way this passage will be understood or make it difficult to accept?
- How can I address those underlying assumptions?
- What invisible rules in our culture "pinch" when we try to walk according to them?
- How does Jesus Christ, salvation, or the application of this passage run counter to culture?
- What about this passage points to a need for personal change?
- What are the biggest issues facing our culture today?
- What do people consider the biggest justice issues?
- How does this passage support and affirm those issues?
- How were the people this passage was written to at cross-purposes with the Commander's intent for this passage?
- How does this passage help us see the cultural issues of today in a new light?
- How can living out the purposes of this passage help us to live better lives?
- How does this passage cure the social ills of today?

CHAPTER 10

DECIDE ON THE COMMANDER'S INTENT

To get to the truth I recommend a plain text Bible and the diligent application of two knees to the floor. Beware of too many footnotes. The rabbis of Israel took to appending notes to the inspired text, with the result that a great body of doctrine grew up which finally crowded out the Scriptures themselves. —A. W. Tozer[i]

The most important thing proclaimers can do is to find God's, our Commander's, intent for a Scripture and let it transform our lives. We then make that intent clear and memorable to others, encouraging them to live it out by the power of the Holy Spirit and in grateful response to Christ's sacrifice.

A primary focus for the thoughtful proclaimer is what the passage says and more important, why it says it. We ask what God has for us to proclaim from His Word at this time and to this people? What is God's primary purpose for this passage of Scripture? Why did God inspire it to be in Scripture? What exactly is the Commander's intent for us and our listeners?

MULTIPLE PURPOSES OF A PASSAGE -> PRIMARY PURPOSE->COMMANDER'S INTENT

Putting our finger on that one primary purpose, the Commander's intent, for any passage often requires meditating on the passage with, as Tozer put it, "two knees on the floor." Other times, it is easy to spot because the writer states the Commander's intent as a universal and timeless principle for everyone. Learning techniques for deciding on the Commander's intent will help us do our jobs better and more easily.

We will learn the top ten (or so) methods for finding the Commander's intent. Choosing which method to use is kind of like trying on clothes. Some methods fit better than others. Others are more appropriate to certain kinds of passages or situations. Clarifying which method is best to use to find the Commander's intent for a story, poem, letter, or prophecy is usually not a one-size-fits-all proposition. We could try to force one method to fit all situations, but why? Looking at the jewel of Scripture from several angles helps us see it better.

You may want to try several different methods until you find the one primary point that relates to all the ideas in our passage, the message of the particular biblical author you are reading, and the situations of your readers. The tricky part can be finding how the Commander's intent differs from passage to passage week in and week out when teaching sequentially through a passage. The method that fit perfectly last week may pinch or be too loose this week.

Don't Panic When the Commander's Intent Is Not Clear

Unfortunately, like any battalion leader reading his or her orders, the Commander's intent might not be perfectly clear to us on occasion and the battle may be at hand. Our assignments are time sensitive; we need a message this week. Despite extensive and thorough exegesis and despite a lot of prayer, we will still sometimes have trouble identifying just one primary Commander's intent that clearly covers all the purposes of the passage. Don't stress; if we are teaching what the Bible says and we end up teaching a subordinate point from the passage occasionally, we will still be teaching the Word of God, and the Holy Spirit working in us can use it to transform others into Christ's likeness. There is no answer key for this test. Finding the Commander's intent is an art, not a science or a grammatical principle. Trust God, the Commander, to pull it together. The important thing is to stick to the passage, not preach on something else, and to preach with one clear ringing chorus, one purpose that came straight from our passage.

When my daughter Laura was in college, she took voice lessons, and whenever she was unsure of her voice and got kind of quiet, her voice teacher would call out (evidently in a loud, high-pitched voice), "Sing out, Lucile!" So, our family joke is that whenever we act unsure or timid, Laura calls out, "Sing out, Lucile!" Though the teacher got Laura's name wrong, Laura got the right message. As much as a thoughtful proclaimer will make every effort to find the proper key, the most important Commander's intent for a passage, it is better to give a clear call, a well-organized message on some point from the passage than to timidly stumble around making no clear point at all or worse, apologizing for what the Bible says. Sing out!

As you become more experienced with this inductive contemplative canonical theological exegesis method, you will find that some types of questions are more relevant to one kind of Scripture and others to another.

At first, skim through all the questions in the ends of the chapters or the Thoughtful Proclaimer Worksheet, prayerfully looking for the keys to the door that will reveal the Commander's intent. If you preach a sequential series through a book, you will have answered many of the questions found in the Thoughtful Proclaimer Worksheet in the Appendix during the first week or two. At the very least, your answers will provide you with more than enough working knowledge to prepare a teaching or message if not a whole book on your passage. The purpose of the thoughtful proclaimer questions is to help you wrap your mind around the passage.

> Do not be anxious about anything, but in everything by prayer and supplication with thanksgiving let your requests be made known to God. And the peace of God, which surpasses all understanding, will guard your hearts and your minds in Christ Jesus. (Philippians 4:6–7)

150

Shepherd or Hired Hand

In John 10, Jesus said He was the good shepherd. He knew his sheep though there were many. He made sure each of them knew Him.[1] He was the gate of the sheepfold deciding what got in and what got out.[2] The reason the Father loved Him, Jesus said, was that He would willingly lay down His life for His flock.[3] Picture Jesus lying across the opening to the sheepfold to keep the sheep safely in and the predators out. Picture Him giving up his life in fighting a wolf that had come to destroy one of the sheep. No one made Him give up His life, but He did so willingly.

Jesus, the perfect Shepherd, told this story to make it clear to the unbelieving religious leaders of his time that they were not acting as good shepherds of the people. You can tell a good shepherd, He continued, because he willingly lays down his life for his sheep.[4] Every day in small ways and sometimes in big ones, a good shepherd lays down his life for his flock.

A hired hand is not a shepherd. When the hired hand sees the wolf coming, he abandons the sheep and runs away. Then the wolf attacks the flock and scatters it. The hired hand cares nothing for the sheep. He works for his pay and nothing more, which isn't wrong necessarily, but a very different mind-set from that of a shepherd.

As leaders and teachers, we daily ask ourselves, Am I a shepherd of the sheep in my care or merely a hired hand? Am I a hired hand who guards and leads the sheep only when it is convenient? Where am I when the going gets tough and the way unclear? Where am I when trouble strikes and things begin to unravel around my flock or in my life? Where am I when the wolf attacks? Will my sheep awake from slumber to find me still lying faithfully in the gate? Am I leading my sheep to places of comfort and peace when all around them storms are raging? Am I up for the challenge of leading them through the tough mountain paths that will take them to the next level spiritually?[5] Are my sheep being fed a balanced and nutritious diet?

Jesus was the perfect shepherd, of course, but the reason the religious leaders got so angry at Him was often the quiet accusations that needled them when He spoke. These religious shepherds didn't catch the metaphor at first. But soon, some of them caught on to the fact that Jesus was talking to them, hired hands who led their sheep without really caring for them.

Jesus' words divide the sheep who know their Master's voice and comprehend His intentions from those who do not want to take the time to really listen. These words also divide the lowly shepherds (who are also wise, tough, brave, and loving) from the hired hands. Are we willing to lay down our lives for the sheep Jesus has put in our care?

A shepherd will carefully guard the gate of the fold to judge what comes in and what goes out. We could simply give an inspirational talk. We could preach on a verse or topic that stands

---

[1] "I am the good shepherd; I know my own and my own know me" (John 10:14).

[2] "So Jesus again said to them, 'Truly, truly, I say to you, I am the door of the sheep. All who came before me are thieves and robbers, but the sheep did not listen to them. I am the door. If anyone enters by me, he will be saved and will go in and out and find pasture'" (John 10:7–9).

[3] "For this reason the Father loves me, because I lay down my life that I may take it up again" (John 10:17).

[4] "I am the good shepherd. The good shepherd lays down his life for the sheep. He who is a hired hand and not a shepherd, who does not own the sheep, sees the wolf coming and leaves the sheep and flees, and the wolf snatches them and scatters them. He flees because he is a hired hand and cares nothing for the sheep" (John 10:11–13).

[5] On this point, I recommend Hannah Hurnard's *Hind's Feet on High Places*.

out to us. But a good shepherd will seek out the best food for his sheep and not leave them to graze on whatever they might come across or wander wherever they see a path. The thoughtful proclaimer, the good shepherd, will work diligently to find God's intent for the overall passage.

The Top Ten Ways to Find the Commander's Intent

The Commander's intent isn't one of the themes of our passage but one sentence that generally covers all the points of the passage. It is general enough to fit every situation that all our listeners will experience regarding it despite individual circumstances. Remember chapter 2 and the story of D-Day? Despite all the variables, the Commander's intent pulled everyone together because they all knew what the end was supposed to look like.

We've torn our passage apart, and we know it well. We've looked at the purposes of the passage as they pertain to the original audience and to our modern audience and to ourselves. We are ready to decide on the Commander's intent for the entire passage. Below are ten methods for taking the work you have done and determining the Commander's Intent from your study.

In the closing chapters, we will turn the Commander's intent into a point for proclamation we can build our sermon or teaching around. Finally, we'll develop a short catchphrase and find an anchor image to make our message stick in our listeners' minds.

THE PURPOSES OF THE PASSAGE ->COMMANDER'S INTENT-> POINT FOR PROCLAMATION ->MESSAGE STRUCTURE-> CATCHPHRASE AND ANCHOR IMAGE

Passage Structure

A good basic way of finding the Commander's intent for a passage if we have marked the beginning and the end of the passage well is to look at the first paragraph.[6] If we have torn our passage down into large idea chunks, we may have found it already. The Commander's intent is quite often in the first sentence of the main paragraph or the first paragraph of a longer section.

This is particularly true of whole books of the Bible. We will often find the book's purpose at the start, sometimes at the end, and sometimes in both places. The difficulty arises in teaching a very long narrative passage when the Commander's intent lies at the beginning of the book and not clearly in the preaching or teaching passage itself. It is also difficult to decide on one Commander's intent in poetry, where the main message of the passage may be repeated in different ways throughout the psalm.

If there are several paragraphs in our chosen passage, sometimes, the main paragraph is the first paragraph, and then the author develops his meaning in the other paragraphs. Other

---

[6] Randal E. Pelton teaches that the subject is often stated in the first sentence of a properly chosen passage.

passages have the Commander's intent right in the middle of a passage (chiastic structure),[7] or the author may use an inductive structure in which the passage builds up to his main message, the Commander's intent, stating it clearly at the end.[8]

Looking for the Commander's intent for 1 Peter 4, I went back to the very beginning of the book and found that Peter was writing to the church suffering trials.[9] They were to live in the hope of the Resurrection, knowing that when genuine faith is tested, it results in Jesus Christ being glorified.

The rest of the letter notes the best way to live under such trials if we are to bring glory to Christ. If I were teaching on 1 Peter 4 specifically, I would want to keep the Commander's intent for chapter 1 in mind since it was the author's reason for writing. Peter said that Christ suffered too so we should think as He did when we are suffering.[10] The rest of the chapter addresses how to do that. What a great teaching series 1 Peter would be!

---

[7] Chiasm is a literary structure that occurs in all kinds of literature, but it is most striking in poetic literature. The word chiasm comes from the Greek letter *chi*, which is written as an *X*. Chiasms have parallel structures, ideas, or lines that are repeated or contrasted on both ends of a passage. In other words, there is a sequence of ideas—A, B, C, D—followed by the reverse sequence of the same or contrasting ideas—D, C, B, A. The center of the passage, the center of the X, will contain the main idea of the passage if indeed the author meant for it to.

There is much you can glean from noticing chiasm, but for our purposes, we are simply concerned with learning to notice chiasms because they are like the bull's-eye on a target; they focus our eyes to the author's central meaning. See Isaiah 1:21–26 for a chiasm with the central point at 23b: "They do not bring justice to the fatherless, and the widow's cause does not come to them." Sometimes, the central meaning is given at the outer ends of the X as in Amos 5:4–6 where "Seek God and live" is the Commander's intent.

[8] A trickier example: any one of the psalmist's points in Psalm 23 would make a good message. However, to be true to God's Word, we are looking for the central theme and why God put it there. The Commander's intent could be in verse 1: "Lift up your soul to God." The rest of the psalm describes how to lift up your soul. You might decide the Commander's intent is in verse 22 (claiming the promises of Israel for the believer in this case): "O God, redeem our troubled lives." Again, the passage describes our prayers as we call for our troubles to be redeemed by God. Still others would claim there is a chiastic structure here, placing the Commander's intent smack dab in the middle: "The one who fears the LORD abides in God's favor." You have to pick just one; you can't have three Commander's intents. Using the structure of the passage as a guide, you can choose: "Lift up your soul to God," "Redeem our troubled lives, O God," or "The one who fears the LORD abides in God's favor."

You can, however, combine these three key points into one overarching sentence that covers the whole chapter; this is perhaps the best solution for a passage like this. Our Commander's intent is for us to: "In reverence ... lift our souls to God praying to Him to redeem us from trouble, and so abide in His favor." This covers both the positive and negative themes of the passage, which can be your points as long as you keep returning to the CI.

One mistake that we could have made is to say "*If* we lift our souls to God, *then* He will redeem us from trouble." But the passage is not offering an if-then proposition. Poetry does not carry promises but general precepts. This is not a promise but rather a guide for prayer. My ESV Bible entitles this psalm "Teach Me Your Paths," and that is one of the nice, shiny lines in the poem. But the titles and headings in our English Bibles are not the inspired Word of God, so we will try not to let them influence our decision.

Looking ahead to chapter 13 where we will turn this Commander's intent into a point for proclamation, we might have as our main sermon point, the point for proclamation, something like, "Put your trust in God." This is an overarching point that will fit the main points of each of the paragraphs (or strophes) in this psalm.

[9] "Blessed be the God and Father of our LORD Jesus Christ! According to his great mercy, he has caused us to be born again to a living hope through the resurrection of Jesus Christ from the dead, to an inheritance that is imperishable, undefiled, and unfading, kept in heaven for you, who by God's power are being guarded through faith for a salvation ready to be revealed in the last time. In this you rejoice, though now for a little while, if necessary, you have been grieved by various trials, so that the tested genuineness of your faith—more precious than gold that perishes though it is tested by fire—may be found to result in praise and glory and honor at the revelation of Jesus Christ" (1 Peter 1:3–7).

[10] "Since therefore Christ suffered in the flesh, arm yourselves with the same way of thinking" (1 Peter 4:1a).

Key Verse or Phrase

Look for the key phrase or a key group of verses in the passage. The key verses should stand out theologically; they may relate to salvation, forgiveness, God, Christ, or something else.

In the narrative passage of Acts 15, Luke was writing about the Jerusalem council and how some people claimed believers had to be circumcised to keep the law of Moses and be saved. The key verses of the chapter in my opinion are 7–11.

> After there had been much debate, Peter stood up and said to them, "My brothers, you know that in the early days God made a choice among you, that I should be the one through whom the Gentiles would hear the message of the good news and become believers. And God, who knows the human heart, testified to them by giving them the Holy Spirit, just as he did to us; and in cleansing their hearts by faith he has made no distinction between them and us. Now therefore why are you putting God to the test by placing on the neck of the disciples a yoke that neither our ancestors nor we have been able to bear? On the contrary, we believe that **we will be saved through the grace of the Lord Jesus, just as they will**." (Luke 15:7-11 emphasis added.)

Voilà! The Commander's intent is that all people, Jew and Gentile, are saved not by keeping the law but when their hearts are cleansed by faith through the grace of the Lord Jesus.

Be careful—sometimes, the shiny memory verse is not the Commander's intent for the passage. Read the entire passage to be sure. Structure always trumps subjective emotional aesthetics when it comes to the Commander's intent. We will not leave that beautiful verse out of our message; rather, our message will use that beautiful verse to support the Commander's intent and point for proclamation. Once we find the Commander's intent, the diamond at the center of our message, we can place the beautiful verses like jewels around it to enhance our message.

For example, in Isaiah 1, the shiny memory, the sparkling jewel is:

> "Come now, let us reason together," says the LORD:
> "though your sins are like scarlet,
> they shall be as white as snow;
> though they are red like crimson,
> they shall become like wool"
> (Isaiah 1:18)

But the Commander's intent, Isaiah's intent in speaking as God's mouthpiece, is that God's children should realize they are guilty before God due to their rebellion. We see this idea first in verse 1, and it is repeated throughout the passage with examples and results of that guilt. Sometimes, as is the case in Isaiah 1, the Commander's intent is not found in the most attractive verses; those verses are the solution, the conclusion, or the application. "Though you are guilty and your sins are like scarlet, God offers to wipe them away." Sometimes the bright, shiny memory verse may be the perfect catchphrase for your message. (See chapter 13 for more on catchphrases. There is a sample Bible teaching in the appendix on Isaiah 1.)

Repeated Themes

Look for repeated words, ideas, and themes. Finding repetition is common in Old Testament narratives. For example, in Joshua 1, "Be strong and courageous" is a repeated phrase. But each time it is used, the sentence concludes differently. In Joshua 1:6, we are encouraged to be strong and courageous because of God's promises. In verse 7, we are to be strong and courageous but be careful to keep the laws of Moses and to keep this Book (the Bible) at the center of our lives. In verse 9, we are to be strong and courageous because God will be with us. Also repeated throughout this passage are the importance of the Book of the Law and the offer of success for those who do what it says. In case we missed the Commander's intent, Joshua repeated it at the end of the chapter in verse 18—"Be strong and courageous."

> Only be strong and very courageous, being careful to do according to all the law that Moses my servant commanded you. Do not turn from it to the right hand or to the left, that you may have good success wherever you go. This Book of the Law shall not depart from your mouth, but you shall meditate on it day and night, so that you may be careful to do according to all that is written in it. For then you will make your way prosperous, and then you will have good success. (Joshua 1:7–8)

Our Commander's intent, then, is "Be strong and courageous by living in the Word of God and believing his promises." Following suit, our point for proclamation catchphrase is, "Be strong and courageous." The points of our message are taken from the remainder of verses 6–9 and our conclusion from verse 18. The application for the message can be built on the modern-day equivalents of moving into the Promised Land even though we are afraid.

Hebrew often uses similar or even identical words to repeat the same idea, whereas English translations may vary word choice to avoid repeating the same word. If you see several words that have similar meanings, check an interlinear Bible, sound out the words, and look for similar sounds, meanings, or alliteration (same sound at the beginning of the word). You might need to check a commentary for elements such as wordplay, similar-sounding words in the ancient language, or other literary devices the original author used in his foreign vernacular that are not evident in English.

Sometimes, we are assisted by a repeated theme throughout the book. For example, the word *rejoice* is repeated nine times in the short book of Philippians. This offers us a clue as to what God intended for the book—though considering Paul's circumstances, rejoice does not capture the theme of every passage in Philippians.[11]

---

[11] Just because a word or theme is repeated several times does not mean it is the only possible theme of every passage in that book, nor does it mean that the Commander's intent for a passage has to include that theme. Philippians 4 reveals how Paul could rejoice despite his circumstances. When I was preparing a teaching on this chapter, I considered several themes: Philippians 4:6–7 (don't be anxious but pray while giving thanks), 4:8–9 (focus on the good things you see and what you have seen in Paul), and 4:10–12 (learn to be content in all circumstances). Verse 13 gave me the key I needed: "I can do all things through Christ who strengthens me." I could have used that statement as my Commander's intent based on the structure of the passage, but it seemed more like the finale than the main point of the passage. So based on repetition, I chose the themes of "peace and contentment" rather than "rejoicing" for chapter 4. My Commander's intent was, "Be content and at peace by looking to Christ who offers us His strength." Since chapter 4 feels kind of tacked on to the end of the book of Philippians, I titled this message: "P.S.: Paul's Secret to Contentment." My major points included, Make peace with others a priority (vv. 2–5), Have peace within yourself (vv. 6–9), and Be at peace with God (vv. 10–19). The Commander's point for proclamation was, "I can do all things through Christ."

"Big Idea"

Haddon Robinson taught that the subject of a passage was the answer to the question, "What is the passage talking about?" The complement to the subject is the answer to the question, "What is the passage saying about the subject?"[ii] Though this is a good starting place for finding the main theme of many passages, the big-idea method does not always equate exactly with the Commander's intent for the passage without adding some other tools, deeper thinking, and more questioning of God's motives for placing the passage in the Bible. The big idea of the passage must be adapted to find the specific purpose of a passage for our specific audience especially in narrative and law portions of the Bible.

The Commander's intent and particularly our point for proclamation is focused not only on the subject and complement or theme but also on transformation and application. However, knowing the theme is often very helpful in identifying the Commander's intent.

To determine the Robinson big idea of a passage, decide on the main subject of the passage and formulate questions to help you decide what the passage is saying about the subject. Ask and answer questions using the interrogatives what, who, when, where, and why. These interrogatives will give you at least five ways to narrow the subject of the big idea of a passage down. Then you will decide what the passage is saying about the subject, and that is the complement. So, for John 3:16 we might say the subject is "God." The interrogative we might choose to narrow down our subject is "what." That gives us, "God what?" Our subject would then be the answer the passage gives us, "God loved." The complement of the big idea is what the passage is saying about the subject. The big idea combines the subject and complement into one statement of the "big idea." For John 3:16 we might have, (subject) "God loved" (complement) "so he sent His son." That is a big idea![12] For more help on this method, see *Biblical Preaching: The Development and Delivery of Expository Messages.*

Theology

Sometimes, we have to work hard to find the takeaway. This is especially true in passages where the main idea seems antithetical to the rest of the Bible. In these cases, we look to theology and study the rest of the canon for help in understanding the Commander's intent. Because our theology is built on Scripture, we can trust that other Scriptures will shed light on what might

---

[12] Jeffrey Arthurs and Randal Pelton, at Gordon Conwell, suggested finding the "big idea" by identifying the subject of the passage and then asking ourselves which question the passage answers about that subject. We considered the following for each passage: 1) the text's "big idea;" 2) the contextual "big idea," which is the "big idea" of the passage in its context or in its book; 3) the canonical "big idea," or the "big idea" in light of the entire Bible; and 4) the homiletical "big idea," which is congruent to our Commander's point for proclamation. For example, for Matthew 8:1–13, you might conclude that the subject is "Jesus."

Text BI: Jesus worked miracles in response to people's faith and to emphasize to His followers that faith was the key to the kingdom of heaven.

Contextual BI: Faith is the key to miracles and to the kingdom of heaven.

Canonical BI: Many will come from the east and the west to the kingdom of God. Those who feel most entitled will be cast out, and those with faith will not only be invited to the wedding banquet of the Lamb but will in fact be the bride of Christ clothed in the righteousness of the saints.

Homiletical BI (and the point for proclamation): Faith is the key.

Commander's intent: Eternal life is offered to all based on faith, not on religious credentials (v. 11–12).

be a troubling subject.[13] This is also very helpful for Old Testament passages. For example, Ezra 9 and 10 discuss marrying outside the Jewish faith. Ezra and all the people were feeling very guilty for having wives and children who were not believers in the Lord and who practiced the religions of neighboring peoples. I might conclude this to mean that if you are a believer married to an unbeliever, you are called to leave your wife and unbelieving children. However, if we look at the theology behind this passage, we see that it is not a call to divorce but to holiness and purity.

Using our cross-references on the subject, we find that in 1 Corinthians 7:12–16, Paul said that if someone became a believer and his or her unbelieving spouse consented to stay with them, the unbelieving spouse was made holy by the believing one.[14] Always consider the theological principles and the historical context. Temper the Old Testament with the New, and inform the New Testament with the Old.

The Book's Purpose

Preaching on Job was great fun, but somewhere in the middle, I began to get lost in all the arguing. So, each week, I returned to the beginning and the ending of the book, which is, as we have discussed, most often where the author gives us his primary message. The Commander's intent for Job might be distilled from these verses: Job 1:21, "The LORD gave, and the LORD has taken away; blessed be the name of the LORD," and Job 42:2ff, "I know that you can do all things, and that no purpose of yours can be thwarted."

Knowing the Commander's intent for the entire book helped to inform me of the Commander's intent of each passage and became the Commander's stealth intent for every passage I taught that veered to the right or left of it. We can more easily understand the passage at hand if we remember that the books purpose has already been stated.

The overall Commander's intent for Job, then, might be that God is big enough to trust. The writer of Job does not explain the causes of all suffering especially when the good suffer; he does not tell us why bad things happen to good people. Job illustrates God's trustworthiness; over time, Job learned that God was big enough to be trusted despite his questions and doubts and the good (but not fully correct) advice from friends. Just as we have often done nothing to deserve suffering, there is nothing we can do to deserve God's gracious gift of salvation.

By now, you have probably concluded that these methods are all very similar. You are right; they are all ways of looking at the same thing, the Commander's intent. The fact that these methods overlap means that when in doubt, you can employ several methods to double-check your choice for the Commander's intent.

---

[13] Speaking on Romans 9:1–18 (which might not have been the best place to divide the passage, but that's what I chose), I experienced a problem. This passage includes the troubling verse "Jacob I have loved, but Esau I hated." I hated that verse. The key to the Commander's intent is found theologically by examining the passage in light of the whole message of Romans and the whole of Scripture. My Commander's intent was "God calls some so that all will come to Him." Verse 17 is key: "For this very purpose I have raised you up, that I might show my power in you and that my name might be proclaimed in all the earth."

[14] "If any woman has a husband who is an unbeliever, and he consents to live with her, she should not divorce him. For the unbelieving husband is made holy because of his wife, and the unbelieving wife is made holy because of her husband. Otherwise your children would be unclean, but as it is, they are holy" (1 Corinthians 7:13–14).

The Ladder of Abstraction—Two Variations

The ladder of abstraction (different from the quagmire of distraction where I sometimes end up) finds the ancient specific situation (e.g., don't muzzle oxen when they are treading grain[15]), moves up the ladder to the institutional or personal norm (treat animals and those who serve us fairly so they do not need to steal or covet), and arrives at the general principle (be fair and kind to all God's creatures). Descending the ladder brings us to the theological and moral principle behind our general principle (love your neighbor as yourself). And at the bottom is the specific principle (treat employees and those who serve you with respect and pay them fairly). Both Kaiser (7) and Sunukjian (8) use variations of the ladder of abstraction as you will see below in "Principalization" and "Truth Outline."

THE LADDER OF ABSTRACTION—PRINCIPALIZATION

Walter Kaiser bridges the gap between "then" and "now" by what he calls principalization. The first step is to determine the subject or focal point of the passage (usually stated directly in the passage). Second, he recommends we seek the emphasis of the passage by identifying the repeated or key words. Third, we determine how the message was structured by the author. Fourth, we decide on a principle for each paragraph (in prose), scene (in narrative), or strophe (in poetry). Finally, express the principles in terms of first person pronouns (e.g., "let us …," "we must …," "it's our job …").[iii]

Principalization can unfortunately end up in creating three or four mini messages instead of one coherent message but it can help you discover the Commander's intent.

THE LADDER OF ABSTRACTION—TRUTH OUTLINE

Related to Kaiser's method is Donald Sunukjian's method.[16] He makes a passage outline (he calls this "Happened") and then transforms it into a truth outline ("Happens") by using the main points of the passage outline and restating them as timeless, universal phrases. Then he distills one "Take-Home Truth" from the truth outline. Finally, the sermon outline ("Happening") is built on these questions: "What do I need to explain?" "Do we buy it?" "What does it look like?"[iv] This is a good, simple sermon outline especially if our take-home truth is the Commander's intent or the point for proclamation for the passage.

Hermeneutical Spiral

Grant Osborne[17] wrote a very detailed method that combined the theological element with the ladder of abstraction.[v] First, he studied the original situation behind the text. Second, he determined the underlying theological truth behind the text (because every passage addresses a deeper doctrine we would call the Commander's intent). Third, he suggested meditating for some time on how these elements relate (which is also part of the thoughtful proclaimer method).

---

[15] "You shall not muzzle an ox when it is treading out the grain" (Deuteronomy 25:4).

[16] Donald Sunukjian is the professor of Christian ministry and leadership and homiletics chair in the Department of Christian Ministry and Leadership at the Talbot School of Theology, Biola University. He has been a senior pastor for fourteen years and a teacher with a passion to see God's Word presented with accuracy, clarity, interest, and relevance.

[17] Grant Osborne was Professor of New testament at Trinity Evangelical Divinity School and specializes in hermeneutics. His book, *The Hermeneutical Spiral: A Comprehensive Introduction to Biblical Interpretation* won the Christianity Today Critics Choice Award in 1993.

Fourth, he sought to discern parallels between the original situation the writer addressed and the experiences of people today.[vi] This can lead us to our point for proclamation. With our thorough inductive exegesis done, this method will produce a good resul.

The Thoughtful Proclaimer Technique

The final technique for finding the Commander's intent is to consider all of the above and distill your thinking by allowing yourself time and space. You may need several hours to meditate on the passage and its cross-references. Study it all. Consider it all. I like to say, let it perk (chapter 10). Try creating a teaching outline using the entire passage using the Commander's intent you chose and see whether your Commander's intent comfortably covers all the passage's purposes. The thoughtful proclaimer technique cannot be rushed. Study your passage as soon as possible and meditate on it, pray, go for a walk, watch a good movie, read a book, read more Scripture, pray some more, take a long shower, and talk to a friend. Often when you talk to a friend and explain what you'll be teaching, you find yourself telling him or her the Commander's intent and you'll think, *That's it!*).

Then ask yourself, *what does God intend for me to tell my people through this passage, and how can they apply it?* A wonderful thing will happen; the Holy Spirit will begin to condense your message into something focused and show you an anchor image, illustrations, and modern-day applications. In this way, you will have plenty of resources to write from once you begin.

Andy Stanley, the senior pastor of North Point Community Church and its five church campuses, said that he prayed before, during, and after he preached, but he had a special kind of prayer when he got stuck in finding what he called the "key point" of a passage. Andy described this prayer.

> I get on my knees and remind God that this was not my idea, it was His ... I confess that every opportunity I have to open His Word in front of people comes from Him and that anything helpful I've ever said came from Him ... Then I ask God to show me if there is something He wants to say to prepare me for what He wants me to communicate to our congregation. I surrender my ideas, my outline, and my topic. Then I just stay in that quiet place until God quiets my heart.[vii]

"We're first-time visitors ... Do you misinterpret Scripture every
Sunday, or is this a special sermon series?"   *viii*

Look for Christ in Every Passage

> And you, who were dead in your trespasses and the uncircumcision of your flesh, God made alive together with him, having forgiven us all our trespasses, by canceling the record of debt that stood against us with its legal demands. This he set aside, nailing it to the cross. (Colossians 2:13–14)

Our message should have one primary intent, the Commander's intent, but it has more than one purpose or reason for being shared. One of these purposes is so all people in our hearing will know Jesus Christ came to save sinners, to save each of us. First, we need to preach the Commander's intent in its scriptural context. Second, we need to preach Christ and the gospel every time because whatever else we say, a grateful response to the gospel is the proper motivation for us to live it out, and the Spirit offers us the power for change.

Since we must speak to people in a way that gives them purpose, hope, and a future, the gospel is the only answer. Preach to show how the watershed event of the cross, the covering of our sins by His blood, and the transformative power of the Holy Spirit inform and make possible the application of the Commander's intent. In a blog entitled "Preaching to the Collective Heart," Timothy Keller said, "Preach the truth, not just your opinion; you should preach the good news, not just good advice; and you should preach to make the truth real to the heart, not just clear to the mind."[ix]

In every passage, look for Jesus Christ; then look for the story of salvation, grace, the reason to change, the way to change, or the fact that we can't change on our own. Look for the symbols of the Bible such as sacrifice, temple, Sabbath, jubilee, circumcision, and the Passover lamb.[x] Preach Christ as the one who delivers from death and triumphs over weakness. Look for the redeemer motif as seen for example in the persons of Ruth and Esther. Talk about the faith or

160

lack of faith demonstrated by biblical characters, and use them as examples to point to faith in Christ. Jesus is everywhere in the Bible; He was there at Creation (John 1); He is the true Israel and the perfect King.[xi]

Look at the story the Bible as a time line. Put the cross in the middle. Everything on both sides of the cross points toward it. Keller said we should get to the point in our preaching and teaching career that we "preach Christ through instinct."[xii] Look for Him everywhere and all the time. Jesus Christ is a better and a more perfect representative than all the characters of the Bible, all of whom were flawed human beings though instruments of God's plan. This comparison of biblical characters to Christ guards against the moral exemplar problem whereby we make characters such as Solomon into characters from a children's story. "As it is written: 'None is righteous, no, not one'" (Romans 3:10). No one, that is, but Jesus.

We all need a reason to want to change. We need the power to be changed. Christ living in us is that power. Gratefulness for Jesus' death on our behalf is our reason for transformation. His Resurrection proves He has the power to shape us more and more into His image. And His Spirit works in our hearts to soften, mold, whisper, and point; making us into vessels for His use. Every message has to provide a place for Him because He is the reason we proclaim.

More about this in chapter 12, "Redemptive Proclamation."

Write the Commander's Intent in One Sentence

In chapter 13, we will talk about deciding on the specific point for proclamation for our particular teaching and for making it memorable. But for now, we should write the Commander's intent in one universal, timeless sentence that incorporates all the points of the passage we will be teaching on. This is what we will keep at the forefront of our minds as we write our message. The Commander's intent is the Scripture's intent, not our message theme; however, it is what we will build our point for proclamation around. This is what we will talk about when our notes blow away. This is what we will remember about this passage. This is God's purpose for the passage. This sentence should be as long as necessary but not too long or too full of details. It can be for us alone, or we can share it as part of our message. (see chapter 13).

Questions for Deciding on the Commander's Intent

- What does the passage's structure (the first, middle, or final verses) tell us about the purpose of the passage?
- What are the key verses in the passage?
- What themes, words, or ideas are repeated throughout the passage?
- What is the main subject of the passage, and what does the passage say about it?
- What is the underlying theological principle of the passage?
- What is the message of the surrounding chapters?
- What is the stated purpose of the book containing our passage? (It should be mentioned in the first and last chapters as well as the book introduction given in a study Bible.)
- What does the rest of the Bible and theology say about the main themes in this passage?
- What is the purpose of this passage in salvation history and the story of redemption?

- What principles can we draw from this passage?
- What truths can we identify in this passage?
- What was the purpose of the original author for this passage?
- What is the purpose of the Holy Spirit for breathing out the passage?
- What is the purpose of the Holy Spirit when the passage is read in our time and culture?
- What is the purpose of the passage for our personal transformation?
- What is the purpose of the passage for our audience's transformation?
- What is the purpose of the book in salvation history and the story of redemption?
- What does God want us to know, do, or be that prompted Him to include this passage?
- What do God's actions surrounding this text imply concerning our actions?[xiii]
- What action is suggested for our community and our relationships with neighbors?[xiv]
- Does this passage contain any implicit or explicit commands of God?[xv]
- What worldly ideals are exemplified by the characters in this text?
- Does this passage provide an example that is opposite of what we consider to be God's commands especially the command to love your neighbor as yourself? How do we reconcile that example?
- Does a character model faith or actions that express how we should live?
- Do events in this text correlate to situations you are familiar with? What are some examples?[xvi]
- What are the needs of your audience or congregation that God intended to address through this passage?
- Where does this passage address our need for the gospel, Jesus Christ, or salvation?

Write out the Commander's Intent for the Passage: Thinking about the Commander's Intent

- Do all the verses/paragraphs/strophes in my passage support my Commander's intent?
- How does the rest of Scripture support my Commander's intent?
- Does my Commander's intent contradict any other Scripture? If it does, how can I rectify that?
- How does my Commander's intent support or reject the cultural ideas of people today where I live?

LET IT PERCOLATE

Occasionally, I go to a coffee shop that takes tea very seriously. When you order tea, they bring you a cup with hot water, a tea bag, a lid, and a timer. You are not supposed to drink your tea until the timer goes off; you must allow it to soak, unless you like watery tea. This step of the thoughtful proclaimer method, "Live—A Transformative Hermeneutic," must include time to soak in what you've learned. Skipping this step will produce a weak sermon. You can tell a weak sermon from a full-flavored one. (You can tell a rushed teacher from a well-rested one too.) This is the "thoughtful" in thoughtful proclaimer.

Live Out the Passage

> And he said, "The kingdom of God is as if a man should scatter seed on the ground. He sleeps and rises night and day, and the seed sprouts and grows; he knows not how. The earth produces by itself, first the blade, then the ear, then the full grain in the ear. But when the grain is ripe, at once he puts in the sickle, because the harvest has come." (Mark 4:26–29)

If the Word of God has not begun to operate on our hearts, we aren't ready to proclaim it to others. The thoughtful proclaimer, as has been said several times in this book, believes the message preparation begins with messenger preparation. Johann Albrecht Bengel (1687–1752), a Lutheran scholar who devoted himself to taking the 30,000 Greek textual variants that existed in his day and creating one single Greek New Testament, said it this way: "Apply yourself wholly to the text; apply the text wholly to yourself."[i]

In *The Dictionary for Theological Interpretation* of the Bible, Kevin Vanhoozer claims that we can't interpret the text accurately if we don't first respond to it: "The inactive reader, by remaining on the level of explanation and never getting to the level of appropriation, short-circuits the process of interpretation."[ii] Brevard Childs wrote,

> But the heart of [theological interpretation] is Christological; its content is Jesus Christ … Therefore the aim of the enterprise involves the classic movement of faith seeking knowledge, of those who confess Christ struggling to understand the nature and will of the One who has already been revealed as Lord. The true expositor of the Christian

Scriptures is the one who awaits in anticipation toward becoming the interpreted rather than the interpreter. The very divine reality which the interpreter strives to grasp, is the very One who grasps the interpreter. The Christian doctrine of the role of the Holy Spirit is not a hermeneutical principle, but that divine reality itself who makes understanding of God possible.[iii]

Allowing the Word to percolate makes our message authentic. This is the step where we wait for the Commander to do His transforming work in our hearts. We need surgery. If the first 10 chapters took us several hours, this one will take the rest of our lives … sorry. Listening to inauthentic proclaimers, those who haven't applied the Word to their own lives, is like listening to the weather report read from behind a desk instead of watching the weather being reported by someone standing on the seashore as the hurricane beats them with wind and rain. We can feel the excitement in the voice of the eyewitness reporter. The words of both reporters may be true, but they are real for only one of them.

> For our appeal does not spring from error or impurity or any attempt to deceive, but just as we have been approved by God to be entrusted with the Gospel, so we speak, not to please man, but to please God who tests our hearts. (1 Thessalonians 2:3–4)

**Pastor Ted always began
each sermon with a question.**   *iv*

Take Time

"We don't want to settle for [serving] microwave snacks but [to] be diligent in preparing a healthy banquet for growing disciples," wrote Scott Gibson in *Preaching with a Plan*.[v] Walter Russell Bowie advised,

Real sermons, which will feed people's minds and hearts, cannot be produced on the spur of the moment any more than ripe grain can be gathered from empty ground. There must have been preparation of the earth, sowing of the seed, patient cultivation, and then a justified trust in the long, silent processes of vital growth before the harvest can be reaped.[vi]

While you must give your tea the proper time to saturate the water, if you leave your tea sitting out too long, it gets cold. The space between preparing for a sermon and giving it should be relatively short, a matter of hours or a few days to retain the heat. Inspiration becomes stale if you don't apply it. Some teachers or preachers wisely complete their studies weeks in advance, but I've never been able to preach month-old messages without heating things up at the last minute. Messages pulled from last year's file feel as though the heat has gone out of them. Planning ahead is always a good strategy, but after you let your message percolate, serve it.

Meditation

No man should stand before an audience who has not first stood before God. Many hours of communion should precede one hour in the pulpit. The prayer chamber should be more familiar than the public platform. Prayer should be continuous, but preaching intermittent. —A. W. Tozer[vii]

Chapter 11 is the meditation step. The go-for-a-walk-and-pray step. The talk-it-over-with-friends step.

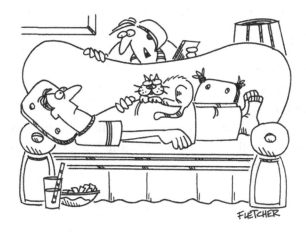

"Are you about finished thinking through the complexities and nuances of Sunday' sermon topic, or should Timmy walk home from school?" [viii]

Take Time Off

The Birth of an Illustration

During this step, the Holy Spirit can inspire us and show us illustrations in what we see and do. Genuine, honest illustrations always feel good to deliver. Illustrations that God shows us and gives us are best. I've never had much success finding illustrations from books though I've invested in several books full of them. There is nothing wrong with recycling an illustration, but it is just more refreshing if we have lived it or recently discovered it ourselves.

I once heard Dr. David Jeremiah speak.[1] He was seventy-five when he gave this message. His sermon included lots of good illustrations and stories about other people, but he also discussed how he had succeeded and how he had failed in personally living out his sermon. He concluded that he had learned from his successes and failures. He used his own struggles of living out the Word of God while managing a busy life as a powerful illustration.

Photographers are inspired by light. Chefs are inspired by ingredients. Proclaimers are inspired by metaphor. We are constantly thinking, *Wow! That would make a great illustration. There's a sermon in that somewhere.* Usually, as I'm letting the passage percolate through my heart, God places an illustration in my path. It may be something I hear, read, or see. It may be a movie, a picture, or a story. It may be current news or an event in my community. Whatever it is, it will be much fresher than a canned illustration written by another person for another time. Allow God time to supply you with the illustrations you will need.

Different proclaimers have different methods of collecting illustrations.[2] Talk to people, read, watch good movies, or catch up on world news. Inform yourself about things that interest your listeners. For example, read about medical and scientific discoveries, read obituaries of well-known people, or look at fresh and unusual statistics.[3] Find out a little about the professions of those you are speaking to. Do fun and interesting things, travel, and talk to all kinds of people. Stay current on things that interest your listeners such as entertainment, culture, sports, and social media. Listen to Christian music (or the kind your audience listens to); sometimes, these songs provide excellent illustrations.

And read Scripture. Many Commander's intents from the Old Testament will be best illustrated by a parable of Jesus or another passage you read during your devotional time. The opposite is true too; a New Testament teaching can be illustrated by a lesser-known Old Testament event. This is how the Holy Spirit works. Scripture is full of stories and poetry that can be used to enrich your message. More often than not, though your daily devotions are on other passages, God will use them to enrich your message—He wrote the whole book after all. When you share illustrations from the Bible, those who are less biblically literate will receive a double portion of truth. A good policy is to continually read the Bible, some New Testament, some Old Testament, and some psalms or books of wisdom each day.

Giving Your Brain a Break Stokes Your Creativity

After I have finished my study and answered my questions, I will often sit with a slice of pizza

---

[1] David Jeremiah is a graduate of Dallas Theological Seminary. He founded Turning Point Radio and Television Ministries. He is the senior pastor of Shadow Mountain Community Church, a Southern Baptist church in El Cajon, California.

[2] Many pastors keep files of illustrations and clippings. Some pastors who plan their messages will have staff members, or volunteers, or friends help them gather illustrations. I find that if I have a day or two, the illustrations come, and they are fresh.

[3] For statistics, try the Pew Research Center (pewforum.org), the Barna Group (barna.com), and Christianity Today (ChristianityToday.com).

to watch a good movie or read a good book. The next thing I know, I'm back at my desk, and I have my entire message written before the end of the evening.

Creativity is like fruit. You buy it hard and bland and leave it out for a bit to ripen and become sweet. If you've ever tried to make guacamole from a newly purchased avocado, you know what I mean. This is impossible unless you like lumpy guacamole, and even then, it won't have much taste. You have to let that avocado ripen for a day or so until it softens a bit. When it's ready, all you need is a fork, some salt, lime juice, and a few chips. The same is true for writing a lesson or a sermon. Give it time to soften, and it will need only a pinch of inspiration and a splash of story to be great.

Take some time to visualize your passage. Pretend you are there. If you are presenting a narrative passage, act it out in your mind. What does it feel like? What does it look like? What does it smell like? What questions does it raise? Put yourself in the place of each of the characters.

Thoughtful Proclaimers Read, Watch, and Listen

One of the most important ways we can grow our creativity and strengthen our messages is to broaden or minds and experiences. We should read widely and well. Read biographies and autobiographies. When you read commentaries, read ones that are written by those who have experienced many things.[4] Watch time-honored and award-winning movies. Read classic literature from a variety of genres.[ix] Make friends. Talk to people from all walks of life. Attend conferences. Get out of the office! This should be fun. The more broadly you think, the more creatively you will proclaim God's message. An interesting person is attractive to others; they will want what you have. Your bright mind will fill your teaching and preaching with interest and light.

[x]

---

[4] That is why I enjoy the NIV Application Commentaries and commentaries by James Montgomery Boice. The writers share their stories, experiences, and ideas.

Sabbath Keeping: Who, Me?

> And he said to them, "The Sabbath was made for man, not man for the Sabbath." (Mark 2:27)

Okay, picture yourself about age sixteen lying in a cozy, warm bed. You just wish you could stay home and sleep, but it's a school day, and that alarm is going to ring any minute and ruin everything. You're not looking forward to trudging through the cold icy morning and waiting for a bus. Then all of a sudden, the door swings open and your mom exclaims, "Snow day!" You have the whole day off, your work is done, and school is canceled until tomorrow, which means you are free to sleep and sled and make snowmen all day long![5] There is not a more wonderful feeling. (If you are from warmer climes, you should consider taking a snow day sometime.)

> See! The LORD has given you the Sabbath; therefore on the sixth day he gives you bread for two days. Remain each of you in his place; let no one go out of his place on the seventh day. So the people rested on the seventh day. (Exodus 16:29–30)

The Sabbath was meant to be a snow day, a gift every week from God. A day when you can do the things you love to do (stop sneaking work in there—God sees you.) All week long, we prepare for that great day. Jesus truly understood the Sabbath. He taught, preached, and visited with friends on the Sabbath. He especially liked to heal people on the Sabbath—I mean, if you could heal people, wouldn't it be fun to do that on the Sabbath?

You may argue, "But we're adults. We have work to do. We can't take a whole day off." Wrong! We can take a Sabbath at least once a week unless there is an emergency—for instance, if someone needs to be healed.

The Sabbath is not a law for believers but God's grace incarnate and offered to all. There are several theological reasons why Sabbath no longer is a commandment but a gift: 1) God is working all the time on our behalf.[6] 2) We always experience Sabbath rest in the sense that we no longer have to strive to please God. The gift of salvation is our rest.[7] 3) The commandment of Sabbath rest was fulfilled in Jesus Christ at the First Advent and will be completed at the Second Advent when we go to be with Him. We find rest for our souls in Christ alone—but we must take time for it.[8] Just as Joshua and the Hebrews entered their rest from wandering in the desert when they entered the Promised Land, we are living "promised" lives and should avail ourselves of God's gift of rest.[9]

---

[5] This illustration is not original. I heard it in an advanced preaching class at Alliance Theological Seminary in Nyack, NY. I don't remember who gave the illustration. My apologies to you if it was your idea! It has stuck with me all these years.

[6] The Jews persecuted Jesus because he was performing this work on the Sabbath. But Jesus answered them, "My Father is working until now, and I am working" (John 5:16–17).

[7] "So then, there remains a Sabbath rest for the people of God, for whoever has entered God's rest has also rested from his works as God did from his. Let us therefore strive to enter that rest, so that no one may fall by the same sort of disobedience" (Hebrews 4:9–11).

[8] "Do not think that I have come to abolish the Law or the Prophets; I have not come to abolish them but to fulfill them" (Matthew 5:17).

[9] "And he said, 'My presence will go with you, and I will give you rest'" (Exodus 33:14).

Though we are not legally bound to take a day off, P. K. Jewett, writing on the Lord's day, offered this encouragement.

> Because believers have not yet [fully] entered the final rest of the life to come, however, they cannot say that this rest in the Lord is only a matter of the heart. An outward sign should correspond to the inner reality; they should cease their labors as a public witness of their renouncing all their works and of their trust in God's grace alone.[xi]

For those of us whose work culminates on the Lord's day, Sunday, take heart; we can celebrate the life, death, and Resurrection of Christ on any day of the week we choose.

> Therefore let no one pass judgment on you in questions of food and drink, or with regard to a festival or a new moon or a Sabbath. These are a shadow of the things to come, but the substance belongs to Christ. (Colossians 2:16–17)

Pastor Chuck spent the first 6 hours researching
how to make his designated rest day more efficient. [xii]

Questions for Meditating on the Passage and the Commander's Intent

Questions to Consider While Your Message Is Percolating

- What has God been saying to me personally through this passage?
- What specific applications for myself and my listeners can I identify regarding the Commander's intent of this passage?
- How is living out the Commander's intent working for me?
- What difficulties have I experienced in living out the Commander's intent? Am I wrestling with God about any aspects of living out His message?
- What has been the hardest part?
- After meditating further on what you have decided is the Commander's intent; consider if it needs to be altered or modified in any way.

- What illustrations of the Commander's intent have I observed in the news or in a book or movie?
- What are people talking about that may be relevant to my message?
- Where have I recently seen an application of the Commander's intent in action?

Creative Meditation Exercises

- Visualize what is happening in the passage.
- If the passage is a sermon, imagine how it sounded to its early audiences. Read it aloud in the translation of your choice.
- If the passage contains a story, visualize its setting, and think about its structure—the beginning, middle (climax), and end.
- Why was this Scripture portion written in this way?
- Tell the story in your own words, and consider telling it as if it were happening today.
- Imagine the sights, the smells, and the sounds.
- If the passage contains theological instruction or a letter, explain it in your own words as you would to a friend who doesn't know the Bible. Better yet, go to lunch with a friend and tell him or her what you think you will say. What's the reaction? What questions does he or she have? What does he or she agree with?
- If the passage is an argument, part of an argument, or part of a sermon or prophecy, map out where this particular point fits into the author's larger argument or larger message. Why did the writer craft the message in this way?
- If the passage is Hebrew poetry, visualize its imagery.
- Write down verses that stand out to you personally and memorize or meditate on them.
- Think deeply about words or phrases and make connections to other Bible passages and stories, creation, nature, events in your life or in the lives of others, and so on.
- Find one simple anchor image that illustrates or reminds people of your Commander's intent. Plan how to describe or present your image.
- If you choose to share slides or video clips, begin gathering photos and videos as well as stories and illustrations.

LOVE: A REDEMPTIVE, PURPOSEFUL HOMILETIC

CHAPTER 12

REDEMPTIVE PROCLAMATION

In him we have redemption through his blood, the forgiveness of our trespasses, according to the riches of his grace, which he lavished upon us, in all wisdom and insight making known to us the mystery of his will, according to his purpose, which he set forth in Christ as a plan for the fullness of time, to unite all things in him, things in heaven and things on earth. (Ephesians 1:7–10)

Two Redemptive Foci in Each Message

The story of Ruth is thousands of years old. It is such great love story that if you've been to very many weddings, you may have heard a line or two from it.[1] It teaches us about two kinds of redemption—one earthly and one heavenly—but both planned and purposed by God for His glory. The Commander's intent of the story is that God is universal in His providence despite initial appearances. Through drought, death, and despair, God reigns and redeems.

All redemption, whether the redemption of a family facing dead ends and destitution or the redemption of a sinner from eternal death to eternal life, can be used by God for His glory. Redemptive proclamation is about teaching others that God can redeem our local, earthly messes in the same way He can redeem us from our sins and purchase us for eternal life. Christ offers us salvation; and He promises to take our disasters and make them into something for His glory.[2]

The story of Ruth and Boaz is the story of a man redeeming the property of a destitute family.[3] Boaz agrees to buy back Ruth's former father-in-law's (Naomi's deceased husband's) mortgaged property. He agrees (that is an understatement) to marry the widowed Ruth and raise their future children in the name of Ruth's late husband. Two lonely people, one wealthy and one poor, are

---

[1] It is always makes me laugh a bit that the verse used at weddings: "For where you go I will go, and where you lodge I will lodge. Your people shall be my people, and your God my God" (Ruth 1:16b) is actually what the widow Ruth says to her mother-in-law, Naomi, after her husband is long dead. It is not what Ruth says to Boaz, her second groom. Another case where knowing the context of your quote is helpful.

[2] "And we know that for those who love God all things work together for good, for those who are called according to his purpose" (Romans 8:28).

[3] Boaz is not the closest relative to Naomi and not the one who would be first in line to redeem or buy back Naomi's husband's lost property. But Boaz is chosen happily by God and his bride-to-be to be the kinsman-redeemer for the family.

united and freed from their loneliness. Ruth and Boaz become not only a happily-ever-after couple, but their family, their descendants (David), redeem a nation in shreds. Most important, their descendent (Jesus Christ) brings redemption to us all.[4]

The story of Zacchaeus is another example of eternal redemption and earthly redemption occurring on the same day. Jesus turned around Zacchaeus's eternal destiny and his earthly destiny in one fell swoop.

> And Zacchaeus stood and said to the Lord, "Behold, Lord, the half of my goods I give to the poor. And if I have defrauded anyone of anything, I restore it fourfold." And Jesus said to him, "Today salvation has come to this house, since he also is a son of Abraham. For the Son of Man came to seek and to save the lost." (Luke 19:8–10)

In the same way that the onlookers grumbled because Jesus was the guest of a sinner like Zacchaeus, many will grumble at proclaimers reaching out to the worst of sinners. But Jesus made it clear, as should we, that He came to seek and save the lost.

Redemptive proclamation is aimed at the gospel, an offer of eternal salvation as well as the offer of earthly redemption for our broken lives. Redemption is aimed at sinners—those who are unsaved and those who have accepted Christ's salvation but who like Paul, you, and me can admit that they still act at times as if they were not fully redeemed.[5]

Redemption as Motivation for Proclamation

Before we go one step further, we must ask ourselves what our motivation is for proclamation. What is the purpose of Bible teaching and preaching? Why proclaim anything at all?

We speak because Christ redeemed us and has called us to offer that redemption to everyone—unbelievers and hurting believers. We speak because we believe that God raised the Lord Jesus from the grave and that He will one day raise us to be in His presence. We are called to extend God's grace to all people. We don't commit ourselves to the work of a proclaimer so we can tell moral stories or encourage people to try to be better. We aren't amateur psychologists or motivational speakers pumping people up with hopeful slogans; we are offering our friends eternal life and sharing God's instruction on how to live life to the fullest. We are assuring them that they are loved by God and demonstrating how to live in that love free from sin despite the fact we all are sinners. We are calling them to do good works, the works God created them to do, and we're showing them how and why that is possible.

To Whom Should We Proclaim?

John A. Huffman Jr., former pastor of St. Andrew's Presbyterian Church in Newport Beach, California, preached this introduction to his Easter sermon some years back. I think his words

---

[4] Ruth and Boaz gave birth to Obed, the grandfather of King David (Ruth 4:21–22), who is the progenitor of Jesus Christ (Luke 3:23–32).

[5] See Romans 7 and 8. "For I delight in the law of God, in my inner being, but I see in my members another law waging war against the law of my mind and making me captive to the law of sin that dwells in my members. Wretched man that I am! Who will deliver me from this body of death? Thanks be to God through Jesus Christ our LORD! So then, I myself serve the law of God with my mind, but with my flesh I serve the law of sin" (Romans 7:22–25).

are still quite relevant. We are called to proclaim salvation to the lost and truth to the saved, but what about those missing in action somewhere in between? Huffman told the story of a pastor who realized his messages were getting stale and so took a part-time job at a Starbucks. To his surprise,

> All 21 people he worked with believed in God. Not one was an atheist. They were all very positive toward God and spirituality. A second surprise was that all were interested in spiritual things, but not in Christians, Christianity, or the church. No one wanted to hear Dan's proofs for God or invitations to come to church or ideas about salvation. Almost everyone thought they knew what Christianity was about and had decided they didn't want it. They were post Christian. At some point along the way, each of them had experienced a breach in trust related to Christianity. Maybe a Christian friend had been hypocritical or pushy. Maybe when they were young they had attended church and found it boring and irrelevant. Maybe they had watched TV preachers and been turned off. Or maybe they had experienced a tragedy—death or sexual abuse or some other trauma—and felt that God had been distant and uncaring.

Richardson said, "Dan wasn't starting at ground zero, but rather at minus-three or four … The biggest thing Dan learned is that people in this generation have a prior question of trust that must be addressed before we can have meaningful spiritual conversations with them."[i]

Besides speaking to Christ followers and those who have never heard the gospel, we must speak to those who have trusted the Christian religion only to find it wanting. They may consider themselves Christian but have gotten lost. Perhaps like the parable of the sower, the cares of the world or the temptations of sin have choked out their faith.[6] Some of our listeners don't trust the validity of God any longer. Some have confessed Jesus Christ as Savior, but somehow, their lives are more broken than ever. Others are seeking faith that works. People are hurting, people are lost, people are angry, and people are disappointed that the faith they grew up practicing no longer seems to work. They want to come back. Are we putting up road blocks?

Put Out Yellow Ribbons Instead of Red Flags—Offer Redemption

In 1973, near the end of the Vietnam War, many soldiers were coming home after a protracted and unpopular campaign. They faced an uncertain future. Would their wives and sweethearts want them back? Were there any jobs waiting for them? Would they return as heroes or pariahs? Amidst all of the angst and uncertainty, one song sold 3 million copies in three weeks.[ii]

The song was "Tie a Yellow Ribbon Round the Ole Oak Tree."[iii] The story behind this song was at least as old as the Civil War. Yellow or white ribbons were worn in a girl's hair as a sign of acceptance of an old love. And ribbons were tied on trees to show that a soldier was welcome home despite the ravages of war.[iv] Tony Orlando and the musical group Dawn helped turn the

---

[6] "And he told them many things in parables, saying: 'A sower went out to sow. And as he sowed, some seeds fell along the path, and the birds came and devoured them. Other seeds fell on rocky ground, where they did not have much soil, and immediately they sprang up, since they had no depth of soil, but when the sun rose they were scorched. And since they had no root, they withered away. Other seeds fell among thorns, and the thorns grew up and choked them. Other seeds fell on good soil and produced grain, some a hundredfold, some sixty, some thirty. He who has ears, let him hear'" (Matthew 13:3–9).

idea of tying a yellow ribbon into American folklore as well as a poignant symbol of welcoming the prodigal home.

The narrator in the song "Tie a Yellow Ribbon" is a man who's been gone three years (likely at war or in prison) and is unsure of whether he will be welcomed home.

> I'm comin' home, I've done my time / Now I've got to know what is and isn't mine / If you received my letter telling you I'd soon be free / Then you'll know just what to do / If you still want me, if you still want me.

The chorus reveals what the sign of welcome and acceptance should be.

> Tie a yellow ribbon round the ole oak tree / It's been three long years, do you still want me? / If I don't see a ribbon, round the ole oak tree / I'll stay on the bus, forget about us, put the blame on me.

In the final verse, he is on the bus heading toward home or maybe continuing past it. Fearing the worst, he says,

> Bus driver, please look for me / 'Cause I couldn't bear to see what I might see / I'm really still in prison and my love, she holds the key / A simple yellow ribbon's what I need to set me free / And I wrote and told her please.

It seems the whole bus is anxious to know. Does this man still have a place to call home? Does the love of his life still want him?

> Now the whole damned bus is cheerin' / And I can't believe I see / A hundred yellow ribbons round the ole oak tree / I'm comin' home.

A bit sappy maybe, but it strikes a chord because we all have been in some sort of prison perhaps of our own making. We have done something wrong. We've left something undone or unfinished. We've run from those who loved us. Will they accept us back? For those who have left the church, the faith, the fold, a place where they knew they were once loved, returning is especially hard.

We must metaphorically tie a yellow ribbon around our churches and Bible studies. Let people who want out of their prisons and into church know they are welcome back no matter how long they've been gone or how far they have strayed.

Sadly, we often put up red caution flags instead. When a friend of mine was considering returning to church after some years hiatus, she checked out several church websites. What she found were big, red warning flags. Rather than statements of faith and lists of classes and Bible studies, she found political agendas. To my friend, these were messages stating what kind of people were not welcome at that church. Red flags such as, "Don't come if you have gay friends (especially if you are gay yourself)," "Don't come if you've had an abortion," "Don't come if you aren't politically conservative," "Don't come if you are divorced—only happy marriages welcome here."

So, whether you eat or drink, or whatever you do, do all to the glory of God. Give no offense to Jews or to Greeks or to the church of God, just as I try to please everyone in everything I do, not seeking my own advantage, but that of many, that they may be saved. (1 Corinthians 10:31–33)

To many, the church has come to be seen as unloving, unjust, and even un-Christian, and those perceptions are the result of ample evidence. Paul's words echo strongly today—whatever you do, do all to the glory of God … that many may be saved.[7]

Does Our Message Tie Yellow Ribbons or Caution Tape around the Gospel?

Consider how your message will welcome the listeners you hope will come this week. Let the Bible speak, and keep blatant politics at bay. Be careful about judging those who have sinned; instead, offer God's grace and redemption. Put no obstacle in the way of salvation.

Can we lovingly let the Bible plan our teaching agenda? Preaching sequentially through God's Word lets God have the say over our message plan. Do we trust the Bible to let it say what it says? If we somehow must preach a topical message (which I don't usually recommend), let's preach through the Bible's nearly five hundred verses on forgiveness.

> But thanks be to God, who in Christ always leads us in triumphal procession, and through us spreads the fragrance of the knowledge of him everywhere. For we are the aroma of Christ to God among those who are being saved and among those who are perishing, to one a fragrance from death to death, to the other a fragrance from life to life. Who is sufficient for these things? For we are not, like so many, peddlers of God's Word, but as men of sincerity, as commissioned by God, in the sight of God we speak in Christ. (2 Corinthians 2:14–17)

Plan to preach and teach redemptively. Preach the gospel every week so those who bring their prodigal sons or daughters to church after weeks of begging them to come will know they will hear the God-ordained message they need. Preach and teach clearly the Commander's intent for each passage in a way that shows how it should be lived out. Sweetly and bravely live out your faith in front of the community, and honestly let your little lights shine by encouraging acts of service. Stand for forgiveness and grace while remaining true to the holy God. Tie yellow ribbons on the church pillars rather than sticking red warning flags in the church lawn, on the church website, and in your messages.

Plan for Divine Intervention in Your Message

Our biblical message should be a three-way conversation. Proclamation is not you and I telling other people things they need to know and do. When we preach and teach we are facilitating a conversation between the people in the pew and their God. They don't need to hear us, they need to hear the Jesus calling. God wants to redeem lost souls.

Redemption means to be delivered from captivity through the payment of a ransom. In

---

[7] 1 Corinthians 10:31–32.

teaching the Bible, we speak of sin as slavery, sinners as slaves,[8] Christ's death as the ransom, and deliverance from the consequences of sin as freedom.[v,9] Redemptive proclamation aims at setting people free from their captivities to all sorts of things—sin, sadness, pain, addiction, and other problems. Redemptive proclamation brings about a divine intervention, an opportunity for God to meet His people where they are and set them free. The objective of redemptive proclamation is to spread an umbrella of redemption over everything we teach or preach.

> The Son of Man came eating and drinking, and they say, "Look at him! A glutton and a drunkard, a friend of tax collectors and sinners!" Yet wisdom is justified by her deeds. (Matthew 11:19)

Wisdom and Christ's example call us to speak to those outside the fold. Sinners tended to gather around Jesus because He offered redemption, and that made religious people grumble. Do we attract sinners or only religious people with our message? Tax collectors and sinners—who were they? Taken separately, tax collectors were those who had sold out and made the system work for them. Many of our parishioners make the economic system work for them to great material advantage and perhaps through less-than-righteous means. The sinners then and now are ungodly people who deserve God's punishment but are unaware of their need. Taken as an idiom, tax collectors and sinners means that Jesus attracted all the people who needed Him most—and that means us too.

> When Jesus had dinner at the home of Matthew, the tax collector, and future disciples, He said to the grumbling religious folks, "It is not the healthy who need a doctor, but the sick. Go and learn what this means, 'I desire mercy, and not sacrifice.' For I came not to call the righteous, but sinners." (Matthew 9:12–13)

Speak Grace, Not Rules

Christ call us to speak grace versus teaching people to live by a set of rules. My children's fifth grade teacher, Mrs. Destroyer,[10] knew how to control a classroom. She had rules, lots of rules, and she knew how to enforce them. If you followed the rules, you were rewarded. If you did not, the entire class was punished. This meant that if one student failed to do everything perfectly, the whole class would miss out on recess. So, if someone forgot to do a math problem, or neglected the questions on the back of the worksheet, or (horror of horrors) just didn't complete their homework at all, there was no recess for anyone. Naturally, everyone hated the student who messed up.

This method of rewards and punishments (recess for perfection and additional work if anyone missed the mark) was integrated into every aspect of every day in Mrs. Destroyer's class. Her students hated her, but they were the best-behaved students I've ever seen.

Her teaching style produced three kinds of students. You will notice that, at least in my experience, it did not produce anyone who couldn't wait to get to school or who found learning

---

[8] John 8:34; Romans 6:15-23; 2 Peter 2:19-20.

[9] John 8:33, 36; Romans 8:21; Galatians 5:1.

[10] Her name has been changed to protect her anonymity.

a joy. It did produce guilt-ridden, legalistic, fearful children. I had one of each in my family and they represent the three responses to religious legalism.

My elder son ignored Mrs. Destroyer's rules because he knew he could never live up to her standards. Perfection was out of his reach, so he decided it was easier to do as he pleased and live with the guilt.

My daughter became a workaholic "people pleaser" to stay on her teacher's good side. At age ten, she would stay up until eleven each night laboring to memorize flash cards. She did all the extra credit she could. I helped her write her spelling sentences (which was quite a challenge even for an adult). The stress she carried was immense; she toiled not to learn but to keep the teacher happy.

My younger son was so afraid of displeasing Mrs. Destroyer and thus ruining the class's day that he wanted to quit school and run away. The strict rewards and punishments system were just too much for him; they made him miserable. He couldn't sleep at night; he worried he had forgotten something in his homework and the whole class would hate him. He plotted how he could jump on a train to New York and live on the streets—all this at age ten.

God is not like Mrs. Destroyer. In fact, Jesus Christ came into the world because the destroyer wants to make quite sure that no one ever gets cosmic recess. It is Satan's plan for the free offer of salvation and forgiveness to be twisted into a mock religion that contrives ways to control people's behavior.

Paul expressed this idea better than I can.

> For the love of Christ controls us, because we have concluded this: that one has died for all, therefore all have died; and he died for all, that those who live might no longer live for themselves but for him who for their sake died and was raised. From now on, therefore, we regard no one according to the flesh. Even though we once regarded Christ according to the flesh, we regard him thus no longer. Therefore, if anyone is in Christ, he is a new Creation. The old has passed away; behold, the new has come. All this is from God, who through Christ reconciled us to himself and gave us the ministry of reconciliation; that is, in Christ God was reconciling the world to himself, not counting their trespasses against them, and entrusting to us the message of reconciliation.
>
> Therefore, we are ambassadors for Christ, God making his appeal through us. We implore you on behalf of Christ, be reconciled to God. For our sake he made him to be sin who knew no sin, so that in him we might become the righteousness of God. Working together with him, then, we appeal to you not to receive the grace of God in vain. For he says, "In a favorable time I listened to you, and in a day of salvation I have helped you." Behold, now is the favorable time; behold, now is the day of salvation. (2 Corinthians 5:14–6:2)

God's servants are not to put obstacles in people's way but to act as Christ's ambassadors to those in need of reconciliation. Our ministry is one of reconciling people to God—people who do not know Christ took on their sins so they could become righteous, and those who struggle to earn their salvation but have come up short. We are ambassadors to all who have never truly appropriated the grace and power offered them by God when they accepted salvation. If we have received God's grace, we are to claim it and pass it on. It is the destroyer, not the Savior, who seeks to produce the guilt, striving, and fear that leads to alienation from Jesus Christ and His church.

God Offers a Different Plan for Motivating Transformation

> But thanks be to God, that you who were once slaves of sin have become obedient from the heart to the standard of teaching to which you were committed. (Romans 6:17)

Employers want to know how to motivate their employees. Parents want to know how to motivate their children. Pastors want to motivate their church members to be better Christians and put more in the collection plate. But the Bible teaches us that real motivation comes from changed hearts, grateful hearts, and called hearts. Guilt, the power of positive thinking, or being told to try harder does not produce lasting change. The grace the Holy Spirit uses to sanctify His people does. We are not obedient to earn favor with God. Believers' obedience grows out of their love for Christ when they recognize it was for their sake that He died. Obedience is the product of gratefulness. We are grateful to no longer be slaves to sin.[11]

> For while we were still weak, at the right time Christ died for the ungodly. For one will scarcely die for a righteous person—though perhaps for a good person one would dare even to die—**but God** shows his love for us in that while we were still sinners, Christ died for us. Since, therefore, we have now been justified by his blood, much more shall we be saved by him from the wrath of God. For if while we were enemies we were reconciled to God by the death of his Son, much more, now that we are reconciled, shall we be saved by his life. More than that, we also rejoice in God through our Lord Jesus Christ, through whom we have now received reconciliation. (Romans 5:6–11 *emphasis added*)

When we are reconciled to God, we become free from guilt, striving, and fear. Our obedience is not motivated by the promise of reward or any other perk. Our obedience grows from thankfulness to Jesus Christ and is the natural outcome of our relationship with Him. He even offers us supernatural power; consider it help with our homework from the parent on high, the power of the Holy Spirit working in and through us. We can never live up to God's standard of holiness no matter how hard we try—"There is no one righteous, no not one." But God offers grace and forgiveness, not guilt. He offers abundant life, not legalism. God offers love that overcomes our fears.

It's More Like Being in Love

Being reconciled to God offers relationship, not religion or legalism. It's more like being in love. I heard of a young woman who married a man, and when she moved into her husband's home, he gave her a list of all the things he wanted done and how he wanted them done. The list provided rules for when he expected her to wake up and just how he wanted his eggs prepared.

---

[11] "You are my friends if you do what I command you. No longer do I call you servants, for the servant does not know what his master is doing; but I have called you friends, for all that I have heard from my Father I have made known to you. You did not choose me, but I chose you and appointed you that you should go and bear fruit and that your fruit should abide, so that whatever you ask the Father in my name, he may give it to you. These things I command you, so that you will love one another" (John 15:14–17).

It detailed how the laundry should be done and what days he expected her to clean and buy the groceries. Dinner was expected a six every night, and the bed was to be turned down at ten. She could go out with friends twice a month but had to be home by ten on those nights. Every detail of the marriage was spelled out. She knew how much money she could spend on herself and how much on groceries. Surely, this woman was blessed to have such an orderly life and a husband who was such a good administrator.

I can't remember what happened to her husband, but perhaps he died of a heart attack such a rigid soul he was. A few years later, this same woman met another man who said he loved her and wanted to marry her. She was at that point a bit older and wiser and decided to find out ahead of time what the rules would be. She asked him which days he would like his laundry done. He said it didn't really matter; maybe they would do the laundry together, and he was happy to do their laundry himself. She wondered just how he liked his eggs, and he assured her that any way she made them he was sure he would like them. Then.he asked her how she liked *her* eggs. Feeling a sweet warmth swell inside her heart, she asked him what her household budget would be, and he informed her that once they were married, everything he had would be hers.

The difference between religion and a relationship is just that—relationship. This second story also illustrates the difference between the motivation of have to vs. get to, the difference between how grace and love transform lives rather than the motivation of guilt, legalism, or fear.

According to the ways of religion, we must keep a list of laws, the laws of the Bible and the laws of our church, and if we keep them very well and are very good, God will bless us. Relationships, on the other hand, mean making eggs for someone just because you love that person and because he or she loves you.

Jesus Illustrates This Amazing Love with Three Stories

Jesus illustrated this relationship-based love in three stories in Luke 15 that epitomize God's attitude toward us. Jesus told these stories to a group that included tax collectors, sinners, and Pharisees (likely the same groups of people, metaphorically speaking, whom we address in our classes, Bible studies, and congregations).

> Now the tax collectors and sinners were all drawing near to hear him. And the Pharisees and the scribes grumbled, saying, "This man [Jesus] receives sinners and eats with them." So [Jesus] told them this parable: "What man of you, having a hundred sheep, if he has lost one of them, does not leave the ninety-nine in the open country, and go after the one that is lost, until he finds it?" (Luke 15:1–4)

Jesus illustrates God's attitude toward the lost and thus informs us what our attitude should be toward those we prepare our teachings and messages for. When one sheep is lost, the shepherd leaves ninety-nine perfectly good sheep without his protection for a time to go after the one who has run away. And when he finds the lost lamb, he carries it home on his shoulders. Though he had ninety-nine in the fold, the shepherd does not rest until the lost one is found.[12] How foolish.

In the second story, a woman has swept her whole house trying to find one lost coin. But when she finds it, instead of putting it away for safekeeping, she spends it on a coin-finding party and invites all her friends.[13] How wasteful.

And in the third story, a father runs to greet a runaway son who has returned home. Though he has lost half his wealth to this wayward son, he kills a fatted calf and throws a lavish party when his family is reunited.[14] How extravagant.

These three stories illustrate the character of God. A shepherd who would go to any length and risks ninety-nine lambs to find the one who is lost. A woman who wastes what she has recovered in celebrating the recovery. A father who not only forgives his wayward son and quietly accepts him back into his home but who celebrates his return openly and lavishly, with only joy and with no embarrassment.

We usually think of the runaway son as the prodigal, and that is how this parable is identified in our Bible subtitles. However, the word *prodigal* is not actually included in most translations. Timothy Keller called God's extravagant attitude towards those of us who are lost "prodigal" and a God who would go to such lengths for secondhand converts a "prodigal God."[vi] My dictionary defines prodigal as (a) characterized by profuse or wasteful expenditures; (b) recklessly spendthrift; and (c) yielding abundantly: luxuriant. A prodigal God is an extravagant spendthrift when it comes to welcoming back those who have left the fold. He would respond in this way even for a barista at Starbucks who had run away from the church.

---

[12] "So he told them this parable: 'What man of you, having a hundred sheep, if he has lost one of them, does not leave the ninety-nine in the open country, and go after the one that is lost, until he finds it? And when he has found it, he lays it on his shoulders, rejoicing. And when he comes home, he calls together his friends and his neighbors, saying to them, "Rejoice with me, for I have found my sheep that was lost." Just so, I tell you, there will be more joy in heaven over one sinner who repents than over ninety-nine righteous persons who need no repentance'" (Luke 15:3–7).

[13] "Or what woman, having ten silver coins, if she loses one coin, does not light a lamp and sweep the house and seek diligently until she finds it? And when she has found it, she calls together her friends and neighbors, saying, 'Rejoice with me, for I have found the coin that I had lost.' Just so, I tell you, there is joy before the angels of God over one sinner who repents" (Luke 15:8–10).

[14] "And he said, 'There was a man who had two sons. And the younger of them said to his father, "Father, give me the share of property that is coming to me." And he divided his property between them. Not many days later, the younger son gathered all he had and took a journey into a far country, and there he squandered his property in reckless living. And when he had spent everything, a severe famine arose in that country, and he began to be in need. So he went and hired himself out to one of the citizens of that country, who sent him into his fields to feed pigs. And he was longing to be fed with the pods that the pigs ate, and no one gave him anything. But when he came to himself, he said, "How many of my father's hired servants have more than enough bread, but I perish here with hunger! I will arise and go to my father, and I will say to him, 'Father, I have sinned against heaven and before you. I am no longer worthy to be called your son. Treat me as one of your hired servants.'" And he arose and came to his father. But while he was still a long way off, his father saw him and felt compassion, and ran and embraced him and kissed him. And the son said to him, "Father, I have sinned against heaven and before you. I am no longer worthy to be called your son." But the father said to his servants, "Bring quickly the best robe, and put it on him, and put a ring on his hand, and shoes on his feet. And bring the fattened calf and kill it, and let us eat and celebrate. For this my son was dead, and is alive again; he was lost, and is found." And they began to celebrate. Now his older son was in the field, and as he came and drew near to the house, he heard music and dancing. And he called one of the servants and asked what these things meant. And he said to him, "Your brother has come, and your father has killed the fattened calf, because he has received him back safe and sound."'" (Luke 15:11–28).

> And he [the run-away] arose and came to his father. But while [the runaway] was still a long way off, his father saw him and felt compassion, and ran and embraced him and kissed him. (Luke 15:20)

In each of Jesus' stories, He illustrated the proper orientation toward the lost and those still at home. Toward those who are faithfully attending church week after week and those who come only occasionally. Toward the younger and the older brother alike. Everyone needs redemption whether redemption that leads to eternal life or the redeeming hand of God healing our bitter hearts and mending our brokenness.

> But [the elder brother] was angry and refused to go in. His father came out and entreated him, but he answered his father, "Look, these many years I have served you, and I never disobeyed your command, yet you never gave me a young goat, that I might celebrate with my friends. But when this son of yours came, who has devoured your property with prostitutes, you killed the fattened calf for him!" And he said to him, "Son, you are always with me, and all that is mine is yours. It was fitting to celebrate and be glad, for this your brother was dead, and is alive; he was lost, and is found." (Luke 15:29–32)

Half his fortune gone, the embarrassment of having a son who had run off and wasted all his money—none of that matters to this father. Every message should be prepared with the same prodigal, wild, spendthrift attitude God has toward all sinners.

Redemptive Messages Have Two Audiences

Remember that Jesus put two brothers in this parable. He had two audiences in mind, two groups listening to him: sinners and Pharisees. In our congregation are two basic types of people who need redemption.[15] The first type is those who have run away from God, the sinners; the second is those who have stayed home and kept the faith but whose lives are not victorious. Like the father who loved both his sons, we must do whatever it takes to win both groups to the truth of Christ. Redemption is for the sinner and the saved because neither is entirely home yet. We speak of abundant life and lavish grace to the younger brother who is lost and the elder brother who is resentful and complaining, not understanding that every fattened calf is always his to claim. This second type includes those who work tirelessly for the church while harboring resentment, addiction, or doubt.

Grace-Filled Applications

Though every message has one Commander's intent, it has at least two applications. One is aimed at those who have come seeking God or perhaps have run from Him. The other is for the believers in the room who have eternal life but have never asked for the fattened calf or claimed their Father's riches. The motivation is the same, however, and that is a loving response to God's offer of salvation and abundant life lived under the power of the Holy Spirit. God's love displayed for us on the cross is our motivation.

One application is for the disappointed, lost, and seeking son, and the other is for the

---

[15] I owe this idea, which changed the way I focus my messages and aim my applications, to Timothy Keller.

self-righteous, entitled, or hypocritical brother—one Commander's intent but a two-pronged application. We offer redemption to the prodigal and the broken brother alike. We offer new life in every message, so we offer hope for the faithful Christians in our pews who need their pain and strife, their broken lives, redeemed by God.

Ask yourself what the application is for the prodigal son—the seeker, the skeptic, the lost one, the rebel, the one who needs salvation, the one who is defeated or feels worthless, the wayward one. Then ask, what the application should be for the older brother, the believing brother, the one like us who is still working out his salvation, being sanctified, but is not perfect yet?

Grateful-Hearted, Spirit-Empowered Transformation

> Therefore, my beloved, as you have always obeyed, so now, not only as in my presence but much more in my absence, work out your own salvation with fear and trembling, for it is God who works in you, both to will and to work for his good pleasure. Do all things without grumbling or disputing, that you may be blameless and innocent, children of God without blemish in the midst of a crooked and twisted generation, among whom you shine as lights in the world. (Philippians 2:12–15)

Bryan Chapell wrote, never preach a "you should" without a "He did." It's not about what we can do for Jesus but what He has done for us and what He wants to do for us. Beware of "be" messages whereby you tell your people to "be" like someone or to "be good" or to "be disciplined" without offering the truth that they can only be more like Christ because He redeemed them, He paid the price for the debt they owe.[vii] We belong to Christ Jesus. Therefore, being good does not gain us favor in God's eyes. We cannot earn our salvation by being good. Never leave that message unstated.[16]

When we call on people to make needed changes, we should point out that all spiritual transformation, though motivated by grateful hearts, is empowered by the Holy Spirit. Every message whether from the Old or New Testament must in some way share the gospel because true spiritual transformation can come only through the power of the Holy Spirit. Unbelievers do not have the power of the Holy Spirit to call on to help them live out God's will for their lives.

> Then he said to me, "This is the word of the LORD to Zerubbabel: Not by might, nor by power, but by my Spirit, says the LORD of hosts." (Zechariah 4:6)

We can do what God calls us to do only by the power of the Holy Spirit. And since we know we cannot do anything in our own strength, we must remind ourselves that we cannot tell others to do anything in theirs. As pastor Bryan Chapell said, no "*sola bootstrapsa*" (just "pull yourself up by your bootstraps") messages.[viii] The Holy Spirit wants to give us the power to live obediently and abundantly.

If a grateful response to the gospel, the warm glow of being loved and wanting to love God back, is our motivation for change, we cannot leave the gospel to be something tacked onto the end; it must permeate our message and be at its heart. Our application is two-pronged, our motivation is the gospel, and our power to transform comes through the Holy Spirit.

---

[16] Bryan Chapell stated that messages that were not Christ-centered or redemptively focused were human centered and presented godliness as a product of human endeavor.

Messengers Made of Clay Giving Messages to Other Jars of Clay

> But we have this treasure in jars of clay, to show that the surpassing power belongs to God and not to us. We are afflicted in every way, but not crushed; perplexed, but not driven to despair; persecuted, but not forsaken; struck down, but not destroyed; always carrying in the body the death of Jesus, so that the life of Jesus may also be manifested in our bodies. (2 Corinthians 4:7–10)

I once observed firsthand how a messenger made of clay could be more effective than one made of silver. After minor knee surgery several years ago, I had a little setback. I was supposed to stay off my feet. At the same time, I had many hospital visits to make. I was embarrassed to wheel myself around in a wheelchair; I felt like a fraud looking for attention since I was only temporarily handicapped. But I dutifully rolled myself into hospital rooms feeling stupid and embarrassed rather than sauntering in wearing a dark suit and looking professional. The reception I received from those who were sick in bed amazed me. They were so glad to see me. They wanted to talk to me. We were both on the same level—my face in the wheelchair was level with theirs in bed. I was able to minister in ways I had never been able to do before because I was broken too.

As messengers, we do well to remember we are jars of clay. We can identify with those who need redemption because we have received redemption and still need Jesus to redeem our cracked and chipped lives. We are broken people addressing other broken people. I'm not commending airing our dirty laundry or making lurid confessions but rather, being humble. We are all people who struggle with self and sin.

We know from experience that our audience is full of broken people. Some have accepted Christ's redemption and forgiveness, others have never heard of it, and others are not quite ready to accept their brokenness and cry out for help. Many are physically ill or caring for others who are ill. Some are out of work. Others have broken marriages. There is suffering of all kinds. I could go on and on because every heart in our congregation is broken or cracked and crying out for God's help.

We proclaim to roomfuls of Christians who are forgiven but not all victorious. The church elder who is secretly having an affair, the deacon who is struggling with alcohol addiction, and the Sunday school teacher whose anger prevents her from sleeping. The pastor who subscribes to pornography, the youth leader whose marriage is collapsing, and the businesswoman who struggles to make ethical decisions. The teenager whose friend is using heroin, the single mother who feels unworthy of love and so looks for it in the wrong places, and the woman with breast cancer whose mother died of cancer and who lives in terror of her own future and is unable to trust God. We all need redemptive messages.

> For all have sinned and fall short of the glory of God, and are justified by his grace as a gift, through the redemption that is in Christ Jesus. (Romans 3:23–24)

Theological Questions for Redemptive Preaching and Teaching

- What seems to be the redemptive-canonical purpose of this passage in light of the Commander's intent and the larger salvation story?
- How does the Commander's intent and the passage as a whole portray the fallen condition of humanity?
- What method of proclaiming Christ and salvation would be most effective considering the Commander's intent?
- In what way is the Holy Spirit convicting us through this passage?
- How can the Holy Spirit empower us to live out the Commander's intent for this passage?
- What is the main redemptive or Christ-centered message of this passage?
- What is the general application of the Commander's intent?
- What is the application for the self-righteous listener?
- What is the application for the wayward or ready-to-repent listener?
- How does Jesus' life, death, Resurrection, or sustaining grace give us a reason to fulfill the application of this passage?
- What is the heart's focus I'm calling for? Do I want my listeners to be good or feel grateful for the goodness of the Lord?
- What is the motivation for change I want to promote?
- How are my listeners empowered to live out this message by the Holy Spirit?

CHAPTER 13

MAKE IT MEMORABLE:
THE POINT FOR PROCLAMATION

And he said to them, "Therefore every scribe who has been trained for the kingdom of heaven is like a master of a house, who brings out of his treasure what is new and what is old." (Matthew 13:52)

In the humorous movie *Planes, Trains, and Automobiles*, the character Neal (played by Steve Martin) is tired of listening to Del (played by John Candy) and gives him this advice:

You know, everything is not an anecdote. You have to discriminate. You choose things that are funny or mildly amusing or interesting. You're a miracle! Your stories have NONE of that. They're not even amusing ACCIDENTALLY! "Honey, I'd like you to meet Del Griffith, he's got some amusing anecdotes for you. Oh, and here's a gun so you can blow your brains out. You'll thank me for it." I could tolerate any insurance seminar. For days I could sit there and listen to them go on and on with a big smile on my face. They'd say, "How can you stand it?" I'd say, "'Cause I've been with Del Griffith. I can take ANYTHING." … And by the way, you know, when you're telling these little stories? Here's a good idea—have a POINT. It makes it SO much more interesting for the listener![i]

Always Have a Point

If you are going to say something on behalf of God—and that is what you are doing when you teach or preach Scripture—you must have a clear point, a point for proclamation. This point is the reason people should take time to listen to you. You should make the point, help people apply it, and give them some good ways and reasons to remember it.[1]

Our goal in proclamation is theological—to enable the people of God to be transformed

---

[1] The most important part of giving a sermon or lesson is to have a point. Make that point. Support that point. Illustrate that point. Convince people of that point. Get the point? There is nothing worse than realizing the teaching we worked hard to prepare all week had no point the audience could discern and needed to hear.

more and more into the likeness of God.[2], [ii] Everyone is bombarded with messages—moral, materialistic, entertaining, and inspirational. But people are counting on us to give them God's message, to have listened and to have heard from Him on their behalf. The message of a sermon or Bible study must come from what God is saying to us through His Word, from the passage we proclaim. We aren't merely reading the passage and providing commentary; we are declaring a message from the Commander regarding the passage. We aren't there to help others with an inspirational dose of self-help or grandfatherly advice and encouragement. We should read our passages and tell our listeners what they need to know from it and why.

In the novel *Gilead*, by Marilyn Robinson, the main character, a pastor, reflects on a woman who had been visiting his congregation (and who eventually became his wife).

> There was a seriousness about her that seemed almost like a kind of anger. As though she might say, "I came here from whatever unspeakable distance and from whatever unimaginable otherness just to oblige your prayers. Now say something with a little meaning in it."[iii]

Whenever I think of this quote, I feel the pastor was talking not only about a parishioner but also about God, who came from His "unimaginable otherness" just to oblige our prayers and inspire our words. We should "say something with a little meaning in it!"

---

[2] "For those whom he foreknew he also predestined to be conformed to the image of his Son, in order that he might be the firstborn among many brothers" (Romans 8:29).

Love Others by Proclaiming the Commander's Intent in One Clear Point

> In this is love, not that we have loved God but that he loved us and sent his Son to be the propitiation for our sins. Beloved, if God so loved us, we also ought to love one another. No one has ever seen God; if we love one another, God abides in us and his love is perfected in us. (1 John 4:10–12)

For those called to proclaim, our preaching and teaching is how we love others best.[3] We are called to serve others with our spiritual gifts. We are God's love and His message made visible and audible. Our inductive exegesis of the particulars of a passage in its canonical context is transformed by the leading of the Holy Spirit into a statement that reflects the Commander's intent for the passage. This statement is communicated to our listeners in the Spirit-filled event of preaching or teaching. For the benefit of our listeners, we condense the Commander's intent for the passage into a general universal idea, the point for proclamation.[4] This point for proclamation is the theme of our biblical expository message. We will aim for it to be clear, redemptive in nature, and applicable for today's listeners.

> The shepherds are senseless
> and do not inquire of the LORD;
> so they do not prosper
> and all their flock is scattered.
> (Jeremiah 10:21)

We discussed shepherding in chapter 10. Thoughtful proclaimers are shepherds of their flocks. Jeremiah and Ezekiel were especially angry at the shepherds of God's people who were supposed to be speaking for God but who did not seek Him for their message. The result of giving their own messages rather than God's was that their flocks became scattered. This is a natural result for anyone called to proclaim who fails to ask God for His message and clearly share it.

> This is how one should regard us, as servants of Christ and stewards of the mysteries of God. Moreover, it is required of stewards that they be found faithful. (1 Corinthians 4:1–2)

Paul called us servants of Christ and stewards of the mysteries of God. We may not all be the most eloquent of preachers, but it is our duty to at least be clear.

A bit later in 1 Corinthians, Paul commended the importance of a clear message over speaking in tongues in a worship setting. Though we are not talking here about speaking in tongues versus prophesying, I believe his argument regarding the clarity of a message can be applied to any unintelligible message pronounced in a worship or teaching setting.

---

[3] Sandwiched between 1 Corinthians 12 on spiritual gifts and 1 Corinthians 14 on the spiritual gift of prophecy compared with the gift of tongues, we read 1 Corinthians 13:1–2: "If I speak in the tongues of men and of angels, but have not love, I am a noisy gong or a clanging cymbal. And if I have prophetic powers, and understand all mysteries and all knowledge, and if I have all faith, so as to remove mountains, but have not love, I am nothing."

[4] See chapters 2 and 10.

If even lifeless instruments, such as the flute or the harp, do not give distinct notes, how will anyone know what is played? And if the bugle gives an indistinct sound, who will get ready for battle? So with yourselves, if with your tongue you utter speech that is not intelligible, how will anyone know what is said? For you will be speaking into the air. (1 Corinthians 14:7–9)

Sound a Clear Call: Have a Point for Proclamation

The thoughtful proclaimer method is distinguished by three distinct precepts for proclamation.

1. Determine the Commander's intent for a substantial portion of Scripture by inductively studying the purposes of the passage, its many contexts, and our audience.
2. Decide on the point for proclamation derived from the Commander's intent, and prepare a teaching or sermon with that as your guiding light and central theme. Use every element of your passage to illuminate and support the point for proclamation. The point for proclamation is relevant and redemptive in application
3. Make your message transformational by including a catchphrase and anchor image (in other words, something auditory and something visual or something that people can see in their mind's eye) that will catch your listeners' attention so they can recall and meditate on your message in the coming hours, days, and weeks. In this way, your message will be like a song with a clear, intelligible tune and a memorable, catchy refrain.

To identify the point for proclamation, we turn the Commander's intent, which can be a very long sentence or short paragraph, into a practical, redemptive proposition for preaching or teaching. At this point, we make the big switch from inductive to deductive thinking. We are done asking questions and mulling over them. We are moving from "What does it say?" and "Why does it say that?" to "This is what it says for us"—to the more direct process of making a statement, a point for proclamation, that is the central tenant of our message and the main precept of our teaching.

To determine the point for proclamation, we will prayerfully stitch together several things in our minds.

- Our Commander's intent which we extracted from the myriad other purposes for that passage being written and placed in the Bible. This is the result of all the questions we have asked of the passage and God.
- Our redemptive homiletic, which considers both the older brother (the faithful believer who has come to church to hear from God or the self-righteous one who does not recognize his need) and the younger brother (the lost soul hoping to come back home or the rebellious one wanting to run from the fold), and any other types of listeners God has impressed upon your mind to speak to today.
- The cultural assumptions of our audience that do not fit with our Commander's intent.
- The gospel message of salvation and the reality of sin. Redemption and hope offered to all.

From these knowns, we will craft our point for proclamation. In this way, our biblical

Commander's intent becomes the purpose of our teaching, God's message for our people in this time and place. God wants us to love our congregations and classes by sharing His message with them in a redemptive, transformational, and practical way.

THE PURPOSES OF THE PASSAGE ->COMMANDER'S INTENT-> POINT FOR PROCLAMATION

The point for proclamation will include the general principle of the Commander's intent and a general application of that principle that fits our listeners. It should support in some way every major point or idea in our biblical passage. It is appropriate for our listeners and their life issues. The point for proclamation is redemptive in tone; it considers people who are hurting, lost, prideful, self-righteous, and looking for help—in other words, people like us.

A Brief Example of finding a Point for Proclamation

Let's use Philippians 2:1–11 and work on an example.[5] The Commander's intent for this passage (built on our contexts and purposes, theology, and a canonical view) might be "Believers should be of one mind with one another, humbly considering the interests of others and using Christ as the example."

The point for proclamation will take into account the transformational message for the mature and self-righteous Christians in the congregation as well as the seeker or the one running from God. We'll also consider our cultural assumptions that encourage us to think of ourselves as more important than others. In the kingdom of God, everything is turned upside down, and we are called to do something that doesn't come naturally—to love one another.

Grateful hearts consider others first. We love others because God loves us. The self-righteous perhaps think they are already doing this and so need an example of when they're not. The seeker may be impressed or disbelieve that believers actually try to live by this principle of putting others first. And the one who wants to come to Christ may be grappling with the idea of putting Christ first let alone putting other people (particularly Christians) first.

Therefore, our point for proclamation in its longer form might be, "You deserve the best life has to offer, but perhaps the best is something other than you thought. Perhaps life's best is found in humbly considering others as more important than yourself. This is what Jesus did." We'll shorten our point for proclamation for the purposes of preaching to "Put the interests of others before your own."

---

[5] " So if there is any encouragement in Christ, any comfort from love, any participation in the Spirit, any affection and sympathy, complete my joy by being of the same mind, having the same love, being in full accord and of one mind. Do nothing from selfish ambition or conceit, but in humility count others more significant than yourselves. Let each of you look not only to his own interests, but also to the interests of others. Have this mind among yourselves, which is yours in Christ Jesus, who, though he was in the form of God, did not count equality with God a thing to be grasped, but emptied himself, by taking the form of a servant, being born in the likeness of men. And being found in human form, he humbled himself by becoming obedient to the point of death, even death on a cross. Therefore God has highly exalted him and bestowed on him the name that is above every name, so that at the name of Jesus every knee should bow, in heaven and on earth and under the earth, and every tongue confess that Jesus Christ is Lord, to the glory of God the Father. " (Philippians 2:1–1).

In the next section of this chapter, we'll think about turning our point for proclamation into a point for proclamation catchphrase, a succinct and hopefully memorable version of our point for proclamation such as "Put someone else's oxygen mask on first," or "You earned it, you deserve it, now add to your joy by giving it away," or "Instead of looking out for number one, point others to the real Number One." You can probably come up with something better.

Finally, skipping to the end of this chapter, we'll consider adding an anchor image, which might be as simple as a picture, description, story, or Bible story that gives your listeners a powerful mental or visual image perhaps of someone standing over the chair of an elderly person with an extended hand. Again, you probably have a better idea.

The Message Structure Is Built around the Point for Proclamation

Our message structure or our sermon outline is built around the point for proclamation, so it is important that the point for proclamation actually reflect the author's main point—God's intent—if He were speaking today. We often hear sermons with good introductions and a Scripture reading, but then, the message veers in another direction, and try as we might to figure out how it all ties together, we become lost. Our listeners will never know where our message is headed if we don't clearly tell them.[6]

If the point for proclamation is truly the point God has for our passage, it will not be difficult to see how the paragraphs or verses of the passage tie into it. Sometimes, this takes some meditation, and other times, it takes modifying our initial point for proclamation to better suit God's message from the whole passage.

A word of warning: knowing the Commander's intent and having a redemptive and relevant point for proclamation does not guarantee a meaningful message. We must show our listeners how the passage says what we claim it does. We must explain our Commander's point for proclamation and help our people apply it. If our message is truly exposing the Word of God, the Bible in their hands is their crib sheet, their sermon notes.

The Point for Proclamation Is the Purpose of Your Message

The authors of *Made to Stick: Why Some Ideas Survive and Other's Die*, wrote, "A well-thought-out simple idea can be amazingly powerful in shaping behavior."[v] Have one well-considered and accurate point for proclamation. Your teaching outline might have three important points, but they all should align with, support, apply, illustrate, or restate your point for proclamation. Whatever structure you use for your message, whatever outline you may have for a lesson, it must have only one primary purpose, one guiding light, one goal, one clear Commander's point for proclamation. And everyone who hears you should be able to tell you what it is.

---

[6] This is why we 1) don't read a bunch of interesting commentaries until we've identified the Commander's intent for the passage; 2) don't write our messages based on a book we are reading rather than the passage we claim to be teaching; 3) do decide on our Commander's intent and basic sermon structure before we decide on the joke we're going to use in the introduction, the title of the sermon, or even the point for proclamation catchphrase (next section). Our preparation must start with the Bible followed by finding the Commander's intent and point for proclamation and deciding on a basic message structure. Then we should read, read, read, look for illustrations, and prepare slides. If we change this order and throw in something we read this week that is inspiring but unrelated to our point for proclamation, we will lose our listeners; worse, we will lose the message God meant for us to teach.

Don't Leave Home without a Catchphrase

Hallelujah! Hallelujah! Hallelujah! Hallelujah! Hallelujah!
For the Lord God Omnipotent reigneth.
Hallelujah! Hallelujah! Hallelujah! Hallelujah!
For the Lord God omnipotent reigneth.
Hallelujah! Hallelujah! Hallelujah! Hallelujah! Hallelujah! Hallelujah! Hallelujah!
The kingdom of this world
Is become the kingdom of our Lord,
And of His Christ, and of His Christ;
And He shall reign for ever and ever,
For ever and ever, forever and ever,
King of kings, and Lord of Lords,

King of kings, and Lord of Lords,
And Lord of Lords,
And He shall reign,
And He shall reign forever and ever,
King of kings, forever and ever,
And Lord of Lords,
Hallelujah! Hallelujah!
And He shall reign forever and ever,
King of kings! and Lord of Lords!
And He shall reign forever and ever,
King of kings! and Lord of Lords!
Hallelujah! Hallelujah! Hallelujah! Hallelujah! Hallelujah

The point for proclamation catchphrase is the "Hallelujah" of the "Hallelujah Chorus."[7] It says a lot about God, but everything it says is captured or summarized by "Hallelujah"—"Praise the Lord!" We want our point for proclamation to pop, so we distill it into a catchphrase that will be memorable. It may take the form of a short parable, a slogan, a slightly altered famous quote, a jingle, or just a powerful word like "Hallelujah!"[8] By giving our message such a handle,

---

[7] The words of George Frideric Handel's "Messiah," which runs about two hours and thirty minutes, were compiled by Charles Jennens from the King James Bible and from the version of the Psalms included in the *Book of Common Prayer*. It emphasizes the writings of Isaiah. It has three parts focusing on the birth, Crucifixion, and Resurrection of Jesus Christ.

[8] Hallelujah is the pronunciation (transliteration) of two Hebrew words: *halal* "I shine" and *yah*, the shortened version of YHWH. So we generally say, "Praise the *LORD*!" (Hebrew *hal le lu+yah*). Note that in many translations the proper name of God YHWH (pronounced yah weh) is spelled LORD all in caps so that it can be distinguished from the usual word LORD.

a phrase that reminds us of the whole, we make it memorable. And if it is memorable, it can be transformational. We want our listeners to think about it all week long.[9]

THE PURPOSES OF THE PASSAGE ->COMMANDER'S INTENT-> POINT FOR PROCLAMATION ->MESSAGE STRUCTURE-> CATCHPHRASE

As you construct your message, you can continue to tweak your catchphrase until you get it just right. Though you need the Commander's intent and the point for proclamation before you can prepare a teaching, you don't need to finalize the catchphrase until you're in the final writing stage. Just don't leave home without it.[10]

My previous career was a medical research scientist. Some of my research involved studying tiny T4 lymphocytes in the blood of patients with and without HIV and the reproductive cycles of cancer cells. To do this, I used a flow cytometer, which worked by shining a laser at individual cells and using the amount and type of light diffracted from the cells to learn things about them. The seven-foot long laser tube had to be focused every morning with crystals and mirrors down to a very fine point so it could hit a single cell at a time. If my laser wasn't perfectly focused, my results would be fuzzy and my conclusions would be inaccurate or even wrong. The laser had to be continually refocused with exacting, smaller-than-pinpoint precision in order for the message I gained from the results to be useful.

The catchphrase is the tiniest point of light, the laser focus on your message. It is not the whole message; it merely points to it. It has to be sharp. It should make people see the message. It should make them think of your point for proclamation.

---

[9] The writer of Kings actually gave us the point for proclamation catchphrase when he told one of his stories of Elijah in 2 Kings 1. Three times in 2 Kings 1, he said, approximately, these words: "Is it because there is no God in Israel that you inquire [elsewhere]?" King Ahaziah had been badly wounded in a fall and had sent messengers to inquire of Baal-Zebub, the God of Ekron, instead of YHWH (the God of Israel) as to whether he would live. Throughout the story, Elijah or his emissary asked this question. By the third time, we understand the point: "Why would God's own people be looking to idols for help instead of YHWH?" So the Commander's intent might be to chide the people of God for trusting in false gods (and just about everything else) instead of YHWH. Also, for the king of Israel to publicly place his trust in another nation's deity was an embarrassment to God and His prophet, Elijah. The writer's point for proclamation might be that God alone is trustworthy; don't trust idols, and don't embarrass God by publicly seeking help from other cult sources when He has always faithfully loved us. The catchphrase, coined by the writer of Kings himself, is "Is it because there is no God in Israel?"

[10] I stumbled onto John Ortberg's sermon "All the Places You'll Go" from (Revelations 3:7–8). He talked about the open door placed before us, an opportunity to do good and have our lives count for eternity. His catchphrase was "All the places you'll go," a play on Dr. Seuss's book "Oh, the Places You'll Go!" One of his illustrations is of Abraham, whom he talked about in Dr. Seuss–like language. He has turned this sermon into his own book.

The best catchphrases include words taken directly from the passage. Is there a key word, theme, or repeated word throughout the passage that would make a laser-sharp catchphrase?[11]

The Catchphrase Is Written after the Message Outline

Don't write your catchphrase until you have written your message outline (see the next chapter). The message structure is based on the passage and the point for proclamation, which is derived from the Commander's intent for the passage. If your catchphrase is catchy, there's a temptation to write your message around it instead of the all-encompassing point for proclamation.

Your point for proclamation has given you a chance to consider where your congregation is and where you want them to be. Your message will show them where they are and where they are going with the aid of a well-defined structure.

Finally, the catchphrase will help them remember the way—it is purely a homiletic device. They can't take the entire message home, but they can take a compact catchphrase home.

Your Catchphrase Will Make Your Point for Proclamation Stick

You would be surprised how hard it is to ensure your listeners are able to remember the point of your message. People have other things on their minds; they lose track of what you are talking about here and there throughout your message. There are internal and external distractions vying for their attention. I cannot overstate the importance of making the point for proclamation clear by using some sort of memorable phrasing, imagery, or story. Use your catchphrase as many times as you can. Use it as a title in the bulletin or on the sign in front of the church. Then find an image that supports or illustrates the idea of your catchphrase and place both on a slide if you use slides. Remember—you should only have one point for proclamation and one catchphrase per message.

In *Communicating for a Change*, Andy Stanley gave five main questions to ask when we are stuck and can't find the central point to preach: 1) What do they need to know? 2) Why do they need to know it? 3) What do they need to do? 4) Why do they need to do it? 5) How can I help them remember?[vi] This corresponds amazingly well with the thoughtful proclaimer method. What they need to know and why they need to know it is the Commander's intent and the point for proclamation. What they need to do is the application derived from the point for proclamation. How we help them remember is the catchphrase and the anchor image. If it helps you to have a second way to think about this process, by all means use Stanley's method.

Warning: don't close your message with any point other than your point for proclamation and/or your catchphrase. We may want to close with an application or story, but your listeners may easily confuse the application or closing story (or anything else that comes at the end of your message) with the main point. Your final words must clarify your point for proclamation or

---

[11] For Romans 14:13–23, the key verse is verse 13: "Therefore, let us not pass judgment on one another any longer, but rather decide never to put a stumbling block or hindrance in the way of a brother." I identified the Commander's intent as follows: "Do what you can, make it your job to put nothing in the way of other people's faith but rather to build others up. Make it your job to help them be who God wants them to be. Make it your job at the very least to not do or say anything that will hinder them spiritually. Don't judge them or confuse them or offend them or lead them astray as they live their life of faith and as they practice their belief in Christ and grow spiritually." My point for proclamation was, "Let's make it our job to make sure that nothing gets in the way of other people's faith and spiritual growth." And my catchphrase was simply "Nothing in the way." My anchor image was a black-and-white picture of my daughter and son-in-law kissing.

emotionally impress it on the hearts and minds of your listeners. You can use a story or a song, but make sure they take home your point for proclamation. Don't inadvertently confuse your audience.

Try asking your congregation or class members what the main point of your message was, but don't be too offended when they get it wrong![12]

The Commander's point for proclamation catchphrase is the handle of the cup; it's a small part of the cup though it is made of the same material. The cup itself is the point for proclamation. The tea is the Commander's intent of the passage.

How to Write a Quotable Catchphrase

A quotable catchphrase makes the passage you taught memorable. Start with your point for proclamation. Consider a proverb or popular saying that sounds almost like what you want to say, and add a twist to make it yours. The title or a line from a praise song or hymn will often fit wonderfully, and you can close with those words to seal the message.

For a message that closely resembled my "Mrs. Destroyer" and "It's More Like Being in Love" sections of this book, I used Jason Gray's song title, "More Like Falling in Love." This was a popular song on Christian radio at the time. It stuck in people's minds, and to seal the deal, I played the song at the end of the message.

The wonderful little book *The Sir Winston Method: The Five Secrets of Speaking the Language of Leadership* by James C. Humes explores how to deliver effective speeches and is chock-full of great ideas for giving your cup a handle.[vii] In chapter 12, "The Magic Quotemaker," Humes explained what goes into a great quote. This book is out of print but worth looking for. Since it is out of print, I'll share some of Humes's secrets. A quotable catchphrase will "like cream … rise to the top." Memorable quotations have elements of familiarity, notability, and memorability. CREAM was the mnemonic Hume used to help us magically create our quotable, memorable catchphrases.

C—Consider contrasts. Jesus used this method in the Beatitudes, for example, "Blessed are those who hunger and thirst for righteousness, for they shall be satisfied."[13] Scripture often contrasts darkness and light: "For it is you who light my lamp; the LORD my God lightens my darkness" (Psalm 18:28).

R—Remember rhymes. Abraham Lincoln said, "Let us have faith that *right* makes *might*." The Bible does not have any rhymes I'm aware of, but you can reword things a bit to make a rhyme.

E—Echo echo. According to Humes, this device has been favored since the days of the Greeks (Aristotle's *Rhetoric* describes it). Benjamin Franklin said, "We must all hang together, or assuredly we shall all hang separately." Jesus said, "So the last will be first, and the first last" (Matthew 20:16; see also Matthew 19:30).

A—Alliteration. Alliteration[14] can be overused as I proved in my promotion of pointing to the purpose of the passage and making the point for proclamation pop. Alliterated sermon outlines are usually frowned upon as alphabetical gymnastics, but when used to help people retain the

---

[12] For example, I spoke on the story of Elijah running for his life from Queen Jezebel in (1 Kings 18:20–20:43). I identified the Commander's intent as "Know me. I am your shepherd. You are my sheep. You can trust in me." My point for proclamation was, "God doesn't guarantee that our lives will be easy, but He does promise He will not leave us." The catchphrase I used had a bit of a familiar ring to it: "When you come to the end of your rope, fall into the everlasting arms."

[13] Matthew 5:6.

[14] The use of the same letter or sound at the beginning of several closely spaced words.

Commander's intent, they can be very effective. The great preacher, Dr. Martin Luther King Jr., used alliteration in his address at the Lincoln Memorial when he pointed to a day when people "will not be judged by the color of their skin, but by the content of their character."

M—Memorable metaphors. Churchill once said, "Dictators ride to and fro upon tigers which they dare not dismount." The psalmist said the one who delighted in the Word was like a tree planted by streams of water.[15]

Hume ended the chapter full of his secrets for writing the best sorts of quotable lines with the reminder to close your talk with a zinger. If your sermon structure or lesson plan will allow for it, close with your "zinger."[viii] Your catchphrase will be most memorable if it's delivered (or repeated) at the end of your message.[16]

Anchor Your Message with an Image

Images act as cement. And no, I don't mean they can sink your sermon! I mean they can glue the message into your listeners' memory. They are ballast for the wandering, distracted brain. Images give our messages an anchor much as catchphrases can. Props, photographs, word pictures, stories, and Bible stories will make your message memorable.[17]

Jesus might not have used a projector, but He had already created the scenes, so He was well equipped to teach through images. He often walked with people through different settings and taught from those places—the path, the vineyard, the fountain. If you are stuck in a room or behind a pulpit with no way to show your audience an image, you can create the image you need in their mind's eye. A word picture has the power to remind us of a point just as well as an actual photograph projected on a screen. Other anchor images include descriptions, charged words (such as *rock*, *cross*, *blood*, or *storm*), a prop, an illustration (example), or a story. When closely tied to your point for proclamation or your catchphrase, these images will make your message stick.[18]

> The LORD told me, "Make a yoke out of leather straps and wooden crossbars and put it on your neck." (Jeremiah 27:2)

A good image is worth many words. The classical prophets—or perhaps God—were masters of image. God directed Jeremiah to make a yoke, the kind oxen use to pull a cart, and to wear it

---

[15] Psalm 1:3.

[16] Sometimes, the catchphrase can be used at the beginning, sometimes throughout the passage, sometimes repeated several times in the last half, and sometimes as the closing. It should be used enough so that no one forgets it.

[17] When I spoke on James 1, my Commander's intent involved knowing the difference between being steadfast in faith and being tossed by the winds of doubt. My point for proclamation was that success was finding what God had for us to do and doing it (being a doer versus a hearer only). Instead of a catchphrase (beyond James's own "Be doers of the word and not hearers only"), I used James's image of the one who doubts being like a wave that was driven and tossed by the wind. I had pictures of giant waves hitting stalwart, unmovable lighthouses, of waves hitting boats, and of a wave hitting an ocean liner and almost turning it on its side. Those slides played at appropriate times as I taught using an outline that closely resembled James's outline.

[18] Bishop Horace E. Smith, MD, used the images of blood cells in his sermon that he turned into a book (or vice versa) called "Blood Works." I heard him preach this at a conference, and he used the catchphrase "Blood works" over and over. See *Blood Works: The Insights of a Pastor and Hematologist into the Wonder and Spiritual Power of Blood* (Friendswood, TX: Baxter Press, 2010).

while he delivered God's message to an international delegation of kings assembled in Jerusalem to discuss the war. He was to tell them they had to unite to serve the enemy, Nebuchadnezzar, king of Babylon, and they should take up the yoke of Babylonian rule. His message was alarming, and his prop added shock value.

> To Zedekiah king of Judah I [Jeremiah] spoke in like manner: "Bring your necks under the yoke of the king of Babylon, and serve him and his people and live. Why will you and your people die by the sword, by famine, and by pestilence, as the LORD has spoken concerning any nation that will not serve the king of Babylon? Do not listen to the words of the prophets who are saying to you, 'You shall not serve the king of Babylon,' for it is a lie that they are prophesying to you." (Jeremiah 27:12–14)

Paul used the altar to the unknown god as his anchor image when he preached at the Areopagus, or Mars Hill, across from the magnificent ruins of the Acropolis in Athens.[19] If you sit where Paul likely preached, you will see the most striking view of the Parthenon, the temple to Athena among the other temples to ancient gods, one of which was unknown. At the time of Paul, the Parthenon was already nearly five hundred years old, an imposing edifice outlined against the sky.

Warning: your anchor image should be simple or it may confuse people. An anchor image is not the same as an illustration or picture that brightens or explains your message. Not every slide in a PowerPoint presentation is an anchor image. Make sure your anchor image is linked closely to your point for proclamation or catchphrase. Images can, on occasion, lead people to the wrong conclusion. Though they are more powerful than words, they are less controlled as to meaning.

An image might mean something different for different people. For example, I had a great image of an owl (the kind that hoots in my back yard in the winter) protecting her owlets while covered in ice and snow. I thought it was an effective anchor image, and my introduction discussed how owls had owlets in the dead of winter (it was winter at the time) so they would have time to grow strong enough to hunt in one season. Despite the cold, the babies were quite safe and warm burrowed in their mother's feathers. The point I was making was that we might not understand why God puts us in difficult situations, but we should trust we are safe and that experience might be needed for us to accomplish His plan. This image worked really well … for a nature talk. But it didn't cement the appropriate memory in the minds of my listeners because I got too involved in discussing the owls. One person came up to me at the end of the message and said, "Nice owl, but I don't get it."

He was right. As an illustration, the owl mother protecting her babies in the dead of winter was a good one, but it was too complicated for an anchor image and caused confusion. Had I made my point and then illustrated it, he probably would have understood. But by the time I had explained the image, people were mentally exhausted and missed the point for proclamation. My point for proclamation was, "If God is for us, nothing can stand against us" from Romans 8:18–39.

---

[19] "For as I passed along and observed the objects of your worship, I found also an altar with this inscription, 'To the unknown God.' What therefore you worship as unknown, this I proclaim to you. The God who made the world and everything in it, being LORD of heaven and earth, does not live in temples made by man, nor is he served by human hands, as though he needed anything, since he himself gives to all mankind life and breath and everything" (Acts 17:23–25).

MY INTERNET SERVICE WAS DOWN LAST NIGHT...
SO, DON'T EXPECT ANY PROFOUND
OFF-THE-CUFF SERMON ILLUSTRATIONS.   *ix*

How Can I Make the Message Memorable and Transformational?

- Restate the Commander's intent as the point for proclamation.
- Determine how your message should be applied—what do they need to do?
- Make sure your point for proclamation is not merely moralistic; it should also call for the enablement of God's grace and the power of the Holy Spirit.
- Write a memorable catchphrase that represents the Commander's intent with a dash of creativity and a pinch of application.
- Choose an image that will anchor your point for proclamation in the minds of your listeners—those who are visually oriented and mentally distracted.

CHAPTER 14

PULL IT TOGETHER

O for a thousand tongues to sing My great Redeemer's praise,
The glories of my God and King, the triumphs of his grace.
My gracious Master and my God, assist me to proclaim,
To spread through all the earth abroad, the honors of thy name.
—Charles Wesley (1707–1788), "O for a Thousand Tongues to Sing"[i]

Proclaimers Wear Many Hats

It is a great privilege to share God's message, but it takes much creative and intellectual work. To excavate (understand, interpret) our passage and build it into a message requires many skills; proclaimers have to wear many hats. I say, "have to," but that's what makes the job fun.

I once attended a NASCAR race. We were very surprised and pleased when the car our company sponsored won by a technicality at the last instant. No one was hurt, but it was exciting as there was a crash—cars rolled and flames shot out. At the victory ceremony, the driver, looking sweaty and exhausted but still smiling, and others on the racing team stood for a long time getting their pictures taken on the victor's stage.

They all donned hats displaying our company's logo and smiled and posed for pictures. We thought that was it, but they quickly threw those hats on the ground and put on new hats bearing the logo and colors of the next sponsor. Then they did the same for yet another sponsor. This continued for about twenty hats, each representing a different sponsor.

> More to be desired are they than gold,
>   even much fine gold;
>   sweeter also than honey
>   and drippings of the honeycomb.
> Moreover, by them is your servant warned;
>   in keeping them there is great reward.
> (Psalm 19:10–11)

Proclaimers must switch hats often and keep smiling though it's unlikely anyone will ever snap our pictures while we're preparing a message. The first hat we don is the miner's helmet with a light to help us dig for gold. The psalmist tells us that gold is highly prized. It is pure, it is rare, and it is valuable. The psalmist also tells us that the precepts of God are perfect—they are sure, they are true, they are always right, and they are pure like gold. Gold nuggets are in Scripture, but they are not always easy to spot. Like pure gold, they must be mined.

Our mining process has been the thoughtful proclaimer's inductive theological exegesis method. Some gold we stumble upon easily, some requires digging deep into the mine of history and grammar, and still other gold requires patient observation and meditation as we swirl the living water of the Word for days and days with both eyes open (okay, we can close them to pray!) looking for those bright spots of gold.

When we mine for gold, we may come across other valuable jewels, but they are not the central purpose, the Commander's intent. These little gems should not be thrown away but set aside as we continue our search for the prize. It can be very difficult to find that nugget of gold that is the Commander's intent, but once we find God's intent for the passage, we have acquired the metal that will build the structure to hold our message. The gold is formed into a piece of jewelry that is best understood as the point for proclamation.

Then we toss down our miner's helmet and put on the jeweler's visor, the one with the magnifying glass that flips down to help the jeweler see clearly to set each of those jewels—the sparkling verses we set aside a moment ago, phrases, key words, stories, characters, and cross-references. With our jeweler's visor on, we will carefully place those jewels in settings of fine gold, the gold of the Commander's intent and the point for proclamation.

We must never carelessly flash those jewels around. Instead, we polish and highlight them in their settings of gold. Using all the creativity and skill of an accomplished jewelry maker, we will keep our fingerprints to a minimum so others can appreciate the purity of the gold.

Next, we will trade the jeweler's visor for a battle helmet as we begin our struggle against spiritual forces attempting to hinder our proclamation and render it ineffective. We are battling to win the hearts and minds of all who will listen to our proclamation. This is not a battle of violence but a battle of love. It is not a battle to destroy but to restore the people to their King.

Finally, we will lay our battle helmet aside and slip on a builder's cap. Wearing our builder's cap, we help people apply the message God has given us to share. We use our words to build, encourage, and bring hope as well as to provide constructive correction. We are building the body of Christ, the kingdom of God. This part of our work goes on and on, week in and week out, as we assist in shaping our listeners carefully and lovingly into God's image.

And one day, we will join our King and Commander on the victor's stage. All those hats will seem like rubbish as we receive our crowns in perfect time to throw at the feet of Jesus.

God's Secret Work: Transforming the Fruits of Our Labors into Something Worth Sharing

The purpose of all our work is not to become Bible experts or sociologists but to grow in our relationship with Jesus Christ while coming to an understanding of His reason for including a particular passage in His Word. We have taken the time as good stewards to learn about those with whom we will share His message. In this way, we can apply the Commander's intent redemptively to our audience. Our careful exegesis has been the means to an end, the end being a message based on the Commander's intent.

At this point, we are prayerfully calling on our gracious Commander to assist us in proclaiming His name. We are preparing to convert our study into a message God can use by His mercy and grace to transform our listeners to be more like Him.

> As for that in the good soil, they are those who, hearing the word, hold it fast in an honest and good heart, and bear fruit with patience. (Luke 8:15)

Structure Your Message

All sermons and excellent Bible teachings must be prepared according to a clear structure. Without structure, we're just pasting together feathers hoping for a duck. We have something that looks like a Bible message, but it's all disorganized fluff, amorphous messages that leave people asking themselves, *that sounded nice, but what did she say?*

Have a structure in mind before you compose your message or teaching; your duck needs bones. I find myself pasting feathers when, instead of working through the proclaimer questions, I start writing my message too early. Or I write at stream of consciousness sort of message and then try to make an outline or structure from what I've written instead of starting with the bones, the structure, first. Other times, I read commentaries and books on my topic before I have decided on the Commander's intent and end up with all kinds of interesting thoughts, a basket of beautiful fluffy feathers I cannot give up, but I have no idea how to glue them together to fit the central purpose of my passage.

There are as many ways to organize messages as there are preachers and teachers. Every passage, every congregation, and every situation calls for something creative, God-inspired, and clear. I've provided a few structural ideas below to get you started. I enjoy the experience of trying new structures. The three-point structure is tried and true (and sometimes even expected). Surprise your listeners by using different structures or by preaching a narrative sermon. Any one of these structures will give you the bones you need.

The Most Basic Structures

I once heard Haddon Robinson (sadly on a CD rather than in person) explain how to preach. He gave three basic instructions for a simple sermon structure. He said (according to my memory) 1) tell them what you want them to know; 2) tell them what you want them to know next; and 3) tell them what you want them to know last. There's your outline. When I wake up in the middle of the night and start to panic because I don't have a coherent outline for a message, I swallow, pray a minute, and remember these simple instructions.

Hint: your congregation will probably remember only step 3, your final point, so make sure it contains the point for proclamation. Tell them the point for proclamation, tell them what the passage says about it, and tell them how they can apply it. Throw in a catchphrase or a memorable image they can take home in their minds and hearts … and done.

Another practical sermon outline was provided in chapter 10 under Sunukjian's Truth Outline, which is 1) What do I need to explain? (See chapters 5–8, 10, 13.) 2) Do we buy it? (See chapters 9, 11, and 12.) 3) What does it look like (the application)?

The No-Brainer Sermon Outline

Another popular preaching outline is this: 1) tell them what you are going to say; 2) say it; and 3) tell them what you said. Make sure what you say is the point for proclamation derived from the Commander's intent. If you use this outline, someone may remember your main point, and that is great! I think that this sermon structure is a little boring, but it is far better than no outline or plan—no outline being by far the most common sermon structure I've observed, unfortunately. Throw in a story or application for good measure.

The Passage Outline Becomes the Sermon Outline

Sermons can be formed around the structure of the passage. This works particularly well in some narrative stories and in some of Paul's writings, which are organized exactly as they should be proclaimed. Though this may seem to be the easiest sermon structure, in practice, it is often poorly done.

Too often, the problem is that speakers use the passage outline for the message outline because they haven't actually determined the Commander's intent and one clear point for proclamation. They have an outline, but it doesn't revolve around God's central intention for that piece of Scripture. Mistakenly assuming that they are preaching an expository message and using Paul's outline, they end up tap-tap-tapping through the passage like a blind man finding his way.[ii] Their listeners are left questioning the point of the message and how they should apply it.[1]

If you decide to use this message structure, make doubly sure to express the point for proclamation clearly. Don't read through the entire passage unless you do so before beginning your message. Too much reading can distract people when it hinders the flow of the message. If you do walk your listeners through the passage, encourage them to keep their Bibles open so they can read along while you highlight or quote the key verses or parts of the passage.[2]

Use creative illustrations, stories, and anecdotes to lighten things up and make the message stick. Remember to include a catchphrase, anchor image, or some other handle to help people remember the purpose of the message. Your introduction should address why they need (and want) to hear what you will say. And your closing should make memorable and clear the Commander's point for proclamation.

Structure Your Message to Explain or Convince: Deductive and Inductive Messages

Traditional sermon structures are deductive or inductive or a variation on one approach or the other. A deductive structure will begin with your point for proclamation and then explain, prove, apply, or convince your listeners of its value or truth. You may say, for example, that Jesus saves and then explain why this is important: 1) we are all sinners; 2) we need forgiveness; and 3) salvation brings us abundant and eternal life.

---

[1] We discussed this before in the section in chapter 2, "The Commander's intent Supports Expository Preaching."

[2] See Appendix G and third person story telling message, "Namaan Wanted More or the Bible study message on Isaiah 1, "Blood on Our Hands."

An inductive message will begin with a problem or question and work toward a solution or conclusion, which is the point for proclamation. For example, if the problems are 1) we are all enslaved to something; 2) everyone is a sinner; and 3) we can't dig ourselves out on our own; 3) the solution/conclusion is that Jesus offers a way and power and life.

You can even combine the inductive and deductive methods by starting with a problem, providing the solution (your point for proclamation), and then applying that solution to demonstrate why it's true or important. The variations are as endless as the passages we can choose to teach.

It occurs to Rev. Billings in the middle of point #2
that point #3 misses the point entirely.

iii

Preaching from the Heart: Structures from Timothy Keller

We may emphasize the issues we identified in our cultural exegesis or the problems we noticed in our text—the areas our listeners will have problems understanding, applying, or agreeing with. When we do, we should introduce them and then resolve them biblically. Timothy Keller offered several ways to turn a sermon proposition, our point for proclamation, into a complete sermon. Keller suggested following these steps (revised to include the terminology of the thoughtful proclaimer method). [iv]

1. Ask the passage several questions about the point for proclamation. Ask what, why, how, when or where questions. Ask why, how, when, or where the Commander's intent is resolved, embodied, or satisfied in Christ. Ask how the Commander's intent works. Ask what the positive effects are of having Christ involved as well as the negative effects of not having Christ involved in our lives or culture. Arrange these questions in your outline. Attach supporting material.
2. Use faceting. Look at the point for proclamation from several different angles or from the perspectives of different types of people or worldviews. Be sure to have an outline.

3. Contrast the point for proclamation with something else. Keller offered this example: if you are speaking on Matthew 25, "Waiting for Jesus," you can talk about the foolish maidens, considering the consequences of their actions, and talk about the wise maidens and what it means to live as they did. You can contrast the kingdom of God with the culture of humankind. You can contrast the Commander's intent with our usual behavior.

4. Expose a problem or controversial but popular assumption. Then answer or solve the problem in stages. The problem or controversial assumption should be solved or rectified by the passage.

In *Preaching with Accuracy*, Randal E. Pelton aptly described a typical Timothy Keller structure as follows: 1) The preaching portion describes or prescribes what Christians should be or do. 2) The preacher explains why we can't do this on our own. 3) The preacher points to Christ, who was or did what we cannot be or do. 4) The preacher explains how faith in Christ and the power of the Holy Spirit can transform us to be or do that thing.

This method begins and ends with application and has the gospel firmly placed at the heart of the message.[v]

First- or Third-Person Narration of a Bible Story

The Bible is full of stories just waiting to be told again and again. Jeffrey Arthurs, professor of preaching at Gordon Conwell Seminary, wrote, "Story is indispensable in embodying and transferring values."[vi] For narrative portions of Scripture, you can actually dramatize the story from the viewpoint of one of the characters. J. Kent Edwards explained how to do this well in *Effective First-Person Biblical Preaching: The Steps from Text to Narrative Sermon*. This style of preaching requires the proclaimer to have a dramatic bent, but it can be especially effective for special services or events. Some preachers even like to use a costume to signify the characters they are portraying.

My favorite preaching style is third-person narrative storytelling, though I usually narrate a story as part of a message rather than the entire message. In third-person storytelling, you are the omniscient narrator instead of a character narrating events according to his or her perspective. Although this method is less dramatic, it requires no acting skills.

I also like to explore how the story would have played out today, which helps keep people alert, makes the story seem real, and highlights the differences and similarities between then and now.

To be an expository sermon, however, our message must focus not only on the plot, action, and characters of a story but primarily on the point for proclamation. We must also have an application. The thoughtful proclaimer will use the story (as well as all the memory devices in his tool kit—repetition, the catchphrase, the anchor image) to direct listeners to the point for proclamation. In this way, a story becomes a sermon in disguise.

Narrative Sermon Structure

A narrative sermon follows a plot rather than an outline. It is not a Bible story but a two-way discussion between the teacher and the student. The plot takes us from a place of equilibrium (everything is okay) to a place of disequilibrium (What's wrong with this picture?) and back to equilibrium (peace through Christ and the power of the Holy Spirit).

Some narrative preaching is inductive by nature and allows the narrative to lead listeners to the point for proclamation. The parables often follow this approach. It is possible to state the point for proclamation at the beginning or to repeat the catchphrase (distilled from the point for proclamation) throughout a biblical narrative sermon.

Upset the Apple Cart à la Eugene Lowry

Eugene Lowry developed a well-loved format for narrative sermon structure. Lowry claimed that every biblical message should present a problem. Something is wrong with the passage, or the way we read it, or the way we live it out, or with the world or our culture generally. In a sense, every sermon involves an itch and a scratch, a human predicament or a felt need that our passage addresses.[vii] We are going along thinking everything is fine and then our apple cart tips over and we have to repack the cart. Our listeners come to us thinking that their lives are fine, that they have reached equilibrium. It is our task to upset their apple carts and help them find a truer equilibrium that nothing can disturb.

Lowry proposed a sermonic or homiletical plot for this narrative sermon structure. Instead of three points and a poem, Lowry's messages were arranged in the following plot stages: 1) upset people's equilibrium (show them that something is wrong, not working, or misunderstood), 2) analyze the discrepancy, 3) disclose the clue to the resolution, 4) experience the gospel as the resolution (or part of it), and 5) anticipate the consequences of following the old way versus the new way.[viii]

Communicate for a Change with Andy Stanley

In their fun little book *Communicating for a Change*, Andy Stanley and Lane Jones presented a structure for relevant sermons.[ix] They use a relational outline rather than an informational one. They call this structure ME-WE-GOD-YOU-WE.

ME—Introduce yourself and the problem with the human condition. Show the need or the problem that you and your listeners have. This is where you introduce the point for proclamation or the problem it will solve.

WE—Join your audience on this journey and cause them to trust you. Find emotional common ground—something you both feel a need for—and connect with them through this need. Encourage them to ask a question or consider a problem. Identify with the different groups of people in your audience.

GOD—Provide a biblical solution to the need you have just raised. This is where you explain what the passage has to say about the problem. Tell your audience what they need to know and why they need to know it. Give them information and motivation for making a change.

YOU—Ask your audience what they will do about the problem identified in the ME and original WE sections and the solution provided in the GOD section. Encourage them to consider how they can apply the point for proclamation in a practical way.

WE—Close with a relevant application for all the groups you addressed in the original WE section. Answer the need you raised, and inspire your audience by showing them how this need will be met if they follow the path you've laid out for them. End your message with a memory device—some way to remember the point for proclamation.

Stanley and Jones's sermon-writing method includes the following steps: 1) determine the goal of your message, 2) identify the point you want to make (for the thoughtful proclaimer method, this point is the point for proclamation), 3) create a map to determine how you will get there (WE-ME-GOD-YOU-ME), 4) internalize the message (see chapter 11), 5) engage your audience, 6) find your voice, and 7) start all over.

Plan Your Structure and Write Your Message

In our home, when the children were small, I attempted to make the rules clear. One day in utter frustration with me, my older son (then a preschooler) began to mimic me: "Number one: 'No snacks without permission.' Number one: 'No food in the family room.' Number one: 'No dessert if you don't eat your dinner.'" I believe this was before I found the remains of several unfinished meals hidden under the moss in the large houseplant next to his chair.

As you can see, propositional outlines can come off stilted and legalistic when presented as disparate points. As you can also see, a good outline does not guarantee a transformational message. Instead of giving point one, point two, and point three, consider having a conversation with your listeners. Use transitional sentences for your message manuscript and notes. You will probably have several points you want to cover, but if they all support your one point for proclamation, you can safely adapt your message into a more intimate style knowing that the entire message really hinges on communicating one idea—the point for proclamation.

Decide on Your Catchphrase Based on the Sermon Outline

Choosing one of these structures, construct the bones of your message. Once you have chosen your message structure, you can write your catchphrase. Jumping the gun is starting the race before the gun has been fired. Wait to write your catchphrase until you've structured your message and know where you're going with it. Then you can use your catchphrase in a variety of ways—as your title, introduction, turning point, conclusion, or sprinkled throughout your message so your listeners will remember your point for proclamation.[3] You have arrived at the starting gate. Grab your catchphrase and go. (See the "Don't Leave Home without a Catchphrase" section in chapter 13 for help writing your catchphrase.)

---

[3] Community Bible study teaching directors and associate teaching directors have been taught to "blink" their main point at least three times in every message.

TODAY'S SERMON "WHATEVER"

"The new pastor is a bit complacent for my tastes."   x

Compile Your Message

There are many ways to write a message once you've identified the point for proclamation. Decide on the best structure to communicate this message to your people. And write. The writing method is up to you. Some write a manuscript, some create a traditional outline, some create a transitional-sentence outline, and others use a few notes. Some deliver their messages using no notes at all.[4] The important thing is that you have something to say, a point for proclamation. You can be poised, articulate, humorous, and even emotional and say absolutely nothing life changing to your audience. For the love of your people, have a point for proclamation and make sure they can't miss it by giving them a catchphrase and an anchor image.

Your teaching or preaching is not a performance or a lecture but a three-way conversation between yourself and your listeners and God; between the Holy Spirit in you and the Holy Spirit in them. Jeffrey Arthurs commended dialogue between the proclaimer and the audience as a way to prepare to preach and as part of the preaching.[xi] You can do this by asking your audience rhetorical questions they can mull over.

Or the dialogue may be more overt. I've heard Timothy Keller detail some of the cultural assumptions that may have blocked his listeners from hearing him out; he addressed these assumptions at the start of his message and asked his audience to momentarily set those cultural assumptions aside and listen to his message. I frequently address issues I know may challenge my listeners early in my message in a dialogical way. For example, "I hear you asking, 'But aren't all

---

[4] If you want help in how to speak without notes, try one of these books: *How to Preach Without Notes* by Charles Koller, *Without a Net: Preaching in the Paperless Pulpit* by William Shepherd, or *Preaching without Notes* by Joseph Webb.

people good?'" I either answer the question or reframe it in a biblical way to diffuse the conflict before it becomes one in someone's mind.[5]

> It is characteristic of the preacher that he simultaneously questions, and proclaims. He must ask along with the congregation, and form a "Socratic community"—otherwise he could not give any reply. But he can reply and he must, because he knows God's answer is Christ. —Dietrich Bonhoeffer, *The Communion of Saints*[xii]

The goal is to communicate God's message to your people the best way possible. I've watched seasoned and well-known preachers read their Easter sermons before crowds of thousands to good effect. All matters of style aside, you need to be comfortable with what God is calling you to do. He can use you best when you prayerfully trust Him with the method. Attempt to make eye contact, use your arms a bit, modulate the tone of your voice to keep people listening, and avoid doing anything to distract or annoy your listeners.[6] However your message is structured or delivered, every part of it should lead your listeners to the point for proclamation.

Simple Slides

I have found that too many slides distracted my listeners; I now use them sparingly. Slides with lots of words are best left for business meetings. Rather, think of slides as billboards. Less is more (less information, fewer slides). Usually, one to five words or a key part of a Scripture verse—a sentence at the most—will suffice. If you must give an outline, present only one point at a time.[7] More than that and your class or audience will be trying to write down the information on every slide rather than listening to you.

But keep in mind that audiences who are used to them generally like slides, and if you suddenly leave them out, your visual learners—often men—will complain. A good rule of thumb is to use a blank, black slide when you want your listeners to connect with you. Remember that Jesus, the prophets, and the apostle Paul all used images in their teaching.

As for pictures, I suggest one per slide. Any text should be presented in a high-contrast color (black, white, or red), and a large font size (36 point). Keep the font style and size consistent throughout the presentation. Avoid changing background colors or images. Simplicity is key to reducing distraction.

---

[5] Jeffrey Arthurs and his cowriter, Andrew Gurevich, gave us further ideas for preaching using a dialogue-style structure. Beyond rhetorical questions and testimony, we can use role play or drama, tell stories that include dialogue, hold a debate, or ask for postsermon feedback. Jeffrey Arthurs and Andrew Gurevich, "Proclamation Through Conversation: Dialogues as a Form for Preaching," *Journal of the American Academy of Ministry* 5, nos. 3 and 4 (Winter/Spring 1997): 35–45.

[6] The top distracting tendencies I've noticed are: 1) pacing like a caged lion at a zoo; 2) stuffing your fists in your pockets; 3) licking your fingers to turn your manuscript pages; 4) smacking the tongue against the roof of the mouth before every important point (this is mine); 5) apologizing for your lack of preparation; 6) standing in one place with your arms hanging limply at your sides while speaking in the same tone and volume for a long time; and 7) my favorite—clicking your laser pointer on and off in your pocket causing an eerie glow to emanate from your side.

[7] Some good books on the use of slides include Slide:ology: The Art and Science of Creating Great Presentations by Nancy Duart and The Naked Presenter: Delivering Powerful Presentations With or Without Slides by Garr Reynolds.

Compelling Truth

> For the love of Christ controls us, because we have concluded this: that one has died for all, therefore all have died; and he died for all, that those who live might no longer live for themselves but for him who for their sake died and was raised. (2 Corinthians 5:14–15)

Once we find the Commander's intent, we aim to make living out that truth a compelling idea. This is not only a matter of clear presentation (though clarity is essential); we also need to make our message transformational. To that end, we have discussed how to make it memorable. Now we will discuss how to make it persuasive.

Take the truth to all SEATS:[xiii] Story, Example, Analogy, Testimony, and Self-Disclosure will help our message be life changing for others.

Stories add gravitas and emotion to our message making it more compelling for the listener. Stories touch people on the heart level.

Examples are a great way to show rather than tell when it comes to application. Provide an example of how your application would appear in action or how the world would appear differently without it.

Analogy is a combination of story, example, and sometimes word picture. An analogy shows how two things are similar. Jesus used a lot of analogies in the form of parables—"The kingdom of heaven is like …"[8]

Testimony implies that you can either borrow a testimony from something you've read, seen, or heard, or you can actually have someone stand up and give a compelling testimony on your transformational point (make sure it is not distracting to your message). Another option would be to use a video clip (but keep it short).

Since you have spent time living out your message, you can share your own testimony as well. Self-disclosure can be a powerful tool, but it is tricky. You must not cause your listeners to lose respect for you; self-disclosure should not be something that would fuel gossip. It is usually most effective when it is very humble.

---

[8] "Again, the kingdom of heaven is like a merchant in search of fine pearls, who, on finding one pearl of great value, went and sold all that he had and bought it. (Matthew 13:45–46)

"The vulnerability of your sermon
inspires me to share my own doubts ...
about the depth of your faith."

xiv

Powerful Illustrations

Illustrations have a special sort of power. You can say things through story that your audience might not be able to swallow whole if you said it straight out. Bryan Chapell closed his book, *Using Illustrations to Preach with Power,* with the following story, which I always remember when I'm tempted to point my long, bony finger at my listeners to drive home my point or application.

> One day Bare Truth came walking into town. What he had to say was very important, but he looked very intimidating with bulging muscles and hard knuckles. Some people remembered when he had hurt them before. As a result, most people went into their houses to wait for Bare Truth to finish his business. Only the strongest of the townspeople did not mind Bare Truth's visits.

> The next day Parable came to town. He looked just like most of the town's people and dressed in ordinary clothes, but he told of all the places he had been and the sights he had seen. All the people loved to visit with Parable. They came out to greet him and invited him into their homes. "Come in and have a cup of coffee and a piece of pie," many offered.

> Bare Truth was upset that Parable got a reception so unlike his own. He went to the other town visitor and said, "Tell me, Parable, why do people greet you with such warmth when I am Truth they should hear?"

> Instead of answering, Parable took off his hat and jacket and put them on Bare Truth. Truth was transformed. He was no less strong. He was no less Truth. But the people saw him in an entirely different light. When he put on Parable's clothes, Truth showed he really was concerned that the people hear him. When the people recognized that Truth cared enough about them to find out what he needed to do to have them listen to him,

211

they listened all the more intently. The very people who had invited Parable for coffee and donuts, now invited Truth, too.

To this day, when Truth has business in town, he puts on Parable's clothes so that the people will hear him and deal with him.[xv]

No matter what you say or how well you say it, if you illustrate it well, your audience will remember your illustrations over other details of your message. For this reason, illustrations are arguably the second most important aspect of your message (the point for proclamation is of course first). Your illustrations should highlight the point for proclamation. Any illustrations of subordinate points in your message should be shorter and less memorable than those that directly support the point for proclamation.

I once spoke on some passage (I don't remember it), and I told a great story about boating and getting stuck and being rescued. It overshadowed my point for proclamation. The audience loved it, but I know they remember that story instead of the point God wanted me to make that day.

Illustrations about yourself are acceptable as long as you don't appear to be bragging. Only the apostle Paul gets to say, "Live like me."[9] Illustrations about yourself and your family do help your audience get to know you and can go a long way toward helping people identify with you and see you as a real person with a life like theirs, not someone who lives and sleeps at the church. Self-deprecating humor is winning if not overused. If you use illustrations about members of your family, get their permission first. Be very careful not to use illustrations involving congregation members. Even if you keep them anonymous, people will begin to worry that you'll be talking about them next.

Tailor your illustration choices to your audience. Make sure they are general enough that everyone can understand them. For example, sports illustrations are wonderful for some audiences, but for a good proportion of most audiences, they will fall flat unless they are presented well. The crowd may roar when you express your support for a local team, but be careful lest you trivialize your message. Sports illustrations should rarely if ever focus on teams, scores, or how to play a sport; rather, they should focus on people or situations. Not everyone cares about baseball, but since everyone interacts with other people, talking about the personal aspects of playing a sport is safe.

The best illustrations are often drawn from Scripture. Consider using one of Jesus' parables or an Old Testament story. It is often said in preaching literature that biblical illustrations do not work today because people are not biblically literate. I strongly disagree; if the illustration fits and is well presented, you've killed two birds with one stone. Your listeners will understand the story and begin to know their Bibles again.

Use caution with television and movie illustrations or interviews. Video clips and interviews work best as introductions or conclusions rather than interruptions to your message. Clips can be helpful, but they tend to take too much time away from the message. The second problem involves your reputation. Once when talking about a song I'd heard on television, I noticed some disapproving smirks in the audience. The television show in which I had heard the song was known for having some off-color episodes. Our reputation is on the line any time we mention or

---

[9] "Brothers, I entreat you, become as I am, for I also have become as you are. You did me no wrong" (Galatians 4:12).

quote television, movies, sports figures, or famous or important people. If you decide to use an illustration that came from a source that might not be church worthy, make a clear note to your audience that you are using this illustration out of the context of its original setting.[10]

An example of a film clip that worked well was one I used to close a message on Acts 4, where the Sadducees, rulers, elders, and the high priestly family were questioning Peter and John's authority to speak for God. I used a film clip from "The Inn of the Sixth Happiness,"[xvi] a 1958 film based on the true story of Gladys Aylward, a British maid who was determined, despite her lowly circumstances, to serve God in China. Gladys, played by Ingrid Bergman, saved up her money to go to the mission field of China during the years leading up to World War II. Gladys experienced great resistance from the mission boards due to her lack of education and status. I compared Peter and John's work as uneducated, common men who effectively shared the gospel to the work of Gladys. I hoped to inspire my class to share the gospel like these three missionaries, Peter, Paul, and Gladys, who though they were not professionals and had never been given ecclesiastical authority to do what they were called to do, stepped out in faith and did it.[11]

Gladys, like Peter and Paul, knew how it felt to have the religious authorities ask, "By what power or what name did you do this?" Who gave you the authority to heal a lame person? Who is giving you the authority to speak for God? There are those who said to Peter and John, as well as to Gladys, "We're in control of that" or "We're in charge." Also, "We just can't have lowly maids and fishermen preaching and teaching." The mission boards made Gladys's road to China almost impossible. She wasn't educated, she wasn't rich, and she wasn't powerful; she was simply called, and she sought to answer her Lord's call. "Have you been told," I asked my audience, "that you aren't educated enough, not powerful enough, not equipped enough, and haven't the authority to follow God's call to proclaim the Word?"

In general, it is a turn-off to say anything hurtful about others with different social, cultural, or political views. I am not talking about softening the message of sin but about loving all God's children because we are all sinners. The only person you can safely make fun of is yourself. Warning: if you are a woman, don't tell jokes about men in groups that contain men. They don't like them, and in fact, they often don't even get them. If you are a man, don't tell jokes that disparage women. They may laugh, but it is not a good policy to be condescending to anyone based on sex, race, or creed. Never disparage other people who identify as Christians (even if you don't think they really are Christians), other churches whose views are not the same as yours, or other denominations. There is never a good reason to cut down Christ's sheep from other folds.[12]

---

[10] The third problem with clips is technology. Even if you have tested and double-tested the system, take my advice and have a backup plan. Be able to describe or tell what you had hoped to show. Don't apologize either—God likely had your message planned that way from the start.

[11] "Now when they saw the boldness of Peter and John, and perceived that they were uneducated, common men, they were astonished. And they recognized that they had been with Jesus. But seeing the man who was healed standing beside them, they had nothing to say in opposition" (Acts 4:13–14).

[12] We've probably all winced as liberals cut down conservatives and called them small minded; or conservatives cut down liberals by claiming they don't follow the Bible. We've heard jokes about Catholics, Pentecostals, Baptists, Episcopalians, Lutherans, Presbyterians and the rest of God's children who see things a bit differently than we do. But hurting others doesn't enhance the work of the Spirit. The only person you should point fingers at is yourself (or your own sex, denomination, etc.).

This undermines the kingdom of God and the work God may be doing in someone else's life unbeknownst to you.

In their book, *Preaching that Connects*, Mark Galli and Craig Brian Larson share with us that prime illustrations are true stories, fictional stories, generic experiences, images, quotes, and facts. These illustrations can be used literally or figuratively.[xvii] The idea of literal stories is easy to understand, but what are figurative stories? They are stories whether true or not that introduce an idea or that point to a truth rather than actually illustrating that truth.[13]

Galli and Larson provided this checklist of illustration sources: Scripture, personal experiences, newspaper, TV news, news magazines, cartoons, personal interviews, TV programs, movies, literature, radio, church history, encyclopedias, Christian magazines, secular magazines, fiction, biography, history, art, quotation books, anecdote and illustration books, and printed sermons.[xviii]

To help make your illustrations more powerful, consider making them specific rather than general and about people rather than things or events. Tell stories rather than making general observations. Use both logical and emotional appeal. True stories usually touch the heart better than hypothetical ones. If possible, show rather than tell. Take time to develop your story a bit rather than just alluding to it.[xix]

Illustrations are helpful to support your point, but an expository Bible message is not a string of statistics, jokes, and emotional stories loosely based on a theme. Overuse of illustrations backfires for two reasons: first, they distract from the point for proclamation, and second, they interfere with the teaching of propositional truth, which should be clearly articulated. It is possible to make your audience feel as though the Holy Spirit is speaking to them by yanking them emotionally, pressing on all their emotional sore spots, and leaving them right where they started—broken people with no hope of redemption or direction for change. It is possible to be inspirational and offer empty encouragement while leaving out the truth of the Word, real hope for eternal life, or a call for repentance from sin.

Make 'em laugh, make 'em cry can be good homiletical advice,[xx] but using emotion to win hearts and minds should be attempted only in the context of a propositional, expository message. Emotion and story are useful for touching hearts in evangelistic settings to encourage spiritual growth and sanctification or to teach the Word in a winning and effective way. Emotional illustrations are very powerful, but they should be used carefully and wisely, not manipulatively. Don't play with people's emotions needlessly—save that power for when it counts to seal the deal with someone's heart.

---

[13] One example of a figurative true story that I once told to a group of children goes like this: "Yesterday, I went into my bedroom and turned on the lights and nothing happened. I counted the lightbulbs, and there were twelve. So I got my keys, drove to Home Depot, and bought twelve lightbulbs. When I got home, I pulled out my ladder and one by one changed all twelve bulbs. Expectantly, I flipped on the switch … Nothing happened. The problem was not bad lightbulbs; it was that there was no electricity. No power. I could change those bulbs again and again, but without power, I would still be in the dark. The Christian life is similar. We can perform good deeds all day long—we can decorate for VBS and bake cookies for the homeless shelter. But without the power of the Holy Spirit, our deeds will not be as effective in changing the world." "Once I discovered the problem, I went down into the basement and flipped the breaker. Light! Just the flick of a switch was all I needed to provide power for all twelve bulbs. Before we run around fussing about doing all sorts of good deeds, stop and ask God what He would have you do. Let's ask Him for the power and wisdom to do it. Ask God to flip the breaker and give you the power you need to light up the world."
This story is figurative because it is comparing electrical power with the power of the Holy Spirit. A literal illustration of the Holy Spirit's power would have been to tell a story of a time when I did something with God's help that turned out to have a far greater than had it only been me doing it.

Illustrations Should Have a SHARP Focus

Your message should focus people's hearts and minds on the point for proclamation. Bert Decker's excellent book *You've God to Be Believed to be Heard: The Complete Book of Speaking in Business and in Life!* provides a list of good ways to SHARPen our illustrations.[xxi]

S—Stories and Examples: Jesus knew the power of story. Sometimes, He didn't even explain a story He told. That was Jesus. We on the other hand should let our listeners know what our story has to do with our teaching subject. Never underestimate the power of a story to transform and help people bring the point of the Commander's intent into sharp focus. When speaking to those who were not His disciples, Jesus taught almost exclusively with story. A powerful story can be your anchor image.

H—Humor: You can use jokes, but better yet, use your own personal brand of humor. Decker says that it is "virtually impossible to dislike someone who makes us laugh." If you have a dry wit, use it. Use self-deprecating humor. Be yourself.

A—Analogy: Analogy is a comparison between two things—for example, nature and the workings of humans. Other types of comparison—contrasts, similes, metaphors—will also help your listeners to understand and remember your point.[14] Some preachers use contrast as their message structure, start down one road and show it doesn't lead anywhere, and change direction with a biblical truth that resolves and applies the passage. Preachers, teachers, and country singers think in metaphor all the time.

R—References and Quotes: These should be recorded and read. (I have been known to misquote a statistic, which is not advisable!) Quotes, facts, data, and statistics add validity to your point for proclamation if not overused. They make you more believable. But the shorter the better. A two-page quote, however moving, will bore your audience. Read just one or two sentences and paraphrase the rest.

P—Pictures and Visual Aids: Visual material can be used to reinforce your message or make it come alive. People remember better what they both see and hear: "Presentations using visual aids are 43% more persuasive than unaided presentations."[xxii] Keep in mind that if you use an anchor image, any other pictures and visual aids should be related to it.

Introductions and Conclusions

Start with a PUNCH

> The heart of the wise makes his speech judicious
> and adds persuasiveness to his lips.
> (Proverbs 16:23)

I once had a man in my class who came, not because he seemed to have any interest in the Bible, but just to please his wife and mother-in-law. Sound familiar? As soon as I stood up, he would stretch his legs out, lean his head back, and close his eyes. I was told that was how he

---

[14] A simile is a metaphor, but a metaphor is not a simile. A simile uses a word such as *like* or *as*. (Psalm 22:14a) "I am poured out like water" is a simile. (Psalm 23:1) "The LORD is my shepherd" is a metaphor.

thought, but I was pretty sure that was how he napped. So, I made it my goal to catch him with something in my introduction that would make him sit up for a minute and open his eyes.

It has been said that you only have thirty seconds to get people to listen and in my experience, that's true for some people; we have thirty seconds to convince them to give us a few more minutes of their time and mental effort. We must gain their attention and hopefully help them identify a need in their lives or something flawed in their thinking. We must convince them that they really want to hear from us today.

Our messages must persuade and transform. Whether we are preachers, teachers, or leaders, our words should have an impact. We should introduce a subject by explaining why it is important. We want our listeners to know why our message matters. By planning ahead, we will know where we want our listeners to be by the time we've finished the introduction. Tell them why it is so important that they showed up this week. Explain what's in it for them.

Introductions and conclusions can ask and answer our listeners' questions: Why did I come here today? Why should I listen? How should I live differently? What should I do? What difference does any of this make to me? What's in it for me?

In *The Naked Presenter,* Garr Reynolds taught that a talk should start with PUNCH.[xxiii] Good openings, Garr wrote, often contain something **P**ersonal, **U**nexpected, **N**ovel, **C**hallenging, or **H**umorous.[xxiv]

P—Share a **personal** story or fact. This helps us to initiate a connection with our listeners. It answers the question "Why did I come here today?" This does not mean we are to recite our resume. Rather, by sharing a bit of ourselves, we lend our topic emotional relevance. (See the "Me" step in chapter 13, "Communicate for a Change with Andy Stanley").

Another great thing about a personal story is that we don't need notes for it. No matter how inexperienced at speaking we are, we can tell opening stories from our lives while maintaining direct eye contact with our audience. We're connected; we're on their island.

Remember that the personal story we tell should illustrate in some way the main point we are trying to make (the point for proclamation) or should begin to cause people to see the need for it.

U—Say or do something **unexpected**. Most people have an attention span of only about ten minutes. However, you can hold their interest longer by starting with something unexpected. Everyone loves a surprise. This might be a quote, a question, a fact, or a surprising thing you do. I remember speaking once very early in my speaking ministry. I was worried about finishing my message in the allotted time. When I noticed the clock, I burst out laughing because I was so relieved to see I had plenty of time for the rest of the message. More than a few people sat up and paid attention partly because my outburst scared them and partly because they feared I was mentally unstable. But at least they listened.

N—Show or tell something **novel**. Some people are listening to you because they want to learn something new or hear something original. Everyone in your audience wants to make a discovery about himself or herself or God's Word. Use a powerful or memorable image to introduce your subject. Include a story or statistic that no one has heard. Or describe the backstory of a hymn or a popular song. Many people like to know something about the biblical location, history, or culture. If you're not going to tell people something they don't already know, why should they come in the first place? Again, this novel item should point to the truth you are proclaiming.

C—**Challenge** their assumptions. Preaching on Acts 1 for Pentecost, I opened with, "You remember from school that energy can be neither created nor destroyed. That is true except when God acts." Challenge their thinking, their intellects, their imagination, their cultural assumptions. People come to your church, study, or class specifically to be challenged, so don't disappoint them. In a Christian setting, the idea of a challenge takes on even more meaning because everything we say and do has eternal significance. If we challenge someone, it should be a spiritual challenge, not merely a moral challenge. Our aim is not to make people better but more like Christ; it is not merely to teach people how to live but to show them how to have eternal life.

H—Use **humor**. Laughter engages and disarms your listeners. Someone once said, "When their mouths are open with laughter, slip in the pill of truth." Garr warned, however, that starting with a joke usually falls flat. He recommended that we forget about jokes and instead make an ironic observation, share an anecdote, or tell a humorous story relevant to our point or topic. Humor taps into people's emotions. Laughter also releases endorphins, and by relaxing both us and our audience, it can assist in changing their perspective. Just be sure your humor is relevant to your subject and appropriate to your audience and setting.

The prophets of the Old Testament always packed a PUNCH. When we read their sermons and writings, we can see that they were masters of the unexpected, the original, and the unforgettable. God taught the prophets how to do this and commanded them to use these methods to convey His message. Consider Jeremiah 19, in which the LORD told Jeremiah to buy a new clay pot from the potter.[15] He was to take some of the elders and the priests and warn them that the God of Israel would bring disaster on them because they had forsaken Him and worshipped other gods. They had even burned their children in the fire as offerings to the idol Baal. Jeremiah led the elders and priests to the valley where they made sacrifices to idols, and while he was speaking, he got their attention by heaving a big clay pot crashing down at their feet.[16]

When God wanted people to listen, He never held back. He struck hard. If you want your introduction to really knock people out, start with a PUNCH.

---

[15] "Thus says the LORD, 'Go, buy a potter's earthenware flask, and take some of the elders of the people and some of the elders of the priests, and go out to the Valley of the Son of Hinnom at the entry of the Potsherd Gate, and proclaim there the words that I tell you. You shall say, "Hear the word of the LORD, O kings of Judah and inhabitants of Jerusalem. Thus says the LORD of hosts, the God of Israel: Behold, I am bringing such disaster upon this place that the ears of everyone who hears of it will tingle"'" (Jeremiah 19:1–3).

[16] "Then you shall break the flask in the sight of the men who go with you, and shall say to them, 'Thus says the LORD of hosts: So will I break this people and this city, as one breaks a potter's vessel, so that it can never be mended. Men shall bury in Topheth because there will be no place else to bury'" (Jeremiah 19:10–11).

According to a recent poll...uh sorry...
according to the Book of Matthew. *xxv*

In Conclusion

Some of the best speakers say they spend most of their time on their introductions and conclusions. For a Bible speaker, I'm not sure that is wise; nonetheless, takeoffs and landings are often how we evaluate and remember the flight. If they are bumpy or late, we remember the trip as uncomfortable.

The problem with conclusions is that they have to be solidly representative of our Commander's intent, contain our point for proclamation, and repeat our catchphrase because whatever we say last is what our listeners will most likely take home.

Mark Galli and Craig Brian Larson shared eight basic methods for concluding a message in their book *Preaching That Connects: Using Journalistic Techniques to Add Impact*. They are as follows.[xxvi]

- Summarize what you've said.
- Paraphrase what you've said (restate your point for proclamation in a new way or by using a metaphor).
- Circle back to your beginning (complete a story that you started at the beginning or complete an image).[17]

---

[17] Pastor Bill Gestal of the Presbyterian Church of Old Greenwich in Old Greenwich, Connecticut, used this technique to great effect one Easter when I filled an entire row with my family and extended family. He started the sermon with the story of a boat containing him and his brother that capsized. He gave a good gospel message. In the end, he (finally) let us know he had been able to save his brother from drowning. Our dinner table was abuzz that Easter as everyone talked about that story and ultimately about the sermon and the offer of salvation that was given.

- Play the refrain (drive home your catchphrase—that line ought to be ringing in people's ears as they leave).
- Illustrate or share a quote, statistic, or surprising fact that will make the message memorable.
- Quote the key text (this works especially well in a deductive-style message where you save the point for proclamation for the end).
- Apply the text (tell a story that brings the application to life).
- End with a challenge or appeal (challenge your audience to do something with what they've heard—this is the transformative element of the message).

For any Bible teacher/preacher, the introduction portion of a message can mean the difference between engaging our audience and causing them to tune us out. The conclusion is even more important, however, because it is often the thing people remember the most clearly. I sometimes make it a little game to ask people I know well what my message was about. They always tell me what I said in conclusion despite the fact that I'd said many other things.

Good conclusions often use emotion to anchor the point in the listener's heart. As long as it is exactly on target and ends with your catchphrase, a good story will work well. Poems and long quotes have gone out of fashion unless they are particularly winning. Whatever method you use, know how you will conclude before you start speaking!

FLETCHER   *xxvii*

Plan for a Response to Your Message

God has given you a message He wants to use in hearts and lives. Plan for ways to help people respond to it. What do you want your listeners to do, be, or feel when they leave? What is the best way to elicit that response? Should you have them respond to an invitation, altar call, or commitment? Would a moment of silence be more appropriate? How about helping them repeat the Commander's intent, the point for proclamation, or the catchphrase? Should you have people standing by ready to pray with or counsel the audience? Is there a song that people could listen to? Better yet, is there one they could sing to verbalize the commitment the message calls for? Often, the prayer or a time of silence at the end of a class or a message can help people articulate in their hearts their response. Though planning for a response is good, the same kind of response shouldn't be repeated so often that it loses its power.

Take care that the response you plan does not disrupt the mood of worship or contemplation the people in your audience are in. Though we want people to respond, the most important response must be in their hearts at least initially. Our call for response must not interrupt this important work. We are also not trying to manipulate, cajole, embarrass, or force people to respond. During the short time people are in the presence of the Holy Spirit and the teacher, they may only have a chance to begin to internalize the message. It is tempting for us to want to see people do something because of what we have said, but what we most want is for them to fully internalize the message first.

The response is not about us but about God working on our listeners. Preaching and teaching are three-way conversations between us and our listeners but more important between our listeners and their Lord. The Holy Spirit, you and I, and our class or congregation are all speaking together on a deeper level. Leave room for God to work and make the message memorable so they will be thinking of it for a long time.

Final Check on Your Message

Every message needs a final haircut before it goes out in public. Everything that is extraneous must be cut away. Anything that isn't relevant to the Commander's intent is not relevant to your message. When my older son was little, he was terrified of getting his hair cut. He would run and hide behind a bush when it was time to get in the car for a haircut. He thought a haircut would hurt. Haircuts don't hurt, but cutting things out of our message because they are not on point does hurt. We have to be tough.

The book *Made to Stick* illustrates this advice by sharing this definition of engineering elegance by the French aviator and author Antoine de Saint-Exupéry: "A designer knows he has achieved perfection not when there is nothing left to add, but when there is nothing left to take away." *Made to Stick* continues: "The designer of simple ideas should aspire to the same goal: knowing how much can be wrung out of an idea before it begins to lose its essence."[xxviii]

If you have time, tell someone else your message. I don't mean preach at them over dinner or give them a Bible teaching with their breakfast cereal, but tell someone else what you are going to say. Use your main structure. Let them talk back. Make it a discussion. It is much better to hear people's comments and questions before you speak rather than later when the toothpaste (your message) has already been squeezed from the tube and can't be put back. Often, their response will not be what you would have anticipated. In any case, you will benefit from hearing the viewpoints of others on your point for proclamation prior to sharing rather than after it's too late.

Thoughtful Proclaimers Move On to the Next Message

> Nice sermon, Pastor. Say, did you hear Charles Stanley [preach] on television this morning?—Haddon Robinson[xxix]

A seasoned pastor once told me that he tried not to think about the message he just gave but rather, he focused ahead to the next week's message. This is good advice. Avoid self-criticism and self-congratulatory backslapping. Turn your attention to the coming week's message. Preaching and teaching, like Christmas morning when the room is full of unwrapped presents and torn paper tossed aside, can leave us feeling depleted and let down. Sometimes, we drive home on a high remembering everything we said fondly and thanking God for making the pieces of a message come together. Other times, we feel washed out, insecure, and maybe a little miffed with God for not pulling a rabbit out of a hat for us. We forgot something. We misspoke. We didn't make our points clearly. People got up and left early. Why was that? No one said they liked the message. What did I do wrong? On such days, we can eat two pizzas or get started on next week's message. I have heard that a certain very famous televangelist, who shall go unnamed, used to eat a half gallon of ice cream on Sunday nights.

But seriously, we have been abiding in the vine and have borne fruit that God called us to share in His name. He turned our fruit into wine. Not every batch is the same, not every bottle gets a perfect score of 10. But it's God's work. If we proclaim God's intent for a passage as clearly and imaginatively as we can, the rest is up to Him. To repeat the Scripture from the beginning of chapter 2, "So shall my word be that goes out from my mouth; it shall not return to me empty, but it shall accomplish that which I purpose, and shall succeed in the thing for which I sent it" (Isaiah 55:11). God gave us His message from His Word, and we proclaimed it to the best of our ability. With that same sense of trust, we must leave the results to Him. Use any despair you might feel to spur you on to do better next week. Read a good book on preaching or teaching (see "Read More about It" in the appendix). But don't lose sleep.

In the parable of the talents, the servant who turned five talents into ten and the one who turned two into four received the same commendation: "Well done, good and faithful servant. You have been faithful over a little; I will set you over much. Enter into the joy of your master."[18]

WHEN PASTORS DREAM.   xxx

---

[18] Matthew 25:14–30.

You Are a Light on a Hill

> You are the light of the world. A city set on a hill cannot be hidden. Nor do people light a lamp and put it under a basket, but on a stand, and it gives light to all in the house. In the same way, let your light shine before others, so that they may see your good works and give glory to your Father who is in heaven. (Matthew 5:14–16)

A lighthouse stands on a hill to guide and warn ships. In conjunction with a ship's charts, the lighthouse marks dangerous shoals and safe harbors. We are lighthouses for people whose charts are the Word of God. We are placed in our positions to warn and encourage. Most important, we are placed there to make clear the offer of salvation available to all people.

A lighthouse bears a very small light. That little light, which would not otherwise be very useful for a distant ship in a storm at sea, is focused and amplified with lenses and mirrors that turn it into something far more powerful and useful. This is the task of a thoughtful proclaimer. We are just people, not outstanding in any way on our own. But when we polish our lenses, clean our mirrors, and keep our glass clear, our little lights will do far more than we can imagine.

Oswald Chambers encourages us with these words.

> If Jesus ever commanded us to do something that He was unable to equip us to accomplish, He would be a liar. And if we make our own inability a stumbling block or an excuse not to be obedient, it means that we are telling God that there is something, which He has not yet taken into account. Every element of our own self-reliance must be put to death by the power of God. The moment we recognize our complete weakness and our dependence upon Him will be the very moment that the Spirit of God will exhibit His power.[xxxi]

Hermeneutical Questions

- Who is my audience, and what are their needs they know about and those they aren't aware of?
- Why did they come here today?
- Why should they listen?
- What difference can this message make to them?
- How should they live differently?
- What should my listeners do now?
- How can I point to the application without being legalistic, moralistic, or nagging?
- In what way do my listeners' cultural assumptions support or conflict with this passage?
- How do the events in this text correlate with events in my community or the world?[xxxii]
- How can I show the difference between what we are called to do in this text and what God has already done for us?
- How can I make clear that our goodness and moral actions are not a way to win favor with God but rather should be done in gratefulness to Jesus Christ?
- How can I show that no one can faithfully perform the actions called for in this text without God's help?

- How will I make clear that we have all fallen short of this goodness but that we can be forgiven by God's free offer of grace?
- How can I demonstrate the living out of these actions by the Holy Spirit's help?
- How do I answer the question my listeners have about the point for proclamation— "So what?"

Homiletical Questions

- What is the best way to structure this message to communicate the point for proclamation to this audience? (Write down your message outline or structure.)
- What is my catchphrase?
- What images, stories, references, or illustrations will I use to support the point for proclamation?
- How will I introduce my message?
- How will I conclude my message?
- How will I make my message stick so my listeners will not forget it?
- How will I allow for a response to God's working through my message?

Preflight Checklist

- Does my introduction connect with my audience and make them want to listen?
- Does my introduction prepare my audience for the message?
- Do I connect with my audience emotionally or culturally at the start of the message?
- Is there an action called for in this passage, and do I include it in my message?
- Have I applied generally and specifically the action called for?
- Is it clear why my listeners should want to act in this way?
- What are the ramifications of not performing the action my message encourages?
- Is God's message my message?
- Do I point out the need for a grateful response to the suffering of Christ on the cross?
- Do I expect people to help themselves or encourage them to call on the Holy Spirit for help?
- Do I state any of my perspectives or opinions as biblical truths rather than what they are?
- Do I waste time discussing ideas that aren't relevant to my message?
- What can I cut out?
- Does my catchphrase lead people away from the meaning of the passage?
- Does my point for proclamation reflect the most significant point in the passage?
- Is the point for proclamation a transformational point, not just a point of fact?
- Is the point for proclamation universally applicable?
- Do all the other points in my outline, stories, and illustrations directly support the point for proclamation?
- Does my conclusion directly support and distill the point for proclamation?
- Do I explain the ramifications of not doing what the Bible says in this passage?

- Does my message speak to the younger brothers (the prodigal sons or daughters) and the self-righteous older brothers (or sisters) in my audience?
- Do I explicitly include the gospel (redemption, forgiveness, hope) in my message?
- Are there any cultural, historical, or other types of differences between then and now that may affect the truth of my point for proclamation?
- Do I give credit for all quotes, ideas, and illustrations? Do I have permission to use all the images I have on screen? Have I obtained the proper licenses for the use of my video clips?

Spooky stories around the Pastor Retreat campfire.

APPENDICES

APPENDICES

READ MORE ABOUT IT

Read More about Personal Preparation

Calvary Road, Roy Hession
Thirsting for God, Gary L Thomas

Read More about Biblical Interpretation

How to Read the Bible for All Its Worth, Gordon Fee and Douglas Stuart
An Introduction to the Bible, Norman Geisler and William E. Nix
The Holman Guide to Interpreting the Bible, David S. Dockery and George H. Guthrie

Read More about Picking a Passage

Preaching with Accuracy: Finding Christ-Centered Big Ideas for Biblical Preaching, Randal E. Pelton
Preaching with a Plan: Sermon Strategies for Growing Mature Believers, Scott M. Gibson
Narrative Art in the Bible, Shimon Bar-Efrat
The Art of Biblical Narrative, Robert Alter
Effective First-Person Biblical Preaching: The Steps from Text to Narrative Sermon, J. Kent Edwards

Read More about Biblical Context

How to Read the Bible Book by Book, Douglas Stuart and Gordon Fee
How to Read the Bible as Literature and Get More Out of It, Leland Ryken
The IVP Bible Background Commentary: New Testament, Craig Keener
The IVP Bible Background Commentary: Old Testament, John H. Walton, Victor Matthews, and
    Mark W. Chavalas
A History of Israel, John Bright
Backgrounds of Early Christianity, Everett Ferguson

Read More about Digging Deep

How to Study Your Bible: The Lasting Rewards of the Inductive Method, Kay Arthur
The New Joy of Discovery in Bible Study, Oletta Wald
Women of the Word: How to Study the Bible with Both Our Hearts and Our Minds, Jen Wilkin
The Navigator Bible Studies Handbook
Methodical Bible Study, Robert A. Traina

Read More about Digging Deep—Word Studies for Those without Greek and Hebrew

Greek for the Rest of Us: Mastering Bible Study without Mastering Biblical Languages, William D. Mounce
Hebrew for the Rest of Us: Using Hebrew Tools without Mastering Biblical Hebrew, Lee M. Fields

Read More about Understanding Your Listeners

The Prodigal God: Recovering the Heart of the Christian Faith, Timothy Keller
Preaching: Communicating Faith in an Age of Skepticism, Timothy Keller

Read More about Redemptive Proclamation

Christ-Centered Preaching: Redeeming the Expository Sermon, Bryan Chapell
Preaching Christ from the Old Testament: A Contemporary Hermeneutical Method, Sidney Greidanus

Read More about Finding the Purpose of Passages

Biblical Preaching: The Development and Delivery of Expository Message, Haddon Robinson
Invitation to Biblical Preaching: Proclaiming Truth with Clarity and Relevance, Donald Sunukjian
Four Views on Moving beyond the Bible to Theology, Stanley N. Gundry, series ed. Gary T. Meadors, gen. ed., Walter C. Kaiser, Daniel M. Doriani, Kevin J. Vanhoozer, William J. Webb
The Big Idea of Biblical Preaching: Connecting the Bible to People, Keith Willhite and Scott M. Gibson, eds.

Read More about Making It Memorable

You've Got to Be Believed to Be Heard: Reach the First Brain to Communicate in Business and in Life! Bert Decker
Made to Stick: Why Some Ideas Survive and Others Die, Chip and Dan Heath
Sir Winston Method: The Five Secrets of Speaking the Language of Leadership, by James C. Humes

Read More about Putting It All Together

The Art and Craft of Biblical Preaching, Haddon Robinson and Craig Brian Larson, eds.

Preaching with Variety, Jeffrey Arthurs

The Homiletical Plot: The Sermon as Narrative Art Form, Eugene Lowry

Preaching That Connects: Using Journalistic Techniques to Add Impact, Mark Galli and Craig Brian Larson

Communicating for a Change, Andy Stanley and Lane Jones

Slide:ology: The Art and Science of Creating Great Presentations, Nancy Duarte

The Naked Presenter: Delivering Powerful Presentations with or without Slides, Garr Reynolds

APPENDIX B

THE THOUGHTFUL PROCLAIMER MESSAGE PREPARATION WORKSHEET

The most important thing that proclaimers of God's Word can do is find God, the Commander's, intent for Scripture and let it transform their lives. Then, they must make that intent clear and memorable to others showing them how to live transformed lives in light of God's message to them and offering them motivation to live out God's intent through the power of the Holy Spirit based on a grateful response to Christ's sacrifice.

This worksheet is a template for you to use in sermon or teaching preparation. Photocopy these pages or download a Microsoft Word file of this document for your use from our website so you can edit it and make your own worksheet that fits your thoughtful exegesis and message-writing style.

You will not write down answers to every question. The questions are to guide your thoughts and keep you from missing something important. Not every question will be needed from every passage. Many of the questions are answered at or near the beginning of your sequential teaching through a book of the Bible.

Date to speak: _____

Passages under Consideration for Message: _____

Specific Key Portion to Proclaim: _____

The Commander's Intent_____

_____

_____

The Point for Proclaiming: _____

_____

The Point for Proclamation Catchphrase: _____

Anchor Image:_____

Message Title: _____

Do not hesitate to proclaim the whole will of God. (Acts 20:27)

If Scripture is my authority and the gospel is my motivating call for change, I can speak with full conviction and confidence.

PRACTICAL PREPARATION

Prepare Yourself—You Are on Holy Ground

The first step in message preparation is messenger preparation.

Confess sins and examine yourself, your motives, your doubts, your family and church problems, the chips on your shoulder that will affect how you read and apply this passage, and consider anyone you need to forgive or ask forgiveness from.

Plan Your Proclamation

1. Plan and portion your Scripture for preaching. Remember to choose large portions, usually about a chapter or more. (See "Questions for Picking Passages" at the end of chapter 4.)
2. Choose a book and divide it into sections. Ask questions of the author and book of the Bible. Note: this need to be done only for the first passage you teach on as long as you can keep it in mind.

BOOK-LEVEL QUESTIONS
- Who wrote this book, and what can we say about the human author?
- Who was this book written to?
- When was this book written?
- Was this book written to or about a special occasion, event, or occurrence?
- Why was this book written? What purpose did the author have?
- What was happening in Israel's, or the church's, or world history at the time this book was written?
- What was happening or was about to happen?
- What is this books place in the cannon of Scripture? History?
- What would be missing from the Bible if this book were not there?
- How does this book fit into the story of salvation?
- How was this book originally meant to be used? (Preached, sung, used for festivals, read aloud, read personally, read in church?)
- How did the author or editors organize or divide this book? Why?
- What is the main message of this book I have chosen to speak on?

3. Choose the parameters for the section you will preach or teach on this week.
4. If your passage is very long (several chapters), consider which specific section is the most representative of the larger message. This may help make your task more manageable.

PRACTICAL PREPARATION QUESTIONS
- What is the passage under consideration this week for my message?
- What are the boundaries of the text to be preached, and why did I choose them? (Generally speaking, ignore chapter and verse and focus on the message of story.)

- Does my passage carry a complete thought? Does it carry the important idea for this section, or is the idea here subordinate to other ideas in the text. If so, do I have a big enough idea?[i]
- Can the surrounding passages stand on their own, or should they be included in this passage I am speaking on?
- Will I be speaking on the same subject next week? Should I combine the two passages?
- What specific portion is meant to carry the main emphasis for the larger passage?
- What is the main message of this passage?
- What verse or phrase contains the Commander's intent for this passage? (Note: it may be way too early for this question, but begin to think about it.)
- Should I include verses from the next passage or previous passages to complete the thought of the passage?
- Do I need to use the spiral-cut method, or does the passage contain a full-enough idea on its own to convey a large idea of the author?
- What are the broad confines of the message? Which verses are included? How much Scripture can I include to support the main message and not get off the topic?
- Are there key words, repeated phrases, or ideas that continue through past my chosen section?
- Am I fairly conveying the author's message in the way I've divided this passage?

5. Remind yourself that you are aiming to find God's intention for this passage rather than finding a passage that you hope supports your idea.
6. Pray for wisdom and guidance from the Holy Spirit as you prepare. The Spirit anoints the preparation as well as the proclamation in a special way. The message preparation is preparing your heart first and foremost.

LISTEN: CONTEMPLATIVE, INDUCTIVE THEOLOGICAL EXEGESIS

Listen! Listen!—Contemplative Exegesis

1. For the first reading or two, just let the Bible speak and respectfully and humbly listen. Don't write anything down.
2. Read the surrounding chapters.
3. Read the passage in many translations and note translational differences. As you read, jot down the questions you have and the questions your readers will have.

PERSONAL QUESTIONS REGARDING THE PASSAGES MIGHT INCLUDE
- What stands out to me about this passage?
- Why would God put this passage in the Bible?
- What is this passage about?
- What questions do I have for God after reading this passage?

- What don't I understand here?
- What parts of this passage or its message don't I like?
- What about this passage goes in a direction opposite from the way most people suppose it should go?
- What is God saying here that is countercultural?
- What is God saying to me personally in this passage?
- Where do I need transformation to live out what God is telling me in this passage?
- What work does the Holy Spirit need to do in my life because of what I've read here?
- What is God saying to me before I am honestly able to say it to others?
- Why did the Holy Spirit inspire this passage?
- What is the Holy Spirit's message from this passage?
- What are the bright, shiny memory verses in this passage?

4. Personally practice *lectio divina*—meditate on the passage.
   a. Lectio—carefully examine and collect the grapes with care. Examine the passage closely. Pay attention to the words and thoughts and how the thoughts are connected. Note their connections and patterns noted.
   b. Meditatio—squeeze the juice from the grapes. Look for the meaning hidden in plain sight in the passage.
   c. Oratio—ferment the juice, talk to God, pray. Ponder in your heart what God's desire for you is from this passage. Pray that God would align your will with His regarding what He is showing you from this passage.
   d. Contemplatio—taste the goodness of God in this message for you. Claim the message. Write it down.
   e. Operatio—apply the message to your life. Begin to live out this passage. See Chapter 11.

5. Make general observations about the passage.

GENERAL OBSERVATION QUESTIONS
- Can I picture the writing or preaching of this passage?
- Do we know who wrote this book? What do we know about him?
- What can we tell about the human author if he is not identified?
- Is the audience this was written to different from the characters in the story?
- Is this book focused on the past, present, or future?
- Did this book cause anything to change or happen when it was written?
- Who are the characters in this story or passage? What are they like? How are they like or different from us?
- What are they doing?
- Where is God in this passage?
- Is this passage written to or for an occasion or circumstance or to address a particular problem? What is it?
- How is this circumstance, occasion, or problem similar to or different from today?
- What do I need to know more about to understand this passage?
- Which questions can I answer from the text and its surrounding context?

- Which questions can't I find the answers to in the book I'm studying? (Make a note of them.)
- What would I want to ask the author of this passage if he were here with me?
- What appear to be the key verses that convey the main meaning in this passage? (Note: the key verses are not necessarily the bright, shiny memory verses.)

6. What is the Bible saying in one paragraph or less?

_____

_____

_____

_____

Context, Context, Context-Contextual Signposts

Here are some questions to get you started. Answer those that are relevant and ignore the rest. Add your own questions of the text.

BOOK OF THE BIBLE
- Who was this book written to? Who was its audience?
- What appears to be its purpose?
- What do you learn about the purpose of this book from the first and last chapters?
- Why was this book written?
- What was its purpose according to commentaries?
- What do I see as the theme of the book that contains my passage?
- Were the people this book is about or the people it was written to religious? Worshippers of YHWH, of Jesus? Of idols?
- How were the people this book was written to different from us?
- How does the purpose of this book relate to us? What might the purpose of this book be for us today?
- If the book is prophetic, what were the circumstances facing the people?

SURROUNDING PASSAGES
- What do the surrounding passages have to do with the one I am working on?
- If this passage is a story, parable, psalm, or proverb, what other stories, poems, or sayings in the same book relate to it?
- How does the main idea of this passage fit into the larger context of the book it is in?
- What does this passage mean to say in light of the larger context and the book it is in?
- Are there repeated words or ideas that help me find the beginning and end to the story?
- Do other connected stories have the same theme or teaching?
- What is the climax of the story?
- What is the conclusion?
- What seems to be the purpose of the story?

CANONICAL CONTEXT
- How does this passage fit into the story of salvation?
- How does this passage relate to the surrounding books of the Bible?
- Why is this book included in the canon?
- What is different about the message of this book than the message of all the other books in the Bible?
- What are the parallel passages in both testaments? What can I glean from them?
- If this book is one of the prophets, what other books expand on the situation, and what do they say?

LITERARY GENRE
- What is the genre of this passage?
- What difference does the genre of this book make to its meaning?
- What literary forms are in the larger genre of this passage?
- Why did God inspire this message to be written in this genre?
- How might the literary form change the way I choose to proclaim this message?

HISTORICAL BACKGROUND
- When was this book written?
- Why were these people being written to or about?
- What was the prevailing historical situation at the time? (Was there war, famine, plenty, etc.?)
- What is happening in the history of Israel, the church, or the world at the time this was written?[ii]
- What was the geopolitical situation at the time of this book?
- What are the people feeling and experiencing?
- How is the meaning of the passage tied to its historical context?
- What is clearly different about then and now?
- What sorts of interpretation may be needed to apply this text to our context?

CULTURAL BACKGROUND
- What were the invisible presuppositions that made up their culture that are very different from the invisible presuppositions that make up ours?
- What difference do they make to God's intent and purpose for the passage?
- How are the people this book was written to like us?
- How are they different from us?
- If this takes place in or describes a geographic location, where is it? What does it look like? What does it feel like? How would that affect their culture?
- Did the people this passage was originally delivered to live in a rural or relatively urban setting? How does that affect the meaning?
- Were they settled or nomadic people?
- Were they living in the pre-temple times, or was there temple worship?
- Were they pre-exilic, in exile, or postexilic?
- Were they in slavery or free?

- Were they Jewish or Christian or both?
- Were they persecuted or not?
- What were their marriage practices?
- In what types of houses did they live?
- How did they raise their families?
- What is the basic social structure in this book—extended family, limited family, nation?
- What were their invisible cultural beliefs?
- Did they worship YHWH and someone or something else? Why?
- What biblical background information on the culture is relevant to this passage?
- How do these observations affect our understanding of this passage?
- How do these observations affect the application of this passage?

REDEMPTIVE THEOLOGICAL QUESTIONS FOR THOUGHT
- What passages from the Old Testament further inform me about this passage? What do they say?
- What passages from the New Testament further inform me about this passage? What do they say?
- What does this passage say about God, Christ, and the Holy Spirit?
- What does this text say about God's love?
- What group or person represents God in this text?
- What does this passage reveal about human brokenness?
- How does this passage point to sin or how we have fallen short of God's purposes for our lives?
- What does this passage say about God's work?
- What does this passage say about God's message to the world?
- What does this text say about God's will for humankind?
- What is God (in each one of the three persons of the Trinity) doing in this biblical text?
- What divine judgment rests on those in this text and why?
- Why did God choose to act in this text?
- What hope does this text imply or offer?
- What does this text say about how God will restore humanity to His purposes?
- What does God do behind the scenes in the larger story of the Bible to accomplish His will regarding the problem in this passage?
- What is said or implied about the future and God's promises?
- How does the idea of covenant play into this passage?
- Are their messianic overtones or types in this passage?
- Does the passage point to blood, forgiveness, or sacrifice?
- Where is grace displayed in this passage?
- What characters might point in some way to Christ?
- What characters point to the need for Christ?
- Where is Christ or forgiveness portrayed?
- Where might Christ be needed?
- Is there a story of redemption here either secular or spiritual?

- How does any story of redemption in this passage relate to Christ?
- How does this passage relate to Jesus Christ's earthly ministry?
- What message from God is this passage relaying?
- Where is the Holy Spirit in this passage? (Is He behind the scenes, or empowering characters, or simply inspiring the author?)
- How can the Holy Spirit empower us to do the thing called for in this passage?
- In what way does this passage speak to the person who may be running from God?
- In what way does this speak to the person seeking God?
- How does this passage speak to those who are sick, suffering, or unable to help themselves?
- In what way does this speak to the religious/legalistic person?
- How does this speak to the self-righteous person (vs. righteousness from God)?
- What does God do in this text to provide or accomplish what is needed?[iii]
- What is God doing in the larger context, canon, or salvation story to accomplish what is needed?[iv]
- What theological truth does this passage convey?
- What does this passage say, imply, or point to about Christ?
- How does this text connect to the cross, Resurrection, or eternity?
- How does our gratefulness to Christ for His offer of salvation cause us to want to live out this text?
- What passage from the other testament might you pair with your passage to deepen your message?

Dig Deep: Ideas

1. Divide the passage into major chunks by idea or plot movement.
   a. If there is a story, give the plot.
   b. If there is a poem, give the major thoughts.
   c. If there is a prophecy, look at the near and far situations addressed and find the major themes.
2. How are the major themes or ideas organized?
3. Outline the passage or draw its plot noting the rising action, climax of the story, and the conclusion.
4. Underline key words, ideas, and connecting words.
5. Turn your outline or plot into a truth outline.

Questions for Digging Deeper

Dig Deep—General Observations
- What appear to be key verses or phrases?
- Diagram the key verse or verses if it will help make it clearer.
- What is the mood of this passage? Why was it written in this mood?
- What is the organizing principle of the passage? Is it inductive, deductive, informally arranged, or arranged with the main thought in the middle?

- Why did the writer organize his thoughts in this way?
- What ideas are repeated and why?

DIG DEEPER BY GENRE
If the passage is didactic:

- After you outline the passage in detail, outline the passage with subject headlines.
- Show how the discussion or argument develops.
- What is the mood of the passage/author?
- Is there any advice? Are there admonitions? Warnings? Promises?
- What are the emphatic phrases?
- Is there figurative language? Why was it used?
- If this is an epistle, what was the situation(s) that are being addressed? Why?
- How are these situations the same or different from our situations today?
- Is the application exactly the same or different today?
- Why did the author organize his ideas as he did?
- What was the most important idea to the author? Where did he put it?

If the passage is narrative:

- Where does this story begins and end (different places, characters, or moods may help)?
- What is the setting of the story? When does this story occur? Where does it occur? What is significant about these observations as far as the bigger picture of Scripture, Israel, or the church is concerned?
- What is the mood of the story?
- Who is the main character or protagonist or principal character?
- Who is the antagonist the one who contends with or opposes the main character?
- Is God a protagonist or antagonist in this story?
- What is the significance of the major character's name?
- What is the conflict or problem that between the protagonist and the antagonist?
- Does the Bible tell us anything about how the character looked? Why?
- What is the rising action? What major events lead to the turning point or climax of the story?
- What is the turning point or main even between the protagonist and antagonist?
- What happens after that, the falling action, the events that lead to a resolution?
- What is the resolution or the conclusion of the story?
- Who has the power in this story? Who is powerless? Who is excluded from power? How does this affect the meaning?
- How does the story resolve or conclude?
- What is the outcome?
- What ideas are highlighted?
- What brought suspense?
- What words are repeated more frequently than usual?
- Where is God in this story? What is He doing? Is He in front of the camera or behind it?

- What is the theme of the story?
- What is the lesson the protagonist learned?
- What could we learn from this story?
- Whom do we want to identify with? Whom do we not want to identify with?
- What message is the author trying to get across?
- What other passages of Scripture link to this story or explain it?

If the passage is a psalm or poetry:

- What types of images or figurative language is used? What do they represent?
- Take note of the parallelism—how does it function (repetition, enhancements)?
- Where in the psalter (if this is a psalm) is it? What are the other psalms around it about?
- Note the literary form—how is it arranged? Try to guess why it is arranged that way. Does it start with a call to worship or praise phrase? Is it arranged alphabetically in Hebrew? (i.e., Psalm 119).
- Why is this message in this genre?
- Divide the passage into strophes or chunks.
- Outline the strophes by topic or image.
- Where is the main topic or intent of the passage mentioned? Is it in the beginning, the end, or the middle?
- How are the strophes arranged? Look at the macro arrangement and the micro arrangement of the strophes.
- Is this psalm a community psalm or an individual psalm? What difference does that make to its meaning?
- What is the mood? Is it one more of praise or lament?
- If praise, is it a song of thanksgiving or a hymn of praise?
- If a hymn of praise, is it to the Creator or Redeemer of Israel, or the world, or the ruler of history?
- Is it a storytelling psalm? A psalm of penitence? A psalm of trust and meditation? A royal psalm? A renewal liturgy? A psalm of ascent, a song of Zion, or an enthronement psalm?
- Note the feelings expressed. Get into the writer's emotions. How was he feeling in each part? Does it change in the psalm?
- Are some of the feelings or phrases troubling to you? Prayerfully note these and then read carefully to see if they are giving emotions to God or are registering trust in His sovereignty.
- Note stories or experiences shared by the psalmist.
- Note key words. How many different words are used for the same basic idea? (Psalm 119 for example has many words for God's Word.)
- Are there theologically loaded power words (like *love* or *justice*) the psalmist uses?
- What is God's name here (God/Elohim—general word for God or LORD/YHWH—personal name for God)?
- How is God portrayed?
- Note strong illusions or illustrations.

- Can the historical context be discovered? Look up historical or grammatical notes to understand the poetry better.
- Are there any parts that could come from other Near East cultures—mythical references such as water or other gods, etc.?
- Do some parts reflect a simple view of the universe as though chariots pulled the sun across the sky?
- Look up the cross-references or notes to other Scriptures. Note that often, other passages will refer to psalms.
- Read the psalms with a Christian perspective. Look for Christ, prophecy, or covenant.

If the passage is prophecy:

- How was this prophecy original offered—preached, spoken, illustrated, written?
- Is there figurative language?
- Can you identify what the figurative motifs are meant to point to?
- Who are the characters?
- What subgenres are included? Why?
- Why did God give this message to the prophet?
- What forms is this prophecy presented in?
- Is it addressed to a priest, a king, or a group of people? What significance does that have?
- If addressed to a group, is it a nation, and international group, or the kingdom of God?
- How was the prophecy fulfilled in its day?
- Does this prophecy also point to a future fulfillment (for example, a return to the land or a messiah)?
- Does this prophecy point even further to the future (for example, the Day of the Lord)?

Dig Deep: Words

1. What word or words needs to be studied because they carry a lot of weight in the passage, are used repeatedly, or have theological significance? Check the words you underlined in your outline. Some words that may require deeper study.
   - key words
   - difficult words
   - repeated words
   - unusual words
   - words with similar meanings repeated
   - words that all start with the same letter (in Hebrew) or that sound the same (in Hebrew, commentaries may be helpful here)
   - words that are pronounced similarly but have different spellings
   - words that have theological import
   - words influencing the meaning of the text

2. Compare that word to see how it is translated in several good translations.
3. Study the original word's meaning. See which meaning fits in the passage at hand. See how that word is used in other places in Scripture (particularly in the book you are studying and other books by that same author). What words in Hebrew (if your word is Greek) or in Greek (if your word is Hebrew) have similar meanings? Look up your word in the Theological Wordbook of the OT (TWOT) or the Theological Dictionary of the NT (TDNT). See chapter 8 for more details and help on this. What significance did your word studies have in discovering the meaning of the text?
4. Using all your translations, your outline, and the things you have learned in this section, write a paraphrase of your passage or the key sections of your passage if it is very long.

LIVE—A TRANSFORMATIVE HERMENEUTIC

Consider Your Audience

1. Identify with the skeptics and doubters. Ask their most challenging questions for them.
2. Go over an imaginary list of listeners—those in your audience and those you wish were. How will they hear this passage? What are their needs, and how does the passage apply?
3. If there are difficulties for you in believing your passage, consider taking a little leap of faith to better apply the passage.

QUESTIONS FOR EXEGETING CULTURE AND OUR LISTENERS
- What kinds of people make up my congregation?
- How does my congregation differ from me in their thinking and understanding of Scripture?
- What has been happening in the world lately that this passage reminds me of?
- What things will my audience have difficulty understanding?
- What things in this passage will my audience disagree with?
- Where does this passage differ from popular theological ideas my congregation or society holds?
- Who is going to stop listening to me and tune out?
- Why should they listen to me?
- Why should they hear this?
- How will I gain their attention or interest?
- What do they need? Do they know they need it?
- How can I make their need for this message clear to them?
- Why is this idea better than the others in other religions or in secular society?
- Could my message sound judgmental, hypocritical, politically incorrect, or mean spirited? How can I address that?
- Would a parable-like story or some other image of the application make the message palatable for my hearers?

- Do I need to translate some ideas or common Christian or biblical words and phrases into a language that laypeople will understand?
- What invisible cultural belief or norm is touched on in our passage?
- What unknown assumptions underlie the way this passage will be understood or make it difficult to accept?
- How can I address those underlying assumptions?
- Where are the hurts in our culture?
- What assumptions in the culture just aren't working? How does Christianity speak to that problem?
- How does Jesus Christ, salvation, or the application of our passage run counter to culture?
- What about this passage points to a need for personal change?
- What are the biggest issues facing our culture today?
- What do people consider the biggest justice issues?
- How does this passage support and affirm those issues?
- How are the people this passage is written to at cross-purposes with the Commander's intent for this passage?
- How does this passage help us see the cultural issues of today in a new light?
- How can living out the purposes of this passage help us live better lives?
- How does this passage cure the social ills of today?

Decide on the Commander's Intent

QUESTIONS FOR DECIDING ON THE COMMANDER'S INTENT
- What does the passages structure, the first verses (or the middle or final verses) tell us about the purpose of the passage?
- What are the key verses in the passage?
- What themes are repeated (words or ideas) throughout the passage?
- What is the main subject of the passage, and what does the passage say about it?
- What is the underlying theological principle of this passage?
- What is the message of the surrounding chapters?
- What is the stated purpose of the book containing your passage? Is it mentioned in the first and last chapters as well as the book introduction given in a study Bible?
- What does the rest of the Bible and theology say about the main themes in this passage?
- What is the purpose of this passage in salvation history and the big story of redemption?
- What principles can you draw from your passage?
- What truths can you identify in your passage?
- What was the purpose of the original author for this passage?
- What is the purpose of the Holy Spirit for breathing out the passage?
- What is the purpose that the Holy Spirit had in mind for this passage when read in our time and culture?
- What is the purpose of the passage for my personal transformation?
- What is the purpose of the passage for my audience's transformation?
- What is the purpose of the book in salvation history and the big story of redemption?
- What does God want us to know, do, or be that caused Him to include this passage?

- What do God's actions surrounding this text imply concerning our actions?[v]
- What action is suggested for our community and our relationship to our neighbor?[vi]
- Are there implicit or explicit command of God here?[vii]
- What worldly ideals are exemplified in this text?
- Does this passage show us an example that is opposite of what we consider God's commands or that is opposite of loving our neighbor as ourselves? How do we rectify that example?
- Is someone's faith or actions a model for how we should live?
- Do events in this text correlate to situations I come in contact with? What are some examples?
- What are the needs of my audience or congregation that God intended to speak to with this passage?

1. Look for Christ in this passage. Where do we see the gospel, Jesus Christ, salvation, or the need for these things in this passage?
2. Write the Commander's intent in a single sentence.

_____

_____

Let the Commander's Intent Permeate Your Life

Take time to meditate on the Commander's intent.

THINKING ABOUT THE COMMANDER'S INTENT
- Do all the verses/paragraphs/strophes in my passage support my Commander's intent?
- How does the rest of Scripture support my Commander's intent?
- Does my Commander's intent contradict any other Scripture? If it does, how can I rectify this?
- How does my Commander's intent support or reject the cultural ideas of people today where I live?

1. Don't forget to rest. Have fun. Have you had a day of Sabbath this week?
2. Live out the Commander's intent.

QUESTIONS TO THINK ABOUT WHILE YOU PERK
- What has God been saying to me personally this week from this passage?
- What specific applications can I imagine for me and my people regarding the Commander's intent of this passage?
- How is living out the Commander's intent working for me?
- What am I wrestling with God about concerning living out His message?
- What difficulties have I had living out the Commander's intent for my passage?
- What has been the hardest part of living out the Commander's intent?
- Have I experienced any place where the Commander's intent needed altering after I've thought about it a bit?

- As I begin to live this out, can I think of some universal or specific application?
- What illustrations of the Commander's intent have I seen in the news or in things I've read or watched?
- Where have I seen the application of the Commander's intent in action recently?
- What are people talking about or what happened in the news recently that needs to be part of my message? Any holidays?

CREATIVE MEDITATION EXERCISES
- Visualize what is happening in the passage.
- If the passage is a sermon, how did it sound when it was spoken or read aloud to its early audiences? Read it aloud in the translation of your choice.
- If the passage contains a story, visualize the setting, think of the beginning, the climax of the story, and the end. Why was it written the way it was?
- Tell the story in your own words. Consider telling the story as if it were happening today. Think about the weather, the smells, the sounds.
- If the passage is theological instruction or a letter, explain it in your own words as you would to a friend who doesn't know the Bible. Better yet, go out to lunch with a friend and tell him or her what you think you will say. What is the reaction? What questions does he or she have? What doesn't he or she agree with?
- If the passage is an argument or part of an argument or a sermon, map out where this particular point in the argument or sermon is in the greater argument being made. Why did the writer craft the message this way?
- If the passage is Hebrew poetry, attempt to visualize the concrete images the author has written.
- Write down verses that stand out to you personally and meditate on them for a while or memorize them.
- Think deeply about phrases or words that remind you of other Bible passages and Bible stories, creation, nature, events in your life or that of others dear to you, and any other connections that come to you.
- Make your Commander's intent image driven; find one simple anchor image that illustrates or reminds people of your main point. This can be a slide if you do slides. Otherwise, plan how to describe some sort of image.
- If you will do slides or video clips, begin to gather pictures and videos along with collecting illustrations.

LOVE—COMPOSE A RELEVANT AND REDEMPTIVE MESSAGE

Decide on the point for proclamation from the Commander's intent for including this passage in the Bible and the people you will be speaking to with this message.

Decide on the Point for Proclamation

HERMENEUTICAL QUESTIONS
- Who is my audience, and what are their needs they know about and those they aren't aware of?
- Why did they come here today?
- Why should they listen?
- What difference does this message make to them?
- How should they live differently?
- What should my listeners do now?
- How can I point to the application without being legalistic, moralistic, or nagging?
- In what way do the culture's assumptions support this passage?
- In what way are my listeners' cultural assumptions different from Scriptures or my own?
- How do the events in this text correlate to events in my community or in the world?[viii]
- How can I show the difference between what we are called to do in this text and what God has already done for us?
- How can I make clear that our goodness and moral actions are not a way to win points with God but are rather done in gratefulness to God?
- How can I show that no one can do the actions called for in this text without God's help?
- How will I make clear that we have all fallen short of these actions but that we can be forgiven by God's free offer of grace?
- How can I demonstrate the living out of these actions by the Holy Spirit's help?
- How do we answer the question that our listener has about our point for proclamation— "So what?"

1. Consider the seekers, the mature, and immature believers in your audience in regard to an application.
2. Write out the point for proclamation sentence.

_____

_____

3. Write an outline or some sort of structure for your message; see chapter 14 for ideas.

Prepare Your Message

HOMILETICAL QUESTIONS
- What is the best way to structure this message to get across the Commander's point for proclamation to this audience?
- Write out your message outline or structure.
- What is my point for proclamation catchphrase?
- What images, stories, references, or illustrations will I use to support the Commander's intent point for proclamation?
- How will I introduce my message?
- How will I conclude my message?

- How will I make my message stick so the people listening can't forget it?
- How will I allow for a response to God's working through my message?

1. Decide on a point for proclamation catchphrase.
2. Find an anchor image.
3. Gather your message resources, pictures, illustrations to point to truths, stories, application examples.
4. Write your conclusion.
5. Write your introduction.
6. Write your message if you choose to speak from a written sheet.
7. Go through and cut everything that doesn't support the point for proclamation from the message. Check it over with the following questions.

Remove Anything Extraneous from Your Message

PREFLIGHT CHECKLIST

- Does my introduction connect with my audience and make them want to listen?
- Does my introduction prepare the audience for the message?
- Do I get on their island emotionally or culturally at the start of the message?
- Is there an action called for in this passage? Did I include it in my message?
- Did I apply generally and specifically the action called for?
- Is it clear why we would want to do the thing called for?
- What are the ramifications of not doing the thing called for in this message?
- Is God's message my message?
- Did I point out the need for a grateful response to the suffering of Christ on the cross?
- Did I expect people to help themselves or encourage them to call on the Holy Spirit for help?
- Is there any part of me or my opinions that I state as biblical truth and not clearly as my opinion?
- Do I waste a lot of time talking about things not relevant to my message? What can I cut out?
- Does the Commander's point for proclamation catchphrase lead people away from the meaning of the passage?
- Does the Commander's point for proclamation truly reflect the most significant point in the passage?
- Is the Commander's point for proclamation a transformational point, not just a point of fact?
- Is the Commander's point for proclamation universally applicable?
- Are all the other points in my outline, stories, and illustrations directly in support of the point for proclamation?
- Does the conclusion directly support and distill the point for proclamation?
- Did I explain what the ramifications of not doing what the Bible says in this passage?
- Does my message speak to the younger brother (the prodigal son) and the self-righteous older brother?

- Is the gospel, redemption, forgiveness, or hope explicitly part of the message?
- Are there any cultural, historical, or other differences between then and now that may affect the truth of my Commander's intent point for proclamation?
- Do I give credit for all quotes, ideas, and illustrations? Do I have permission to use all the images I have on screen? Have I obtained the proper licenses for the use of my video clips?

THE THOUGHTFUL PROCLAIMER
METHOD IN BRIEF

The Thoughtful Proclaimer Method in Brief

Prepare

1. Confess sins and examine yourself, your motives, your doubts, your family and church problems, the chips on your shoulders that will affect how you read and apply this passage, and consider anyone you need to forgive or ask forgiveness from.
2. Plan and portion your Scripture for preaching.
   a. Choose a book and divide it into sections.
   b. Choose the parameters for the section you will preach or teach on this week.
3. Remind yourself you are aiming to find God's intention for this passage.
4. Pray for wisdom and guidance from the Holy Spirit.

Listen—Contemplative Exegesis

1. Listen! Listen!
   a. Read the passage in many translations and note translational differences
      i.   Ask personal questions
      ii. Ask general questions
   b. Read the surrounding chapters.
   c. Practice Lectio Divina—meditate on the passage
      i.   Lectio—carefully examine and collect the grapes
      ii. Meditatio—squeeze the juice from the grapes
      iii. Oratio—ferment the juice, talk to God, pray
      iv. Contemplatio—consider the goodness of God in giving this message
      v.   Operatio—apply the message to your life.
   d. What is the Bible saying in one paragraph or less?

2. Consider the Contexts
   a. Consider the purposes of the book of the Bible the passage is from.

b. Consider the immediate surrounding chapters and how they relate to this passage and inform it.

c. Consider the rest of the Bible and what it has to say about the more important themes in this passage. Look at cross-references, and consider theology, geography, typology, messianic references, and covenant.

d. Consider how the literary genre of the passage influences the meaning.

e. Consider how the historical setting of this book informs us of its purposes.

f. Consider how the culture of the people this book was written to (the people, their secular leaders, and religious leaders) plays into its meaning for them and for us.

3. Dig Deep: Ideas
   a. Write an outline of the passage.
   b. If there is a story, give the plot.
   c. If there is a poem, give the major thoughts.
   d. If there is a prophecy, look at the near and far situations addressed and find the major themes.

4. Dig Deep: Words
   a. What word or words needs to be studied because they carry a lot of weight in the passage, are used repeatedly, or have theological significance?
   b. Find the original Greek, Hebrew, or Aramaic word behind your word and study that.

Live—Transform Your Heart and Mind

1. Consider your audience and the culture we live in and how they relate to this passage.
2. Decide on the Commander's intent.
3. Take time to percolate and meditate on the Commander's intent, and rest.

Love—Compose a Relevant and Redemptive Message

1. Consider the seekers, the mature, and immature believers in your audience in regard to the Commander's intent.
2. Decide on the point for proclamation from the Commander's intent for including this passage in the Bible and the people you will be speaking to with this message.
3. Write an outline or some sort of structure for your message.
4. Write a point for proclamation catchphrase.
5. Find an anchor image.
6. Gather your message resources, pictures, illustrations to point to truths, stories, application examples.
7. Write your conclusion.
8. Write your introduction.
9. Write your message if you choose to speak from a written sheet.
10. Cut out anything that doesn't support the point for proclamation and make it clear and compelling.

THOUGHTFUL PROCLAIMER ONE-PAGER FOR EXPERT

Thoughtful Proclaimer One-Pager for Experts

Prepare:

Confess, examine, pick passage, pray.

Listen: Read:

Question, meditate, summarize. Do contemplative exegesis. Consider the contexts: book, Bible, genre, history, culture old and new, redemption for sinners (both lost and found).

Dig Deep: Ideas

Outline, plot, divide into thought hunks, consider near and far meanings.

Dig Deep: Words

Significant words in original languages defined.

Live: Consider the Commander's Intent

Focus on your audience, God's purposes, and personally living out the passage.

Love: Have a point and make it clear

Decide on the point for proclamation for your message, the message structure, and the redemptive application for all the different people.

Compile illustrations, stories, samples of applications.

Write a takeoff, landing, and plot your course in between.

Make the message sticky with a point for proclamation, a short catchphrase, and anchor image.

SAMPLE OF PLANNING A BIBLICAL SERIES

Sample of Planning a Church-Wide Biblical Series

Jeremiah Church-Wide Series: 22 Weeks of Message Ideas and Special Services

Topic	Major Reference	Comment	Use
Jeremiah's Call	Jeremiah 1:4–11	Jeremiah's call; Jeremiah's self-image irrelevant to the LORD; predestination; God's promise of help to do His bidding; faithfulness; God is more interested in who you are than what you do; I knew you; reluctance; when God calls us, He gives us the words/tools (Moses)	first week of autumn—may be divided into opening sermon series of three weeks

Almonds Branches and Boiling Pots	Jeremiah 1:11–19	God's sovereignty, universality, covenants; God is in charge	Early fall or early spring
Cisterns and Fountains	Jeremiah:1–19	Forsaking your first love; running after the wrong things; God's spiritual provision and our rejection of it; courtroom scene	Thanksgiving or as it falls in the calendar.
The Weeping Prophet	Jeremiah 13	Linen belts; compassion and prayer; Jeremiah wept for his people, had compassion for them, and prayed for them after God said there was no hope; Jeremiah encouraged them to pray for others	
Can a Leopard Change Its Spots?	Jeremiah 13:1–11, 22–25, 18:11–12, 31:18–19	Forgiveness; repentance; linen belts story	
New Beginnings	Jeremiah 18	The Potter; God as Creator authority; our need for flexibility; being "mud"; fresh starts	
Throwing Pots	Jeremiah 19	God's justice; "God Uses Cracked Pots"	

True Worship/Seeking God with All Your Heart	Jeremiah 29:13–14	The Temple of the LORD	
How to Be a Christian Without Being Religious	Jeremiah 7:1–15, 9:24–25, 26:1–24, 29:1–14, esp. 29:11–13	God's concern with hearts, not form; seeking God with all your heart	Confirmation or Commissioning service
Once in David's Royal City	Jeremiah 23:1–8, 33:15–16	Prophecy of Jesus	Advent
New Year's Resolutions/ Following the Call	Jeremiah 20:7–13	Jeremiah's complaint; God's promises	New Year
Ain't Nothing Like the Real Thing, Baby	Jeremiah 23	True vs. False prophets; learning to distinguish false Christianity and preaching; the reason for being well versed in Scripture and theology; being watchful	May be a short sermon series
Everlasting Love	Jeremiah 31:1–20, esp. v. 3	Consolation; God's compassion; hope for future; promises	Service of encouragement after death or catastrophe
Purifying Silver	Jeremiah 6:27–30	Assessing what's valuable; heat to remove impurities; getting rid of the impurities	
Worshipping the Wrong Thing	Jeremiah 44 especially vv. 16–20	The Queen of Heaven cult; idolatry in our lives; rebellion from God	

Who's Bragging?/In God We Trust	Jeremiah 9:22–23, 17:5–8	Wisdom, valor, and understanding; not depending on riches; putting our roots in the right place	
Believing in God with All Your Kidneys	Jeremiah 17:9–11	The hidden depths of the heart and emotion; what is belief? What is faith?	Valentine's Day
Seduced by God	Jeremiah 20:7–13	Struggling with our calls; following the LORD; the pitfalls and the suffering	
Live Like a King	Jeremiah 22:13–19; Haggai 1:3–11	Story of Jehoiakim and his palace; what makes a great person; how do good things slip through our fingers?	Beginning of Lent
Be Wise	Jeremiah 23:16–22	False security; staying in the Word; being faithful in prayer; being able to see falseness	
Finding God	Jeremiah 29:1–32, esp. vv. 11 and 13	Coping with spiritual depression	
Writing on the Walls (of Your Heart)	Jeremiah 31:27–40	The new covenant; the Holy Spirit; New Jerusalem	Pentecost

Jeremiah Special Events/Retreats

Special Talks	Major Reference	Comment	Use
Being a Fool (for God) and Loving It	Jeremiah 27:1–28:17	Jeremiah and the yoke, being willing to do what it takes to get the point across to those who need to hear it	A devotional
How Not to Invest in Real Estate	Jeremiah 32	Jeremiah buys a field; is anything too hard for God? Sticking by what you believe to be right; hope	Adult retreat
Landscaping for Success	Jeremiah 17:5–13	The difference between desert shrubs and willow trees; amassing riches unjustly; paying employees fairly; trees with deep roots; fountains of living water	Adult retreat
Don't Give a Fig	Jeremiah 24:1–10, 25:1–14	Two baskets of figs; giving God the best/first fruits; worshipping the works of our hands; what is an idol; workaholics; doing what we do as for the LORD	Adult retreat
Integrity	Jeremiah 34:8–22	Reclaiming the freed slaves; integrity; fairness; doing the right thing; treating people with respect; knowing what God's Word calls us to do	Business person's devotional
Coloring Within the Lines	Jeremiah 23:21, 42:1–22	Jeremiah is consulted about the future (Egypt); knowing the LORD's will/waiting/doing what He tells us; story of the people asking about going to Egypt; waiting on the LORD; not running ahead; listening when the Word comes	Talk for mature believers
Playing Second Fiddle/When Hard Work Doesn't Pay Off	Jeremiah 32:12–16, 36:4–32, 43:3, 45:1–5	Being Baruch in Jeremiah's world; God's charge to Baruch; Baruch's contribution; learning to be a gracious support person; finding our place in the world	Encouraging retreat message for lay leaders, volunteers

Jeremiah Classes and Bible Studies

Children's Sunday School-upper grades	Children's References	Some story ideas	Use
Intrigue and Suspense in the Old Testament/ The Life of Jeremiah	Start in Jeremiah 1 and do the stories and parables only–for example in Jeremiah 37:1–41:3	Zedekiah consults Jeremiah, Jeremiah in the Cistern, Ebed-Melech the Ethiopian rescues Jeremiah, weak leadership of Zedekiah, fall of Jerusalem, Zedekiah Death, Gedaliah's murder	Story Series for upper elementary school (2nd–5th)

Adult Bible study	References:	Discussion	Use
Intrigue and Suspense in the Old Testament/ The Book of Jeremiah	Start with chapter 1 and the call and work through each chapter; some chapters may want to be skipped, others will need several weeks	Provide Scripture passage and discussion questions for class or churchwide small groups	Adult Bible study or Sunday school class or small groups

In-Depth Bible class	Idea	Class Themes (Use Jeremiah for examples)	Use
Understanding the Old Testament	Use the book of Jeremiah and its background and genres as a springboard for a college-level adult study on the Old Testament	Timeline of Israel, prophecy, bio of Jeremiah, history of writing of OT-LXX, MT etc., covenants, pre- and post-exilic theology, poetry and laments, monarchy, maps, etc. Culminate with class trip to Israel—pay the teacher's way	A weeknight class for advanced biblical study

DIG DEEP: IDEAS—SAMPLE GRAMMATICAL OBSERVATIONS

Observations from Philippians 4:4–9

Outline of Philippians 4:4–9

⁴ Rejoice in the Lord
        always.
I will say it again: <u>Rejoice</u>!
⁵ Let your gentleness be evident
             to all.
The Lord is near.
⁶ Do not be <u>anxious</u>
     about <u>anything</u>,
  but in <u>everything</u>,
       by <u>prayer</u> and <u>petition</u>,
      with thanksgiving,
        <u>present</u> your <u>requests</u> to God.
⁷ And the <u>peace</u> of God,
    which transcends all understanding,
      will <u>guard</u> your <u>hearts</u>
        and your <u>minds</u>
          in Christ Jesus.

⁸ Finally, brothers,
whatever is <u>true</u>,
whatever is <u>noble</u>,
whatever is <u>right</u>,
whatever is <u>pure</u>,
whatever is <u>lovely</u>,
whatever is <u>admirable</u>—
if anything is <u>excellent</u>
or praiseworthy

—think about such things.
⁹ Whatever you have learned
         or received
         or heard from me,
         or seen in me
                  —put it into practice.
And the God
      of peace
            will be with you.

Passage Analysis

ADVICE, ADMONITIONS, WARNINGS, PROMISES
- (Imperative Advice) "Rejoice in the Lord always. I will say it again: Rejoice!" (v. 4).
- (Imperative Advice) "Let your gentleness be evident to all" (v. 4).
- (Warning or Advice/Comfort) "The Lord is near" (v. 4).
- (Imperative Advice) "Do not be anxious about anything" (v. 6).
- (Imperative Advice) "In everything, by prayer and petition, with thanksgiving, present your requests to God" (v. 6).
- (Imperative Advice) "Whatever is true, whatever is noble, whatever is right, whatever is pure, whatever is lovely, whatever is admirable—if anything is excellent or praiseworthy—think about such things" (v. 8).
- (Advice) "Whatever you have learned or received or heard from me, or seen in me—put it into practice" (v. 9).

REASONS, RESULTS
- "Do not be anxious about anything, but in everything, by prayer and petition, with thanksgiving, present your requests to God" (v. 6).
- "And the peace of God, which transcends all understanding, will guard your hearts and your minds in Christ Jesus" (v. 7).
- (Possible) "Let your gentleness be evident to all. The Lord is near" (v. 5).
- Or "The Lord is near" (v. 5).
- "Do not be anxious about anything, but in everything, by prayer and petition, with thanksgiving, present your requests to God" (vv. 5–6).

CONTRAST, COMPARISONS, ILLUSTRATION
- (Comparison or Repetition) "whatever is true, whatever is noble, whatever is right, whatever is pure, whatever is lovely, whatever is admirable—if anything is excellent or praiseworthy" (v. 8).
- (Comparison or Repetition) "learned or received or heard from me, or seen in me" (v. 9).
- (Comparison or Repetition) "hearts" and "minds" (v. 7).

REPETITION AND PROGRESSION OF IDEAS
- (Repetition) "Rejoice in the Lord always. I will say it again: Rejoice!" (v. 4).

- (Repetition) "prayer," "petition," "present your requests to God" (v. 6).
- (Repetition) "peace of God" (v. 7); "God of peace" (v. 9).

Mood, Emphatic Tenses, Figurative Language

Atmosphere, tone, mood: The tone is imperative: "Rejoice," "let your gentleness be evident," "do not be anxious," "let your requests be made known to God," "think about such things." Paul is full advice, and as usual, in Philippians, he is rejoicing! He also talks about the peace of God twice.

Emphatic phrases: See the imperative phrases above. But all the phrases are emphatic in this portion. Two standout emphatic phrases are "the Lord is near" and "Rejoice in the Lord always. I will say it again: Rejoice!"

Figurative language: Figurative phrases include "the Lord is near" (v. 5) and "in everything" (v. 6). "Present your requests to God" and "guard your hearts and your minds" are possibly figurative. Paul uses several nominative adjectives in verse 8— "whatever is true, whatever is noble, whatever is right, whatever is pure, whatever is lovely, whatever is admirable—if anything is excellent or praiseworthy ..."

Main Points of Philippians 4:4–9
- **Paragraph 1 (vv. 2–3)** Agree with one another and help others to do the same.
- **Paragraph 2 (vv. 4–7)** The peace of God will guard your hearts if you rejoice; be gentle, stop worrying, and pray.
- **Paragraph 3 (vv. 8–9)** Think about good things and put into practice what you have learned.

Examples of questions raised in studying the grammar and syntax for Philippians 4:4–9
1. In verse 5, what does "the Lord is near" mean? See question 8.
2. Does "the Lord is near" correspond to verse 5 or 6, or is it an independent phrase?
3. What does it mean to bring all our requests "by prayer and petition, with thanksgiving" to God (v. 6)?
4. What is meant by "the peace of God ... will guard [our] hearts" (v. 7)?
5. Did Paul's emphatic writing style ever lose its power when read aloud, or did he build from less-emphatic phrases in the beginning of Philippians to more emphatic at the end?
6. What did Paul mean by verse 8: "Finally, brothers, whatever is true, whatever is noble, whatever is right, whatever is pure, whatever is lovely, whatever is admirable—if anything is excellent or praiseworthy—think about such things"? Is it as simple an exhortation as it sounds, or is there some deeper underlying or theological meaning? (I have often used this as comfort to my children when they were afraid of having bad dreams but wondered if I had taken it out of context.)
7. How are we to let are gentleness be evident to all? Why just our gentleness and not our justice or our peacefulness?
8. What does it really mean to pray and "petition, with thanksgiving"? Are we to be thankful for what we already have or for the answers to prayer we can expect? (Verse 6 has been my favorite since a woman I respected mailed it to me in high school.)

9. "Finally" in 4:8 resembles the "Finally" in 3:1. Some say this exemplifies a Greek style of writing, while others say it means that parts of more than one letter to the Philippians were combined when they circulated. Which is true? Can we ever know?

Appendix G

SAMPLE MESSAGES

Sermon on Zephaniah

Passage: Zephaniah
Key Verse(s):

> "I will utterly sweep away everything
> from the face of the earth," declares the LORD
> (Zephaniah 1:2)

> The great day of the LORD is near,
> near and hastening fast;
> the sound of the day of the LORD is bitter;
> the mighty man cries aloud there.
> (Zephaniah 1:14)

> Seek the LORD, all you humble of the land,
> who do his just commands;
> seek righteousness; seek humility;
> perhaps you may be hidden
> on the day of the anger of the LORD.
> (Zephaniah 2:3)

> On that day it shall be said to Jerusalem:
> "Fear not, O Zion;
> let not your hands grow weak.
> The LORD your God is in your midst,
> a mighty one who will save;
> he will rejoice over you with gladness;
> he will quiet you by his love;
> he will exult over you with loud singing."
> (Zephaniah 3:16–17)

Purposes of the Passage in Context

Purpose of the passage as it stands: The Day of the Lord is near, so seek the Lord, seek righteousness, seek humility, and perhaps you may be hidden.

PURPOSE OF THE PASSAGE IN CONTEXT OF THE MINOR PROPHETS: The Day of the Lord is near, so seek the Lord, but know that one day the Lord will bring all people unto himself.

PURPOSE OF THE PASSAGE IN THE CONTEXT OF THE CANON:

The Day of the Lord will come like a thief in the night. We do not know the day or the time, but we know that one day there will be a new heaven and a new earth, where those who are in Christ will reign with Him.

COMMANDER'S INTENT: Humble yourself, seek the Lord, and do good for the Day of the LORD is near.

POINT FOR PROCLAMATION: Knowing the Day of LORD is near should cause us to live for God. We should seek the LORD, righteousness, and humility.

CATCHPHRASE: Live like there's no tomorrow.

INTRODUCTION: How would we live differently if we kept in mind that the Day of the LORD is near?

CONCLUSION: Encourage people to consider how they will live differently now that they have this message in mind.

REDEMPTIVE CHRIST-CENTERED FOCUS: God is in our midst, the mighty one who will save. Christ offers forgiveness so we need not fear the end of our lives or the end of the world. Seek the LORD.

GRATEFUL HEART FOCUS: Live humbly and righteously because we don't know the future. We do know God's promises are good for all those who call on Him to be saved.

APPLICATION FOR YOUNGER BROTHER: Repent and live humbly because no one knows when the end will come.

APPLICATION FOR OLDER BROTHER: Live righteously and honestly, and humble yourself before God. Seek justice for others.

Zephaniah Sermon: Live Like There's No Tomorrow

Şirince, Turkey (show pictures of the town):
Last Easter Sunday, our family was visiting Pergamum in Turkey. After a day looking at that once great city that is now nothing but ruins, we were driven up into the mountains to a quaint village called Şirince (pronounced [she rin je]).

As we drove up the winding road into the village, we noticed there were many cars parked on the side of the road; Turkish tourists were walking on trails and up into the hills. The tiny place was packed. I asked our tour guide why that was. My assumption was that it was Easter Sunday and everyone was out celebrating. He said no, 98 percent of Turkey was Muslim, so these gatherings of families and hikers were just people celebrating a nice, sunny spring day.

DOOMSDAY ŞIRINCE (with pictures of shop signs happily announcing the end):
"But," our guide continued, "You should have been here four months ago, on December 21, 2012. The place was packed with thousands of people." (Less than a thousand people live there

normally. Why? The Mayan calendar completed its 5,125-year cycle on December 21, 2012, and many people thought that the world would end on the day the Mayan calendar ended. Şirince, a small village near the ruins of the ancient Greek city of Ephesus, was believed to be one of the few places on earth that would survive the end of the world because the Virgin Mary was said to have risen to heaven from near there.

The shop owners and hoteliers of Şirince were delighted that the end was near. They stocked up on doomsday trinkets and souvenirs.

But Jesus said, "Concerning that day and hour no one knows, not even the angels of heaven, nor the Son, but the Father only" (Matthew 24:36).

IF YOU KNEW YOU HAD ONLY ONE DAY TO LIVE, WHAT WOULD YOU DO? "LIVE LIKE YOU WERE DYING."

My daughter's favorite country singer is Tim McGraw (picture), and when his estranged father found out he was dying of cancer, he came back into Tim's life. Later, McGraw sang a song for his father called "Live Like You Were Dying."[ix] (Play a bit of the song.)

The words of the song explain how a man with only a short time left on earth lives differently than the rest of us. The first thing he did was all the things on his bucket list! Mountain climbing, fishing, taking chances riding a bull. And he took the time to spend time with the ones he loved doing the things they loved.

When the time is short, when it really sinks in you have only a short time left, what do you do? Let me share some of my favorite lines from the song about how to live like you're dying:

> I loved deeper, and I spoke sweeter, and I gave forgiveness I'd been denying.
> I was finally the husband that most the time I wasn't.
> And I became a friend a friend would like to have.
> I finally read the good book and I took a good long hard look
> At what I'd do if I could do it all again.
> And he said, "One day I hope you get a chance to live like you were dying.
> Like tomorrow was a gift and you've got eternity to think of what you did with it."[x]

HOW WOULD *YOU* LIVE IF YOU KNEW THE WORLD WAS ENDING TOMORROW?

We generally think of doing all those things we always wanted to do and never got around to doing or were never brave enough to do. But really, how would we live? How should we live, knowing that at best, life is short? How do we live knowing that the Bible says that the whole world will come to an end one day?

How should we live if this might be our last day on this earth?

What does the Bible say about living in the face of the knowledge of the end?

Well, it turns out, the "good book," as Tim McGraw calls it, has a lot to say about living like we're dying and a lot to say about what the end of the world will look like and how we should live in light of these facts.

Turn with me to Zephaniah (find Matthew and flip backward). The prophet Zephaniah tells us how to live in light of the fact that one day—and we won't know when that day is—but one day, the world will come to an end. Zephaniah tells us how to live in light of this certainty. Zephaniah tells us how to live like there's no tomorrow.

The saying "Live like there's no tomorrow," for those who are unfamiliar, is usually interpreted as "do whatever you want because if there's no tomorrow, there will be no consequences." But I tell you, if there is no tomorrow, then tomorrow, we will meet our Maker. How do we want to live in light of that fact?

The world might tell us to do all the things we always wanted to do but never quite got around to doing. It might be good advice to love deeper and forgive more and spend time with our families and loved ones. But Zephaniah shares some eternal advice.

Zephaniah says the world will end one day. He calls this day "the great day of the LORD," and here's how it will really look.

> "I will utterly sweep away everything
> from the face of the earth," declares the LORD.
> "I will sweep away man and beast;
> I will sweep away the birds of the heavens and the fish of the sea,
> and the rubble with the wicked.
> I will cut off mankind from the face of the earth,"
> declares the LORD.
> (Zephaniah 1:2–3)

> The great day of the LORD is near—
> near and hastening fast;
> the sound of the day of the LORD is bitter;
> the mighty man cries aloud there.
> A day of wrath is that day,
> a day of distress and anguish,
> a day of ruin and devastation,
> a day of darkness and gloom,
> a day of clouds and thick darkness,
> a day of trumpet blast and battle cry
> against the fortified cities
> and against the lofty battlements.
> (Zephaniah 1:14–16)

WHAT WAS IT LIKE IN THE PROPHET ZEPHANIAH'S TIME?

The prophet Zephaniah lived about six hundred years before Christ in the days of King Josiah. His prophecy was to Judah, primarily Jerusalem, where people were worshipping idols and foreign Gods besides the LORD and sometimes in addition to the LORD.

The prophets, like Zephaniah, warned the people they were facing a future cataclysmic event in which Nebuchadnezzar would carry their people to Babylon (which actually happened in 597 BCE) and eventually crush Jerusalem (which happened in 587 BCE). The prophet is calling this event, when the Babylonians overrun their nation and capture their people and destroy their land, the Day of the LORD.

Zephaniah's prophecy came startlingly true. We've heard so many so-called prophecies of the end of the world that we are desensitized to them. But Zephaniah's came true just as he said.

Be silent before the LORD God!
For the day of the LORD is near;
the LORD has prepared a sacrifice and consecrated his guests.
And on the day of the LORD's sacrifice—
I will punish the officials
and the king's sons
and all who array themselves
in foreign attire.
(Zephaniah 1:7–8)

The LORD had prepared a sacrifice…and it was them.
How should we live in light of the fact that we do not know if there will be a tomorrow?

Seek the LORD,
all you humble of the land,
who do his just commands;
seek righteousness;
seek humility;
perhaps you may be hidden
on the day of the anger of the LORD.
(Zephaniah 2:3)

Zephaniah's message was to those who lived in Judah and would be experiencing judgment, but it also instructs us how to live in light of the fact we do not know what tomorrow may bring.

God says that if there's no tomorrow, you should:

Seek the Lord.
Seek righteousness.
Seek humility.

Live like there's no tomorrow: seek humility

The people's pride is what made God the most angry. It wasn't bad enough that they sought after idols instead of seeking the LORD. It wasn't bad enough that they were unrighteous.

This shall be their lot in return for their pride because they taunted and boasted against the people of the LORD of hosts.

The LORD will be awesome against them;
for he will famish all the gods of the earth,
and to him shall bow down,
each in its place, all the lands of the nations.
(Zephaniah 2:11)

This is the exultant city
that lived securely,
that said in her heart,
"I am, and there is no one else."

What a desolation she has become,
a lair for wild beasts!
Everyone who passes by her
hisses and shakes his fist.
(Zephaniah 2:15)

Woe to her who is rebellious and defiled,
the oppressing city!
She listens to no voice;
she accepts no correction.
She does not trust in the LORD;
she does not draw near to her God.
(Zephaniah 3:1–2)

The nerve! Boasting against God! It wasn't enough that they said, "I am, and there is no one else." It was the fact that they wouldn't listen to anyone who spoke of God or trusted the Lord.

God hates pride. If there is no tomorrow, our pride is something we must focus on.

Zephaniah said that those who had some chance of being spared from Nebuchadnezzar's attack were the humble of the land, those who performed God's commands.

LIVE LIKE THERE'S NO TOMORROW: SEEK RIGHTEOUSNESS

Zephaniah warned the people of Jerusalem that because of their unrighteousness, when their world was destroyed, they would not be spared.

At that time I will search Jerusalem with lamps,
and I will punish the
men who are complacent,
those who say in their hearts,
"The LORD will not do good,
nor will he do ill."
Their goods shall be plundered,
their houses laid waste.
Though they build houses,
they shall not inhabit them;
though they plant vineyards,
they shall not drink wine from them.
(Zephaniah 1:12–13)

I will bring distress on mankind,
so that they shall walk like the blind,
because they have sinned against the LORD;
their blood shall be poured out like dust,
and their flesh like dung.
Neither their silver nor their gold
shall be able to deliver them
on the day of the wrath of the LORD.
In the fire of his jealousy,

all the earth shall be consumed;
for a full and sudden end
he will make of all the inhabitants of the earth.
(Zephaniah 1:17–18)

THE DAY OF THE LORD HAS AT LEAST TWO MEANINGS

One meaning is any major judgment God brings on the world. So, Zephaniah spoke of the Day of the Lord in his time, the coming of the Babylonian army.

The other meaning of the Day of the Lord has more finality. This is the future Day of the Lord when Christ returns.

And that final Day of the Lord is the one that makes us want to live like there's no tomorrow.

LIVE LIKE THERE'S NO TOMORROW: SEEK THE LORD

We can seek the Lord in the "good book" as Tim McGraw suggests.

Another prophet, Isaiah, put it this way:

Seek the LORD while he may be found;
call upon him while he is near;
let the wicked forsake his way,
and the unrighteous man his thoughts;
let him return to the LORD, that he may have compassion on him,
and to our God, for he will abundantly pardon.
(Isaiah 55:6–7)

The prophet Amos put it very simply:

For thus says the LORD to the house of Israel:
"Seek me and live."
(Amos 5:4)

Zephaniah's advice for how to live like there's no tomorrow can be summed up in this: "Seek the Lord."

BELIEVING IN JESUS CHRIST IS THE PRIMARY WAY WE SHOULD LIVE LIKE THERE'S NO TOMORROW.

This means living every day in light of the fact that tomorrow might be eternity and knowing we are ready to be with Jesus Christ.

Let me read you Paul's advice about how to live like there's no tomorrow. He's writing to the people of Thessalonica from 1 Thessalonians 5:1–4 and 8–11.

Now concerning the times and the seasons, brothers, you have no need to have anything written to you. For you yourselves are fully aware that the day of the Lord will come like a thief in the night. While people are saying, "There is peace and security," then sudden destruction will come upon them as labor pains come upon a pregnant woman, and they will not escape. But you are not in darkness, brothers, for that day to surprise you like a thief...But since we belong to the day, let us be sober, having put on the breastplate of faith and love, and for a helmet the hope of salvation. For God has not destined us for

271

wrath, but to obtain salvation through our Lord Jesus Christ, who died for us so that whether we are awake or asleep we might live with him. Therefore encourage one another and build one another up, just as you are doing. (1 Thessalonians 5:1-4, 8–11)

The Day of the Lord, as you can see, is not a frightening thing but an encouraging hope for the believer. Though some must live in fear of the Day of the Lord, those of us who have salvation, who believe in Jesus Christ as our Savior, are not afraid of it. Even though we may not have always been humble or acted perfectly, if we have sought the Lord, called on Him, and trusted Him, we have no need to fear.

The people of Judah receive the same promise from Zephaniah near the end of his book. For those who seek the Lord who put their trust in Him, Zephaniah concluded,

> For at that time I will change the speech of the peoples to a pure speech, that all of them may call upon the name of the LORD and serve him with one accord. (Zephaniah 3:9)

> On that day you shall not be put to shame because of the deeds by which you have rebelled against me; for then I will remove from your midst your proudly exultant ones, and you shall no longer be haughty in my holy mountain. But I will leave in your midst a people humble and lowly. They shall seek refuge in the name of the LORD. (Zephaniah 3:11–12)

So, live like there's no tomorrow

Like the country song says, live like you know you're dying.

Even if the return of the Lord is delayed, we're all dying—every day.

So live righteously, live humbly, and maybe love people more deeply, speak more sweetly, and offer forgiveness.

Be the husband/wife you want to be.

Live every day like you know you're dying, like there's no tomorrow.

Remember that for all of us, eternity is right around the corner. So be continually humble, live rightly, and most important, seek the Lord—call on Him for salvation and you will have no fear concerning the end of the world.

The LORD your God is in your midst,
a mighty one who will save;
he will rejoice over you with gladness;
he will quiet you by his love;
he will exult over you with loud singing.
"I will gather those of you who mourn for the festival,
so that you will no longer suffer reproach.
Behold, at that time I will deal with all your oppressors.
And I will save the lame and gather the outcast,
and I will change their shame into praise
and renown in all the earth.
At that time I will bring you in,
at the time when I gather you together;
for I will make you renowned and praised
among all the peoples of the earth,
when I restore your fortunes
before your eyes," says the LORD.
(Zephaniah 3:17–20)

Sample Third-Person Storytelling—2 Kings 5

COMMANDER'S INTENT: Submit to God and you will have enough. Taking more will lead to having less.

WHAT IS THE NEED ADDRESSED: We always want more—more respect, more money, more assurances.

POINT FOR PROCLAMATION: Submission is all we need. God has offered us everything we need for our salvation.

CATCHPHRASE: It is enough.

Naaman Wanted More

Everything around us tells us we need more. Advertisers and businesses want to create a need, something that they can sell us. They want to give us something else we think we must have. We find out from advertising what we are supposed to want.

When the iPhone 6 came out, I thought I really needed it. My old phone wasn't working well. My eyes were getting bad, and I needed a bigger screen. I had an upgrade available on my phone from Verizon, and I convinced myself I needed an iPhone 6. I ended up driving to another state and wandering around several stores to get the phone, get it set up on Verizon, and then get it backed up and programmed for my use.

I was so excited. I had my iPhone 6. And guess what? It's pretty much exactly the same as my old phone. It still breaks when I drop it. The camera didn't work at all. I wasted a lot of time and spent more money than was necessary to fix my old phone. Worse than that, I wasted a lot of mental and emotional energy wanting, craving, and thinking about something just because Apple convinced me I had to have it.

What do you really need? What is it that you think you have to have? Do you need a bigger house? A better job? More respect? What would you do for it?

Now I know we all really do have true needs, and our story tonight is about someone named Namaan, who had both real and superficial needs. He had real needs—he was sick and needed healing. But he almost lost out on being healed because of his need for self-importance. He was second string, and he needed—he wanted—to feel important. He also had a third need, which he didn't even recognize, and that was a need for God.

In 2 Kings 5 is the story of the commander of Syria whom YHWH favors with the victory over Israel. This is a low time in Israel's history as the people are not following God. So low that God is favoring the enemy, Syria. King Ahab, the king of Israel, is the worst enemy of all.

Naaman is the commander of the Syrian army. He is also the king of Syria's right-hand man. But Namaan suffers from leprosy. An incurable disease. His wife's little Israelite servant girl tells her that there is a prophet in Israel who can cure Naaman. So, the Syrian king, whom Naaman cares for, sends Naaman, his army commander, to Israel for healing. But rather than going to a lowly prophet of Israel, they go, of course, to the powerful King of Israel. Naaman has his camels loaded with gold and gifts and expensive presents and a letter from the king of Syria on his behalf. He travels quite a long distance to see the king of Israel.

Now, the king of Israel, Ahab, does not have a good relationship with Syria, with God, or with the prophet of Israel, Elisha, for that matter. So, when Naaman shows up asking to be healed,

Ahab, who knows he can't cure anyone, becomes upset and frightened. He tears his clothes in anguish and agitation. Ahab thinks this is some sort of trick by the king of Syria to make him look bad. Maybe Naaman is a spy. Ahab doesn't know what's happening, and he is terrified.

Elisha hears that Naaman has gone to King Ahab rather than coming to him. In response, Elisha asks, "What? Is it because there is no prophet in Israel that you are in a panic, Ahab?" So Naaman, the Syrian commander, finally comes to the prophet of Israel, the prophet of God, where he should have come first. He drives up with his gold and gifts, his horses and chariots to Elisha's house and knocks.

Elisha is a little put out that Naaman visited King Ahab first instead of him, the prophet of Israel. So instead of rushing to the door and bowing down in respect, Elisha keeps things in perspective. Elisha is not about to bow down to the enemy, a Syrian commander. I like to picture Elisha sitting on his couch changing television channels looking for a good football game (that's just me and my imagination), and he ends a messenger (probably his servant Gehazi) to answer the door. The messenger is to give Commander Naaman and his grand entourage a message.

"Elisha's busy. He says to go dip yourself in the Jordan River seven times and you'll be fine."

Naaman is so angry. He is an important person. He has come a long way. He has a letter from the conquering king, the king of Syria. He has a boatload of expensive gifts. He thought that surely the prophet would come out of his house and stand in front of him and call on the name of YHWH in a deep voice and wave his hands dramatically over the leprosy and cure him.

Instead, this prophet has some servant instruct him to dip in a nasty creek. Naaman marches off in a rage. This is not how he had pictured his healing at all. Naaman has a real need for healing. But he has a worse need that he has not yet recognized. Naaman needs to be willing to submit to someone. Naaman needs to submit to God.

Finally, a servant of Naaman, a servant wiser than himself, bravely comes forward to talk some sense into him. He reminds Naaman that the prophet has spoken the Word on behalf of God, and if Naaman will just simply submit himself to Israel's God and to the prophet of God, maybe he will be healed. The servant asks Naaman to do the small thing that he was asked to do. The servant asks him to be willing to submit himself to someone else instead of hoping for a big, dramatic healing.

Naaman submits himself to the lowly washing in the muddy Jordan, and in that act of submitting to God, he is cleansed of his leprosy. Naaman is convinced Elisha is a man of God. He returns and says to Elisha, "Behold, I know that there is no God in all the earth but in Israel." Naaman asks Elisha to accept a gift of thanks for healing him. Elisha, the prophet of Israel, will not accept gold and gifts from Naaman. Elisha knows that it was God, not himself, who healed Naaman. Elisha has all he needs and will take no more.

Yet surprise of surprises, Naaman humbly asks Elisha for something else. He asks for dirt. Naaman wants to bring dirt home from Israel so he can worship the God of Israel when he is in a temple to a foreign God. He asks pardon for having to perform his job, which is taking care of the king of Syria while the king worships the false god Rimnon.

Elisha pardons him and lets him know that he can worship the true God in a foreign land and even in a foreign temple. Elisha sends him, probably with the load of dirt, back home.

But Gehazi, the servant of Elisha, is pretty mad about missing out on the gold and presents.

That's well enough for Elisha, he thinks, but I'm not a rich man. I'm not going to work for Elisha forever. I want some of the gold. Elisha's crazy for not taking it.

So Gehazi finagles his way into getting some gold. He's given gold that weighs as much as two people, so probably around three hundred pounds. He also asks for a couple of outfits to wear. He's going to need a new wardrobe now that he's rich. Gehazi lies to Naaman, saying that Elisha needs the clothes for someone else.

Elisha is again seen as a shrewd judge of character. He knows exactly what Gehazi has done. It's probably hard to bring home three hundred pounds of gold without anyone noticing.

"Where have you been Gehazi?" Elisha asks. Elisha then asks Gehazi if this was a time to take great wealth from the enemy. His first point: "Gehazi, do you steal from your conquering enemy when your enemy bows down humbly before you and asks for help?" And second: "Gehazi, when our enemy has so humbled himself before YHWH and his prophet that he asks for two mule loads of dirt so he can worship the God of Israel on Israeli soil despite returning to Syria, should we rob him?"

Gehazi, in his greed, has destroyed the good name and the reputation of the God of Israel and the prophet Elisha. Elisha curses Gehazi and his descendants with leprosy forever.

God provided the way for Naaman to be cleansed. He merely required him to humble himself in the presence of a lowly prophet. This wasn't good enough for Naaman. God provided a way for Naaman to be cleansed of his disease by dipping himself in a river rather than experiencing a dramatic healing. This wasn't good enough for Naaman either.

Finally, when Naaman submitted to God and admitted that God's ways were good enough, not only was he cleansed but he also found God.

Gehazi, on the other hand, knew God and was well cared for by his master, but wanted more. He wanted to be rich. He wanted what he thought he deserved, some of that gold. Nothing was good enough for Gehazi, so he and his family were cursed for his greed.

What do we feel we're missing? Security? Respect? Health? What do we wish we had? What has God not given us that we want?

What do we really deserve? When we buy a new car, people say, "You deserve it—you work so hard." When we have an ice cream cone, people say, "You deserve it after a long, hard day." Usually, I want to scream, "No. I don't deserve it. It is just a gift, a blessing, or in the case of the ice cream, too much of something I really didn't need."

What would it look like if we took what God offered and were thankful for it? What has God given me? What has he given you? I'm reminded of an old song: "Count your blessings, name them one by one. Count your blessings, see what God has done." We don't deserve anything, actually. In fact, everything we have is a gift.

When Naaman, the commander for the king of Syria, won the battle against Israel, the Bible says it was not because he was so mighty but because he was favored by God. How has God favored us? What if God removed his favor? Do we express thanks for God's favor?

Is your life so good you don't need God? Have you ever thought what your life would be like if God withdrew his favor?

When we submit to Jesus Christ and take a little step of faith like Naaman's submissive step into the Jordan River, we can be cleansed too. Not from leprosy but from our guilt and sin. When like Gehazi we pridefully crave a little more, not trusting God, we end up with nothing, or worse. We end up without the Savior, without our sins being cleansed, and without the gift of eternal life.

Do I have enough? Do I need to submit to God and take that little step of faith? What little step do I need to take? Do I need to be grateful for things I thought were mine because of my hard work but now understand they are really due to God's great favor?

What if I go home tonight with a cleansed heart and a memento of what happened here—maybe a couple bags of dirt? —maybe I need to make a commitment to worship God like Naaman made. Let's worship God with a grateful heart, exclaiming, "Thank you, God. I have enough."

At Passover, some Jewish people remember God's many blessings with a song they sing called Daiyyeinu. Daiyyeinu means, "It would have been enough." After each great gift of God they repeat, "Daiyyeinu—it would have been enough."

Five Stanzas of Leaving Slavery
1. If He had brought us out of Egypt. It would have been enough.
2. If He had executed justice upon the Egyptians. It would have been enough.
3. If He had executed justice upon their gods. It would have been enough.
4. If He had slain their firstborn. It would have been enough.
5. If He had given to us their health and wealth. It would have been enough.

Five Stanzas of Miracles
1. If He had split the sea for us. It would have been enough.
2. If He had led us through on dry land. It would have been enough.
3. If He had drowned our oppressors. It would have been enough.
4. If He had provided for our needs in the wilderness for forty years. It would have been enough.
5. If He had fed us manna. It would have been enough.

Five Stanzas of Being with God
1. If He had given us Shabbat. It would have been enough.
2. If He had led us to Mount Sinai. It would have been enough.
3. If He had given us the Torah. It would have been enough.
4. If He had brought us into the land of Israel. It would have been enough.
5. If He built the temple for us. It would have been enough.

Five Stanzas for Believers
1. If you gave us your son Jesus, who gave up the glory of heaven and came as a baby, taking the form of a slave. Say it with me: "It would have been enough."
2. If you sent your son, your only son, to the cross to die for the dark sins of the world, for our sins. It would have been enough.
3. If you brought Jesus to life again and He reigned with you in heaven, where He brings our prayers before you. It would have been enough.
4. If you gave us your Holy Spirit to be with us, comfort us, and guide us in truth. It would have been enough.
5. If you are come again at the Second Advent to conquer death and sin. It would have been enough.

IT IS ENOUGH. WE HAVE ALL WE NEED.

Sample Bible Study Message

Isaiah 1

COMMANDER'S INTENT: We have all rebelled and are all guilty before God. God offers forgiveness to those who will repent.

POINT FOR PROCLAMATION: We have blood on our hands. Christ's blood can wash it away.

CATCHPHARASE: There has been a great rebellion against God, and the people of God have blood on their hands.

Blood on Our Hands

It's been over twenty years since one of the most highly publicized arrests and trials in history. The trial lasted 135 days, and the verdict was televised and seen by more than 150 million people.[xi] The trial of O. J. Simpson hinged on a bloody glove.

In a surprising twist during the trial, Simpson held up his hand to pull on the glove he supposedly had worn when he killed his ex-wife and her friend.

The blood-stained glove did not fit. O. J. Simpson, former famous football player for the Buffalo Bills, was therefore found not guilty of killing his ex-wife and another man. All because the glove didn't fit.

Blood on your hands is a powerful proof of guilt.

Let's enter another courtroom scene.

The courtroom is heaven. God is the righteous and holy Judge. The people of Israel are now brought into the courtroom, and we have front-row seats at the trial not only of the century but also of eternity as it unfolds.

There is a surprising twist. Something unexpected. God is not only the judge but also the prosecuting attorney, and Isaiah is his mouthpiece.

The verdict has been drawn. Isaiah brings the prosecution, and he pronounces the verdict for the Judge.

Speaking for the judge, Isaiah restates the charges. Israel has repeatedly broken the law. Having offered Israel mercy over and over, the Judge seems to have lost His patience.

God, the Holy One of Israel, sends his mouthpiece Isaiah to convey His judgment. But there is no attorney for the defense. There is no need for one since the Judge is not only perfect in righteousness but He is also the loving Father of the accused!

Isaiah Announces the Charges: Hear Ye, Hear Ye!

> Hear, O heavens!
> Listen, O earth!
> For the LORD has spoken:
> "I reared children and brought them up,
> but they have rebelled against me."
> (Isaiah 1:2 NIV)

278

How had the people rebelled against God?

> The ox knows its master,
> the donkey its owner's manger,
> but Israel does not know,
> my people do not understand.
> (Isaiah 1:3 NIV)

Isaiah speaks on God's behalf, declaring, "Your hands are full of blood!" (vv. 15–16). There has been a great rebellion, and the people of God have blood on their hands. Therefore, they are pronounced guilty as charged.

First, Isaiah repeats the charges.

> Woe to the sinful nation,
> a people whose guilt is great,
> a brood of evildoers,
> children given to corruption!
> They have forsaken the LORD;
> they have spurned the Holy One of Israel
> and turned their backs on him.
> (Isaiah 1:4 NIV)

Then, Isaiah describes in detail their sentence for rebelling against the Holy One of Israel.

> Your whole head is injured,
> your whole heart afflicted.
> From the sole of your foot to the top of your head
> there is no soundness—
> only wounds and welts and open sores,
> not cleansed or bandaged
> or soothed with olive oil.
> Your country is desolate,
> your cities burned with fire;
> your fields are being stripped by foreigners right before you,
> laid waste as when overthrown by strangers.
> (Isaiah 1:5b–7 NIV)

In an ironic twist, the righteous Judge has sentenced the guilty party not only to the punishment they deserve but also to the punishment they requested. They have turned from God; they have metaphorically run from His care. They have spurned and rejected their Protector, so He will leave them to fight their own battles and live on their own.

> Daughter Zion is left like a shelter in a vineyard,
> like a hut in a cucumber field,
> like a city under siege.
> (Isaiah 1:8 NIV)

As we watch this trial unfold, we get the sense that the people of Israel have faced these same charges repeatedly. They have been pretending to be upright citizens deserving of the blessings of those who are part of the kingdom of God while all the time mocking the very desires of the Judge and King.

The Judge has seen them in his courtroom begging for mercy many times before. They have feigned respect and pretended to bow down in homage to the Holy One of Israel, but they have been dishonest about their worship.

The righteous Judge declares:

> The multitude of your sacrifices—what are they to me? …
> I have more than enough of burnt offerings,
> of rams and the fat of fattened animals;
> I have no pleasure in the blood of bulls and lambs and goats.
> When you come to appear before me,
> who has asked this of you,
> this trampling of my courts?
> Stop bringing meaningless offerings!
> Your incense is detestable to me.
> New Moons, Sabbaths and convocations—
> I cannot bear your worthless assemblies.
> Your New Moon feasts and your appointed festivals
> I hate with all my being.
> They have become a burden to me;
> I am weary of bearing them.
> When you spread out your hands in prayer,
> I hide my eyes from you;
> even when you offer many prayers,
> I am not listening.
> Your hands are full of blood!
> (Isaiah 1:11–15 NIV)

Another Perspective on This Scene

What of all this courtroom drama? I thought God was our loving Father. Why would a loving Father not listen to his children? Why would He hide His eyes when they are in pain?

What Isaiah is describing could perhaps be pictured as an unruly teenager who though loved dearly and raised by kind and loving parents has run wild and broken every moral, ethical, and spiritual rule his parents have given him. He has defied his parents repeatedly and denied any help to his siblings who were in need, and then he comes creeping home on Mother's Day with a stolen Mother's Day card and a plea for a loan from Mom and Dad.

Even the dogs in the house have more respect for their masters than that child has for his parents. Even the animals in the barn know who gives them their grain.

These prayers our loving God is rejecting in verse 15 are not prayers of apology or repentance or prayers spoken to a holy God in humility. These are the prayers of those who have chronically rebelled against God, rejected Him, and now expect His supernatural blessing though they have made no real effort to change.

And this has happened many times before.

God, in this image of Him as a loving but fair parent, says He is not listening anymore. Like an earthly parent unable to bear the sight of his child begging for what he could have had all along if he hadn't rebelled and walked away, God has to cover His eyes when Israel comes to Him in prayer while still living in open rebellion.

There has been a great rebellion against God, and it is the people of God who have blood on their hands.

Back to the Trial—Let's Look at the Scene of the Crime and See What Rebellion Looks Like.

We have to ask, what could anyone do to make God turn His head? What could be so bad? What have these Israelites done to make a loving God cover his eyes when they pray?

In verse 17, Isaiah provides some details on the scene of the crime. What exactly does rebellion against God look like? It's not what you would think.

Israel's great rebellion against God is described clearly—twice—in this chapter, first in verses 16–17 and again in verse 23.

> Take your evil deeds out of my sight!
> Stop doing wrong, learn to do right!
> Seek justice, encourage the oppressed.
> Defend the cause of the fatherless,
> plead the case of the widow.
> (Isaiah 1:16–17 NIV)

In the form of literary parallelism that is very common in Hebrew poetry (which is how the book of Isaiah was written), Isaiah states the general crime and then gets more specific. His words are a spiral, driving deeper and deeper to the point. He provides specific examples of how Israel (or we) can stop doing evil and begin to do good. He says, "Seek justice, encourage the oppressed." Then, "Defend the cause of the fatherless, plead the case of the widow."[1] Justice and encouragement are inherent in God's nature. His true followers can do no less than seek to do justice and encourage the oppressed.

This great rebellion is not about what they have done. This great rebellion, the blood on their hands, is about the things they have left undone.

The crimes for which they are being convicted are not working for justice in the world, not encouraging those who are oppressed, not defending causes that support the fatherless, not pleading for widows—in short, not supporting and caring for those in their midst that needed them to show God's love and mercy. That is the blood on their hands.

There has been a great rebellion against God, and the people of God are guilty. They have blood on their hands. They have shown their utter disdain for God by leaving things undone.

The people of God stand convicted.

Often, when we hear words like *widows* and *fatherless*, we think they speak to a different time. A time when widows didn't get Social Security. A time before orphanages. You know, back when things were really bad. Before we were civilized.

---

[1] Isaiah 1:17 (NIV).

Here's how it stands now. Let's pick just one issue of serious rebellion, not caring for the fatherless. In the United States, "an estimated 24.7 million children (33%) live without their biological father."[xii] "57.6% of black children ... [are] living without their biological fathers."[xiii]

God has spoken. Just like the Israelites, we do not know what we have done. Like them, we do not understand the gravity of our sins. But we can see the effects on society of this terrible sin of omission, of not caring for our own children, and especially for the fatherless among us.

The words *orphans and widows* stand for all the oppressed—just as in verse 2, "Hear, O Heavens! Listen, O Earth!" implies that this is a message not just for some but for everyone.

Another Surprising Twist—The Rebels Are Offered Redemption

The O. J. Simpson trial is memorable for its surprising end. Simpson was acquitted because the bloody glove, the one bearing his blood and the blood of the murder victims, did not fit his hand. But in our case, the glove fits. The blood of our victims is on our hands. No lawyer, no tampering with the evidence, nothing can acquit us of our guilt.

The guilt of the church, of believers, of you and me for ignoring these issues is staggering. Our entire society is wounded from head to toe. There is violence everywhere. We chose to abandon God's commands, and God has let that run its course. We are getting what we asked for.

Basic Old Testament theology is consistent with verses 19 and 20.

> If you are willing and obedient,
> you shall eat the good of the land;
> but if you refuse and rebel,
> you shall be eaten by the sword;
> for the mouth of the LORD has spoken.
> (Isaiah 1:19–20)

If we were Israelites reading this passage in Isaiah's day, we would know that verse 25 is talking about God's judgment—smelting away the impurities of the silver, the dross, with high heat.

> I will turn my hand against you
> and will smelt away your dross as with lye
> and remove all your alloy.
> (Isaiah 1:25)

The only way for them to cleanse their sins is through trouble and tribulation. The message to the people of Israel is that they have sinned and deserve the punishment of the sword. Their rebellion against God will bring death by another nation. If they turn from their rebellion to God, He won't send in the Assyrian army. Purification is a painful thing.

All these thousands of years later, we face other enemies. But notice that this policy still applies. If we follow the rules and do good, things will go better for us than if we don't.

But the book of Isaiah is not in the Bible to warn us, "The Assyrians are coming," though perhaps the things we've omitted to care for have produced great problems in our society.

The message for us today is far more important. Our rebellion against God still brings death. Eternal death. The Israelite Paul, writing several hundred years after Isaiah, made it very clear:

"For the wages of sin is death, but the free gift of God is eternal life in Christ Jesus our Lord" (Romans 6:23).

Make no mistake—God is still just as holy as He was when Isaiah called Him the Holy One of Israel, which he does twenty-five times in this book written some seven centuries before Jesus Christ.

And we are guilty of leaving things undone. Of not caring for the elderly, the poor, the refugee, the single mother, the fatherless child, the orphan, the unloved.

Even those of us who have faith in Jesus Christ must admit we have left things undone that God wants us to do. The glove fits. Our disobedience means we deserve death. We have rebelled, and there is blood on our hands.

Now for the gem. The big surprise of this passage lies in verse 18. Isaiah's message, inspired by the Holy Spirit and coming directly from the mouth of God, fits perfectly with the message of the gospel in the New Testament (hence the double meaning of verse 18 that Isaiah himself probably did not fully know).

> "Come now, let us reason together," says the LORD:
> "though your sins are like scarlet,
>   they shall be as white as snow;
> though they are red like crimson,
>   they shall become like wool."
> (Isaiah 1:18)

The word *reason* here means more than just "to argue"; it also means, "to decide a case in court." This is consistent with the legal terms we see in verse 17 such as justice, correct, and plead. But instead of the Judge pronouncing the deserved sentence, He offers pardon![xiv] Our Judge has offered us, the convicted ones, the opportunity not only for pardon but also for a record wiped clean of guilt through the One who took on our penalty of death.

Yes, that is right. The Judge is not acquitting us of guilt. We are in fact guilty and deserve the sword. But God, the righteous Judge, is sending His Son to die, to take the sword, and to take the painful, purifying punishment in our place.

As 1 John 1:7b declares, "The blood of Jesus his Son cleanses us from all sin."

The only way to cleanse the blood from our hands is by the cleansing blood of Jesus Christ.

But Wait—There's More

That is the surprise conclusion to the trial. But God's Son, Jesus Christ, does more than that. He offers us His Spirit. At the very moment, we turn from our rebellion and repent of our sins, both those we've done and the things we've left undone, at that very moment the Holy Spirit, the Spirit of the Holy One of Israel, comes to dwell in us and give us His power by which we can continue our repentance. Stop the rebellion. Learn to do right!

> Stop doing wrong,
> learn to do right!
> Seek justice,
> encourage the oppressed.

Defend the cause of the fatherless,
plead the case of the widow.
(Isaiah 1:16b–17 NIV)

The whole message of Isaiah 1 is reiterated by Jesus in the book of Matthew.

"Teacher, which is the great commandment in the Law?" And he said to him, "You shall love the Lord your God with all your heart and with all your soul and with all your mind. This is the great and first commandment. And a second is like it: You shall love your neighbor as yourself. On these two commandments depend all the Law and the Prophets."(Matthew 22:36–40)

God has called us, His rebellious children, to Himself. And He willingly provides a way to wash the blood from our hands with His blood. But just as in those days of Israel and Isaiah, we are called to stop rebelling and turn back to God. To seek justice, encourage the oppressed, defend the cause of the fatherless, and plead the case of the widow.

There has been a great rebellion against God, and the people of God have blood on their hands. But the blood shed on the cross is able to cleanse the blood from our hands if we will turn to Him.

ENDNOTES

Glossary

i   Norman L. Geisler and William E. Nix, *A General Introduction to the Bible*, revised and expanded. (Chicago: Moody Press, 1986), 202.

ii   Arthur G. Patzia and Anthony J. Petrotta, *Pocket Dictionary of Biblical Studies* (Downers Grove, IL: InterVarsity Press, 2002), 45.

iii Richard L. Mayhue, "Rediscovering Expository Preaching" in *Rediscovering Expository Preaching* (Dallas: Word Publishing, 1992), 12–13.

iv Stanley Grenz, David Guretzki, and Cherith Fee Nordling, *Pocket Dictionary of Theological Terms* (Downers Grove, IL: InterVarsity Press, 1999).

v   Arthur G. Patzia and Anthony J. Petrotta, *Pocket Dictionary of Biblical Studies* (Downers Grove, IL: InterVarsity Press, 2002), 60.

vi Bruce Corley, Steve Lemke, and Grant Lovejoy, *Biblical Hermeneutics: A Comprehensive Introduction to Interpreting* Scripture, 2d ed. (Nashville: Broadman & Holman, 2002), 310–11.

vii Ibid.

Chapter 1: Thoughtful Proclaimers Are Changed by the Word

i   Snyder, James L. *The Life of A. Word. Tozer: In Pursuit of God* (Bloomington, MN: Bethany House, Baker Publishing 2009, Kindle Edition 2011), 14.

ii   Ibid., 68.

iii Ibid., 9.

iv Ibid., 8.

v   Frank Heile, "What is the main difference between resonance and interference," Quora, 3/21/2013, Word.quora.com/What-is-the-main-difference-between-resonance-and-interference (accessed 4/25/2016).

vi John R. Stott, *Understanding the Bible* (Grand Rapids, MI: Zondervan, 2011), Locations 2610–2612, Kindle.

vii N. T. Wright, "How Can the Bible Be Authoritative?" from "The Laing Lecture 1989" and the "Griffith Thomas Lecture 1989," originally published in *Vox Evangelica*, vol. 21 (1991), 7–32, http://ntwrightpage.com/Wright_Bible_Authoritative.htm (accessed 4/22/2016).

viii Wikipedia, "Charles Hodge," March 2016, https://en.wikipedia.org/wiki/Charles_Hodge (accessed 3/30/16).

ix Charles Hodge, *Systematic Theology*, vol. 1 (Oak Harbor, WA: Logos Research Systems, 1997), 10.

x   N. T. Wright, "How Can the Bible Be Authoritative?" from "The Laing Lecture 1989," and the "Griffith Thomas Lecture 1989"; originally published in *Vox Evangelica*, vol. 21 (1991), 7–32, http://ntwrightpage.com/Wright_Bible_Authoritative.htm (accessed 4/22/2016).

xi   William Shakespeare, *Hamlet*, act 1, scene 3.

xii   Dennis Fletcher. Copyright July 2016. Used with permission.

xiii   Vern S. Poythress, *Reading the Word of God in the Presence of God: A Handbook for Biblical Interpretation* (Wheaton IL: Crossway, 2016), 512, Kindle Edition.

xiv   Gordon D. Fee and Douglas Stuart, *How to Read the Bible for All Its Worth: A Guide to Understanding the Bible*, 3d ed. (Grand Rapids, MI: Zondervan, 2003), locations 574–75, Kindle.

xv   Gordon D. Fee and Douglas Stuart, *How to Read the Bible for All Its Worth: A Guide to Understanding the Bible*, 3d ed. (Grand Rapids, MI: Zondervan, 2003), locations 574–75, Kindle.

Chapter 2: Discover the Commander's Intent

i   Chad Storlie, "Manage Uncertainty with Commander's Intent," Harvard Business Review (Nov. 3, 2010), https://hbr.org/2010/11/dont-play-golf-in-a-football-g/ (accessed 5/5/2016).

ii   Chip Heath and Dan Heath, *Made to Stick: Why Some Ideas Survive and Others Die* (New York: Random House, 2008), 26–28.

iii   Air University, "Military Decision Making Process," http://Word.au.af.mil/au/awc/awcgate/army/fm101-5_mdmp.pdf (accessed 5/5/2016); and Maj. Richard Dempsey and Maj. John M. Chavous, "Commander's intent and Concept of Operations," U.S. Army in Military Review (Nov. and Dec. 2013).

iv   Chip Heath and Dan Heath, *Made to Stick: Why Some Ideas Survive and Others Die* (New York: Random House, 2008), 26–28.

v   C. Plantinga Jr., *A Sure Thing: What We Believe and Why* (Grand Rapids MI: Bible Way CRC Publications, 1986), 67; quoted in J. Kent Edwards, *Deep Preaching: Creating Sermons That Go Beyond the Superficial* (Nashville: B&H Publishing, 2009), 18, Kindle.

vi   Chip Heath and Dan Heath, *Made to Stick: Why Some Ideas Survive and Others Die* (New York: Random House, 2008), 26–28.

vii   Ibid.

viii   D. G. Barnhouse, "On Expository Preaching," in Clarence Stonelynn Roddy, ed., *We Prepare and Preach: The Practice of Sermon Construction and Delivery* (Chicago: Moody Press, 1959), 29; quoted in J. Kent Edwards, *Deep Preaching: Creating Sermons That Go beyond the Superficial* (Nashville: B&H Publishing, 2009), 18, Kindle.

ix   J. Kent Edwards, *Deep Preaching: Creating Sermons That Go beyond the Superficial* (Nashville: B&H Publishing, 2009), 18, Kindle.

x   Haddon Robinson, *Biblical Preaching: The Development and Delivery of Expository Messages*, 2d ed. (Grand Rapids, MI: Baker, 2001), locations 214–16, Kindle.

xi   R. Albert Mohler, "As One without Authority," Albert Mohler.com, http://www.albertmohler.com/2008/12/12/as-one-with-authority (accessed 6/6/2016).

xii   Haddon Robinson, quoted by Richard L. Mayhue, "Rediscovering Expository Preaching," in *Rediscovering Expository Preaching* (Dallas: Word Publishing, 1992), 12.

xiii   Walter Russell Bowie, *Preaching* (Nashville: Abingdon, 1954), 124–25; quoted in Scott M. Gibson, *Preaching with a Plan: Sermon Strategies for Growing Mature Believers* (Grand Rapids, MI: Baker Publishing, 2012), 97–98.

xiv   Chip Heath and Dan Heath, *Made to Stick: Why Some Ideas Survive and Others Die* (New York: Random House, 2008), 26–28.

xv   Dennis Fletcher. Copyright 2015. Used with permission.

Chapter 3: Practice Inquisitive Exegesis

i   Gordon Fee, *New Testament Exegesis: A Handbook for Students and Pastors*, 3d ed. (Louisville: Westminster John Knox Press, 2002), 5.

ii   Ibid., 1.

iii   Ibid., 181.

iv   Kevin Vanhoozer, *Theological Interpretation of the Old Testament: A Book-by-Book Survey* (Grand Rapids, MI: Baker Academic, 2008), 537, Kindle.

v   Eugene Lowry, *The Homiletical Plot: The Sermon as Narrative Art Form*, expanded edition (Louisville, KY: Westminster John Knox Press, 2001), 44.

vi   Lesslie Newbigin, *Foolishness to the Greeks: The Gospel and Western Culture* (Grand Rapids, MI: Eerdmans, 1986), 56–57.

vii   Lesslie Newbigin, *Foolishness to the Greeks: The Gospel and Western Culture* (Grand Rapids, MI: Eerdmans, 1986), 783–87, Kindle.

viii   Timothy Keller, "Preaching to the Collective Heart," (blog) January 30, 2013 (accessed 4/22/16), http://www.timothykeller.com/blog/2013/1/30/preaching-to-the-collective-heart.

ix   Ibid.

x   Ramsey and Suenens, *The Future*, 13–14. In John Stott, *Between Two Worlds: The Art of Preaching in the Twentieth Century* (Grand Rapids, MI: Eerdmans, 1982), 179.

xi   Charles Spurgeon, *Lectures*, Third Series, 54, in John Stott, *Between Two Worlds: The Art of Preaching in the Twentieth Century* (Grand Rapids, MI: Eerdmans 1982), 149.

xii   Timothy Keller, "Preaching to the Collective Heart," (blog) January 30, 2013 (accessed 4/22/16), http://www.timothykeller.com/blog/2013/1/30/preaching-to-the-collective-heart.

xiii   Brevard Childs, Biblical Theology of the Old and New Testaments: Theological Reflection on the Christian Bible (Minneapolis: Fortress Press, 2011), 86.

Chapter 4: Plan Your Proclamation

i   Scott M. Gibson, Preaching with a Plan: Sermon Strategies for Growing Mature Believers (Grand Rapids, MI: Baker Publishing, 2012), 48.

ii   "Sandy Hook shooting: What happened?" CNN, Dec., 2012 (accessed 4/15/16), http://www.cnn.com/interactive/2012/12/us/sandy-hook-timeline/.

iii   Hurricane Sandy, October 29.

iv   Warren Wiersbe, *The Dynamics of Preaching* (Grand Rapids, MI: Baker, 1999), 55, in Scott M. Gibson, *Preaching with a Plan: Sermon Strategies for Growing Mature Believers* (Grand Rapids, MI: Baker Publishing, 2012), 121, Kindle.

v   Dennis Fletcher. Copyright. Used with permission.

vi   Scott M. Gibson, *Preaching with a Plan: Sermon Strategies for Growing Mature Believers* (Grand Rapids, MI: Baker Publishing, 2012), 17.

vii   DayDay Porchulav speaking in David Kennard's documentary: *A Year in Burgundy*, Dir. David Kennard, 91 min., Inca Productions, 2013.

viii   Dennis Fletcher. Copyright. Used with permission.

ix   Dennis Fletcher. Copyright 2016. Used with permission.

x   Walter C. Kaiser Jr., *Toward an Exegetical Theology: Biblical Exegesis for Preaching and Teaching* (Baker Publishing, 1998), 167–68, Kindle.

xi   Walter C. Kaiser Jr., *Toward an Exegetical Theology: Biblical Exegesis for Preaching and Teaching* (Baker Publishing, 1998), 169–71, Kindle.

xii   Johannes P. Louw and Eugene Albert Nida, *Greek-English Lexicon of the New Testament: Based on Semantic Domains* (New York: United Bible Societies, 1996), 414.

xiii Paul Scott Wilson, *God Sense: Reading the Bible for Preaching* (Nashville: Abingdon Press, 2001), 32.

xiv Norman L. Geisler and William E. Nix, *A General Introduction to the Bible*, rev. and expanded (Chicago: Moody Press, 1986), 339 ff.

xv Rob Portlock. Copyright 1999. Used with permission.

xvi Robert Alter, *The Art of Biblical Narrative* (Basic Book, 1981), 13.

xvii Dennis Fletcher. Copyright. Used with permission.

xviii Paul Scott Wilson, *God Sense: Reading the Bible for Preaching* (Nashville: Abingdon Press, 2001) 69–71.

xix Randall E. Pelton, *Preaching with Accuracy: Finding Christ-Centered Ideas for Biblical Preaching* (Grand Rapids, MI: Kregel, 2014) 33–37.

Chapter 5: Listen! Listen!

i Paul Scott Wilson, *God Sense: Reading the Bible for Preaching* (Nashville: Abingdon Press, 2001), 30.

ii Thomas G. Long, *Preaching and the Literary Forms of the Bible* (Philadelphia: Fortress, 1989), 28.

iii Haddon Robinson, *Biblical Preaching: The Development and Delivery of Expository Messages*, 2d ed. (Grand Rapids, MI: Baker, 2001), locations 252–53, Kindle.

iv Guigo the Carthusian, *Guigo II: Ladder of Monks and Twelve* Meditations (Kalamazoo, MI: Cistercian Publications, 1979), 67–68, in Tim Gray, *Praying* Scripture *for a Change: An Introduction to Lectio Divina* (Westchester, PA: Ascension Press), 30.

v Ibid., 430, Kindle.

vi Tim Gray, *Praying* Scripture *for a Change: An Introduction to Lectio Divina* (Westchester, PA: Ascension Press, 2009), 216–17, Kindle.

vii Tim Gray, *Praying* Scripture *for a Change: An Introduction to Lectio Divina* (Westchester PA: Ascension Press, 2009), 36.

viii Ibid., 35.

ix George Verwer, Messiology: The Mystery of How God Works Even When It Doesn't Make Sense to Us (Chicago: Moody, 2016) 2.

x Rob Portlock, Copyright 1988. Used with permission.

xi J. I. Packer, *God Has Spoken: Revelation and the Bible*, 2d ed.; new material, 1993 (Grand Rapids, MI: Baker Book House), 1979), 21.

xii Gordon D. Fee and Douglas Stuart, *How to Read the Bible for All Its Worth: A Guide to Understanding the Bible*, 3d ed. (Grand Rapids, MI: Zondervan, 2003), 775, Kindle.

xiii Oletta Wald, *The Joy of Discovery in Bible Study* (Minneapolis: Bible Banner Press, 1956); quoted in *The Navigator Bible Studies Handbook* (Colorado Springs: NavPress, 1974), 118, Kindle.

xiv John F. Walvoord and Roy B. Zuck, *The Bible Knowledge Commentary: An Exposition of the* Scriptures (Wheaton, IL: Victor Books, 1985).

xv *The ESV Study Bible* (Wheaton, IL: Crossway Bibles, 2008).

xvi Dennis Fletcher. Copyright. Used with permission.

Chapter 6: Context, Context, Context

i Greg Kouki, "Context is Crucial: Never Read a Bible Verse," In Plain Site, 2001 (accessed 4/22/2016), http://www.InPlainSite.org/html/contextis_crucial.html.

ii Randal E. Pelton, "Preaching the Literary Forms of the Bible" (D. Min. lecture, Gordon Conwell, Hamilton, MA, May 2014).

iii Brevard Childs, *Biblical Theology: A Proposal*, Facets ed., Facets Series (Minneapolis: Fortress Press, 2002), 79–80.

iv Ibid., 66–67.

v Ibid., 86.

vi Walter Kaiser, *Toward an Exegetical Theology: Biblical Exegesis for Preaching and Teaching* (Baker Publishing, 1998), 4237–38, Kindle.

vii Baruch Halpern, "Erasing History: The Minimalist Assault on Ancient Israel," *Bible Review* (December 1995), 35.

viii Walter C. Kaiser, *Toward an Exegetical Theology: Biblical Exegesis for Preaching and Teaching* (Grand Rapids, MI: Baker Academic, 1981), 134.

ix Ibid.

x Mike Graves, *The Sermon as Symphony: Preaching the Literary Forms of the New Testament* (Valley Forge: Judson Press, 1997), 6. See also Bruce Corley, Steve Lemke and Grant Lovejoy, *Biblical Hermeneutics: A Comprehensive Introduction to Interpreting* Scripture, 2d ed. (Nashville: Broadman & Holman, 2002), 398.

xi Richard Oster, *1 Corinthians, The College Press NIV Commentary* (Joplin, MO: College Press, 1995), 1 Corinthians 15:33.

xii D. A. Carson, *Exegetical Fallacies*, 2d ed. (Grand Rapids, MI: Baker Publishing, 1996), 1354, Kindle.

xiii Ibid.

xiv Gordon D. Fee and Douglas Stuart, *How to Read the Bible for All Its Worth: A Guide to Understanding the Bible*, 3d ed. (Grand Rapids, MI: Zondervan, 2003), locations 1619–20, Kindle.

xv Mike Graves, *The Sermon as Symphony: Preaching the Literary Forms of the New Testament* (Valley Forge: Judson Press, 1997), 6.

xvi Thomas Long, *Preaching and the Literary Forms of the Bible* (Philadelphia: Fortress, 1989), 51.

xvii Vern S. Polythress, Reading the Word of God in the Presence of God: A Handbook for Biblical Interpretation (Chicago, IL: Crossway, 2016), 35.

xviii W. D. McDonald, "Theology and Culture," in David F. Wells and Clark H. Pinnock, eds., *Toward a Theology for the Future* (Carol Stream, IL: Creation, 1971), 239, 241; quoted in Walter C. Kaiser, *Toward an Exegetical Theology: Biblical Exegesis for Preaching and Teaching* (Baker Publishing, 1998), 4186–87, Kindle.

xix Craig Keener, *The IVP Bible Background Commentary: New Testament* (Downers Grove, IL: InterVarsity Press, 1993), 26.

xx Scott Masear. Copyright 2015. Used with permission.

xxi Paul Scott Wilson, *God Sense: Reading the Bible for Preaching* (Nashville: Abingdon Press, 2001), 13.

xxii Timothy Keller, *Preaching: Communicating Faith in an Age of Skepticism* (New York: Viking, 2015), 86–90.

xxiii Brevard Childs, Biblical Theology of the Old and New Testaments: Theological Reflection on the Christian Bible (Minneapolis: Fortress Press, 2011), 87.

xxiv Graeme Goldworthy, *Christ-Centered Biblical Theology: Hermeneutical Foundations and Principles* (Downers Grove, IL: IVP Academic, 2012), 123.

xxv Ibid.

xxvi Bryan Chapell, *Christ-Centered Preaching*, 2d ed. (Grand Rapids, MI: Baker Publishing, 2005), 315.

xxvii Elyse Fitzpatrick in Jessi Strong, "Words of Assurance," *Leadership Journal* (July–August 2016), 25–28.

xxviii Ibid.

xxix Ibid.

xxx Stanley Grenz, David Guretzki, and Cherith Fee Nordling, *Pocket Dictionary of Theological Terms* (Downers Grove, IL: InterVarsity Press, 1999).

xxxi Walter Kaiser, *Preaching and Teaching from the Old Testament: A Guide for the Church* (Grand Rapids, MI: Baker Academic, 2003), 10.

xxxii Arnold G. Fruchtenbaum, *Messianic Christology: A Study of Old Testament Prophecy Concerning the First Coming of the Messiah* (Tustin, CA: Ariel Ministries, 1998), 11.

xxxiii Ibid.

xxxiv Ibid., 5–6.

xxxv Sidney Greidanus, *Preaching Christ from the Old Testament: A Contemporary Hermeneutical Method* (Grand Rapids, MI: Eerdmans, 1999), 262.

xxxvi Elizabeth Achtemeier, *Preaching from the Old Testament* (Louisville: Westminster/John Knox Press, 1989), 123–32.

xxxvii Gordon MacDonald, "Feeling as God Feels: Habakkuk 1–3," *Christianity Today International*, 2009; PreachingToday.com.

xxxviii Nick Hobart. Copyright 2001. Used with permission.

xxxix Jeffrey Arthurs, *Preaching with Variety: How to Re-Create the Dynamics of Biblical Genres* (Grand Rapids, MI: Kregel, 2007), 64.

xl Ibid., 67.

xli Ibid., 68.

xlii Paul Scott Wilson, *God Sense: Reading the Bible for Preaching* (Nashville: Abingdon Press, 2001), 31.

xliii Ibid., 69–71.

xliv Ibid.

xlv Ibid.

xlvi Ibid.

xlvii Ibid.

xlviii Ibid.

xlix Ibid.

l Ibid.

li Ibid.

lii Ibid.

Chapter 7: Dig Deep—Idea Level

i Frederick C. Mish, "Preface," *Merriam-Webster's Collegiate Dictionary* (Springfield, MA: Merriam-Webster, 2003).

ii Fredrick J. Long, *Kairos: A Beginning Greek Grammar* (Mishawaka, IN: Fredrick J. Long, 2005), 1.

iii Ramesh Richard, *Preparing Expository Sermons: A Seven-Step Method for Biblical Preaching* (Grand Rapids, MI: Baker Books, 2001), 37.

iv Ibid., 38.

v Ibid., 65.

vi Charles Dickens, *A Tale of Two Cities* (1859), 1.

vii Robert Alter, in Thomas Long *Preaching and the Literary Forms of the Bible* (Philadelphia: Fortress, 1989), 67.

viii Jeffrey Arthurs, *Preaching with Variety: How to Re-Create the Dynamics of Biblical Genres* (Grand Rapids, MI: Kregel, 2007), 71.

ix Strong, James. *Enhanced Strong's Lexicon* (Woodside Bible Fellowship, 1995).

x Coppes, Leonard J. "3 אָבָה." in *Theological Wordbook of the Old Testament*, eds. R. Laird Harris, Gleason L. Archer Jr., and Bruce K. Waltke (Chicago: Moody Press, 1999).

xi *The Navigator Bible Studies Handbook* (Colorado Springs: NavPress, 1974), 94–102, Kindle.

Chapter 8: Dig Deep—Word Level

i George Guthrie, "How to Study Your Bible" "Word Studies" at BiblicalTraining.org (accessed April 2016), http.www://biblicaltraining.org/library/Word-studies/how-to-study-your-bible/george-guthrie.

ii John Joseph Owens, *Analytical Key to the Old Testament* (Grand Rapids, MI: Baker Book House, 1989). And Francis Brown, Samuel Rolles Driver, and Charles Augustus Briggs, *Brown-Driver-Briggs Hebrew and English Lexicon* (Oxford: Clarendon Press, 1977).

iii Ludwig Koehler, Walter Baumgartner, M.E.J. Richardson, and Johann Jakob Stamm, *The Hebrew and Aramaic Lexicon of the Old Testament* (Leiden: E. J. Brill, 1994–2000), חֶסֶד.

iv Ibid., and Francis Brown, Samuel Rolles Driver, and Charles Augustus Briggs, *Enhanced Brown-Driver-Briggs Hebrew and English Lexicon* (Oxford: Clarendon Press, 1977).

^v   William D. Mounce, *Mounce's Complete Expository Dictionary of Old and New Testament Words,* eds. William D. Mounce, D. Matthew Smith, and Miles Van Pelt (Grand Rapids, MI: Zondervan, 2006).

^{vi}   *The Lexham English Septuagint,* eds. Brannan, Rick, Ken M. Penner, Israel Loken, Michael Aubrey, and Isaiah Hoogendyk (Bellingham, WA: Lexham Press, 2012).

^{vii}   *Theological Wordbook of the Old Testament,* ed. Harris, R. Laird, Gleason L. Archer Jr., and Bruce K. Waltke (Chicago: Moody Press, 1999).

^{viii} Gerhard Kittel, Gerhard Friedrich, and Geoffrey William Bromiley, *Theological Dictionary of the New Testament* (Grand Rapids, MI: Eerdmans, 1985).

^{ix}   R. Laird Harris, "698 חסד" in *Theological Wordbook of the Old Testament,* ed. Harris, R. Laird, Gleason L. Archer Jr., and Bruce K. Waltke (Chicago: Moody Press, 1999).

^x   Allen C. Myers, *The Eerdmans Bible Dictionary* (Grand Rapids, MI: Eerdmans, 1987), 710.

^{xi}   Dik LaPine. Copyright 2003. Used with permission.

^{xii}   Walter C. Kaiser, *Toward an Exegetical Theology: Biblical Exegesis for Preaching and Teaching* (Baker Publishing, 1998), 1552–54, Kindle.

^{xiii} William Arndt, Frederick Word Danker, and Walter Bauer, *A Greek-English Lexicon of the New Testament and Other Early Christian Literature* (Chicago: University of Chicago Press, 2000), χάρις, ιτος, ἡ.

^{xiv}   Ibid.

^{xv}   Spiros Zodhiates, *The Complete Word Study Dictionary: NT* (Chattanooga, TN: AMG Publishers, 2000).

^{xvi}   D. A. Carson, *Exegetical Fallacies,* 2d ed. (Grand Rapids, MI: Baker Publishing, 1996), 251–52, Kindle.

^{xvii} William D. Mounce, Greek for the Rest of Us: Mastering Bible Study without Mastering Biblical Languages (Grand Rapids, MI: Zondervan, 2003), 212–14.

^{xviii} D. A. Carson, *Exegetical Fallacies,* 2d ed. (Grand Rapids, MI: Baker Publishing, 1996), 252–53, Kindle.

^{xix}   *UBS Handbook Series* (New York: United Bible Societies).

^{xx}   Cleon L. Rogers Jr. and Cleon L. Rogers III, *The New Linguistic and Exegetical Key to the Greek New Testament* (Grand Rapids, MI: Zondervan, 1998).

^{xxi}   Abraham Kuruvilla, *Privilege the Text!: A Theological Hermeneutic for Preaching* (Chicago: Moody Publishers, 2013), 981–83, Kindle.

^{xxii} Ibid.

^{xxiii} Haddon Robinson, *Biblical Preaching: The Development and Delivery of Expository Messages,* 2d ed. (Grand Rapids, MI: Baker, 2001), 262–63, Kindle.

Chapter 9: Consider the Audience: Cultural Context

ⁱ   Lesslie Newbigin, Foolishness to the Greeks: The Gospel and Western Culture (Grand Rapids, MI: Eerdmans, 1986), 862–64, Kindle.

ⁱⁱ   Dietrich Bonhoeffer, *Ethics* (Simon and Schuster.com), 121.

ⁱⁱⁱ   Dennis Fletcher. Copyright 2016. Used with permission.

^{iv}   Timothy J Keller, "Accepting the Judge," *The Timothy Keller Sermon Archive.* (New York: Redeemer Presbyterian Church, 2013), preached January 23, 2000.

^v   Timothy J. Keller, *The Timothy Keller Sermon Archive* (New York City: Redeemer Presbyterian Church, 2013). Keller was paraphrasing Miroslav Volf, *Exclusion and Embrace: A Theological Exploration of Identity, Otherness, and Reconciliation* (Nashville, TN: Abingdon Press, 1996), 304.

^{vi}   John A Kern, *The Ministry to the Congregation* (New York: Wilbur B. Ketcham, 1897), 404; quoted in Scott M. Gibson, *Preaching with a Plan: Sermon Strategies for Growing Mature Believers* (Grand Rapids, MI: Baker Publishing, 2012), 18.

^{vii}   Karen Swallow Prior, "When the Abortion Doctor I Protested Was Killed by a Sniper: The shaken conscience of a pro-life activist," *ChristianityToday.com,* March 18, 2016 (accessed 5/2/16), http://www.christianitytoday.com/ct/2016/april/shaken-conscience-of-pro-life-activist.html.

^{viii} Timothy Keller, *Preaching: Communicating Faith in an Age of Skepticism* (New York: Viking, 2015), 116.

ix   Ibid., 119.

x   Ibid.

xi   Dennis Fletcher. Copyright 2016. Used with permission.

Chapter 10: Decide on the Commander's Intent

i   James L. Snyder, *The Life of A. W. Tozer: In Pursuit of God* (Bloomington, MN: Bethany House, Baker Publishing 2009) 219, Kindle.

ii   Haddon Robinson, *Biblical Preaching: The Development and Delivery of Expository Messages*, 2d ed. (Grand Rapids, MI: Baker, 2001), 490, Kindle.

iii   Walter Kaiser, *Four Views on Moving beyond the Bible to Theology* (Grand Rapids, MI: Zondervan, 2009), 23–25.

iv   Donald R. Sunukjian, *Biblical Preaching: Proclaiming Truth with Clarity and Relevance* (Grand Rapids, MI: Kregel, 2007), 134–35.

v   Grant Osborne, *The Hermeneutical Spiral: A Comprehensive Introduction to Biblical Interpretation*, 2d. ed. (Downers Grove, IL: IVP Academic, 2006), 167.

vi   Ibid.

vii   Andy Stanley and Lane Jones, *Communicating for a Change: Seven Keys to Irresistible Communication* (Colorado Springs: Multnomah Books, 2006), 184–85.

viii Dennis Fletcher. Copyright 2016. Used with permission.

ix   191 Timothy Keller, "Preaching to the Collective Heart," blog, January 30, 2013 (accessed 4/22/16), http://www.timothykeller.com/blog/2013/1/30/preaching-to-the-collective-heart.

x   Timothy Keller, *Preaching: Communicating Faith in an Age of Skepticism* (New York: Viking, 2015), 81.

xi   Ibid., 82–85.

xii   Ibid., 86–90.

xiii Paul Scott Wilson, *God Sense: Reading the Bible for Preaching* (Nashville: Abingdon Press, 2001) 109–11.

xiv   Ibid.

xv   Ibid.

xvi   Ibid.

Chapter 11: Let It Percolate

i   Kevin J. Vanhoozer, Dictionary for Theological Interpretation of the Bible, Kevin J. Vanhoozer, Craig G. Bartholomew, Daniel J. Treier, and N. T. Wright, eds. (London; Grand Rapids, MI: SPCK; Baker Academic, 2005), 24.

ii   Kevin J. Vanhoozer, *Is There a Meaning in This Text?: The Bible, the Reader, and the Morality of Literary Knowledge* (Grand Rapids, MI: Zondervan, 1998), 396.

iii   Brevard Childs, *Biblical Theology of the Old and New Testaments: Theological Reflection on the Christian Bible* (Minneapolis, MN: Fortress Press, 2011), 86–87.

iv   Dennis Fletcher. Copyright. Used with permission.

v   Scott Gibson, *Preaching with a Plan: Sermon Strategies for Growing Mature Believers* (Grand Rapids, MI: Baker Publishing, 2012), 29, Kindle.

vi   Walter Russell Bowie, *Preaching* (Nashville: Abingdon, 1954), 63; quoted in Scott M. Gibson, *Preaching with a Plan: Sermon Strategies for Growing Mature Believers* (Grand Rapids, MI: Baker Publishing, 2012), 33.

vii   A. W. Tozer, God Tells the Man Who Cares, God Speaks to Those Who Take Time to Listen (Camp Hill, PA: WingSpread Publishers, 2010), 41.

viii Dennis Fletcher. Copyright. Used with permission.

ix   Gordon MacDonald, *Ordering Your Private World* (Nashville: Thomas Nelson, 2003), 128.

x   Dan Pegoda. Copyright. Used with permission.

xi   P. K. Jewett, "LORD's Day" *The International Standard Bible Encyclopedia, Revised*, ed. Geoffrey Bromiley (Eerdmans, 1979–1988).

xii   Dennis Fletcher. Used with permission.

Chapter 12: Redemptive Proclamation

i   John A. Hauffman Jr., "What Starbucks, Harry and You All Have in Common (Heb. 2:2–3)," Preaching, March 10, 2009 (accessed 4/15/16), http://www.preaching.com/resources/articles/11600669.

ii   "Mr. Yellow Ribbon and his Anthem of Hope," AsiaOne, Wednesday, July 23, 2014 (accessed 7/ /2016), http://news.asiaone.com/news/Singapore/mr-yellow-ribbon-and-his-anthem-hope.

iii   Irwin Levine and L. Russell Brown, "Tie a Yellow Ribbon Round the Ole Oak Tree," Peermusic Publishing, Southern Music Publishing, Spirit Music Group, 1971.

iv   Gerald E. Parsons, "How the Yellow Ribbon Became a National Folk Symbol," The American Folklife Center, The Library of Congress, Research Centers, Online Collections (accessed 7/25/2016), http://www.loc.gov/folklife/ribbons/ribbons.html.

v   Spiros Zodhiates, *The Complete Word Study Dictionary: New Testament* (Chattanooga, TN: AMG Publishers, 2000).

vi   Timothy Keller, *The Prodigal God: Recovering the Heart of the Christian Faith* (New York: Riverhead Books, 2008), 1.

vii   Bryan Chapell, *Christ-Centered Preaching: Redeeming the Expository Sermon*, 2d ed. (Grand Rapids, MI: Baker Academic, 2005), 289–295, 318–19.

viii Ibid., 289.

ix   Erik Johnson. Copyright 1988. Used with permission.

Chapter 13: Make It Memorable: The Point for Proclamation

i   *Planes, Trains, and Automobiles*, written and directed by John Hughes (Paramount Pictures, 1987); quote from IMDB, "Plains, Trains, and Automobiles: Quotes" (accessed 4/22/2016), http://www.imdb.com/title/tt0093748/quotes.

ii   Abraham Kuruvilla, *Privilege the Text!: A Theological Hermeneutic for Preaching* (Chicago, IL: Moody Publishers, 2013), 26.

iii   Marilynne Robinson, *Gilead: A Novel* (New York: Farrar, Straus and Giroux, 2004), 24, Kindle.

iv   Rob Suggs. Copyright 1992. Used with permission.

v   Chip Heath and Dan Heath, *Made to Stick: Why Some Ideas Survive and Others Die* (New York: Random House, 2008), 479–80, Kindle.

vi   Andy Stanley and Lane Jones, *Communicating For a Change: Seven Keys to Irresistible Communication* (Colorado Springs: Multnomah Books, 2006), 191.

vii   James C. Humes, The Sir Winston Method: The Five Secrets of Speaking the Language of Leadership (New York: William Morrow, 1991), 88–101

viii Ibid., 100–01.

ix   Dennis Fletcher. Copyright. Used with permission.

Chapter 14: Pull It Together

i   Lexham Press, *Logos Hymnal Media Resource* (Bellingham, WA: Lexham Press, 2009).

ii   Walter Russell Bowie, *Preaching* (Nashville: Abingdon, 1954), 124–25; quoted in Scott M. Gibson, *Preaching with a Plan: Sermon Strategies for Growing Mature Believers* (Grand Rapids, MI: Baker Publishing, 2012), 97–98, Kindle.

iii   Dan Pegoda. Copyright 1985. Used with permission.

iv   Timothy Keller, "Preaching to the Heart: Reading, Preparation, Conversation, and Preaching," one of a series of Forums at the Ockenga Institute Pastors' Forum, Wednesday April 5, 2006; accessed 6/5/2016 at *static1.1.sqspcdn.com/../Keller+-+Ockenga+Lectures+on+Preaching+to+the+Heart.pdf.*

v   Randal E. Pelton, *Preaching with Accuracy: Finding Christ-Centered Big Ideas for Biblical Preaching* (Grand Rapids, MI: Kregel Publishing, 2014), 121.

vi   Jeffrey D. Arthurs, "Preparing to Preach Old Testament Narratives," in *Preaching the Old Testament*, ed. Scott Gibson (Grand Rapids, MI: Baker, 2006), 73.

vii   Eugene Lowry, *The Homiletical Plot: The Sermon as Narrative Art Form*—Expanded Edition (Louisville Westminster John Knox Press, 2001), 19.

viii   Ibid., 26.

ix   Andy Stanley and Lane Jones, *Communicating For a Change* (Colorado Springs: Multnomah Books, 2006), 46–49.

x   Dennis Fletcher. Copyright. Used with permission.

xi   Jeffrey Arthurs and Andrew Gurevich, "Proclamation Through Conversation: Dialogues as a Form for Preaching," *Journal of the American Academy of Ministry*, vol. 5, nos. 3 and 4 (Winter/Spring 1997): 35–45.

xii   Dietrich Bonhoeffer, *The Communion of Saints*, reprinted in Jeffrey Arthurs and Andrew Gurevich, "Proclamation Through Conversation: Dialogues as a Form for Preaching," *Journal of the American Academy of Ministry*, vol. 5, nos. 3 and 4 (Winter/Spring 1997), 35.

xiii   Jeffrey D. Arthurs and Randal E. Pelton, "Preaching the Literary Forms of the Bible," D.Min. lecture at Gordon Conwell, Hamilton, MA, May 2014.

xiv   Dennis Fletcher. Copyright 2014. Used with permission.

xv   Adapted from a story told by Annette Harrison in "Tell Me a Story," by Joseph Schuster in St. Louis Home (May 1989), 17–18. Quoted in Bryan Chapell, *Using Illustrations to Preach with Power*, revised edition (Wheaton, IL: Crossway, 2001), 176.

xvi   *Inn of the Sixth Happiness*, directed by Mark Robson, screenplay by Isobel Lennart, novel by Alan Burgess (20th Century Fox CinemaScope, 1958).

xvii   Mark Galli and Craig Brian Larson, *Preaching that Connects: Using Journalistic Techniques to Add Impact* (Grand Rapids, MI: Zondervan, 1994), 57–70.

xviii   Ibid.

xix   Ibid.

xx   Martin Sanders, "Preaching 101" (Class notes, Alliance Theological Seminary, Nyack, New York).

xxi   Bert Decker, You've Got to Be Believed to be Heard: The Complete Book of Speaking in Business and in Life! (New York: St. Martin's Press, 2008), 227–34.

xxii   Ibid., 234.

xxiii   Garr Reynolds, *The Naked Presenter: Delivering Powerful Presentations With or Without Slides* (Berkley, CA: New Riders, 2010), 64–68.

xxiv   Ibid.

xxv   David Harbaugh. Used with permission.

xxvi   Mark Galli and Craig Brian Larson, *Preaching that Connects: Using Journalistic Techniques to Add Impact* (Grand Rapids, MI: Zondervan, 1994), 130–32.

xxvii   Dennis Fletcher. Copyright. Used with permission.

xxviii   Chip Heath and Dan Heath, *Made to Stick: Why Some Ideas Survive and Others Die* (New York: Random House, 2008), 445–47, Kindle.

xxix   Haddon Robinson, *Making a Difference in Preaching* (Grand Rapids, MI: Baker Books, 2002), 109.

xxx   Scott Masear. Copyright 2015. Used with permission.

xxxi   Oswald Chambers, *My Utmost for His Highest*, Chaplain's ed. (Grand Rapids, MI: Discovery House Publishers, 1992), entry for May 5.

xxxii   Paul Scott Wilson, *God Sense: Reading the Bible for Preaching* (Nashville: Abingdon Press, 2001) 109–11.

xxxiii   Dennis Fletcher. Copyright 2015. Used with permission.

Appendix

[i] Randal E. Pelton, *Preaching with Accuracy: Finding Christ-Centered Ideas for Biblical Preaching* (Grand Rapids, MI: Kregel, 2014), 33–37.

[ii] Paul Scott Wilson, *God Sense: Reading the Bible for Preaching* (Nashville: Abingdon Press, 2001) 31.

[iii] Ibid., 69–71.

[iv] Ibid.

[v] Ibid., 109–11.

[vi] Ibid.

[vii] Ibid.

[viii] Ibid.

[ix] Timothy Nichols and Craig Wiseman, "Live Like You Were Dying" (BMG Bumblebee, Warner-Tamerlane, 2004).

[x] Tim McGraw, excerpted from the "Introduction." In *Live Like You Were Dying* by Tim Nichols, Craig Wiseman, and Michael Morris (Nashville: Rutledge Press, Thomas Nelson) location 15–32, Kindle.

[xi] Colleen Currey, "10 Classic Images That Explain the O.J. Simpson Trial," *ABCnews.go.com* (accessed June 12, 2014).

[xii] Survey "Living Arrangements of Children under 18 Years/1 and Marital Status of Parents by Age, Sex, Race, and Hispanic Origin/2 and Selected Characteristics of the Child for all Children 2010." Table C3. U.S. Census Bureau, Current Population, internet release date November 2010 (accessed September 24, 2015), Fathers.com/statistics-and-research/the-extent-of-fatherlessness.

[xiii] "Family Structure and Children's Living Arrangements *2012,* Current Population Report" U.S. Census Bureau July 1, 2012 (accessed September 24, 2015), Fathers.com/statistics-and-research/the-extent-of-fatherlessness.

[xiv] Warren Wiersbe, *Be Comforted*, "Be" Commentary Series (Wheaton, IL: Victor Books, 1996), 21.

INDEX

Pelton, Randall 288
Peter 5, 33, 47, 80, 141, 142, 154, 213
Peter, First 55, 65, 153
Peter, Second 55
Philemon 55
Philippians 11, 21, 27, 55, 80, 140, 150, 155, 184, 191, 261, 263, 264
picking a passage 229
places 2, 15, 19, 20, 46, 50, 77, 81, 82, 89, 93, 94, 111, 116, 125, 143, 147, 151, 152, 166, 185, 194, 197, 211, 241, 244, 267
Planes, Trains, and Automobiles 187, 293
Plantiga, Cornelius Jr. 22, 286
Plantinga, Cornelius Jr. 22
plot 29, 48, 49, 110, 205, 240, 252, 253
poetry 8, 33, 46, 48, 54, 70, 82, 83, 84, 85, 86, 109, 112, 117, 152, 158, 166, 170, 243, 247, 281
Point for Proclamation xiii, xiv, xvii, xx, xxi, xxii, 18, 21, 22, 23, 24, 49, 65, 82, 91, 152, 153, 154, 155, 156, 161, 187, 189, 190, 191, 192, 193, 194, 195, 196, 197, 198, 199, 201, 202, 203, 204, 205, 206, 207, 208, 209, 212, 214, 215, 216, 218, 219, 220, 223, 224, 233, 247, 248, 249, 250, 252, 253, 266
Portlock, Rob 66, 288
Poythress, Vern 86, 286
preach to the heart 34
presuppositions xx, 11, 12, 29, 87, 105, 238
primary purpose xiii, xxi, 113, 149, 192
principalization 158
proof-texting 44
prophecy xxiii, 8, 18, 80, 82, 84, 86, 99, 100, 114, 117, 118, 149, 189, 240, 243, 252, 268
prophetic 51
prophets 2, 10, 39, 52, 54, 55, 78, 79, 80, 81, 86, 87, 89, 91, 95, 98, 99, 100, 101, 105, 118, 134, 168, 194, 243, 257, 260, 267, 268, 271, 274, 275, 276, 284
proverb 14, 21, 51, 83, 84, 104, 196, 237
Proverbs 14, 37, 39, 40, 51, 54, 62, 84, 96, 215
psalm 32, 83, 85, 104, 112, 113, 117, 152, 153, 237, 242
psalms 51, 112, 117
Psalms 12, 15, 24, 25, 32, 36, 38, 39, 40, 51, 54, 55, 84, 95, 96, 98, 108, 117, 126, 143, 153, 166, 193, 196, 197, 200, 215, 242, 243
purpose xiii, xiv, xv, xvi, xvii, xix, xx, xxi, xxii, xxiii, 4, 6, 7, 8, 10, 14, 15, 16, 18, 19, 20, 21, 22, 25, 26, 28, 29, 30, 31, 33, 34, 48, 49, 50, 56, 65, 72, 75, 76, 77, 80, 81, 83, 84, 87, 89, 91, 92, 98, 99, 103, 104, 105, 106, 109, 110, 111, 112, 133, 141, 145, 148, 150, 152, 153, 156, 157, 160, 161, 162, 173, 174, 186, 190, 191, 194, 196, 201, 202, 203, 221, 234, 237, 238, 239, 245, 251, 252, 253, 266
original purpose 56
purpose of the passage xiv, xvi, 20

Q

questions xiii, xiv, xv, xvi, xvii, xx, xxi, 5, 6, 12, 19, 20, 24, 28, 29, 30, 31, 33, 34, 62, 67, 68, 70, 71, 72, 73, 74, 87, 90, 104, 106, 140, 141, 142, 143, 144, 145, 146, 147, 150, 157, 158, 166, 167, 169, 170, 190, 195, 202, 204, 208, 209, 216, 220, 233, 234, 235, 236, 237, 244, 247, 249, 251, 260, 263. *See* exegesis:Inductive Theological Exegesis; *See* exegesis:Inductive Theological Exegesis
quotes 215, 293

R

reconcile 30, 91, 162
redemption xvi, xvii, xxi, 2, 16, 20, 30, 36, 70, 75, 78, 91, 106, 117, 144, 153, 160, 161, 162, 173, 174, 177, 178, 183, 184, 185, 214, 224, 239, 240, 242, 245, 250, 253
redemptive xiv, 7, 65, 78, 81, 95, 103, 106, 171, 173, 177, 178, 183, 184, 186, 189, 190, 191, 192, 202, 230, 239, 247, 252, 253
relational outline 206
relationship xiv, 4, 24, 64, 100, 121, 125, 180, 181, 201, 246, 274
relevant xvi, 15, 23, 29, 31, 32, 35, 39, 40, 51, 71, 104, 106, 150, 158, 170, 175, 192, 206, 216, 217, 220, 223, 237, 239, 247, 249, 252
resonance 3, 143, 285
resonate 92
response 10, 84, 88, 146, 156, 183, 219, 220, 223, 249, 275
Revelation 12, 33, 35, 39, 55, 83, 109, 288
Reynolds, Garr 209, 216, 231, 294
Richard, Ramesh 109, 290
Robinson, Haddon 20, 21, 23, 24, 37, 62, 134, 156, 188, 202, 220, 230, 286, 288, 291, 292, 293
Romans xxi, xxiii, 3, 5, 7, 11, 13, 14, 15, 17, 22, 52, 53, 55, 80, 84, 97, 157, 161, 173, 174, 178, 180, 185, 188, 195, 198, 283
Ruth 54, 83, 160, 173, 174
Ryken, Leland 229

Printed in the United States
By Bookmasters